Climate
Finance

Nuno Fernandes

British Library Cataloguing in Publication Data

A catalogue record for this book is available from the British Library

Library of Congress Cataloguing in Publication Data

Fernandes, Nuno

    Climate Finance

    Includes bibliographical references and index

    ISBN: 9789899885431

    1. Corporations—Finance. 2. International business enterprises—Finance. 3. Corporate Finance

To Isabel, Francisco, and Luísa

ESG is the latest expansion of a CFO's role in the roaring 2000s. *Climate Finance* offers a one-stop shop to explain how finance can impact the ESG agenda and ultimately create a brighter future.

Alexandre Pouille, Europe CFO, AB InBev

Climate change is the challenge of this century and has become the dominant issue shaping finance. Close to 40% of global financial assets are now managed with an eye to environmental and climate impacts. Nuno Fernandes provides the most cutting-edge and complete coverage of all the main climate finance issues. The book is very approachable with clear takeaways. It is a perfect introduction for practitioners and MBA students looking to deepen their knowledge of this important area.

Patrick Bolton, Professor of Finance, Columbia Business School

Nuno Fernandes' book on climate finance is a comprehensive and insightful guide to the complex world of financing the transition to a carbon neutral, sustainable future. Its in-depth analysis of the current state of the industry and its clear explanation of the various financial instruments and mechanisms available to support clean energy projects make it a must-read for anyone looking to understand and take action on the pressing issue of climate change.

Stephane Biguet, Executive Vice President & Chief Financial Officer, SLB

Nuno Fernandes provides an incredibly comprehensive overview and explanation of the various components and actors driving the development of climate finance. Covering both analytical frameworks and case studies, his contribution provides a solid foundation and excellent introduction to this important topic. It is a must-read for those who want to understand the role, opportunities, and challenges of finance in the climate-neutral transition.

Emma Navarro, Executive Director, the European Climate Foundation. Independent Board Director, Iberdrola España. Former Vice-President, the European Investment Bank

Nuno Fernandes covers one of the most important topics of our day with this book. This fact-based book highlights great case studies and real examples to reinforce key themes. Clearly, the "Climate Finance" topic is in constant evolution, but this book provides the necessary foundation and understanding to navigate through this ever-changing landscape.

Daniel Shook, Chief Financial Officer, IMI plc

Nuno Fernandes takes on one of the major challenges we face today: climate change. Climate change imposes a limit on pollution generation and the exploitation of natural resources. We therefore have to think about how society's response can be financed. Why is this difficult? Climate change does not hit everybody at the same time, which makes the question of how to finance it over time and through economic agents hard to answer. That's what Nuno does the best. As he has done before, Nuno develops a careful, in-depth approach to the topic. A must-read, surely, for central bankers.

Mário Centeno, Governor, Banco de Portugal

For practitioners and academics, it is a challenge for finance to tackle climate change challenges and opportunities. This book provides practical and applied concepts that are firmly grounded in reality. Professor Nuno Fernandes guides readers through the possible routes and roles of financial actors and instruments for the climate and environmental objectives. He does so in a pragmatic, thorough, and rigorous fashion. A must-read for all engaged in understanding climate finance!

Isabel Ucha, Managing Board, Euronext NV, CEO Euronext Lisbon

The implications of climate change for society are serious. The financial dimensions are huge and diverse. Policymakers and companies are figuring out how to tackle it. Nuno Fernandes provides a holistic and balanced way to fully grasp this complex and relevant phenomenon by analyzing and integrating the views of companies, shareholders, investors, capital markets, and regulators. An excellent book to understand and diagnose the connections between climate change and finance.

Jordi Canals, IESE Foundation Professor of Corporate Governance

An important and timely book that addresses complex matters about which there is a lack of knowledge. Many individuals and organizations, especially in the financial sector, need enlightenment and guidance on the topics covered in this book. *Climate Finance* fills this gap.

Vítor Bento, President, Portuguese Banking Association

Climate Finance is a must-read, a primer on one of the most challenging subjects for the decades ahead. Companies, investors, governments, and regulators must adapt and contribute to finding new solutions. Prof. Nuno Fernandes delivers a comprehensive and balanced assessment of the current situation and the alternatives to pursue.

Paulo C. Pereira, Founding Partner, Perella Weinberg Partners

Climate Finance is essential reading. It provides a comprehensive overview of the new risks and opportunities that are transforming the finance industry, and the critical role of finance in the race to net zero.

Marco Becht, Executive Director, European Corporate Governance Institute

A must-read that should be of great interest to industry leaders, policymakers, banks and asset managers, scholars, and students alike. Nuno Fernandes presents the role of capital markets and market-based finance as a pillar to the necessary responses from the private sector in tackling the challenges ahead. Supported by scientific articles and practical examples, the author presents an unbiased characterization of the demand and supply of capital, leading to some answers to current and future challenges.

Nuno Barroca, Vice-Chairman of the Board of Directors, Corticeira Amorim

Nuno Fernandes provides the definitive guide for all trying to find their way in sustainable finance! Finance must be a part of any effort to better our world. *Climate Finance* covers the main points for all finance professionals to get started and advance!

Michel Galeazzi, Partner, Evoco AG

Climate Finance opens a new dimension of financial analysis. It helps identify the actors and their possible vested interests. It clearly shows the enormity of this challenge. It should be a required textbook in business schools worldwide and used by decision-makers who can no longer ignore the short-term and long-term impacts of the constraints of life on this planet.

João Talone, Chairman of the Board, EDP

Climate finance is no more a greenfield after Professor Fernandes' book. This book is a practical and inspiring study that will appeal to anyone interested in climate finance. In fact, I am convinced that climate is an issue that should matter to anyone interested in finance.

Narciso Perales, CEO, Banco Pichincha Spain

Nuno Fernandes has long been a reference for me. In this timely book, he explores the world of climate finance and how the financial sector and companies are contributing to solve this worldwide crisis. It will be a new reference for all managers and boards.

Gonçalo Morais Soares, CFO and Member of the Board REN – Redes Energéticas Nacionais

Nuno Fernandes offers a holistic perspective on the intricate interface between sustainability and financial markets. It is an insightful look at how the "green" funding gap should be addressed by capital supply and demand. It explores the different challenges faced by actors on both sides as they raise funding, develop sustainability-related strategies, and manage risks. A succinct yet comprehensive book about the big picture in a critical, emerging area of the financial system.

Stilpon Nestor, Founder of Nestor Advisors

Climate change presents an enormous challenge not only to humanity´s survival but to the way our economies are organised around the world. In the process of corporate transformation that will have to take place, private capital will play a lead role. Nuno Fernandes is the right person to guide us through the levers of this transformation, to show us how existing corporate structures will have to adapt and investors mobilised. This is the topic for our times and this book provides the much needed framework for decision makers. A must-read.

João Moreira Rato, Chairman of the Portuguese DMO during the Euro crisis and President of the Portuguese Institute for Corporate Governance

Climate change is a threat to humanity. It has been described as the biggest market failure in history. Correcting that failure is not an option, but rather an absolute need. To address this, there is a fundamental role for the corporate sector, with risks and opportunities that demand top management's capacity to take hard decisions. *Climate Finance* is a must-read, an outstanding contribution, for the timing, rigorous coverage, and depth of issues covered.

Luís Laginha de Sousa, Chair of the Management Board, CMVM

Mitigating and adapting to climate change has been at the forefront of the world's agenda. Business as usual is not good enough. We need fundamental changes in the way financial agents understand their roles as investors, issuers, intermediaries, regulators, and citizens. This is why it is important that clear, well-structured, and accessible textbooks, like Nuno Fernandes's *Climate Finance*, make their way into MBA classrooms – and into corporate boardrooms – as soon as possible.

Pablo de Ramón-Laca, former Director General, the Spanish Treasury and Financial Policy

This book builds a comprehensive framework that helps the reader understand the various components of climate-related financial issues. Nuno Fernandes masterfully assembles evidence from markets and academic studies, complemented by practical case studies from leading companies around the world. It is a great resource for market practitioners as well as lay readers who want to understand the risks and opportunities associated with climate change. I expect the book to be a standard reference for courses in sustainable finance.

Kalok Chan, Wei-Lun Professor of Finance, Chinese University of Hong Kong

Professor Nuno Fernandes provides a comprehensive overview of how climate change challenges the financial management of companies and how it modifies the views and actions of investors in regard to the allocation of capital. Combining scientific rigor (by providing evidence from markets and academic studies) with practical relevance (by addressing the key issues that the finance world needs to tackle), this book is an outstanding contribution that redefines the role of finance in this age of transformation toward a more sustainable society.

António Gomes Mota, Professor at ISCTE and Chairman of the Board of EDP Renewables

Any thoughtful finance practitioner would be well served by reading this book with its sharp focus on the financial dimensions of climate change. Professor Fernandes is careful not to get caught up in moral debates but instead focuses on the implications for finance from a variety of angles, including government and fiscal policy, capital market considerations, corporate strategy, supply chain, and governance. The book is an excellent read and a welcome addition to the conversation.

Brad Greve, Chief Financial Officer, BAE Systems

Climate change and financial impact! There are significant ramifications depending on the course of action taken. Read this book and learn from one of the best.

Anton G. Van Beek, CEO, DOW Western Europe

ABOUT THE AUTHOR

Nuno Fernandes is Professor of Finance at IESE Business School. He is also the Chairman of the Board of Auditors at the Portuguese Central Bank (Banco de Portugal), Non-Executive (Member of Audit Committee) at the European Investment Bank, and a Research Associate of the European Corporate Governance Institute. His areas of interest are climate finance, mergers and acquisitions, corporate governance, banking, financial strategies, and corporate finance.

Professor Fernandes regularly advises companies and financial institutions in Asia, Europe, Latin America, and the Middle East. He has delivered speeches and workshops for well-known companies around the world with audiences ranging from 10 to 1,000 people. Blending real-world examples and practical tips, Professor Fernandes customizes his content to clients' objectives so that audiences leave the room energized and inspired to change the status quo, thus creating lasting impact for the organization.

A regular contributor to international media – including *The Financial Times, Forbes*, and *The Wall Street Journal* – Professor Fernandes is the author of several books, including *Finance for Executives: A Practical Guide for Managers* (second edition), and *The Value Killers: How Mergers and Acquisitions Cost Companies Billions—And How to Prevent It.*

In the past, Professor Fernandes was the Dean of Católica-Lisbon, and Professor of Finance at IMD in Switzerland. He has received numerous teaching and research awards and has been published in leading international academic journals, including the *Journal of Financial Economics, Review of Financial Studies, Journal of International Business Studies, Journal of Financial Intermediation, Journal of Applied Corporate Finance, The Journal of Portfolio Management*, and *Harvard Business Review*. In 2022, he won the "Outstanding Teacher" award, in The Case Centre's Worldwide Competition, also known as "business education's Oscars." He earned his PhD in Management (Finance) from IESE Business School and a degree in Economics from Universidade Católica Portuguesa.

Introduction: A Primer on Green Finance

What This Book Is About

This book focuses on the intersection between climate change and finance.

It aims to provide a comprehensive overview of the various facets of climate-related financial issues. The real-world impacts of climate change are reshaping stakeholders' expectations. Although government policies play a role in tackling climate change, businesses are not waiting and watching. They understand that they need to participate, and contribute, in different ways.

Finance is about linking demand for capital to suppliers of capital. Defined in this broad sense, finance (including financial players such as shareholders, debtholders, capital markets, regulators/central banks, and boards) has an important role to play in tackling the challenges ahead.

A big funding gap exists between what we have right now (the Paris Agreement signatures) and what we need to have in the future (the actual infrastructure, supply chains, and corporate frameworks to deliver on those agreements). It is clear that bridging this gap should now be the priority for executives, board members, and shareholders. For instance, the world's largest investor, Larry Fink, Chief Executive Officer of BlackRock, has already issued several warnings in his 2018 (and later) letters to shareholders. Many more long-term investors, including pension funds, sovereign funds, and others, are increasingly concerned that failure to act could endanger the long-term returns on their assets.

Corporate action will be crucial for obtaining the funds needed to fulfill the carbon neutrality goals, and most of the required investment will come from the private sector. Market-based finance is a key pillar in this process. Capital markets, the intermediary between savings and corporate investments, can be used to close the investment gap.

Therefore, in this book, I will explore this topic from both the demand and supply sides:

- o Demand, or "the need for capital": Here, I look at the corporate side, covering investment and financing needs; the roles of executives and boards, voting advisors, and rating agencies; how climate risks are addressed at the corporate level; supply chain aspects; etc.
- o Supply of capital: Here, I examine the roles of actors such as suppliers of capital, various equity investors, sovereign funds and other large institutions, passive/active shareholders, various debt investors, and central bank/bank supervisors; various certification schemes and standards; challenges to integration in asset management; etc.

Finance is about the exchange of capital over time, with some attendant degree of uncertainty. Climate change issues also involve temporal trade-offs, with a high degree of outcome uncertainty.

Climate change, as well as the government policies related to it, poses risks to companies, banks, governments, and investors, but also opens up opportunities. Apart from managing the direct impacts of climate change on their operations, companies will also have to adapt to how society responds to climate change. They will have to deal with changes in regulations, technologies, markets, consumer reactions, and other effects. Overall, no company is immune to climate change risks and opportunities, as they affect the competitive environment and the global macroeconomic outlook. Also, certain industries and companies may be more affected than others.

Underpinning this book is a careful study of the evidence for the links between financial actions and climate change. This means that instead of providing a one-sided argument by carefully cherry-picking the data or presenting a case study that works only in a certain environment, I try to use large-scale evidence. In all the topics, I present insights from research that spans different periods and uses diverse methodologies covering thousands of companies operating in multiple countries. As far as possible, I rely on studies published in the most rigorous finance, management, science, and economics journals. These journals have high standards of publication and reject more than 90% of the submitted papers; moreover, each paper published in these journals is closely scrutinized (its methodology and data, and also its implications for business practice).

Each section presents relevant frameworks, as well as evidence from markets and academic studies. The academic studies are complemented by practical case studies featuring leading companies and investors, as well as interviews with senior executives from various countries working with a variety of organizations and industries.

What This Book Is Not About

This is not a book about climate change. Rather, it is a book about how finance, from both the corporate side and the capital markets side, can work as an important force to prevent further increases in global warming, mitigating its impact on our lives and helping us adapt to its already inevitable effects. It focuses on what managers and investors can do to promote sound financial management and will also help them understand the impact of their decisions on the climate transition.

This is not a book with a one-sided narrative. It is dangerous to have a siloed, one-dimensional view of the world. Thus, I will show that there are grounds for reasonable doubt about many conclusions found in the literature. There are also false claims about environmental performance – greenwashing – that are dangerous and reduce confidence in various climate change mitigation instruments. Whenever possible, the book tries to answer questions, but several questions that can stir up controversy will regrettably remain open.

In many areas, it is important to understand that there are two sides to every argument. There are good examples of serious research with controversial results. This is not unexpected, and we need to be aware of it. However, it also means that it may not be possible to provide a definitive answer to every question. We soon realize the futility of trying to frame cut-and-dry statements such as the following:

- o "This will increase your profits and positively impact the planet – it is a win-win."
- o "Investing in shares with high environmental, social, and governance (ESG) ratings leads to excellent returns."
- o "Companies that issue green instruments always pay lower interest costs."
- o "Banking regulators penalize banks that have 'brown' loans in their portfolios."

More nuanced answers will sometimes be unavoidable. The reality is that all that glitters is not gold. It is important for companies to avoid greenwashing and not fall into the trap of taking easy shortcuts that typically do not pay off in the long run.

This is not a book focused only on investing in sustainable assets. Many authors have focused on asset management alone. However, climate finance is about much more than investing. Often, most of the discussion is centered on ESG investing, and its performance, or how asset managers should invest taking climate change into account. In this book, I provide a comprehensive overview of the various elements and actors that make up the broad field of climate finance. Besides investors, it includes companies, and also several service providers and facilitators of the investment value chain (e.g., asset managers, banks, index providers, rating agencies, disclosure-standards-setting organizations, and regulators) who will have to respond to new demands.

This is not a book about reinventing capitalism, or refunding our society. Of course, we must think about the broad societal impacts of corporate and financial actions. However, the premise of this book is that we must fix the problems under our current system. We do not have the time to reinvent the wheel. We have a capitalist system in which people save money, which when invested in pension funds or in other assets will hopefully provide for a comfortable retirement. Capital markets exist to channel funds from those with money, to those with entrepreneurial ideas. Therefore, those with money do not have to be creative. By using capital markets, they can channel their money to those with ideas, and it is by developing these ideas that economic growth, job creation, technological development, and also financial returns for investors are generated.

Objectives

Climate change is not a *possible* future risk. It has already started to impact human life, but the worst effects are yet to come. Avoiding those extreme impacts represents an unprecedented challenge for humanity. Besides posing risks, climate change also offers business opportunities, and companies can act to enhance their competitiveness. New business models will arise, new products and services will be demanded, and financing sources have begun adapting to this change.

A huge level of investment is required to meet the Paris Agreement goals. Given the magnitude of the challenge, it is clear that public investment alone will not be enough. Private sector funds need to be channeled into the new investment opportunities. Banks and financial investors can serve as enablers of a smooth transition and help properly allocate capital and risks. Every type of investor will be involved, in different ways: by investing in private equity funds or directly in projects, buying bonds or equities, or investing in global funds that diversify their savings.

The book covers all the financing activities of companies, both through the debt side and the equity side. It also addresses the financial market aspects of these activities. This means, for example, analyzing the following topics through a climate lens: bank loans, supply chain finance, raising equity or debt in capital markets, investing in different assets, mergers and acquisitions, corporate governance, and so on. Several financial instruments are novel, and some aspects of their structure and best practices are still being developed. The book provides practical and applied concepts that are firmly grounded in reality. Further, it also covers the scientific evidence – when it exists – on each topic.

Some other objectives of the book include the following:

- o Bridge the gap between traditional corporate finance and the investment world, with a focus on climate-related issues.
- o Provide frameworks for readers to help them better understand the field, and how finance and climate are linked.

o   Provide some answers, but also food for thought for decision-makers, on what should be the top priorities for managers, investors, and anyone interested in this area.

o   Allow the reader to assess his or her contributions, risks, opportunities, and personal role in the coming transition.

o   Help investors and companies make more informed capital allocation decisions by appropriately incorporating all risks.

o   Present a balanced view, showcasing the arguments for different sides, as well as the evidence in favor of or against certain actions, products, and investments.

o   Provide visibility on up-to-date research, frameworks, and data.

If some of these objectives are achieved, perhaps this book will be able to move the needle just a little in tackling the global challenges we face.

How This Book Is Structured

Carbon emissions, and other sources of pollution, raise Earth's temperature by reducing its ability to absorb heat and expel it outside the atmosphere. This book starts by considering this problem (from the point of view of different stakeholders), and then turns to the finance solutions. It tries to present a "neutral" or "balanced" view of this world through research evidence, numerous interviews with experts in different areas, and multiple case studies.

The book is divided into six chapters, each analyzing a different topic. There are obvious linkages across the chapters, and many topics in different chapters could reasonably be considered part of one, or another, chapter.

Chapter 1 provides an overview of the problems we face. It describes the impacts of climate change, stakeholder reactions, regulatory developments, and some global economic implications. This introductory chapter is intended as a primer on the circular relationship between the environment, corporate actions, and financial markets. It provides useful background information and helps frame the chapters that follow.

Globalization of capital markets, international financial flows, and investors that aim to diversify their portfolios globally to generate long-term returns are all positive forces that help address this world challenge. Thus, finance can be a major force for change. The subsequent chapters of this book focus on these roles and impacts in detail, from the company and investor/market perspectives.

Chapter 2 discusses the risks, opportunities, and costs of climate-related effects. Climate change can have serious impacts on economic growth and development levels, access to resources, and the quality of human life around the world. It affects all countries, but in different ways, and with different timing. Various economic models estimate that failure to act will increase the overall costs and risks of climate change until they account for a significant percentage of the global GDP. Further, some countries are more vulnerable than others. The cost of stabilizing climate change is significant, but the scientific evidence suggests that the alternative is much worse. This chapter introduces some measurement frameworks that will be further developed in subsequent chapters. We discuss the problem of stranded assets and the challenges for both advanced and emerging market economies. Finally, the chapter analyzes how the assessment of these climate-related risks and opportunities can lead to very different business models and valuations of companies.

The next two chapters focus on the "demand for capital." In particular, they cover debt and equity financing across many different dimensions.

Chapter 3 evaluates the climate change impact on debt financing, including various aspects of the debt side of the balance sheet. Activity in the sustainable finance market has grown exponentially in recent years. This chapter overviews recent advances in green financial products, and also their challenges and limitations. This includes green bonds, transition bonds, project finance, and novel forms of bank financing such as green loans, sustainability-linked loans, and supply chain finance. The chapter also highlights how environmental sustainability factors are being incorporated into creditworthiness assessments performed by banks and credit rating agencies.

Chapter 4 focuses on the equity financing side of the balance sheet. It starts by introducing the various actors involved in equity finance (privately held companies, private equity, family firms, public capital markets), summarizing how climate issues can affect them. In addition, this chapter discusses mergers and acquisitions, and how they are affected by climate issues. It also covers the pressure exerted by the ultimate owners/investors, including recent trends in shareholder voting on ESG issues; other cutting-edge topics in corporate governance; shareholder activism; and the role of the board in environmental issues.

Chapter 5 highlights the impact of capital markets and investors, or the "supply of capital." Capital markets play a key role in financing the transition to a green economy. Investors play an important role in lowering the carbon footprint and redirecting capital flows to environmentally sustainable projects and innovative technologies. Some of these investors hold key positions in the world economy, and can significantly influence corporate actions. In this chapter, we discuss how ESG issues and climate risk considerations are being integrated into the business strategies of key players in capital markets. The chapter also covers topics such as ESG rating agencies, the metrics applied to evaluate companies' climate risk vulnerability and sustainability footprint, ESG stock market indices, investor preferences, and the balance between risk and return in investments. It then zooms in on the different strategies used by investors, including institutional investors such as pension funds, sovereign wealth funds, infrastructure funds, mutual funds, and passive investments in exchange-traded funds.

Chapter 6 discusses the impact of global policies on accelerating the transition and helping achieve the overall climate objectives. This chapter discusses the incentives that governments can give to the private sector and financial markets to promote the transition to a low-carbon economy. Although finance (and the various financial actors) can play a role in mobilizing savings toward climate-related goals and investments, policies and regulations also play a role. A first step is to introduce a fiscal policy that incorporates the pricing of externalities, which is related to carbon taxes and fuel subsidies. It is important to recognize that political economy aspects are involved. Some countries are more vulnerable to climate change, and other countries will face higher transition costs and disruptive social problems along the way. Other important elements include the international framework for disclosure and transparency regulations (including the taxonomies, such as the EU Taxonomy), other financial market regulations, and the response of multilateral institutions to the threat of climate change. This chapter also discusses the role of the central banks, and how they are integrating climate considerations into their monetary policy instruments, financial stability, and banking system regulatory frameworks.

Overall, we have a huge task ahead of us, which grows in magnitude by the day. Without significant private financing, we won't get there. However, we should also not overestimate the objective of "doing good for the world" as a driving force of financial flows. It is important to realize that maximizing risk-adjusted returns is likely to remain the primary consideration for the vast majority of investors. In addition, we need effective and coordinated policy measures and regulatory interventions to link the necessary climate investments with economic returns.

Target Audience

This book covers topics and frameworks rigorously, balancing investor and corporate needs. In addition, it also balances practitioner and academic insights. The variety of material and approaches will interest a broad audience, including the following:

- o Corporate managers who want to understand the risks, as well as opportunities, associated with climate change and financial markets.
- o Investors who want to educate themselves on climate change and its implications for their portfolios.
- o Executives and members of boards of directors who want to understand the implications of climate change for corporate finance strategies.
- o Regulators, central bankers, and supranational institutions.
- o Consultants, lawyers, auditors, bankers, advisors, and other financial intermediaries who want to keep abreast of this broad field.
- o Entrepreneurs and business leaders who want to understand where to go for the money they need.

- o Faculty members teaching sustainability- or climate-related courses.
- o Students interested in a textbook that explains how the worlds of finance and climate intersect.
- o Readers with a general interest in climate and finance.

The Book's Website

www.FinanceForExecutives.net/Climate-Finance-Book

Acknowledgments

Writing this book has been a genuine pleasure, above all for the opportunity to discuss ideas with, and learn from, so many people during the different stages of the book. I have greatly benefited from my regular interactions with hundreds of participants in executive education and MBA programs who come from diverse backgrounds, including board members, CEOs, and CFOs of many companies around the world; classroom sessions; development of company-specific programs; corporate workshops; consulting; and even informal conversations. I am grateful to them for inspiring many of the ideas in the book.

I owe a big thank-you to the large number of executives and academics who gave generously of their time, shared their knowledge with me, and allowed me to interview them and learn from their insights into many of the challenging topics this book covers. Also, many business professionals and researchers were kind enough to read earlier drafts of the book, correct mistakes, comment on the content, and suggest additional thoughts and insights, all of which helped shape *Climate Finance* into the book that you now hold in your hands. For all the above valuable support that has enriched the book immeasurably, I would like to express my profound gratitude to Adam Roscoe, Ahmad Rahnema, Aiswarya Choppali, Alain Dargham, Aldo Romani, Alex Pouille, Álvaro Nascimento, Andrew Karolyi, Andrew McDowell, Aniket Poojary, Anton Van Beek, António Gomes Mota, Brad Greve, Bruce Burrows, Carsten Staecker, Cherie Bong, Chuks Umeche, Cyrille Urfer, Dan Shook, David Atkin, David Blumer, Deriam Chirinos, Duarte Silva, Emma Navarro, Fabian Fiege, Fabrizio Ferraro, Filinto Martins, Gabriela Figueiredo Dias, Geraldine Matchett , Giulio Banchini, Gonçalo Morais Soares, Halit Gonenc, Hernando Cortina, Isabel Ucha, Javier Dias Gimenez, Jeffrey Baccash, João Moreira Rato, João Talone, Joaquim Cadete, John Sutherland, Jordi Canals, Jorge Martínez, José Leitão, José Manuel Campa, Justo Gomez, Kalok Chan, Katharina Klohe, Katja Pluto, Kevin Anselmo, Larissa Švábová, Liana Logiurato, Lucía García, Luís Laginha de Sousa, Marco Becht, Margarida Abreu, Mark Konyn, Mark Hermle, Marta Teixeira, Mauro Giacosa, Max Horster, Michel Demare, Michel Galleazi, Mike Rosenberg, Narciso Perales, Nuno Amado, Nuno Barroca, Olivier Jaeggi, Óscar Figueiredo, Pablo de Ramón-Laca, Patrick Bolton, Paulo Cartucho Pereira, Phil Rosenzweig, Rafael Cisneros, Raj Patara, Ron Steijn, Shubo Nag, Simon Henry, Stilpon Nestor, Vinoshen Vinayagam, Vitor Bento, and Werner Hoyer.

I am extremely grateful to my research assistants, Filippo Bonanno and Brenda Torres, for their amazing help and support along this journey. They have been instrumental in helping me navigate the complexities of the topics, and bring this project from the very early stages to this final form. They have read every chapter, scanned and gathered data from many data sources, checked formulas, calculations, cases, and exhibits. They have delivered with a great attitude and acceded to all my demands, which were not few! Of course, in no way are they responsible for any errors that may remain in this book. These are all my sole responsibility. I am also extremely grateful to my editor, Santhosh Matthew Paul, who has been consistently encouraging, directing, and pushing my work forward. His attention to detail, good suggestions, and overall high standards played a crucial role in ensuring that complex concepts will be understood by readers of all levels.

This book could not have been written without the love and support of my family. I want to dedicate this book to my mom, who was alive when I started the journey, but did not live to see it finished. I know she would have been prouder than I am for having written this book, especially given her passion for the topic of climate change. I also dedicate this to my father, who I'm sure will read it just because I wrote it, and will proudly share it. My two teenagers helped me with their patience and uncomplainingly sacrificed time with their dad on account of my work on this book. Francisco had to put up with his dad typing away for long hours instead of trying to beat him on PES. Luísa had to wait for a long time to finish watching some Netflix series with me. Besides being an amazing (and award-winning) photographer, Luísa is very creative and managed the entire cover design process. Finally, my wife, Isabel, unsparingly gave of her time and energy to support my writing. She has read and commented on different drafts of this book, and has always been a sounding board and source of ideas for my work.

Contents

Chapter 1
What Is the Problem?

This chapter provides an overview of the problem we face. We document the evidence for climate change and introduce its physical effects, summarizing the link between climate change, natural disasters, and economic effects (of varying magnitudes) around the world.

Globalization has brought about many positive outcomes such as unprecedented growth, less poverty, less inequality, diversified financial portfolios, high living standards, increased consumption, improved longevity, and better health. However, the increased economic growth and consumption, exponential growth in global population, expanding trade, and improved living standards have all contributed to a greater demand for natural resources, and above all for energy.

The connection between human activity and climate change has now been recognized by policymakers, who are pushing for policy actions to facilitate the transition to a lower-carbon economy. We also highlight the role and impact of the business and financial sector in this transition.

We describe the impacts of rising carbon emissions, stakeholder reactions, and regulatory developments, as well as some global economic implications. Our coverage includes not only the Paris Agreement, but also the role of environmental, social, and governance (ESG) issues, which have become an important factor in business decisions. Moreover, we describe some problems that can arise through abuses of the "green" concept (*greenwashing*).

1.1   THE PHYSICAL EFFECTS OF CLIMATE CHANGE

This section focuses on the evidence for climate change and its impacts. We document the most relevant environmental risks and the physical impact of climate change. We also present a snapshot of some phenomena that demonstrate how global warming has impacted human health and safety.

1

1.1.1 The Early Evidence on Global Warming

In 1859, John Tyndall tried to verify the existence of gases in the atmosphere that could trap the heat generated by the sun's rays. His laboratory work identified several gases that did just that, although at the time the scientific community was interested not in global warming but in the possibility that a different composition of the atmosphere could explain the ice ages, whose causes were unknown.

In the late 19th century, the Swedish scientist Svante Arrhenius (1896) argued that Earth's temperature was regulated by the atmospheric concentration of carbon dioxide. This led him to hypothesize that human activities could influence climate by producing this gas. Meanwhile, a colleague, Högbom, had calculated the quantity of carbon dioxide (CO_2) emitted by industrial and natural sources. With this data, Arrhenius estimated that global temperatures could increase by 5–6° C if the overall CO_2 concentration doubled; according to his data, and the trends prevailing at the time, it would perhaps take 3,000 years for that to happen.

The experts of the time, however, rejected Arrhenius's hypothesis, arguing that it grossly simplified the climate system (they also relied on laboratory tests that later proved to be incorrect). Thus, only a small minority of the scientific community thought it worthwhile to study a hypothetical anthropogenic greenhouse effect.[1]

In the very early 1900s, under the influence of Arrhenius's studies, Ekholm (1901) was the first to use the term *greenhouse effect*. Analyzing temperature data from more than 100 weather stations, Callendar (1938) argued that there was a link between the artificial production of CO_2 emissions and the recent increase in global temperature.

Since the early 1950s, several studies have reported evidence of global warming. Kaplan (1952) calculated the stratospheric heating and cooling rates caused by CO_2. Similarly, Plass (1956) showed that the average surface temperature of Earth would increase by 3.6° C if the CO_2 concentration in the atmosphere doubled. Almost contemporaneously, Revelle and Suess (1957) warned that the greenhouse effect of CO_2 emissions "may become significant during future decades if industrial fuel combustion continues to rise exponentially."

1.1.2 Recent Evidence on Rising Temperatures

Public concerns about the effects of human activity on climate change intensified during the 1980s, when scientists extracted ice cores from ice caps, using their chemical content as direct archives of atmospheric gases in the different eras (Masson-Delmotte et al., 2006).

---

[1] That is, an effect that results from human activities. Carbon emissions can also be caused by volcanos and other natural events.

More advanced engineering equipment (such as satellites) enabled scientists to observe the changes in the surface of the large ice sheets, both in the Arctic and Antarctic hemispheres, due to global warming. Mass loss from the Antarctic and Greenland ice sheets, and from mountain glaciers, has accelerated over time, primarily due to rising atmospheric and oceanic temperatures (Golledge et al., 2019). The effect of ice sheet melting goes far beyond rising ocean levels; it also changes ocean circulation and alters the sea temperature, driving extreme weather events.

To measure global warming and empirically estimate its determinants and effects, the National Oceanic and Atmospheric Administration (NOAA) built the Land-Ocean Temperature Index.[2] Annual temperature anomalies began increasing since the 1970s, and in 2020 the index registered a temperature anomaly of 0.98 °C above the baseline. Further, the data clearly show a positive relationship between global warming and CO_2 emissions over the period (see Section 1.3).

Figure 1.1 Land-Ocean Temperature Index: temperature anomalies

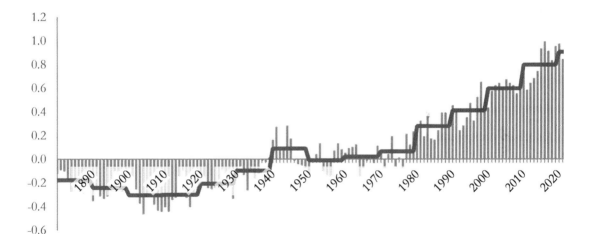

Source: National Oceanic and Atmospheric Administration.

These results are consistent with the evidence reported by the Intergovernmental Panel on Climate Change (IPCC[3]) that average temperatures are currently around 1 °C above the

---

[2] The index uses data collections of temperatures (in °C) over different land and ocean locations around the globe. It measures temperature anomalies since 1880, using the 20th century average as the baseline. Therefore, an index equal to 0.98 in 2020 means that the temperature that year was warmer than the baseline by 0.98 °C.
[3] The IPCC is the United Nations entity assessing the science related to climate change. It was established by the United Nations Environment Programme (UNEP) and the World Meteorological Organization (WMO) in 1988 to keep policymakers abreast of the current state of knowledge about climate change.

preindustrial levels. The IPCC also reports that "each of the last four decades has been successively warmer than any decade that preceded it since 1850."

1.1.3   Rising Ocean Levels and Acidification

Global warming contributes to rising ocean levels in two ways. One, glaciers and ice sheets around the world melt and add water to the ocean. Two, the volume of the ocean expands as the water becomes warmer.

Sea level rise causes both natural and economic damage. Coastal ecosystems are already affected by rising sea levels and other climate-related phenomena. Rising sea levels also increase the coastal risk for community livelihoods, habitability, agriculture, and infrastructure. Some island states, coastal cities, and deltaic coasts are seriously threatened by sea level rise.

To monitor the global sea level for climate policy purposes, the National Aeronautics and Space Administration (NASA) and Centre National d'Etudes Spatiales (CNES) launched the TOPEX/Poseidon satellite mission in 1992.[4] Its data showed a significant increase in the Global Mean Sea Level (GMSL) anomaly[5] of approximately 0.4 cm per year. The IPCC (2021) suggested a 0.37 cm per year rise in seawater in the past few decades. A study by the Royal Society (2020) showed that if future CO_2 emissions maintain the trajectory observed during the past century, the ocean level would rise by a further 40 to 80 cm by 2100.

Coastal regions and low-lying areas face extreme risks from sea level rise. Like many other features of the climate system, increases in sea level are not uniform around the world. More than 600 million people – around 10% of the global population – are estimated to live in coastal areas that are less than 10 m above sea level (United Nations, 2017). The World Economic Forum (2019) has predicted that the following cities could disappear by 2100: Jakarta (Indonesia), Lagos (Nigeria), Houston (United States), Dhaka (Bangladesh), Venice (Italy), Bangkok (Thailand), New Orleans (United States), Rotterdam (Netherlands), and Alexandria (Egypt). Several island states such as Tuvalu, Kiribati, and the Marshall Islands in the Pacific Ocean are predicted to disappear even more quickly. They are part of the Vulnerable 20 (V20), a group of countries that are highly vulnerable to a warming planet.[6]

---

[4] CNES is the French space agency; the TOPEX/Poseidon satellite mission was followed by the Jason-1 (2002–2008), Jason-2 (2009–2015), and Jason-3 satellite missions (2016–present).

[5] A sea level anomaly (as defined by the NOAA's National Ocean Service) occurs when the five-month running average of the interannual variation is at least 0.1 m (4 inches) greater than or less than the long-term trend (eliminating the average seasonal effects).

[6] The V20 includes Afghanistan, Bangladesh, Barbados, Bhutan, Costa Rica, Ethiopia, Ghana, Kenya, Kiribati, Madagascar, Maldives, Nepal, Philippines, Rwanda, Saint Lucia, Tanzania, Timor-Leste, Tuvalu, Vanuatu, and Vietnam.

Among developed nations, the United States is the country with the largest population whose homes are at risk of flooding due to rising sea levels. For example, in Miami, 40,000 and 98,000 homes are predicted to be at risk in 2060 and 2100, respectively.

Other adverse consequences of rising sea levels include an increase in the frequency and intensity of storms and coastal flooding. Under a "business as usual" scenario, Kirezci et al. (2020) estimate that the increased risk of flooding by 2100 will affect 48% of the world's land, 52% of the global population, and 46% of global assets.

Besides rising, the ocean is becoming hotter, more acidic, and less oxygenated, with dire consequences for biodiversity. The oceans have warmed by about 0.1 °C per decade. The warming is larger near the surface and varies around the globe. The acidification of the ocean poses significant challenges to biodiversity and fish stocks. Many ocean species will not survive the higher temperatures and acidity levels (e.g., coral reefs and polar ecosystems).

1.1.4　Climate Change and Natural Disasters

Climate change is associated with increasingly frequent and intense natural disasters ranging from droughts and wildfires to hurricanes and coastal flooding (IPCC, 2014). The occurrence of natural disasters[7] has intensified decade by decade since the early 1970s. The number of extreme weather events rose from a yearly average of 66 during the decade 1970–1979 to 286 during 2010–2019.

Figure 1.2 Annual reported natural disasters (excluding earthquakes, landslides, and volcanic eruptions)

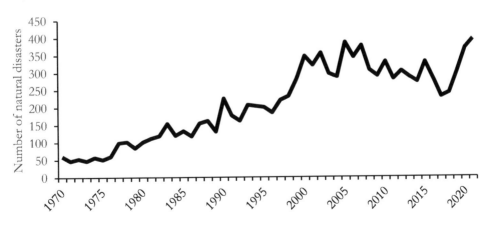

Source: EM-DAT, OFDA/CRED International Disaster Database, Université Catholique de Louvain.

---

[7] The natural disaster count includes droughts, extreme temperature, extreme weather, floods, and wildfires. Volcanic eruptions, landslides, dry mass movements, and earthquakes are excluded from the count.

Natural disasters such as floods, hurricanes, prolonged drought, tornadoes, earthquakes, and tsunamis (also called extreme weather events) are associated with economic losses. In 2020, direct economic losses from natural disasters amounted to US$268 billion (Aon, 2021). The cumulative direct economic losses from natural disasters between 2000 and 2020 amounted to about US$5 trillion, (approximately equal to 5% of the world's GDP in 2020).

Extreme weather events do not have the same social and economic impacts in different regions of the world. Some countries are more sensitive, in terms of the direct cost of damage, lives lost, and destruction of employment and production capacity. Asian emerging market economies bear 30% to 50% of the global economic losses from natural disasters induced by climate change. In 2019, approximately 74% of the population affected by natural disasters lived in Asia, 24% in Africa, and only 2% in Europe and the Americas.

In another estimate from Paun et al. (2018) measured during 2007–16, average annual costs incurred globally due to climate-related events amounted to 0.14% of the GDP. However, in countries such as Thailand, Pakistan, Vietnam, the Philippines, and Oman, the costs were above 1% of their GDP per year.

Low-income countries are much more affected than advanced economies by the occurrence of natural disasters because they do not have the financial resources for reconstruction, have generally weaker and older infrastructures, and are often reliant on foreign aid or financial support. As Jim Yong Kim[8] pointed out: "Severe climate shocks threaten to roll back decades of progress against poverty. Storms, floods, and droughts have dire human and economic consequences, with poor people often paying the heaviest price." Emerging economies – and the Asian ones in particular – are more vulnerable to climate change than advanced economies for a variety of reasons:

- o *Geographic location:* Emerging economies are located in regions whose latitudes make them more prone to extreme weather events such as hurricanes, floods, and prolonged drought. Moreover, the largest economic centers of these countries are often coastal or deltaic cities (e.g., Bangkok, Mumbai, Manila, Djakarta, Ho Chi Min City, and Hanoi), which increases their vulnerability to ocean and river floods, hurricanes, and tsunamis.
- o *Size of the urban population:* Many capital cities are megacities (with more than 15 million inhabitants), characterized by widespread poverty and a significant slum population. The impact of natural disasters is much more significant for poor households than for others because they tend to live in the most vulnerable areas, often with weak housing standards and limited or no access to credit or insurance (Hallegatte et al., 2017).
- o *Economic structure:* Compared to advanced economies, emerging market economies have large agricultural sectors. For example, in 2017, most South American

---

[8] President of the World Bank Group (2012–2019).

countries' labor force was employed in agriculture (between 10% and 20%), and in the Asian-Pacific regions this figure was between 20% and 40%. Given their geographical exposure, these countries are expected to experience a drop in agricultural productivity (Cline, 2008). Further, as a large portion of the labor force has outdoor jobs, extreme weather events can undermine the work conditions (and health) in those regions.

o *Less resilience:* The economies of poorer regions are generally less resilient to extreme weather events than those of richer economies. Many U.S. states (such as California or Florida) are often hit by extreme climate events such as hurricanes and wildfires, but the effects are not as long-lasting as in emerging market countries. The difference in resilience to similar climate events between U.S. cities and cities located in emerging market countries lies essentially in the different levels of economic development, quality of construction, and provision of public goods, such as flood control systems or other infrastructures that are difficult to finance from private funds (Rogers et al., 2012). Given the lack of government financial resources, often very large urban agglomerations with millions of inhabitants in emerging market countries lack adequate infrastructures to protect assets and citizens from extreme weather events.

KEY LEARNING POINT

Natural disasters and extreme weather events are associated with significant economic losses. But the burden is not equally distributed, with some countries suffering much more damage from these events.

1.1.5 Other Environmental Impacts

Climate change has been observed to lead to several changes in the climate system that have been accelerating over the past decades:

o *The melting of ice sheets and glaciers:* The Greenland and Antarctic ice sheets have been melting, and so have glaciers all over the world. In the Arctic, for instance, ice sheets have been melting gradually every season. It is very likely that, before 2050, the Arctic will fully melt during one of these summers.

o *Changing precipitation:* The precipitation patterns in many areas have shifted. In many regions, this development is already altering hydrological systems and affecting the quantity and quality of water resources. The changes in rain patterns are not uniform. In higher latitudes and some areas of the Pacific, they are likely to increase and lead to extreme precipitation events, including intense storms and flooding. However, in most other areas, the mean precipitation will decrease, affecting water levels and land productivity.

○ *Reduction in crop yields:* Studies covering a wide range of regions show global negative impacts of climate change on crop yields (despite observing positive impacts in some regions).

○ *Heat waves:* Heat waves will occur with greater frequency and longer duration. They pose several challenges to human beings, including forest fires, decreased land productivity, and damage to human health and productivity.

Nature contributes to the economy. That is why economists sometimes use the term *natural capital.* Nature also provides inputs for our economic production system, such as breathable air, drinking water, reasonable living temperatures, and land to grow vegetables. These inputs are as vital as other inputs such as labor and capital. Natural capital also provides other services, such as decomposing waste products into nutrients, reduction of CO_2 and other gases to maintain global temperatures at reasonable levels, and other "regulating and maintenance services" (Dasgupta, 2021). Like any other type of capital, natural capital can contribute to economic growth. As we extract resources from nature and do not replenish them, nature's capacity to provide economic returns will decrease over time, and so will the flow of its valuable environmental services.

KEY LEARNING POINT

Natural capital can contribute to economic growth.

Biodiversity

Climate change, besides directly affecting human health and different regions around the world, is also a threat to biodiversity and ecosystem functioning. Figure 1.3 shows the decline in global biodiversity – the Living Planet Index – by region during 1970–2016.[9] Biodiversity decreased globally by more than 60% during this period, especially in Latin America and the Caribbean region.

---

[9] According to the World Wildlife Fund for Nature (WWF), the Living Planet Index (LPI) measures the abundance of almost 2,100 species of mammals, birds, reptiles, amphibians, and fish across the globe.

Figure 1.3 Decline in global biodiversity (1970-2016)

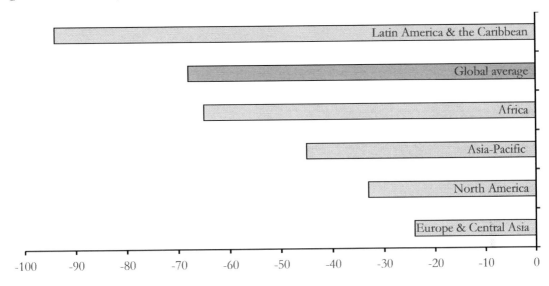

Source: World Wide Fund for Nature.

Land usage

Agricultural land represents 37% of the global land surface.[10] As the population grows, more natural resources are needed to sustain current lifestyles. In this framework, healthy soil management is crucial for ensuring sustainable agricultural production.[11] Soils have been subject to various changes related to human activity. Modern agriculture uses chemical fertilizers and pesticides to increase crop yields.[12] Besides degrading the soil, improper use of pesticides and fertilizer can also have a severe impact on water and air contamination (Park et al., 2012; Malaguerra et al., 2012). During the last several decades, the global use of pesticides and fertilizers (which can have a negative impact on the environment, if not properly planned and used) has substantially increased. Between 1990 and 2017, pesticide application (per unit of cropland, measured in kilograms per hectare) increased from 1.5 kg/ha to more than 2.6 kg/ha (FAO). In light of these figures, Goal 12 of the United Nations (UN) Sustainable Development Goals (SDGs) is to "achieve the environmentally

[10] According to World Bank estimations, agricultural land is the share of land area that is arable, under permanent crops (such as fruit trees, cocoa, rubber, coffee, and vines), and under permanent pastures.
[11] FAO defines soil degradation as the *change in the soil health status resulting in a diminished capacity of the ecosystem to provide goods and services for its beneficiaries.*

[12] It is important to realize that every year, the world loses millions of hectares of farmland due to desertification and drought, which creates additional pressure to generate a greater yield from the remaining cropland.

sound management of chemicals and significantly reduce their release to air, water and soil in order to minimize their adverse impacts on human health and the environment."

Human health

Climate change also affects human health by altering the epidemiology of climate-sensitive pathogens (Mirsaeidi et al., 2016). Worsening air quality and the increased incidence of allergens can worsen existing diseases, while climate-related changes in allergens and in vectors can cause new diseases (Joshi et al., 2020). Furthermore, climate change contributes to increasing ground-level ozone (smog) and particulate matter air pollution, which directly impact respiratory health (Siebelts, 2017).

The global phenomenon of wildfires, which consume forests and release fine dust, is assuming worrying proportions in many regions. During the last decades, the countries of Southeast Asia have been especially badly affected by air pollution (commonly called haze) arising from the burning of vegetation by plantation owners seeking to expand their cultivable plots of land (Jones, 2006).

Haze pollution became particularly visible in 2015, when several fires originating in Indonesia generated an air pollution crisis that posed serious public health threats to neighboring countries such as Singapore, Malaysia, Brunei, Vietnam, Cambodia, and the Philippines. Crippa et al. (2016) estimate that high particulate matter concentrations from fires during 2015 were responsible for the persistent exposure of 69 million people to unhealthy air quality conditions in equatorial Asia. Such persistent exposure to particulate matter concentrations is associated with a significant impact on human health in terms of respiratory conditions. Sheldon and Sankaran (2017) found that an Indonesian fire increases Singaporean polyclinic attendance for respiratory diseases.

Figure 1.4 South East Asia: annual death tolls due to outdoor pollution

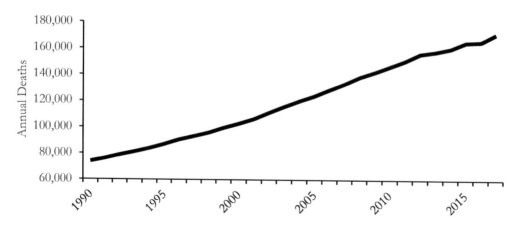

Source: Institute for Health Metrics and Evaluation (IHME).

Water usage

Freshwater reserves are fundamental for life on Earth. The earliest civilizations developed in fertile river valleys, where the conditions were right to support large, settled populations (Kraft Rector, 2016). Given this historical dependence, human settlements worldwide are concentrated near freshwater ecosystems, with over half of the world's population living within 20 km of a permanent river (Combes, 2003).

Water use increases as a function of population growth, economic development, and changing consumption patterns. Global freshwater use increased from approximately 600 billion m[3] in 1901 to 4 trillion m[3] in 2014, a dramatic increase mainly due to the BRICS[13] countries, which in 2010 accounted for 43% of global water use.

Figure 1.5 Global freshwater use by region (1901–2014)

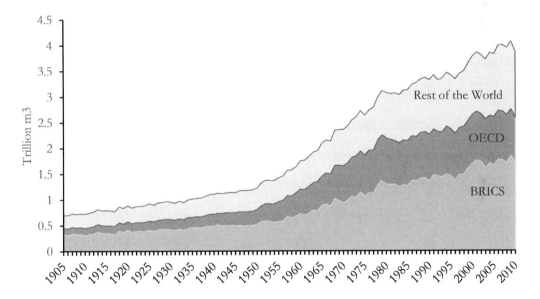

Source: Global International Biosphere-Geosphere Program.

Agriculture accounts for 70% of global water use. Given the expected increase in food demand, the UN estimates that the intensification of food production will increase the use of water by 15%.[14] The increase in global use of freshwater has already shrunk the world's freshwater resources per capita by 55% (between 1962 and 2014). In some countries, such as Iran, Mexico, Brazil, India, Indonesia, Turkey, and Vietnam, renewable freshwater resources per capita has shrunk by more than 60%.

---

[13] BRICS is an acronym for Brazil, Russia, India, China, and South Africa.
[14] World Water Development Report 2018.

Deforestation

Deforestation refers to the decrease in the areas of Earth covered by forests. This phenomenon has been extensively observed in tropical areas, and it is of particular concern in regard to climate change, as forests can absorb a significant share of CO_2 in the atmosphere. The containment of deforestation is an important strategy to prevent further climate change.

According to the Food and Agricultural Organization (FAO; data World Bank), between 1990 and 2018, forest areas [15] reduced by 3.2%. However, this reduction was not homogenous, and in absolute terms, it was concentrated in large countries such as Brazil and Indonesia, where forest areas decreased by approximately 900,000 and 250,000 sq. km, respectively.

Figure 1.6 Reduction in forest area: top 10 countries (1990–2018)

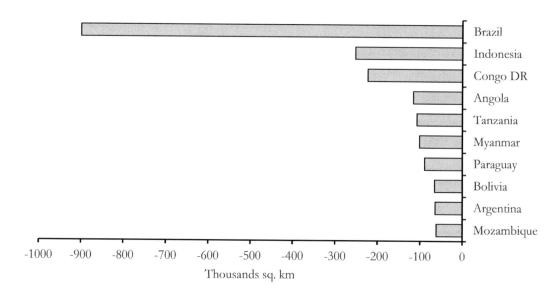

Source: The World Bank.

---

[15] FAO defines forest area as land spanning more than 0.5 hectares with trees higher than 5 m and a canopy cover of more than 10%, or trees able to reach these thresholds in situ. It does not include land that is predominantly under agricultural or urban land use.

1.2 GLOBALIZATION AND DEVELOPMENT

Globalization is not a new phenomenon. Rather, the world has witnessed different phases of globalization (advances and retreats) since the mid-1800s.

Economists and economic historians trace back the first wave of globalization to the period 1870–1914 (Morys et al., 2008). In this phase, global economic integration developed under the industrialized European colonial powers, in particular, France and Great Britain, and was interrupted by the outbreak of WWI in 1914 (Williamson, 1997).

The second phase of globalization occurred in the period between the end of WWII and the end of the Bretton Woods System in 1971–1973. During this period, a new wave of globalization started under the General Agreement on Tariffs and Trade (GATT), a mechanism designed to ensure that countries did not reintroduce protectionist measures after tariffs were lowered.

Since the 1980s, we have entered the third phase of globalization, during which global economic integration accelerated. On the one hand, governments in advanced economies promoted market deregulation and free trade. On the other hand, as China (and others) embraced the market economy and the communist system in Eastern Europe started to disintegrate, an increasing number of countries began to participate in the global economic system. Over this period, tariffs on manufactured goods continued to decline, and many developing countries undertook major trade and economic liberalizations. As their economies boomed, developing countries progressively became important global suppliers of goods and services and significant global consumers. Business leaders expanded the operations of their companies abroad, entered new markets, acquired companies overseas, diversified their stock portfolios globally, created global multinational corporations, hired talent globally, and sold their products and services around the world and not just in the country where they were born. All of this has worked well in many dimensions.

1.2.1 International Trade

In this third phase of globalization, new global institutions such as the World Trade Organization (WTO) were established to govern international trade and protect foreign direct investment (FDI) by multinational corporations. Since the WTO agreement came into force at the end of the Uruguay Round in 1994, international trade and foreign direct investment increased across the world, spurring economic growth in less developed countries.

The global export of goods increased by more than 500% during 1990–2020, from below $4 trillion to approximately US$20 trillion before the outbreak of the COVID-19 pandemic.

Figure 1.7 Global export of merchandise

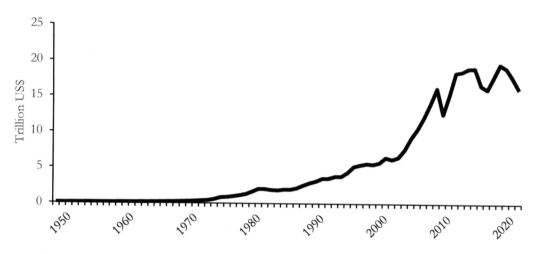

Source: World Trade Organization.

During the same period, the global export share[16] of emerging market economies from Asia, Africa, America, and Eastern Europe increased substantially, from 27% to 46%. Within the group of emerging market economies, the global export share of Asian emerging market economies increased from less than 9% to 34%. At the same time, the global export share of the Group of Seven (G7)[17] economies declined substantially from 46% to 29%.

Another feature of globalization is international capital flows. As globalization advanced, not only did trade increase, but FDI also surged. In fact, the volume of FDI as a percentage of the world's GDP more than tripled from the 1970s (0.5%; World Bank) to the 2000s (above 3%). The increase in global FDI inflows mainly benefited the emerging economies from Asia and Latin America, which in 2019 received approximately 30% and 10% of the global FDI, respectively.

1.2.2 Industrialization and Economic Growth

The third phase of globalization led to increased economic integration in less developed economies. These countries experienced a substantial rise in population, economic development and living standards, a shift of employment from agriculture to industry, and increased urbanization.

---

[16] Exports from a region as a percentage of the sum of all the exports worldwide.
[17] The G7 comprises Canada, France, Germany, Italy, Japan, the United Kingdom, and the United States.

Over a period of 50 years, the world more than doubled its population, and a significant part of the growth came from Asia. The increased population has created additional demand for resources such as food and energy.

Figure 1.8 World population

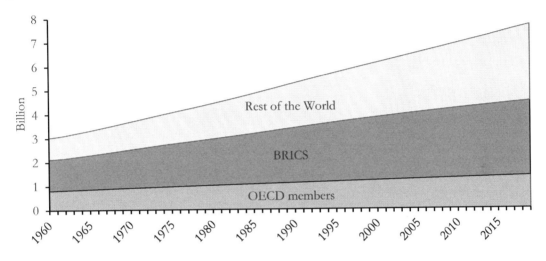

Source: The World Bank.

Another important trend was the change in employment patterns. Between 1991 and 2019, the global employment in agriculture as a percentage of total employment shrank from 43% to 26%.

Figure 1.9 Global employment in agriculture as a percentage of total employment

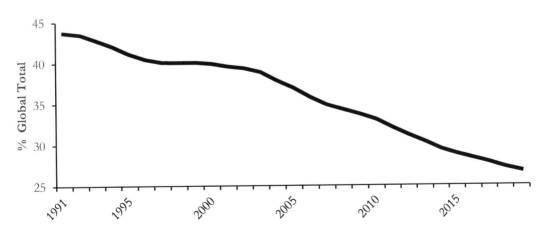

Source: The World Bank.

At the same time, employment in industry as a percentage of total employment decreased from 28% to 22% in the Organization for Co-operation and Economic Development (OECD) group, and from 31% to 24% in the European Union. However, despite the dramatic reduction of employment in industry in the advanced economies, at the global level, employment in industry increased from 21% in 1994 to 23% in 2019. This "paradox" can be easily explained by looking at employment in industry in emerging markets, for instance, from BRICS and Next-11 countries.[18] In China, employment in industry as a percentage of total employment increased from 22% in 1994 to 28% in 2019. In India, it rose from 15% to 25%.

Figure 1.10 Employment in industry as a percentage of total employment

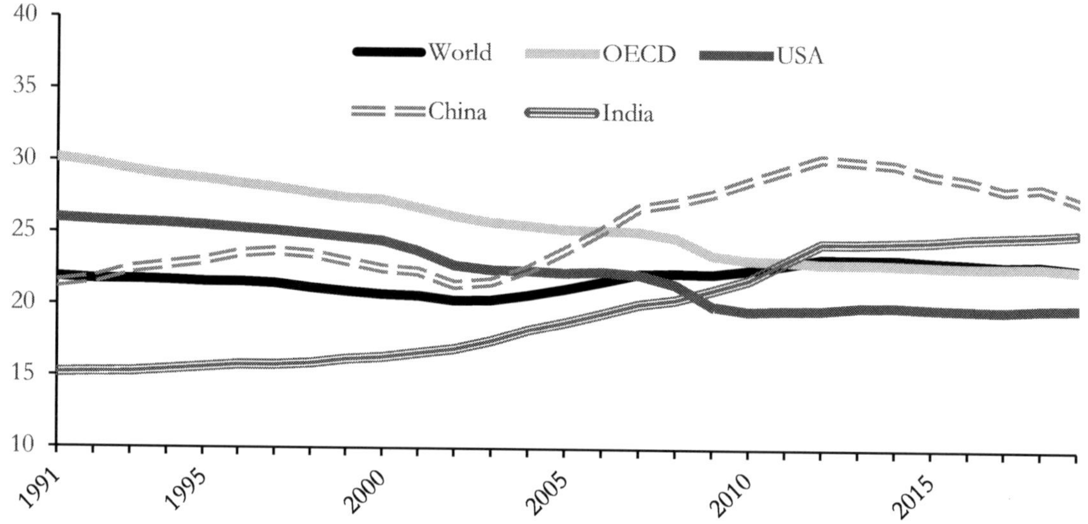

Source: The World Bank.

Structural changes across most emerging market economies let to internal migration from rural areas to cities. Between 1994 and 2019, the global urban population increased from 44% to 55%, mostly in emerging markets. For instance, in China, the urban population increased by more than 30% during this period.

1.2.3 Economic and Human Development

Figure 1.11 shows the evolution of the global GDP and the contributions of selected advanced and emerging market economies. Over the years, the contribution to the global

---

[18] Next-11 countries are a group of countries (South Korea, Mexico, Bangladesh, Egypt, Indonesia, Iran, Nigeria, Pakistan, the Philippines, Turkey, and Vietnam) that Goldman Sachs designated as the "next BRICs."

GDP of the advanced economies from the OECD has progressively shrunk. In 1960, the advanced economies represented more than 2/3 of the global output. In 2019, more than half of the global output was from non-OECD economies.

Figure 1.11 Global GDP (constant 2020 US$ billion)

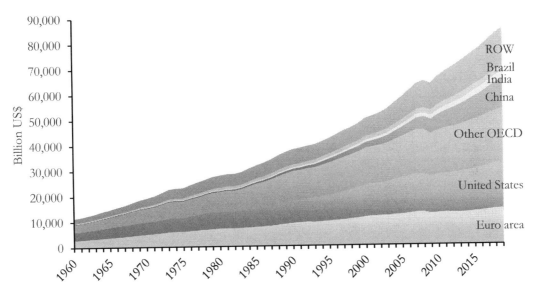

Note: ROW = rest of the world.
Source: The World Bank.

This trend drove extremely high growth in GDP per capita in selected regions, especially in the emerging economies. For example, GDP per capita increased 5 times in South Asia and 32 times in China.

Table 1.1 GDP per capita rebased to 100 in 1990

Country	1970	1990	2000	2010	2020
Brazil	17	100	143	430	259
China	36	100	302	1,431	3,283
European Union	12	100	109	213	221
India	31	100	121	369	524
Latin America & Caribbean	24	100	176	362	289
Middle East & North Africa	13	100	105	244	207
North America	22	100	149	205	260
South Asia	33	100	126	350	508
Sub-Saharan Africa	33	100	97	253	229
World	19	100	129	223	254

Source: The World Bank.

This strong economic growth also led to impressive progress in global poverty reduction. The percentage of the world's population living below the poverty line (defined as US$1.9 per day 2011 PPP adjusted) decreased from 36% in 1990 to 10% in 2015. Over the same period, China reduced the share of its population living below the poverty line from 65% to 0.7%. A similar pattern was observed in many emerging market countries, especially in Asia (from 60% in 1990 to 1% in 2019) and Latin America (from 16% in 1990 to less than 4% in 2019).

Figure 1.12 Poverty rates in China

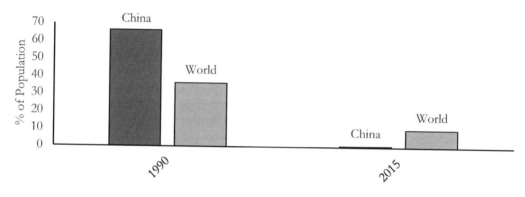

Source: The World Bank.

This remarkable reduction in global poverty was accompanied by substantial improvements in human development indicators such as life expectancy, infant mortality, and literacy rates. The global infant mortality rate more than halved, decreasing in all the regions of the world between 1994 and 2019.[19] Substantial progress was also recorded in the literacy rate, which improved throughout the world.

Table 1.2 Social development (infant mortality, life expectancy, literacy rate)

Region	Life expectancy		Mortality rate		Literacy rate	
	1960	2019	1994	2019	1990	2019
East Asia & Pacific	48.4	76.3	39.3	11.9	80.4	95.8
Europe & Central Asia	67.0	78.0	37.1	10.0	95.5	99.0
Latin America & Caribbean	56.1	75.6	36.6	13.9	84.4	94.3
Middle East & North Africa	46.4	74.3	43	18.1	57.9	79.3
South Asia	42.1	69.6	82.8	33.1	45.5	73.0
Sub-Saharan Africa	40.4	61.6	102.8	51.7	51.8	65.5
World	52.6	72.7	61	28.2	74.3	86.5

Source: The World Bank.

---

[19] The World Bank measures the infant mortality rate as the number of infants dying before reaching one year of age, per 1,000 live births in a given year.

1.3   THE RISE IN CO_2 EMISSIONS AND CLIMATE CHANGE

The data in the previous section highlighted some of the key impacts of globalization that occurred after 1960, namely, an increase in trade, income, and living standards, and a reduction in poverty around the world. Significant changes in urbanization, employment sectors, and consumption also occurred.

Overall, the increasing world population lives better than in the post-WWII era, but also consumes more resources. According to the data provided by the Carbon Dioxide Information Analysis Centre (CDIAC) and Global Carbon Project (GCP), annual global CO_2 emissions increased from basically 0 in 1750 to 5 billion tons in 1950. Since then, it has risen to more than 36 billion tons in 2021.[20]

Figure 1.13 Global CO_2 emissions over time

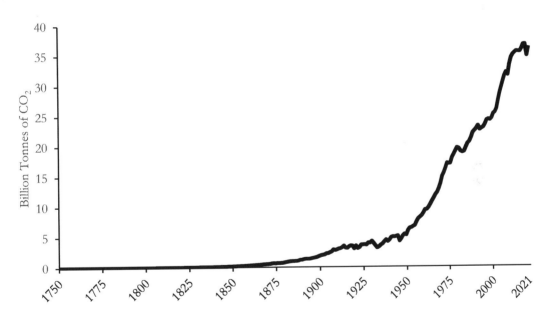

Source: Global Carbon Project and Carbon Dioxide Information Analysis Center.

The sources of CO_2 can be split into two groups: (1) production by natural processes such as respiration, organism decomposition, fires, and volcanic eruptions and (2) production by

---

[20] CO_2 is one of the main agents of climate change, but it is not the only one. Other gases are generated by humans, such as methane (CH_4), nitrous oxide (N_2O), ozone (O_3), and chlorofluorocarbons (CFCs), that amplify the greenhouse effect.

human activities (anthropogenic production) such as land exploitation and burning fossil fuels for general economic activity.

Since the Industrial Revolution in the second half of the 18th century, the burning of increasing quantities of coal, oil, and gas; destruction of forests; and the transformation of land use (increasing use of cropland for animal farming and meat production) were the key reasons for the accumulation of greenhouse gases[21] (GHGs) in the atmosphere.[22]

1.3.1 Geographical Variation in Emissions

Given the rapid economic development documented in earlier sections, the demand for energy increased worldwide, especially in the emerging market economies. Most of the increase in demand for fossil fuel energy during 1970–2018 came from these economies. For example, the annual consumption of fossil fuels grew on average by almost 10% a year in Bangladesh and by more than 6% a year in Iran, China, India, and Indonesia during 1970–2019.[23] Canada was the G7 country that recorded the largest average annual increase in fossil fuel consumption (approximately 1.5%), followed by Japan (1.3%), the United States, and Italy (each approximately 0.5%). During the same period, the average annual fossil fuel consumption decreased in all the other European countries of the G7 (Germany, France, and the United Kingdom).

Overall, emissions of CO_2 started to accelerate during the 1980s and recorded a surge during the early 2000s.[24] Between 1970 and 2019, global tons of CO_2 emissions more than doubled. This increase was not uniform across countries. For instance, CO_2 emissions in China and India increased by more than 1000% between 1970 and 2019. Even more sizeable increases in tons of CO_2 emissions have been observed in other smaller emerging market economies such as Bangladesh (2,153%). All the other emerging market countries such as Saudi Arabia (+1,273%) and Vietnam (+694%) followed the same pattern.

---

[21] GHGs trap heat in the atmosphere. These gases include carbon dioxide (CO_2), which accounts for almost 80% of them; methane (CH_4); nitrous oxide (N_2O); and fluorinated gases (F gases). The effect of heat trapping is known as the greenhouse effect (EPA, 2022).

[22] The consensus that anthropogenic production of GHGs is the cause of recent global warming is shared by more than 90% of published climate scientists (Cook et al., 2016).

[23] Source: BP Statistical Review of World Energy.

[24] The direct effects of globalization on global CO_2 emissions have been empirically analyzed in a wide body of academic literature and technical reports, and are mainly linked to the increased energy consumption embedded in the production of goods and international trade (Xie et al., 2020; Zaidi et al., 2019; Hasanov et al., 2018; Liu and Bae, 2018; Chen and Chen, 2011; McAusland, 2008).

Figure 1.14 Selected advanced and emerging markets: percentage change in CO_2 emissions

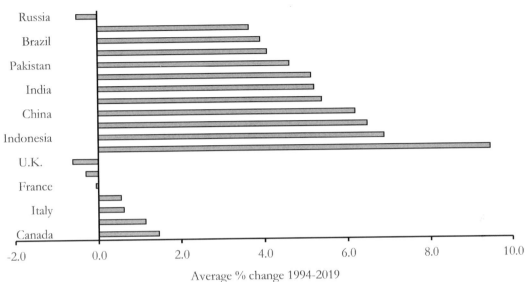

Average % change 1994-2019

Source: Global Carbon Project and Carbon Dioxide Information Analysis Center.

Looking at recent data (from 2018), global emissions of CO_2 amounted to about 37 billion tons. The largest polluter was China (31% of global emissions), followed by the United States (14%), the EU-27 (7%), and India (7%). Russia contributed to 4% of global emissions.

Figure 1.15 Share of global CO_2 emissions by country

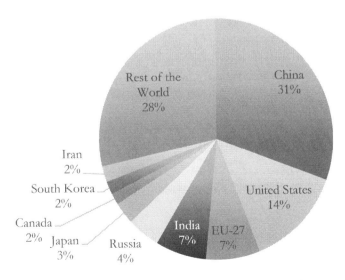

Source: Carbon Dioxide Information Analysis Center and Global Carbon Project, in 2018.

The figures change radically if we focus on the stock of emissions by country during the same period (instead of annual emissions flows). If today the biggest emitters are emerging markets such as China and India, most of the historical emissions were generated in developed markets.

Figure 1.16 Share of the stock of global emissions (1970–2020)

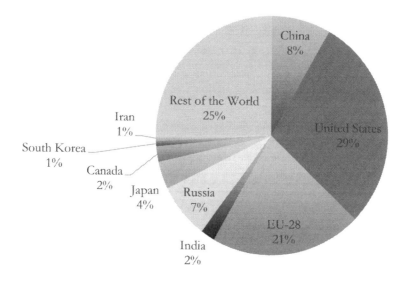

Source: Carbon Dioxide Information Analysis Center and Global Carbon Project.

1.3.2 Metric Tons of CO_2 Emissions per Person

Besides the global level of emissions, it is important to analyze the emissions data per person. In the debate about CO_2 emissions and climate change mitigation, it is important to understand population dynamics, and the metric tons of CO_2 emissions per person, in different regions. For example, in China – the largest global polluter in absolute terms – CO_2 emissions per inhabitant in 2018 was half that in the United States. However, China's population is almost four times larger than that of the United States, and thus its total emissions is larger. Similarly, India in 2018 was responsible for 7% of global emissions, while Indian emissions per capita were approximately 12% of the emissions per capita in the United States. The largest volume of emissions per capita is in Saudi Arabia. The EU-28 (5.7 metric tons per capita) was the advanced economy with the lowest volume of CO_2 emissions per capita, but this amount is still much higher than the average in emerging markets.

Table 1.3 Emissions per capita (metric tons)

Country/region	Per capita emissions
Saudi Arabia	18
United States	14.2
Canada	14.2
Russia	10.8
Japan	8.2
China	7.4
EU-28	5.7
Turkey	4.7
Brazil	2.2
Vietnam	2.6
India	1.8

Source: Carbon Dioxide Information Analysis Center and Global Carbon Project, in 2018.

These data have raised serious concerns about global sustainability in the near future. For example, if China had the same amount of CO_2 emissions per capita as the United States, in 2018 the global emissions of CO_2 would have been 30% higher. Similarly, if India polluted as much per person as the United States, global emissions would have been 56 billion tons (an increase of 43%).

Overall, the data on emissions show the following:

o   When looking at the stock of global emissions, the majority of accumulated pollution was generated by advanced economies, such as Europe, the United States, and Japan. When looking at changes, emerging markets are responsible for most of the increase in emissions over the past few decades.

o   As emerging market countries developed, the level of pollution they generate increased.

o   If emerging economies follow the same development trajectory we have seen historically in advanced economies, the levels of pollution will skyrocket. Thus, the green transition in these emerging economies has immense implications for global climate change.

KEY LEARNING POINT

In recent years, emerging markets have been responsible for most of the increase in emissions. However, the majority of accumulated emissions was generated by advanced economies.

1.3.3 Global Emissions by Sector

As Figure 1.17 shows, in 2018, sectors that contributed more to global emissions were energy[25] (approximately 57%), transport (16%), and agriculture, forestry and land use (19%).[26]

Figure 1.17 Annual contribution to global CO_2 emissions by sector

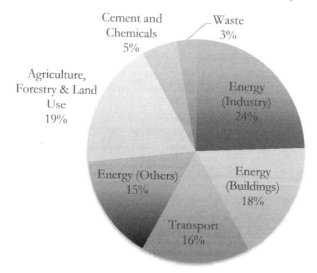

Source: CAIT Climate Data Explorer via Climate Watch (https://ourworldindata.org/emissions-by-sector), in 2016.

Transport accounts for around one-fifth of global CO_2 emissions. Road travel accounts for three-quarters of transport emissions (passenger vehicles 45%, road cargo freight 30%). Aviation and shipping account for 12% and 11% of transport emissions, respectively.[27]

Agriculture is under enormous pressure to produce more – and healthier – food, while also reducing its impact on the environment. The world population is expected to reach 10 billion by 2050, and food production will need to rise to meet future needs. A delicate balance will

---

[25] The sum of energy in industry, buildings, agriculture and fishing, fugitive emissions, and unallocated fuel combustion.

[26] Industry includes the production of minerals, chemicals, metals, pulp, paper, food, drink, refrigeration and air conditioning, aerosols and solvents, semiconductor and electronics manufacture, and electrical equipment. Energy includes public heat and electricity production; other energy industries; fugitive emissions from solid fuels, oil, and gas; manufacturing industries and construction; and other fuel combustion.

[27] Our World in Data (https://ourworldindata.org).

have to be struck between preserving natural resources and making sufficient quality food available and affordable.

1.3.4 Global Emissions by Fuel Type

In 2018, the main two sources of CO_2 emission associated with energy and industrial production were coal (accounting for 40% of global emissions) and oil (accounting for 34% of global emissions). The remaining sources were gas, cement, and flaring. The contribution of each fuel to global CO_2 emissions has changed since 1980. In fact, during 1980–2018, CO_2 emissions produced by coal increased from 36% to 40% while emissions produced by oil decreased from 46% to 34%.

Figure 1.18 Annual contribution to CO_2 by fuel type

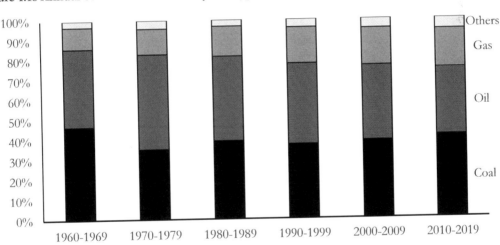

Source: Global Carbon Project and CDIAC.

The contributions to global CO_2 emissions associated with the use of different sources of fuels vary across countries and regions. In 2020, China and India consumed more than 60% of the world's coal, which represents a very significant input to their energy production. Within developed markets, in countries such as Canada, France, Italy, and the United Kingdom, emissions associated with the use of coal represented about 10% of their total emissions. The share of emissions from coal was higher in the United States, Germany, and Japan.

Table 1.4 Coal consumption by country in 2020

Country	Consumption in exajoules
China	82.3
India	17.5
United States	9.2
Japan	4.6
South Africa	3.5
Russian Federation	3.3
Indonesia	3.3
South Korea	3.0
Vietnam	2.1
Germany	1.8
World	**151.4**

Source: BP's Statistical Review of World Energy 2021.

KEY LEARNING POINT

The increase in emissions from coal reflects the larger use of coal in emerging markets since the 1980s.

1.4   THE ROAD TO THE PARIS AGREEMENT

Today, there is a global consensus on the relevance of anthropogenic global warming and its consequences, but it was not always like this. Over the last three decades, several intergovernmental events such as the Kyoto Protocol and Montreal Protocol contributed to a global consensus on the need for action.

In December 2015, more than 190 countries adopted a historic climate agreement. The Paris Agreement was a historic step in the global battle against global climate change because it commits governments to reducing greenhouse gas emissions, with a collective target of −50% by 2050 compared to 1990 levels. The agreement aims to arrest the temperature rise, and the signatories commit to "holding the increase in the global average temperature to well below 2 °C above pre-industrial levels and pursuing efforts to limit the temperature increase to 1.5 °C above pre-industrial levels."

The Paris Agreement requires individual countries to present their commitments – Nationally Determined Contributions (NDCs) – in their climate plans. The objective is to periodically strengthen the voluntary reduction targets set by individual countries. Countries were asked to submit their NDCs in 2020, and every five years thereafter. The signatories have also pledged to fund the transfer of clean technologies to countries unable to transition to the green economy on their own. The agreement itself is legally binding, but legal scholars have some doubts about its practical consequences.[28]

In the remarks at the closing of the Conference, the UN secretary Ban Ki Moon declared: "Mesdames, Messieurs. All my congratulations. The Paris Agreement on climate change is a monumental triumph for people and the planet."[29]

1.4.1 IPCC Report: Scenarios on Global Warming

Over the years, the various IPCC reports have evolved in terms of the certainty of their conclusions, the weight of supporting scientific evidence included, and the wealth of presented data, conclusively establishing the reality of anthropogenic climate change and global warming. The reports typically start with the observed changes in the climate system and their causes, and then move on to future climate changes, the risks, and the impact around the world. Besides global warming, many other changes have been predicted in the climate system. These include changes in earth and sea level temperatures, the water cycle, ocean quality and sea level, biodiversity, food systems, human health, and other dimensions.

The report then talks about future pathways for adaptation, mitigation, and sustainable development. That is, depending on the response options (global mitigation and adaptation policies), several emissions scenarios are presented, and the consequences of these scenarios for the climate system.

In 2019, atmospheric CO_2 concentrations were the highest in the last two million years, and concentrations of methane (CH_4) and nitrous oxide (N_2O) were the highest in the last 800,000 years (IPCC, 2021). The IPCC 2021 report states that without rapid and large-scale reductions in GHG emissions, the goal of limiting warming to around 1.5 ° C or even 2 ° C above the pre-industrial levels by 2050 will be out of reach.

The IPCC presents several scenarios that vary according to the concentration of emissions in the atmosphere. Some scenarios are more stringent and involve significant mitigation. Other scenarios feature very high GHG emissions, implying that no additional effort to restrict emissions has occurred. There are also several intermediate scenarios.

The IPCC (2021) has published a report that describes the possible evolution of global warming through 2050 and 2100 under the different scenarios of CO_2 and GHG emission patterns:

---

[28] The UN 2015 Paris Agreement is a "legally binding international treaty on climate change." Yet the treaty does not impose penalties (fees, fines, or embargos) on parties that violate its terms. Also, no international court is ready to enforce compliance. https://www.un.org/sg/en/content/sg/statement/2015-12-12/secretary-generals-remarks-closing-cop21

[29] Statements United Nations, 2015.

1. Emissions decline toward the goal of net zero around 2050 or, later, followed by different levels of negative net CO_2 emissions (SSP1-2.6).
2. Emissions remain at the current levels (SSP1-1.9).
3. Intermediate boost in emission values, which remain at the current levels until the middle of the century (SSP2-4.5).
4. Substantial increase in emissions values (SSP3-7.0).
5. Emissions double by 2100 or 2050 (SSP5-8.5).

Table 1.5 reports the increase in global surface temperature under the different CO_2 (and other GHG) emissions scenarios.

Table 1.5 Global warming under different emissions scenarios

Scenario	Near term 2021–2040		Mid-term 2041–2060		Long term 2081–2100	
	Best estimate (°C)	Very likely range (°C)	Best estimate (°C)2	Very likely range (°C)3	Best estimate (°C)4	Very likely range (°C)5
SSP1-1.9	1.5	1.2–1.7	1.6	1.2–2.0	1.4	1.0–1.8
SSP1-2.6	1.5	1.2–1.8	1.7	1.3–2.2	1.8	1.3–2.4
SP2-4.5	1.5	1.2–1.8	2.0	1.6–2.5	2.7	2.1–3.5
SSP3-7.0	1.5	1.2–1.8	2.1	1.7–2.6	3.6	2.8–4.6
SSP5-8.5	1.6	1.3–1.9	2.4	1.9–3.0	4.4	3.3–5.7

Source: IPCC (2021).

1.4.2 Net Zero

Net zero will occur when the stock of CO_2 emitted into the atmosphere by human activities will equal that removed from the atmosphere by human activities over the same period of time. Therefore, achieving "net-zero emissions" implies that any CO_2 released into the atmosphere by a company's activities is balanced by an equivalent amount that is removed. To achieve the net-zero emissions goal, apart from reforestation, new technologies such as Carbon Capture and Storage (CCS) systems "are available to capture and store the carbon dioxide generated during the process of power generation and industrial production. Capture technologies are mostly applicable to power plants and large industries and will open the way for large-scale production of low-carbon or carbon-free electricity and fuels for transportation, as well as for small-scale or distributed applications" (IPCC, 2005: 117).

In a report published in 2019, the IPCC estimates that to stabilize global warming to 1.5 °C above the pre-industrial era as established by the Paris Agreement, GHG emissions must be reduced to zero by 2050. Whereas the achievement of "gross zero" means the cessation of GHG emissions, the achievement of the net zero goal means that the stock of CO_2 emitted in the atmosphere by human activities should be equal to that removed from the atmosphere by human activities. Jim Skea, co-chairman of the Working Group III of the IPCC, declared that "limiting warming to 1.5 °C is possible within the laws of chemistry and physics but doing so would require unprecedented changes." For example, a net zero goal entails greater adoption of low-emission and carbon-free technologies, electrification of transport, and reduction of land-use change (IPCC, 2018). As of 2021, together with companies, cities, and financial institutions, 131 governments have committed to, or are considering committing to, net zero emissions by 2050. Further, 164 out of the 191 countries that signed the Paris Agreement have submitted their action plans – Nationally Determined Contributions – to achieve the net-zero objective.

Commitments to net-zero emissions differ from country to country. At the end of 2020, the countries that had set legally net zero emissions binding targets were the United Kingdom, Sweden, France, New Zealand, and Denmark. For example, in 2019, the UK Parliament passed legislation to legally commit the government to achieving a net-zero emissions target by 2050.

In the Global Assessment of Net Zero Targets, the Energy & Climate Intelligence Unit (Black et al. 2021)[30] in partnership with the University of Oxford estimated that countries with net-zero targets together produce 68% of the world's GDP, are responsible for 61% of the global emissions of GHGs, and represent 51% of the global population.

The costs of the net-zero transition will not be equally shared by corporates and consumers across countries and regions. Rather, most of the adjustment burden will be borne by regions and corporates with carbon-intensive product portfolios and operations and low levels of technological sophistication.

KEY LEARNING POINT

The costs of the net-zero transition will not be equally distributed.

1.4.3 Science Based Targets Initiative (SBTi)

After signing the Paris Agreement, various countries agreed to take action to keep temperature increases well below 2 °C. To achieve this, countries can formulate policies and regulations for companies producing significant amounts of carbon emissions, to achieve net-zero emissions objectives. Ultimately, to comply with various policies, satisfy differing stakeholder expectations, and help achieve the goals of the Paris Agreement, companies will need to change the way they produce, and thereby reduce their emissions.

---

[30] The Energy and Climate Intelligence Unit is a nonprofit organization that supports informed debate on energy and climate change issues in the United Kingdom.

The Science Based Target initiative (SBTi) is a partnership created by the Carbon Disclosure Project (CDP), UN Global Compact, World Wide Fund for Nature (WWF), and World Resources Institute (WRI) after the Paris Agreement was signed. This initiative helps companies align their objectives of carbon emissions reduction with the Paris Agreement by following targets based on science.

The Paris Agreement set the limit for global temperature rise to below 2 °C, preferably 1.5 °C, compared to pre-industrial levels. The ultimate goal of the SBTi is to help companies engage in the change needed to achieve the goal set by the Paris Agreement by defining targets that are considered "science based" and in line with the above limits. Specifically, the SBTi proposes the following[31]:

- o Define and promote best practices in emissions reductions and net-zero targets in line with climate science.
- o Provide technical assistance and expert resources to companies so that they set science-based targets that are in line with the latest climate science.
- o Bring together a team of experts to assist companies with independent target assessment and validation.

To limit the temperature increase on Earth, the maximum CO_2 emissions allowed worldwide must comply with the carbon budget. Following the Paris Agreement, the carbon budget will be the maximum amount of carbon emissions that we, as a society, can allow to maintain the temperature within the established limits.

There are different ways of reducing carbon emissions. Firms can become carbon neutral by drastically reducing their carbon emissions, or by investing in projects that absorb CO_2 (this is called *offsetting*). If the amount of carbon emissions that a company offsets is the same as the amount it releases, that company is known as a carbon neutral firm, based on the concept given by the United Nations Framework Convention on Climate Change (UNFCCC, 2021).

The achievement of either carbon neutrality or net zero is determined by the actions taken by the company to reduce emissions (UNFCCC, 2021). A company's net-zero target requires decarbonization (no carbon is emitted by the company) if carbon offsets are not used.

The SBTi does not accept carbon offsetting to achieve a previously settled target.[32] For a science-based target to be recognized by the SBTi, decarbonization has to be included at a date that aligns with the Paris Agreement – but without using carbon offsets: "Offsets are

---

[31] SBTi official website: https://sciencebasedtargets.org.
[32] A problem with carbon offsetting is the credibility of the projects chosen to absorb carbon. Indeed, often there is no certainty that the action selected to offset carbon will reduce emissions by the desired amount (see further details in Section 1.5.3 on greenwashing).

only considered to be an option for companies wanting to finance additional emission reductions beyond their science-based target (SBT) or net-zero target."[33]

The first step to joining the SBTi is registering and submitting a standard commitment letter. After this, the company has 24 months to present its targets for validation. Next, the SBTi will approve the settled targets, and these must be made public within six months. For the SBTi to approve the company's target, it should be computed based on one of these methodologies:

- o The Absolute Contraction Approach (ACA) requires each company to reduce its emissions by the same amount that is globally required to achieve the temperature goal. Two-thirds of the targets approved by SBTi in 2020 were set using this method (see the SBTi website: https://sciencebasedtargets.org).
- o The Sectoral Decarbonization Approach (SDA) divides the 2 °C carbon budget among different sectors, and within each sector, companies can set their science-based emission reduction targets based on, for example, their percentage contribution to the total sectoral activity.

Also, every year the company should disclose its emissions and review the progress made toward its targets. Moreover, the targets should be updated every five years.

In 2022, the companies that joined the SBTi increased to almost 2,800 (more than 70% of the companies joined the initiative between 2021 and 2022). These companies represent a combined market capitalization of over $38 trillion.

Figure 1.19 Companies joining the SBTi per year

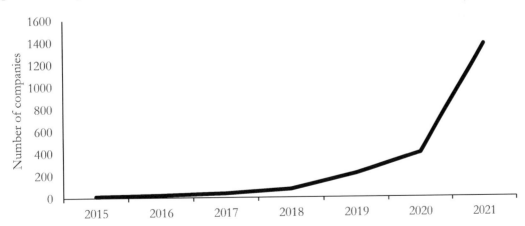

Source: SBTi official website (https://sciencebasedtargets.org).

---

[33] SBTi official website: https://sciencebasedtargets.org.

According to SBTi (2020), member companies reduced their collective emissions by 25% between 2015 and 2019. More than 1,200 of the member companies (41% of the total, with a combined US$8.6 trillion in market capitalization) have committed to science-based targets aligned with 1.5 °C. The study reveals that there has been excellent progress in developed countries, with the OECD countries at the forefront. For instance, in Europe, one-third of the companies with high emissions have committed to the SBTi. However, looking at the specific category of energy and industry, companies committed to the SBTi represented only 3.6% of global greenhouse emissions as of October 2020 (SBTi, 2020).

Wipro and STBi

Wipro is an Indian multinational corporation that provides services related to technology and consulting. In October 2018, STBi approved Wipro´s targets, and Wipro became the first Indian IT company to join the STBi.

The measures included in the targets include replacement of motors, improvement of air-conditioning fans, supplier rationalization, and agreements to purchase renewable energy.

Since 2015, its renewable energy consumption increased by 40%. Also, it reduced 28% of Scope 1 and 2 emissions (The CSR Journal, 2021).

SBTi-approved targets pledged by October 2020 amounted to a total emissions reduction of 28.8 million metric tons annually, "equivalent to taking 6.2 million cars off the road each year."[34] However, their calculations show that this represents only 0.1% of the amount needed to reach net zero, which spotlights the long and arduous path ahead.

Investors and financial institutions play an important role in encouraging companies to establish targets to reduce emissions. According to the Carbon Disclosure Project (2020), 96% of the surveyed companies agreed that general investor pressure influenced their decision to join the SBTi (see also Section 4.4 on shareholder activism and Section 5.4 on the strategies followed by different investors). Moreover, stock exchanges such as the London Stock Exchange and Euronext are coordinating their actions with the goals established by the Paris Agreement, and using targets validated by the SBTi.

The SBTi is not immune to the danger of greenwashing (see Section 1.5.3). The Corporate Climate Responsibility Monitor (CCRM, 2022) evaluated 25 companies representing 10% of the total revenue of the world's largest 500 companies. They suggested that only a small proportion of the companies planned to commit to the settled targets, and the companies' plans suffered from significant omissions and lack of clarity.

It is important to distinguish between the different scopes of emissions and understand why some companies do not meet the planned targets. According to the Greenhouse Gas

---

[34] STBi (2020).

Protocol (https://ghgprotocol.org), carbon emissions from a company's operations and economic activity are typically grouped into three different categories:

○ Scope 1: Direct emissions from production.
○ Scope 2: Indirect emissions from consumption of purchased electricity, heat, or steam.
○ Scope 3: Other indirect emissions from the production of purchased materials, product use, waste disposal, outsourced activities, etc.

Scope 3 CO_2 emissions are therefore defined end to end. They include supplier-related emissions as well as consumers' emissions related to the use of the product/service. As a result, Scope 3 emissions include all indirect emissions that the company is responsible for in its value chain,[35] and in most cases represent the majority of the emissions of a company. This means that if a company commits to a certain Scope 1 emissions target and achieves it, it may cover only a small part of its actual carbon footprint.

KEY LEARNING POINT

Carbon emissions can be computed under three different categories: Scopes 1, 2, and 3.

The importance of clear plans and targets: an example from Carrefour

Carrefour is a French global retailer, and most of its carbon emissions arise from product packaging and supply. This company joined the SBTi in 2020, committing to reduce almost half of its Scope 1 and 2 emissions by 2040 and 29% of its Scope 3 emissions by 2030. However, according to a report by CCRM (2022), most of the targets defined by the company were unclear and therefore lacked credibility. They highlighted the fact that the emissions covered (Scopes 1 and 2) represented only approximately 2% of the total emissions of the company, and its Scope 3 emissions (which include the indirect emissions of all the products sold in their stores) targets and plans lacked credibility because they did not include sufficient information.

Another important difficulty relates to the methodology used by the SBTi to record the impact of the established targets. Bjørn (2021) suggests that the SBTi should "be more transparent about which of these methods was used to assess each company's targets," and clarify why it used the selected methodology. The SBTi (2020) report recognizes that companies must be more transparent. It finds that 13% of the committed companies did not make public the progress they had made toward their target, and 43% reported their progress but with inadequate data or in a nonstandard way.

---

[35] See Section 3.6 for an additional discussion on supply chain issues.

1.4.4 United Nations Sustainable Development Goals

In September 2000, leaders of 189 countries within the framework of the UN signed the Millennium Declaration, with which they committed to achieving eight Millennium Development Goals (MDGs) by 2015. The goals ranged from halving extreme poverty to promoting gender equality and from ensuring environmental sustainability to reducing child mortality. In September 2015, the UN conceived a "blueprint to achieve a better and sustainable future for all," which was formally known as the 17 Sustainable Development Goals (SDGs), within the framework of the 2030 Agenda for Sustainable Development. The SDGs were signed by all the 193 member states of the UN.

The SDGs represent an urgent call for action by the international community in global partnership to address pressing global challenges ranging from food security to gender inequality and from education to climate change. The SDGs "recognize that ending poverty and other deprivations must go hand in hand with strategies that improve health and education, reduce inequality, and spur economic growth – all while tackling climate change and working to preserve our oceans and forests."[36] The 17 goals to be achieved by 2030 are the following:

1. No Poverty: End poverty in all its forms everywhere.
2. Zero Hunger: End hunger, achieve food security, improved nutrition, and promote sustainable agriculture.
3. Good Health and Well-Being: Ensure healthy lives and promote well-being for all at all ages.
4. Quality Education: Ensure inclusive and equitable quality education and promote lifelong learning opportunities for all.
5. Gender Equality: Achieve gender equality and empower all women and girls.
6. Clean Water and Sanitation: Ensure availability and sustainable management of water and sanitation for all.
7. Affordable and Clean Energy: Ensure access to affordable, reliable, sustainable, and modern energy for all.
8. Decent Work and Economic Growth: Promote sustained, inclusive, and sustainable economic growth, full and productive employment, and decent work for all.
9. Industry, Innovation, and Infrastructure: Build resilient infrastructure, promote inclusive and sustainable industrialization, and foster innovation.
10. Reduced Inequalities: Reduce inequality within and among countries.
11. Sustainable Cities and Communities: Make cities and human settlements inclusive, safe, resilient, and sustainable
12. Responsible Consumption and Production: Ensure sustainable consumption and production patterns.

---

[36] https://sdgs.un.org/goals.

13. Climate Action: Take urgent action to combat climate change and its impacts.
14. Life Below Water: Conserve and sustainably use the oceans, seas, and marine resources for sustainable development.
15. Life on Land: Protect, restore, and promote sustainable use of terrestrial ecosystems, sustainably manage forests, combat desertification, halt and reverse land degradation, and halt biodiversity loss
16. Peace and Justice, Strong Institutions: Promote peaceful and inclusive societies for sustainable development, provide access to justice for all, and build effective, accountable, and inclusive institutions at all levels.
17. Partnerships for the Goals: Strengthen the means of implementation and revitalize the global partnership for sustainable development.

Some of these goals are economic, whereas others are societal or environmental. Several SDGs are interrelated. For instance, combating climate change (Goal 13) is clearly linked to other goals such as 2 (food), 7 (energy), 11 (cities), and 12 (sustainable consumption and production).

The ambitiousness of the goals and targets means that all sections of society – the corporate sector, in particular – will be involved in the effort. Sachs (2012) argues that achieving the SDGs requires not only the provision of resources, technology, and innovation but also leadership in the corporate sector, regardless of the company's size.

The involvement of the corporate sector means that the SDGs represent an opportunity for investors too. The selection of the SDGs to invest in depends, of course, both on investors' goals and on the attractiveness and availability of the related investment targets. Not all SDGs offer the same investment opportunities.

KEY LEARNING POINT

SDGs are a clear example of the interrelationships between the challenges humankind faces, which are at the same time economic, societal, and environmental.

1.5 ESG, CLIMATE CHANGE, AND STAKEHOLDER EXPECTATIONS

ESG characteristics have become an important factor in business decisions. In this section, we focus on climate change and other ESG components to provide an overview of how the expectations of different stakeholders are changing. We also introduce *greenwashing*, one of the ways in which the "green" concept can be abused.

1.5.1 Sustainability and Stakeholder Expectations

Concern about climate change has not only grown in the scientific community but also in social circles. Mass media and environmental activism events have helped raise awareness throughout society. For example, in 2007, former U.S. vice-president Al Gore and the IPCC were awarded the Nobel Peace Prize for their contributions to the environmental movement.

Calls for action to address the climate crisis come from company stakeholders (customers, employees, etc.), world leaders, governments, regulators, shareholders, and financial investors. As a matter of fact, the Oxford English Dictionary's Word of the Year in 2019 was "climate emergency." Calls for action to address climate challenges are intensifying and involve a wide range of stakeholders, from regulators to consumers.

Concerns about environmental issues are spreading to consumers. In December 2019, an online survey of 19,964 consumers across 28 developed and developing countries (Ipsos, 2019) showed that about 70% of the respondents had changed the products and services they used due to environmental concerns. Similarly, Capgemini (2019) surveyed 7,520 retail consumers and found that 79% of them had already changed or were about to change their purchase preferences owing to sustainability concerns.

The younger generation is increasingly concerned about climate change. The Deloitte Global Millennial Survey 2020 (Deloitte 2020) revealed that environmental issues were one of the top concerns of millennials. Moreover, more than half of the surveyed millennials declared that they had changed their consumption habits or transport choices as their contribution to improving the planet. PwC (2021) reported similar findings: 60% of the millennials surveyed had begun choosing products from companies with environment-friendly policies. In addition, the generational wealth transfer will make millennials owners of significant financial assets in the future, and they would therefore be concerned about these issues.

Charm et al. (2020) of McKinsey analyzed a sample of more than 22,000 consumers across 10 countries (Brazil, China, France, Germany, India, Japan, Mexico, Russia, the United Kingdom, and the United States) and found that 79% of the surveyed consumers aspired to reduce the environmental impact of their consumption by taking actions such as choosing products with sustainable packaging.

Greta Thunberg and the Fridays for Future initiative

The environmental campaigns of the Swedish teenager, Greta Thunberg, showcased the global concern of the new generation about climate change.

On August 20, 2018, Greta Thunberg, then an unknown 15-year-old from Stockholm, decided not to go to school until September 9, the date of the Swedish elections. Her goal was to ask the government to respect the Paris agreements on CO_2 emissions reductions. After the polls, Greta went back to school, but she began to strike every Friday to force the authorities to take notice of climate change. It was the beginning of the Fridays for Future initiative.

In 2019, the Swedish activist teenager was invited to hold conferences at Davos during the World Economic Forum and the UN's Climate Action Summit in New York. Greta Thunberg's speech at the UN Summit was accompanied by the September 2019 Global Climate Strikes, a series of international strikes, where 7.5 million people gathered at 6,000 events in 185 countries to mobilize against the perceived government inaction on climate change issues.

Kronthal-Sacco and Tensie (2019) analyzed 36 product categories and more than 71,000 stock keeping units (SKUs) that accounted for more than 40% of consumer packaged goods (CPG) sales in the United States between 2013 and 2018. They found that 50% of the CPG growth from 2013 to 2018 came from sustainability-marketed products.

These changes in consumption attitudes affect the way companies design their strategies, as they strive to meet the consumer demand for more responsible products. Consequently, large companies, such as automotive companies, are also asking their suppliers to be more environment-friendly.

Employees of some large corporations have begun taking steps to change the corporate attitude toward climate change. For example, in April 2019, 8,700 Amazon employees signed an open letter asking the company's CEO – Jeff Bezos – to take actions to address climate change challenges and reduce the company's carbon footprint. In September 2019, the internal, informal group called Amazon Employees for Climate Justice organized a march, in 25 cities and 14 countries, to urge the company to assist climate change mitigation efforts. This march took place in the context of the climate strikes organized within the global framework of the climate activism association Fridays for Future led by Greta Thunberg. After Amazon's employees announced their decision to take part in the global demonstrations, employees from other Silicon Valley firms such as Google, Facebook, Square, and Twitter announced that they would join the initiative (Matsakis, 2019).

Employee engagement with corporate climate policies did not involve only Amazon or large U.S. corporations. In September 2019, German labor unions backed Fridays for Future strikes and called on workers to participate in the climate demonstrations to urge governments to accelerate the transition process toward a low carbon economy (Syndicat European Trade Union, 2020).

KEY LEARNING POINT

The pressure exerted by consumers and social movements, and even by companies' own employees, is increasing the motivation to produce more environment-friendly products and formulate different commercial and production strategies.

1.5.2 ESG Components

ESG factors have become more important over the past decade. Broadly speaking, ESG is about the incorporation of environmental, social, and corporate governance factors into business decisions and policymaking.

The growing interest of investors in ESG factors reflects the fact that environmental, social, and corporate governance issues can affect the performance of companies, and create additional risks and opportunities. Therefore, companies and investors should give these factors due consideration in their decision-making. Further, the growing societal awareness of the risks posed by climate change, diversity in companies and boards, and responsible conduct toward different stakeholders, for example, employees, have made ESG more important.

The Origins of ESG

The ESG concept is connected to an old idea: corporate social responsibility (CSR). Domini, the founder of Domini and KLD, summarized it as follows: "The strategy and mechanics of social investing evolved out of faith-based standards for investments, moved through the early environmental movement, the influence of the war in Vietnam, the civil rights struggle in the United States, and came of age during the synthesis of international efforts geared toward alleviating suffering in South Africa" (Domini, 2001).

From 1970 until 2000, with the exception of some retail investors and religious institutions, responsible investing remained a niche market in asset management.

Efforts to promote corporate social responsibility began several decades ago and have accelerated more recently. In the 1990s, the United Nations formed a partnership with the financial sector: The United Nations Program Finance Initiative (UNEP FI). This group launched several initiatives in the area of sustainable finance and was later responsible for the launch of the Principles for Responsible Investing (PRI). The PRI initiative was sponsored by the then UN Secretary-General, Kofi Anan, and was initially signed by a group of pension funds, a sovereign fund (from Norway), and a re-insurance company (Munich Re) drawn from nine countries. The number of signatories has currently grown to over 3,000, with assets under management of more than US$100 trillion.[37]

The Different Components of ESG

ESG issues concern many different stakeholders. There is not a complete list of all the different aspects of sustainability, but there are several important components within each of the ESG pillars:

  o Environment (E): This concerns the company's impact on the environment and ecosystems. It includes items such as carbon emissions and vulnerability to climate change, and also other themes such as natural resources, the circular economy, pollution and waste management, water usage, biodiversity, deforestation, and land use.
  o Social (S): This includes topics related to human capital; product safety; customer privacy and data security; relations with customers, suppliers, the community and civil society; and others. It includes issues such as human rights, employee relations and engagement, labor practices, diversity, political contributions and corruption, child labor, community relations, supply chain, and product responsibility.
  o Governance (G): This refers to the company's mechanisms to safeguard the interests of long-term shareholders. It includes topics such as the board structure, management effectiveness, disclosure practices, protection of shareholder rights, corruption, takeover defenses, independent directors, executive compensation, and other corporate behaviors.

Within ESG, environmental factors have attracted the most attention, as the need to transition economies and financial systems to a low-carbon economy has gained traction. Also, awareness of the risks associated with climate change has increased in recent years.

Environmental factors are the core focus of this book, although many of the issues discussed here intersect the different sustainability areas.

---

[37] See Section 5.4.3 for more details on the PRI.

Table 1.6 The scope of ESG issues

	Themes	Examples of ESG issues
Environment	Climate change	Carbon emissions (Scope 1, 2, 3)
		Vulnerability to climate events
	Natural resources	Water usage
		Biodiversity & land use
		Raw material sourcing
		Energy efficiency
	Pollution & waste	Toxic emissions (besides CO_2)
		Waste management
		Packaging material
		Electronic waste
Social	Human capital	Labor management
		Human capital development
		Employee engagement, inclusion, diversity
		Supply chain labor standards
		Health & safety in the workplace
	Product liability	Product safety & quality
		Privacy & data security
		Product labelling
		Selling practices
	Stakeholders	Controversial sourcing
		Government relations
		Community relations
Governance	Corporate governance	Ownership & protection of shareholders
		Executive compensation
		Board & management processes, and quality
		Disclosure practices
	Corporate behavior	Business ethics
		Corruption
		Manipulation of earnings
		Competitive behavior
		Tax transparency

What ESG Means Today

Sustainable finance is sometimes defined as the incorporation of ESG considerations into financial decisions. These decisions can be corporate actions (such as capital allocation or financing decisions) or investor choices (where to allocate capital).

There is an economic rationale for sustainable finance. Firms may choose to invest in ESG in response to investor or consumer expectations, thereby reducing their cost of capital, or improving their profit margin. Investments in ESG may also lead to lower costs and lower future risks. Further, companies may decide to become more ESG friendly to comply with regulatory requirements. That is, the growing interest in ESG reflects the view that sustainability factors are not merely "nice to have," but that they are related to corporate performance and risks (see Section 5.3).

For investors, information on how firms are incorporating ESG principles is crucial for their decision-making. The various ESG issues can have a material impact on companies' performance and risk. Over the past decades, we have seen the consequences of governance failure at banks and large companies. We have also seen how social risks can lead to financial instability and greater political risk.

Sustainable finance, and environmental issues, are increasingly part of various financial market practices. Data on ESG are used by investors when building their portfolios, and many investment funds track assets using sustainable criteria. Sustainable investing was originally linked to publicly listed companies and equity markets, but over the years it has developed beyond these asset classes. Nowadays fixed income investors, private equity funds, infrastructure players, hedge funds, and many others are signatories of the PRI and apply its principles to their activities. Credit rating agencies and banks are beginning to factor environmental risks into their credit assessments. A growing number of companies issue green bonds (and other sustainability instruments) through a certification process that assures the proceeds will be used for environmental projects.

However, investors and companies face many challenges, such as the need for consistent methodologies and reporting standards, and stricter requirements to prevent greenwashing behaviors. Other challenges include the current high costs of ESG reporting, which can be complicated and burdensome for smaller companies.

The sustainable finance field has many different players that integrate ESG into their products and services:

- o Issuers: Both on the debt and equity sides, issuers can incorporate sustainability considerations into their operations and capital market deals.
- o Investors: The owners of capital bear the ultimate risk and reward of companies' investments and are increasingly incorporating non-financial factors into their decision-making. These owners can be individuals or institutional investors such as sovereign funds, insurance companies, pension funds, endowments, and foundations.
- o Service providers: These are involved in the investment value chain and include index providers, rating providers, asset managers, data providers, auditors, and second-party opinion entities.

- o Policy and regulators: Several policy entities are involved in these areas, such as disclosure-standard-setting organizations, stock exchanges, capital market regulators, and central banks.

Chapters 3 and 4 cover the issuers' perspective, on the debt and equity sides. Chapter 5 is dedicated to investors, with substantial coverage of the role of institutional investors, who are the driving force behind significant change in many areas. They can achieve this through their investment policies, through the way they engage with companies (through dialogue with executives and board members, and also by their votes), and as important players in the public policy debate and evolution of regulations. Given their fiduciary duty, many of these investors have a more long-term orientation than most. Being PRI signatories and institutional investors, they acknowledge that they must act in the best long-term interests of their beneficiaries.

1.5.3 The Dangers of Greenwashing

In 1986, Jay Westervelt, an American environmentalist, was visiting the Fiji Islands. His hotel asked customers to reuse towels, to protect the local sea areas and coral reefs. However, he argued that the hotel's real goal was to cut costs. For instance, that hotel had expanded into near-sea areas, with scant regard for coral reefs. He called greenwashing a pretense of concern for the environment, whereas the main purpose is to increase profits. According to the Cambridge Dictionary, the purpose of greenwashing is "to make people believe that your company is doing more to protect the environment than it really is." The Oxford English Dictionary defines it as the "disinformation disseminated by an organisation so as to present an environmentally responsible public image."

CSR may have a positive impact on businesses, from market share to company reputation, and even on firm value. Recent trends also show that the more well-established consumer preference for sustainable products is now beginning to be translated into investor preference for sustainable financial assets. Because of these expected benefits, the number of firms marketing their CSR credentials has been growing steadily over the past 20 years. This increase in CSR awareness intensifies the risk that firms may choose to engage in strategic disclosure and communication to appear "greener" than they are. Such practices are generally referred to as greenwashing.

There are numerous examples of greenwashing, such as companies that make false claims of eco-friendly benefits. TerraChoice, an environmental marketing company, reported that out of almost 5,000 "green" products sold in the United States and Canada, more than 95% were "guilty" of one of the seven sins of greenwashing[38]:

---

[38] https://www.ul.com/insights/sins-greenwashing.

1. Hidden trade-off: A claim that a product is "green" based on a narrow set of attributes without paying attention to other important environmental issues

2. No proof: A claim that cannot be substantiated with easily accessible information, and that is not confirmed by a reliable third-party certification

3. Vagueness: A claim that is so poorly defined that its real meaning is likely to be misunderstood by the consumer

4. Worshiping false labels: A claim that gives the impression of a third-party endorsement where none exists

5. Irrelevance: A claim that may be truthful, but which is unhelpful to consumers seeking environmental-friendly products

6. Lesser of two evils: A claim that may be true, but that distracts consumers from the greater environmental impact of the product as a whole

7. Fibbing: A claim that is simply false

Chevron's pledge of "ever-cleaner energy"

In 2010, the U.S. oil giant Chevron launched the global CSR campaign "We Agree" in response to the criticisms of oil companies by environmental activists, highlighting the actions the company had taken to produce energy responsibly and support communities wherever it operated. In its advertising, Chevron stated that it "agreed" with the need for energy companies to operate in an environmentally sustainable way.

In 2011, Chevron's subsidiary, Texaco, was accused by the Ecuadorian court of dumping billions of gallons of toxic material into the Amazon river. In 2012, the court fined Chevron US$8.6 billion for damage caused to the Amazon rainforest and the resident communities.

In February 2021, three nonprofit organizations—Earthworks, Global Witness, and Greenpeace USA— jointly filed the first-ever greenwashing complaint to the Federal Trade Commission (FTC). In its complaint against Chevron, the three environmental networks claimed that "Chevron, the world's second largest polluter, is under scrutiny over social media, television and other marketing campaigns that consistently misrepresent its image to appear climate-friendly and socially responsible, while its business operations overwhelmingly rely on climate-polluting fossil fuels, which disproportionately harm communities of color."

As the popularity of green business practices increases among companies' stakeholders, the temptation to "greenwash" a company's business also increases. Some examples include the following:

o   In 2020, the Italian oil major ENI was fined €5 million by the Competition and Market Authority for misleading commercial practices regarding the marketing of its palm-oil-based diesel – EniDiesel+ – which was claimed to "green" in an advertising campaign.

- o   In June 2020, IKEA was accused by the British environmental group Earthsight of being a large buyer of illegally harvested Ukrainian wood for its furniture.
- o   In 2019, the clothing retailer H&M was accused of greenwashing by the Norwegian Consumer Authority for its "Recycling Scheme," which consisted of taking back customers' old clothes in exchange for a coupon to buy new clothes. A large portion of the unwanted clothes taken back by H&M was sent to developing countries, where these clothes could not be processed for disposal.

Greenwashing can be damaging in many ways. First, there are possible litigation costs associated with it. Second, consumers and other stakeholders may significantly penalize a company that is found to be indulging in greenwashing. The reputational impact of being caught greenwashing is high.

KEY LEARNING POINT

Greenwashing is "to make people believe that your company is doing more to protect the environment than it really is."

Empirical research generally shows that the long-run costs of greenwashing exceed the short-term benefits arising from misleading communication strategies. Du (2015) studied publicly traded firms in the Chinese stock market that were included in the greenwashing list by the *Southern Weekly* financial newspaper. They found a negative relationship between greenwashing exposure events and firms' financial performance, measured using the cumulative abnormal return (CAR)[39] associated with the exposure of greenwashing. Berrone et al. (2017) built an indicator for environmental legitimacy and studied how this was affected by the discrepancy between "talk" and "walk" on a longitudinal dataset (1997–2001) containing 325 publicly traded U.S. firms in polluting industries. The analysis essentially suggests that companies that "walk the talk" gain environmental legitimacy, whereas greenwashing tarnishes a firm's environmental legitimacy. Yu et al. (2020) studied a sample of 1,925 companies from the MSCI All Country World Index over the period 2012–2016 and found that the scrutiny from independent directors, institutional investors, and cross-listings are the main corporate governance factors that deter greenwashing. Several studies have demonstrated the negative relationship between greenwashing and trust in companies.[40] Also, there is evidence that greenwashing not only affects the company

---

[39] An abnormal return is defined as the difference between the actual return of a stock and its forecasted expected return. The CAR is the sum of all these differences over a specific period of time, usually limited to a few days.

[40] Among others, Chen et al. (2014), Aji and Sutikno (2015), and More (2019) have provided evidence on how greenwashing can erode trust in a company.

involved in it but can also have spillover effects on other related companies (Wang et al., 2020).

Greenwashing in finance

Finance also faces the problem of greenwashing, which can exist at the company or investor level. At the company level, greenwashing can exist if, for instance, funds raised for green projects (sometimes with favorable financing conditions) are ultimately allocated to finance conventional, or even polluting, projects. Green bonds and sustainable loans (see Sections 3.1 and 3.3) are two ways in which companies can link their finances to environmental outcomes. Unfortunately, some companies have issued green bonds without using the proceeds for green purposes. Another type of greenwashing that can occur at the company level is related to wrong corporate governance practices (see Section 4.3).

Companies can undertake internal actions to reduce their emissions. They can also work with suppliers and other parts of their supply chain to reduce their total carbon footprint. The SBTi (see Section 1.4.3) attempts to corroborate the targets that companies set to become carbon neutral. Initially, this seemed to be a solution to greenwashing. However, the lack of clarity around some targets makes it difficult to check their accuracy. Further, the goals provided by companies (and subsequently approved by the SBTi) do not always take into account the full carbon footprint of a company (that is, Scope 3 emissions).

Companies can also become "carbon neutral" by using offsets. In this method, the company pays for projects that absorb the same amount of emissions that it generates. However, for the offsets to be effective in achieving the stated goals, it is important that the offsetting projects be real and verifiable. Proper validation of offsetting certifications could also reduce greenwashing.

Many global banks have made commitments to climate action. Whether or not banks actually act or simply talk without doing anything concrete is an empirical question that is discussed in Chapter 3. The Rainforest Action Network (2021) used data from Bloomberg to assess banks' involvement in corporate lending and underwriting transactions between 2016 and 2020. The report suggests the top 60 global investment banks financed over 2,300 companies in the oil industry, despite their claims related to portfolio decarbonization and sustainability. In this, and in many other cases, one has to be careful in distinguishing historical data from the future trajectory. The absolute amount of loans is a stock, determined by historical decisions. However, it is important to complement this information with flow data, that is, the current activity level of each bank, and what the lending trends imply for the expected future lending portfolio.

Investors are increasingly demanding investment products that incorporate ESG factors. Chapter 5 focuses on capital markets, and describes the different strategies, products, and developments across different types of investors.

Given this growing investor interest, greenwashing is a relevant concern and could occur if institutional investors make false claims about the "greenness" of their investment products and strategies to attract more clients, but do not actually fulfil their promises. According to *The Economist* (2021), 20 of the world's largest ESG funds hold on average 17 fossil fuel producers, and many of them have even invested in coal mining companies. Sustainable funds often use ESG ratings (see Section 5.1) to determine their portfolio investments. In this case, the danger of greenwashing comes from the lack of clarity regarding the ESG criteria and ratings. Also, it could be a case of greenwashing if a portfolio manager says the portfolio invests in companies with positive environmental impact, and ultimately invests only in companies that, although having very low carbon emissions, have no investments or activities related to the carbon transition. The voting behavior of institutional investors could also lay them open to accusations of greenwashing (see Section 4.3). For example, greenwashing could occur if an asset manager announces certain policies but does not vote in line with them and offers no explanation for this discrepancy.

Besides green claims by investors who later invest in "non-green" assets, greenwashing practices in the financial industry can be favored by the myriad of definitions and methodologies applied by the providers of ESG scores.[41] If these are just box-ticking exercises, they may lead to inconsistent and irrelevant outcomes. The variability and imprecision of industry ESG definitions and terms can also confuse investors. Importantly, many passive funds track indices (see Section 5.5) created on the basis of these scores. Another problem is the lack of proper disclosures, both at the company and investment levels, which also increase greenwashing risks (see Section 6.3 on disclosure).

> **The Saudi Arabia government's bond and BlackRock ESG index funds**
>
> In recent years, Saudi Arabia has been one of the most polluting countries in the world, with more than 18 metric tons of annual CO_2 emissions per capita.
>
> BlackRock and Legal & General Investment Management (LGIM) raised more than $1 billion with ESG index funds that buy emerging market government debt. The fifth-largest position held by these ESG index funds was Saudi Arabia, whose government actually also owns the biggest oil company in the world. The large weight of Saudi Arabia government bonds in these ESG index funds was due to Saudi Arabia scoring better than other emerging market economies in human capital, education, and life expectancy, even though it had very low environmental scores.

Overall, at the portfolio management level, greenwashing occurs when firms say one thing and do something else. Several different behaviors can constitute greenwashing:

---

[41] As described in Section 5.1, the majority of metrics underlying environmental ratings (or ESG ratings in general) are computed using different methodologies. In many cases, the degree of correlation of these metrics is low.

o   Portfolio management practices that are inconsistent with disclosures about ESG
     approaches: This includes possible lack of adherence with global ESG frameworks
     although a firm claims adherence with them, as evidenced by, for instance, fund
     holdings dominated by assets with low ESG scores, which can be inconsistent with
     the firm's stated approaches. (See Section 5.3 for a description of various sustainable
     investment strategies.)

o   Misleading claims regarding ESG approaches, including not being able to reconcile
     a fund's actual holdings with public statements made to consumers: An example is
     the lack of proper controls to guarantee implementation of clients' wishes regarding
     negative screening of certain industries or assets.

o   Passive funds having a "green" or ESG-related name, but tracking an index that is
     not ESG focused. (See Section 5.2 for the challenges to sustainable stock indices.)

o   Biases in performance advertising and marketing, especially related to ESG issues:
     This can happen if marketing materials selectively report returns, risk, and
     correlations, without disclosing methodological issues that can explain them, or
     without including all expenses and fees in their reported performance. It is important
     to be careful with exaggerated statements and to remember that in the long run risk
     is correlated with expected returns (see Section5.3). This means that assets with
     lower risk should generate lower expected returns, even if during a transition period
     prices may be adjusted upward.

o   Proxy voting that is inconsistent with funds' stated goals/policies: For instance,
     issuing public statements regarding the method for assessing proxy proposals, but
     not implementing it later (see Section 4.3 on voting and governance topics).

Bank of New York ESG funds

In May 2022, the U.S. Securities and Exchange Commission (SEC) fined the Bank of New York Mellon
US$1.5 million for ESG misstatements.

The bank had publicly advertised that all investments in certain funds had undergone an ESG quality
review. However, the SEC found several investments in those funds did not have an ESG quality review.
An SEC official commented: "… funds are increasingly offering and evaluating investments that employ
ESG strategies or incorporate certain ESG criteria, in part to meet investor demand for such strategies
and investments. [The bank] did not always perform the ESG quality review that it disclosed using as part
of its investment selection process for certain mutual funds it advised."

Preventing greenwashing/actions to avoid it

Without a proper regulatory framework, several green finance concepts run the risk of being
mere marketing strategies, with no actual environmental or sustainability benefits. False
claims of "green" assets or funds may lead to reputational risk. They may also erode trust in

financial instruments (such as green bonds) that if used well can actually be very helpful for companies and their investors in the actual battle against climate change.

To prevent greenwashing, various guidelines (for companies and funds) are being developed by security market regulators worldwide. These cover aspects such as the labels used by investment funds and benchmarks, proper application of standards, improved disclosure, and a clear connection between stated goals and actual internal practices. Some examples include the following:

- o In the European Union, the European Securities and Markets Authority (ESMA) released the "Sustainable Finance Roadmap 2022-2024," aimed at promoting transparency in financial markets and addressing greenwashing. Also, the European Union announced the Sustainable Finance Disclosure Regulation (SFDR) and the EU Sustainable Finance Action Plan. This EU Plan contains several forms of regulation, including which activities or assets can be called sustainable, as well as standards for green bonds, climate-related indices, and sustainable funds. Section 6.4 further discusses this topic.
- o In the United Kingdom, the Financial Conduct Authority (FCA) published a guide for consumers to identify a sustainable investment fund in 2021. Moreover, it created a UK Green Taxonomy that provides guidelines for sustainable investments and products.
- o In the United States, the Securities and Exchange Commission (SEC) has examined investment firms and whether they accurately disclose their ESG investing approaches, and have implemented processes consistent with their stated aims.
- o In Switzerland, the Swiss Financial Market Supervisory Authority (FINMA) created a guide for preventing greenwashing.
- o The Financial Services Agency in Japan proposed the creation of guidelines that will be mandatory for companies when reporting non-financial information.
- o China's regulators have a Green Bonds Projects Catalogue, created by the People's Bank of China (PBOC), the National Development and Reform Commission (NDRC), and the China Securities Regulatory Commission (CSRC), that gives issuers a criterion to follow when they want to classify a bond as green.
- o South Africa Sustainable Finance Initiative created a Draft Green Finance Taxonomy in 2021 that very closely follows the criteria of the EU Taxonomy mentioned above.

At the company level, Chapters 3 and 4 focus on topics related to the debt financing, equity financing, and corporate governance practices that relate to greenwashing. Some of the possible practices of greenwashing include reporting-level greenwashing, which can include disclosure of misleading or false environment-related information about the company's future strategy, or financing using "sustainable" instruments but investing the proceeds in "brown" projects.

Walmart setting targets

In 2016, Walmart's targets for reducing emissions were approved by the STBi. In an analysis by Carbon Market Watch in 2022, they declare that these goals settled by Walmart focused mainly on Scopes 1 and 2, which covered only 9% of their emissions. Although Walmart did create a plan called "Project Gigaton" to address Scope 3, a lack of transparency makes it is unclear what impact this project is going to have.

At the investment management level, some of the recommended policies and procedures to prevent greenwashing include the following:

- Making clear and understandable disclosures regarding the funds' approaches to ESG investing. Disclosures should be simple and clear, explaining the role of the portfolio manager and any other organization involved.
- Using marketing claims that are accurate, unbiased, and demonstrate consistency with internal practices.
- Disclosing information on how a given strategy aligns with the stated goal, with information on how to measure and monitor the impact.
- Explaining how investments are evaluated, using goals derived from the stated ESG policies. ESG factors can be considered along other factors, but this should be consistently articulated.
- Having clear links between the ultimate investors' goals and needs, and the investment policy that is chosen for them.
- Having clear procedures that address ESG investing across all key aspects of the firms' relevant practices. This includes being clear on ESG issues, and how they are applied, at different phases of the investment process (research, selection of assets, monitoring, etc.).
- Proper staffing of internal control departments, including compliance personnel who are knowledgeable about specific ESG-related practices
- Disclose measurable non-financial information at both the fund and firm levels.

DWS accused of greenwashing

DWS is a German asset manager with almost €900 bn of assets under management (AuM). In its 2020 annual report, DWS claimed that more than half of their assets were using ESG criteria.

BaFin, the German financial markets regulator, launched an investigation into DWS in the summer of 2021 after the German asset manager's former head of sustainability alleged that it was misrepresenting how it used ESG metrics to analyze companies. Other accusations were that DWS portfolio managers were using and relying on external ESG ratings, without performing any further checks. As a result of the announcement of the investigation, DWS's stock price fell by more than 13%.

REFERENCES: CHAPTER 1

Aji, H.M., and B. Sutikno. 2015. "The Extended Consequence of Greenwashing: Perceived Consumer Skepticism." *International Journal of Business and Information* 10 (4): 433.

Aon. 2020. "Weather, Climate & Catastrophe Insight." 2020 Annual Report.

Berrone, P., A. Fosfuri, and L. Gelabert. 2017. "Does Greenwashing Pay off? Understanding the Relationship between Environmental Actions and Environmental Legitimacy." *Journal of Business Ethics* 144 (2): 363–79.

Bjørn, A., S. Lloyd, and D. Matthews. 2021. "From the Paris Agreement to Corporate Climate Commitments: Evaluation of Seven Methods for Setting 'Science-Based' Emission Targets." *Environmental Research Letters* 16 (5): 054019. https://doi.org/10.1088/1748-9326/abe57b.

Black, R., K. Cullen, B. Fay, T. Hale, J. Lang, S. Mahmood, and S.M. Smith. 2021. "Taking Stock: A Global Assessment of Net Zero Targets." *Energy & Climate Intelligence Unit and Oxford Net Zero* 23.

Callendar, G.S. 1938. "The Artificial Production of Carbon Dioxide and Its Influence on Temperature." *Quarterly Journal of the Royal Meteorological Society* 64 (275): 223–40.

Capgemini. 2019. "How Sustainability is Fundamentally Changing Consumer Preferences."

Carbon Disclosure Project. 2020. "CDP Science-Based Targets Campaign. Final Progress Report: 2020 Campaign."

CCRM. 2022. "Corporate Climate Responsibility Monitor 2022." https://newclimate.org/resources/publications/corporate-climate-responsibility-monitor-2022.

Charm, T., A. Grimmelt, H. Kim, K. Robinson, N. Lu, and Mayank. n.d. "Consumer Sentiment Is Diverging across Countries | McKinsey." Accessed August 1, 2022. https://www.mckinsey.com/business-functions/growth-marketing-and-sales/our-insights/a-global-view-of-how-consumer-behavior-is-changing-amid-covid-19.

Chen, Z. M., and G. Q. Chen. 2011. "An Overview of Energy Consumption of the Globalized World Economy." *Energy Policy*, 39 (10): 5920–28. https://doi.org/10.1016/j.enpol.2011.06.046.

Chen, Y.-S., C.-L. Lin, and C.-H. Chang. 2014. "The Influence of Greenwash on Green Word-of-Mouth (Green WOM): The Mediation Effects of Green Perceived Quality and Green Satisfaction." *Quality & Quantity* 48 (5): 2411–25.

Cline, W.R. 2008. "Global Warming and Agriculture." *Finance & Development* 45 (001).

Combes, S. 2003. "Protecting Freshwater Ecosystems in the Face of Global Climate Change." In *Buying Time: A User's Manual for Building Resistance and Resilience to Climate Change in Natural Systems*, edited by Hansen, L. J., Bringer J. L., and Hoffman, J. R. Berlin: World Wildlife Fund Climate Change Program.

Cook, J., N. Oreskes, P.T. Doran, W.R.L. Anderegg, B. Verheggen, E.W. Maibach, J.S. Carlton, et al. 2016. "Consensus on Consensus: A Synthesis of Consensus Estimates on Human-

Caused Global Warming." *Environmental Research Letters* 11 (4): 048002. https://doi.org/10.1088/1748-9326/11/4/048002.

Crippa, P., S. Castruccio, S. Archer-Nicholls, Gissela B. Lebron, M. Kuwata, A. Thota, S. Sumin, et al. 2016. "Population Exposure to Hazardous Air Quality Due to the 2015 Fires in Equatorial Asia." *Scientific Reports* 6 (1): 1–9.

Dasgupta, P. 2021. "Final Report - The Economics of Biodiversity: The Dasgupta Review." https://www.gov.uk/government/publications/final-report-the-economics-of-biodiversity-the-dasgupta-review.

Deloitte. 2020. "Resilient Generations Hold the Key to Creating a 'Better Normal.'". The Deloitte Global Millennial Survey 2020.

Domini, A.L. 2001. *Socially Responsible Investing: Making a Difference and Making Money.* Dearborn Trade Publishing.

Du, X. 2015. "How the Market Values Greenwashing? Evidence from China." *Journal of Business Ethics* 128 (3): 547–74.

Ekholm, N. 1901. "On the Variations of the Climate of the Geological and Historical Past and Their Causes." *Quarterly Journal of the Royal Meteorological Society* 27 (117): 1–62.

Golledge, N.R., E.D. Keller, N. Gomez, K.A. Naughten, J. Bernales, L.D. Trusel, and T.L. Edwards. 2019. "Global Environmental Consequences of Twenty-First-Century Ice-Sheet Melt." *Nature* 566 (7742): 65–72.

Hallegatte, S., A. Vogt-Schilb, M. Bangalore, and J. Rozenberg. 2017. *Unbreakable: Building the Resilience of the Poor in the Face of Natural Disasters.* Washington, DC: World Bank. https://doi.org/10.1596/978-1-4648-1003-9.

Hasanov, F.J., B. Liddle, and J.I. Mikayilov. 2018. "The Impact of International Trade on CO2 Emissions in Oil Exporting Countries: Territory vs. Consumption Emissions Accounting." *Energy Economics* 74: 343–50.

IPCC. 2005. *IPCC Special Report on Carbon Dioxide Capture and Storage.* Cambridge University Press.

IPCC. 2014. Climate Change 2014: *Synthesis Report. Contribution of Working Groups I, II and III to the Fifth Assessment Report of the Intergovernmental Panel on Climate Change* [Core Writing Team, R.K. Pachauri and L.A. Meyer (eds.)]. IPCC, Geneva, Switzerland, 151 pp.

IPCC. 2018. "Strengthening and Implementing the Global Response." In *IPCC Special Report on Global Warming of 1.5°C.*

IPCC. 2021. "Summary for Policymakers." In: *Climate Change 2021: The Physical Science Basis. Contribution of Working Group I to the Sixth Assessment Report of the Intergovernmental Panel on Climate Change.* Cambridge University Press.

Ipsos. 2019. "Climate Change and Consumer Behavior: Global changes in Consumer Behavior in Response to Climate Change." Survey conducted for the World Economic Forum.

Jones, D.S. 2006. "ASEAN and Transboundary Haze Pollution in Southeast Asia." *Asia Europe Journal* 4 (3): 431–46.

Joshi, M., H. Goraya, A. Joshi, and T. Bartter. 2020. "Climate Change and Respiratory Diseases: A 2020 Perspective." *Current Opinion in Pulmonary Medicine* 26 (2): 119–27. https://doi.org/10.1097/MCP.0000000000000656.

Kaplan, L.D. 1952. "On the Pressure Dependence of Radiative Heat Transfer in the Atmosphere." *Journal of Atmospheric Sciences* 9 (1): 1–12.

Kirezci, E., I.R. Young, R. Ranasinghe, S. Muis, R.J. Nicholls, D. Lincke, and J. Hinkel. 2020. "Projections of Global-Scale Extreme Sea Levels and Resulting Episodic Coastal Flooding over the 21st Century." *Scientific Reports* 10 (1): 11629. https://doi.org/10.1038/s41598-020-67736-6.

Kraft Rector, R. 2016. *The Early River Valley Civilizations*. New York: Rosen Publishing.

Kronthal-Sacco, R. and Whelan, T. (2019) Sustainable Share Index: Research on IRI Purchasing Data (2013-2018). PowerPoint Presentation. NYU Stern.

Liu, X., and J. Bae. 2018. "Urbanization and Industrialization Impact of CO2 Emissions in China." *Journal of Cleaner Production* 172 (January): 178–86. https://doi.org/10.1016/j.jclepro.2017.10.156.

Malaguerra, F., H.-J. Albrechtsen, L. Thorling, and P.J. Binning. 2012. "Pesticides in Water Supply Wells in Zealand, Denmark: A Statistical Analysis." *Science of The Total Environment* 414 (January): 433–44. https://doi.org/10.1016/j.scitotenv.2011.09.071.

Masson-Delmotte, V., G. Dreyfus, P. Braconnot, S. Johnsen, J. Jouzel, M. Kageyama, A. Landais, et al. 2006. "Past Temperature Reconstructions from Deep Ice Cores: Relevance for Future Climate Change." *Climate of the Past* 2 (2): 145–65. https://doi.org/10.5194/cp-2-145-2006.

Matsakis, L.. 2019. "Thousands of Tech Workers Join Global Climate Change Strike | WIRED." September 20, 2019. https://www.wired.com/story/tech-workers-global-climate-change-strike/.

McAusland, C.. 2010. "Globalisation's Direct and Indirect Effects on the Environment." In *Globalisation, Transport and the Environment*, by OECD, 31–53. OECD. https://doi.org/10.1787/9789264072916-4-en.

Mirsaeidi, M., H. Motahari, M.T. Khamesi, A. Sharifi, M. Campos, and D.E. Schraufnagel. 2016. "Climate Change and Respiratory Infections." *Annals of the American Thoracic Society* 13 (8): 1223–30. https://doi.org/10.1513/AnnalsATS.201511-729PS.

More, P.V. 2019. "The Impact of Greenwashing on Green Brand Trust from an Indian Perspective." *Asian Journal of Innovation and Policy* 8 (1): 162–79.

Morys, M., G. Daudin, and K.H. O'Rourke. 2008. "Globalization, 1870-1914." 395. *Economics Series Working Papers*. Economics Series Working Papers. University of Oxford, Department of Economics. https://ideas.repec.org/p/oxf/wpaper/395.html.

Park, S., P. Croteau, K.A. Boering, D.M. Etheridge, D. Ferretti, P.J. Fraser, K.-R. Kim, et al. 2012. "Trends and Seasonal Cycles in the Isotopic Composition of Nitrous Oxide since 1940." *Nature Geoscience* 5 (4): 261–65.

Paun, A., L. Acton, and W.-S. Chan. 2018. "Fragile Planet: Scoring Climate Risks around the World." HSBC Bank.

Plass, G.N. 1956. "The Carbon Dioxide Theory of Climatic Change." *Tellus* 8 (2): 140–54.

PwC. 2021. "PwC's Global Consumer Insights Survey 2021." PricewaterhouseCoopers. https://www.pwc.com/gx/en/industries/consumer-markets/consumer-insights-survey/archive/consumer-insights-survey-2021.html.

Rainforest Action Network. 2020. "Banking on Climate Chaos: Fossil Fuel Finance Report 2021."

Revelle, R., and H.E. Suess. 1957. "Carbon Dioxide Exchange between Atmosphere and Ocean and the Question of an Increase of Atmospheric CO2 during the Past Decades." *Tellus* 9 (1): 18–27.

Rogers, P.P., K.F. Jalal, and J.A. Boyd. 2012. *An Introduction to Sustainable Development*. Routledge.

Royal Society. 2020. "14. How Fast Is Sea Level Rising?" https://royalsociety.org/topics-policy/projects/climate-change-evidence-causes/question-14/.

Sachs, J.D. 2012. "From Millennium Development Goals to Sustainable Development Goals." *The Lancet* 379 (9832): 2206–11.

SBTi. 2020. "From Ambition to Impact: How Companies Are Cutting Emissions at Scale with Science-Based Targets." SBTi. https://sciencebasedtargets.org/sbti-progress-report-2020.

Sheldon, T.L., and C. Sankaran. 2017. "The Impact of Indonesian Forest Fires on Singaporean Pollution and Health." *American Economic Review* 107 (5): 526–29. https://doi.org/10.1257/aer.p20171134.

Siebelts, J. 2017. "Climate Change & Respiratory Health." Chicago: Respiratory Health Association. https://resphealth.org/news/library/climate-change-respiratory-health/.

Syndicat European Trade Union. .2020. "German Unions Back Fridays for Future Campaign." ETUC | European Trade Union Confederation. https://www.etuc.org/en/german-unions-back-fridays-future-campaign.

The CSR Journal. 2021. "Top Indian Companies Committed to Science Based Targets Initiative (SBTi)." November 4. https://thecsrjournal.in/sbti-top-companies-india-science-based-targets-climate-change/.

The Economist. 2021. "Sustainable Finance Is Rife with Greenwash. Time for More Disclosure." https://www.economist.com/leaders/2021/05/22/sustainable-finance-is-rife-with-greenwash-time-for-more-disclosure.

UNFCC. 2021. "Climate Neutral Now: Guidelines for Participation | UNFCCC." https://unfccc.int/documents/271233.

United Nations. 2017. "The Ocean Conference | 5-9 June 2017." https://oceanconference.un.org/about.

Wang, H., B. Ma, and R. Bai. 2019. "The Spillover Effect of Greenwashing Behaviours: An Experimental Approach." *Marketing Intelligence & Planning*.

Williamson, J.G. 1997. "Globalization and Inequality, Past and Present." *The World Bank Research Observer* 12 (2): 117–35.

Xie, Q., X. Wang, and X. Cong. 2020. "How Does Foreign Direct Investment Affect CO2 Emissions in Emerging Countries?New Findings from a Nonlinear Panel Analysis." *Journal of Cleaner Production* 249 (March): 119422. https://doi.org/10.1016/j.jclepro.2019.119422.

Yu, E.P., B. Van Luu, and C.H. Chen. 2020. "Greenwashing in Environmental, Social and Governance Disclosures." *Research in International Business and Finance* 52: 101192.

Zaidi, S.A.H., M.W. Zafar, M. Shahbaz, and F. Hou. 2019. "Dynamic Linkages between Globalization, Financial Development and Carbon Emissions: Evidence from Asia Pacific Economic Cooperation Countries." *Journal of Cleaner Production* 228 (August): 533–43. https://doi.org/10.1016/j.jclepro.2019.04.210.

Chapter 2
Measuring and Valuing Climate Effects

This chapter focuses on the impact of climate change on companies' activities, profitability, and value. It describes the two key climate change risks – physical risk and transition risk – and their economic impacts. The effective management of climate-change risks may also create opportunities.

In this chapter, we introduce the problem of stranded assets, extreme weather events due to climate change, and the challenges for both advanced and emerging market economies. We also analyze how the assessment of these risks and opportunities can lead to very different asset valuations.

2.1   ECONOMIC CONSEQUENCES OF CLIMATE CHANGE

2.1.1 Global Economic Impacts

Climate change is no longer a future risk. Solid scientific evidence confirms its present-day effects, and we are already seeing changes to natural resources and natural events (see Chapter 1). Climate risks also threaten companies, industries, and markets with the following socioeconomic consequences:

- o   Slowdown of economic growth: In the short run, destructive climate events such as tornadoes, hurricanes, tsunamis, and extreme heatwaves damage infrastructure and other assets. In the long run, economic growth stalls as overall productivity decreases, natural capital is depleted, and costs associated with weather and environmental changes increase.

- o Increased inflation: Commodities prices become more volatile, and can drive up food, water, and energy prices.
- o Supply chain disruptions: Production chains for goods and services can be disrupted.
- o Gap between high- and low-exposure countries:
  - o Balance of payments: Countries with high exposure to climate factors will be at greater risk. Their exports can decrease, as companies could decide to source goods from lower-risk locations.
  - o Investment levels and employment: Countries with high exposure to climate factors will be at greater risk. Their production capacity could take a hit, as companies could decide to source goods from, and move their facilities to, lower-risk locations.
  - o Inequality: Less developed countries are likely to be more affected by climate change due to their geographical location and weaker infrastructure, which is typically more vulnerable to risks. Further, these countries have poorer populations, whose living standards are likely to be severely impacted by climate change.
- o Increased health costs and health problems: Higher temperatures and changing weather patterns will increase the incidence of health problems, especially respiratory diseases. Costs to national health systems will consequently rise.
- o Decreased labor productivity: A labor force subject to extreme environmental conditions exhibits reduced capacity, productivity, and supply.

In 2006, Nicolas Stern concluded that climate change was "the world's greatest market failure" (Stern, 2007). His book *Economics of Climate Change: The Stern Review* estimated that if global actions to contain climate change were not taken, the overall costs and risks of climate change would be equivalent to losing at least 5% of the global GDP each year by 2100. In some scenarios, the costs could rise to 20% of the GDP or more. Other estimates suggest that unmitigated climate change will reduce the global real GDP per capita by more than 7% by 2100 (Kahn et al., 2019), and some estimates suggest that unmitigated global warming will lead to a 25% decline in the global GDP by 2100 (IMF, 2019). BlackRock estimates that if no climate change mitigation measures are taken, the result will be a cumulative loss in global economic output of 25% over the period 2020–2040 (and a 2.3% lower GDP level in 2040). Moreover, the costs are increasing over time because the greater accumulation of emissions in the atmosphere will require correspondingly stronger interventions to stabilize global temperatures (Burke et al., 2015).

Estimates suggest that the impacts of climate change are geographically asymmetric. That is, climate change and the associated extreme weather events affect regions and countries differently, both in terms of output losses and human safety. The adverse economic effects of global warming will affect low-income countries the most (Diffenbaugh and Burke, 2019; Dell et al., 2012; Hsiang et al., 2017; IMF, 2017). In the absence of mitigation, the temperature in Asia is expected to increase by 6 °C by the end of the century (Asian

Development Bank, 2017). As a consequence, the region will face more tropical storms, pollution, severe flooding, and decreased agricultural productivity. Overall, this suggests a more unequal world, in which low-income countries suffer the most.

Understanding the consequences of climate change for countries, industries, and companies helps predict economic effects and identify priorities and action plans.

2.1.2 Global Investment Needs

It seems clear that long-term economic growth and wealth will be significantly affected by climate change. The overall results will also depend on the transition path to a low carbon economy, which is fraught with uncertainty and entails costs. Infrastructures such as energy, transport, water, and telecommunications are the backbone of our economies. Meeting the mitigation and adaptation[42] objectives of the Paris Agreement will require substantial shifts in the world's infrastructural base, over many decades. The various estimates of the investments in infrastructure required to sustain economic growth while meeting mitigation goals are very significant:

o A report from Ceres (Fulton and Capalino, 2014) suggests that we will need an additional US$1 trillion per year of investment in clean energy through 2050 to limit the global temperature rise to no more than 2 °C.

o IRENA (2019) estimates that – globally – the total investment needed to convert the energy system to renewable power needs to be twice as high as currently foreseen, reaching US$22.5 trillion by 2050. Further, energy efficiency requires a US$1.1 trillion investment per year. Similarly, IRENA (2020) estimates that to meet the internationally agreed climate goal, an investment of US$800 billion per year in renewable energy will be required until 2050.

o The International Energy Agency (IEA) estimates that the cumulative investment needed to stay on the path to 2° C global warming is above US$50 trillion (IEA and OECD, 2015)

o The UN Sustainable Development Goals (SDGs) require an annual investment of US$5 to 7 trillion, a significant part of it in developing countries (Doumbia and Lykke, 2019).

o Bloomberg New Energy Finance (BNEF) estimates that investments in energy supply and infrastructure will have to more than double. In their report for 2021, investments were estimated at US$1.7 trillion per year, which will be required to reach between US$3.1 trillion and US$5.8 trillion per year in 30 years (BloombergNEF, 2021).

---

[42] Adaptation addresses the physical impacts of climate change and actions to minimize the damage it causes. Mitigation focuses on the causes of climate change, and on the concrete actions to reduce GHG emissions.

- o The International Monetary Fund (IMF) published a study in June 2021 (IMF, 2021) stating that investment needs to increase from 0.5% to 4.5% of the GDP in the next decade.
- o In 2021, The World Economic Forum confirmed, in a report titled "Financing the Transition to a Net-Zero Future," that investments needed to be increased by US$50 trillion by 2050 to meet the net-zero targets.
- o McKinsey created a hypothetical scenario in which the need for investments worked out to US$3.5 trillion per year, "equivalent to half of global corporate profits, one-quarter of total tax revenue, and 7 percent of household spending" (Kumra and Woezel, 2022).

The evidence also suggests that delays in policy execution can lead to a disorderly transition, which will be much more costly in terms of adjustment/transition.

2.2   CLIMATE RISKS AT THE CORPORATE LEVEL

Climate risk impacts businesses in different ways. An example of a short-term risk is exposure to extreme weather events. New consumer tastes and expectations can also affect businesses. In addition, the clear perception that regulations are in a state of flux and that investors themselves have begun to incorporate long-term climate risks in their decision-making poses long-term risks to many businesses.

Besides the growing, and now commonly accepted, evidence for global warming and its relationship with GHG emissions, other factors have led business stakeholders to think more carefully about climate risks. For instance, over the past decade, several businesses have suffered significant losses because of climate change and its inherent risks. Examples of companies that suffered because of climate risks (or related extreme weather events) are the following:

- o October 2011: Ford closed a plant in Thailand due to flooding that had affected its supply chain and operations. The effects of the Thailand floods spread through global supply chains. The operating profit of Toyota was reduced by more than US$1 billion due to plant closures and problems with supplies in East Asia. Even in the United States, production had to be suspended in several plants.
- o February 2021: S&P Global Ratings downgraded the credit ratings of U.S. oil producers Exxon Mobil, Chevron, and ConocoPhillips due to the "pressure to tackle climate change." The agency warned it was considering further downgrades due to energy-transition-related risks.

o September 2021: Typhoon Chanthu forced a two-week closure of the Chinese ports of Shanghai and Ningbo, which suffered catastrophic trading losses of over US$1 billion.

The bankruptcy of PG&E

One of the first climate change bankruptcies was perhaps the California utility company PG&E Corp (NYSE:PCG). In 2019, PG&E filled for bankruptcy in the face of potential liabilities of US$30 billion or more on account of wildfires that swept its service areas in 2017 and 2018. Analysts and scientists suggested that global warming worsened the effects of droughts in California, making wildfires more likely. The full-year 2019 net loss was US$7.7 billion. For pension funds, asset managers, and other investors that held stakes in PG&E equity, as well as for its debtholders, this clearly showed how climate risk can affect the financial industry and investor returns.

Environmental risk can lead to large losses for companies, and consequently losses for their suppliers of capital (either debt or equity). Losses from climate-related risks can be large, nonlinear, and difficult to estimate. However, it is clear that they affect financial markets through the impairment of assets, lower collateral values, operating performance losses, and lower economic growth, all of which affect companies' financials.

Two clear channels of climate-related risks have been identified:

1. Physical risks are linked to damage to assets from extreme weather events. In Section 1.1.4, we reviewed the large losses associated with extreme weather events. Physical risks also encompass the broader impact of climate trends, such as global warming, lower productivity of agricultural assets, water scarcity, and rising sea levels.

2. Transition risks are related to changes in relative prices and widespread economic disruption because of changes in technology, market sentiment, regulations, and policies during the adjustments to a low-carbon economy. In an abrupt transition to a cleaner energy economy, important reassessments of risks and valuation levels will occur across sectors. Investors also fear the likely rising costs of noncompliance with environmental standards, which can translate into legal and reputational risks for investors and companies.

Investors are asking how they should incorporate climate risk in their activities. This requires an understanding of both the physical risks associated with climate change, as well as longer-term risks related to the transition. Short-term risks are related to direct exposure of assets to physical risks, whereas long-term risks are related to the impacts of global warming.

Figure 2.1 The different climate effects

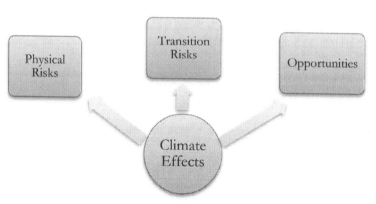

Transition risk and physical risk are different and can affect companies (and countries) in very different ways. Physical risk has a large geographic component, because it affects all companies operating in a certain location in similar ways. However, transition risk affects companies in different ways, depending on their industry and overall carbon footprint.

KEY LEARNING POINT

Physical risk and transition risk are different and affect companies differently.

2.3 PHYSICAL RISK

Physical risk includes the direct effects of climate change, which can disrupt operations and destroy assets. The physical effects of climate change on our planet were described in Section 1.3. Global warming impacts human life, ecosystems, and resource availability (due to consequences for farmland, water shortages, and rising sea levels). Also, as explained in Chapter 1, global warming increases extreme weather events, which are becoming more frequent, more intense, and more regular. Natural disasters are becoming more frequent, and caused cumulative losses above US$5 trillion between 1980 and 2018.[43]

Physical risk is of two types: acute and chronic risks. Acute physical risks are posed by the increased severity of extreme weather events such as floods, hurricanes, wildfires, and

---

[43] Source: Munich Re.

droughts. Chronic physical risks are posed by longer-term shifts in climate patterns such as higher temperatures, sea level rise, changes in precipitation, water scarcity, and heat waves.

Physical risks can impact companies' operations, markets, and supply chains. The location of a company's assets and its exposure to extreme weather events will have different impacts at the operational level. Some of the ways in which climate change affects companies include the following:

- o   Sea level rise will expose assets to the risk of increased coastal flooding, which damages property and industrial assets. It will increase costs as protection, relocation, and backup facilities have to be provided.
- o   Exposure to hurricanes and typhoons can severely damage property and industrial plants, and sometimes the losses are irreversible. Significant relocation costs may also be incurred.
- o   Intense rain and storms can expose assets to floods and landslides, compromising key infrastructures and damaging property.[44]
- o   Higher temperatures can decrease labor force productivity and cause health problems. Sectors involving outdoor activity (e.g., construction, tourism, agriculture, sports, and leisure) will be hardest hit by extreme weather events such as storms, floods, hurricanes, and typhoons.
- o   Climate change events (heat waves, storms, droughts, river and coastal flooding, water availability, and others) lower agricultural productivity and thus threaten food supply chains.
- o   Water supply shortages will impact companies, particularly those in the agricultural and industrial sectors. Water costs will increase.
- o   Temperature increases can drive up energy costs, increasing the risk of power outages.

Thus, the company-level impact depends on the country of operation, the industry segment, and also on firm-specific factors, such as how sensitive a company is to each risk factor and how it is managing the risks. For instance, companies with energy- and water-intensive processes will be more affected than others in less resource-intensive sectors.[45] Also, some sectors, such as agriculture and tourism, are more sensitive to weather fluctuations, and their traditional markets will also change. In managing risks, a key concept is the idea of *adaptation*. Adaptation efforts attempt to minimize the impacts of climate change. These actions (at the

---

[44] Seetharam (2017) conducted an event study on the stock price responses to the top 122 natural disasters that occurred in the United States between 1980 and 2014. The results show a significant negative impact of disasters on stock returns, and a significant loss of market capitalization by firms due to natural disaster exposure.

[45] About 90% of water withdrawals is used in the agricultural and industrial sectors. https://smarterbusiness.co.uk/blogs/the-top-5-industries-that-consume-the-most-water/

country or company level) aim to reduce vulnerability to the effects of climate change and the attendant damage.

In terms of regions, Asia is particularly vulnerable as more than 80% of its population lives in zones with the highest global climate risk, where temperature rises are much higher than average (6 °C by the end of the century in the absence of mitigation action, according to the Asian Development Bank).

Pearl River Delta coastal flooding

Sea level rise can submerge land that is currently home to more than 500 million people. River delta regions are economically important, and especially vulnerable in Asia.

The Guangzhou region (in southeast China), which is a densely populated hub of economic activity, is vulnerable to sea level rise. Indeed, the whole Pearl River Delta area (which includes cities such as Guangzhou, Shenzhen, and Zhuhai) is expected to experience a much higher than average sea level rise (a more than 30 cm rise in relative sea level by 2030, against an average of 8 cm globally). The region has a high concentration of oil infrastructure assets that belong to the China National Offshore Oil Corporation (CNOOC) and other Chinese energy companies.

These oil platforms, power plants, refineries, and other energy infrastructures are long-lived, high-value assets that cannot be easily moved. Thus, they will require substantial protection from rising seas, or they will need to be decommissioned. This creates uncertainty about the long-term value of those assets, and signals increased operating and maintenance costs for their companies and for the region as whole.

Different country-level climate indicators are available. For instance, HSBC (Paun et al. 2018) analyzed 67 countries on different factors and estimated an overall score for the physical risk of each country. The scores are based on exposure to higher temperature levels, water availability, and extreme weather events. Sensitivity to extreme events includes the social and economic costs, which include death, loss of livelihood, and post-event rebuilding costs. Table 2.1 shows the countries that are most/least exposed to physical impacts.

However, there are other estimates of country-level physical risk. In general, these are country-level scores that aggregate different variables to obtain physical and transition risk scores. There is, however, no standard methodology yet, and the indices differ in the number of categories of risk used, aggregation of subtopics, and the choice of individual metrics for each variable.

The University of Notre Dame developed the Notre Dame Global Adaptation Initiative Index (Chen et al., 2015). This index covers physical risk for 192 countries. It is based on a large set of equally weighted variables, covering not only the country's vulnerability but also its readiness to adapt.

Table 2.1 Country-wise exposure to physical risk

Higher physical risk	Lower physical risk
Qatar	Ireland
Israel	United States
Bahrain	New Zealand
Kuwait	Norway
UAE	Sweden
Saudi Arabia	Estonia
Oman	Chile
Kenya	Finland
Nigeria	Russia
Egypt	Canada

Source: HSBC (Paun et al. 2018).

The European Investment Bank (EIB) has also developed a model for evaluating country-level climate risk (Ferrazzi et al., 2021). The EIB computes the exposure of countries to physical and transition risks, and the scores are used to manage the exposure of the EIB portfolio to climate risk. EIB Climate Risk Country scores cover 184 countries. The physical risk scores are based on a large number of variables that are aggregated to cover the acute and chronic risks as well as the adaptation capacity of each country. The transition risk scores are based on the country's exposure and mitigation.[46]

Importantly, a company's exposure to climate risks extends well beyond where it is headquartered. Physical climate risk can be direct or indirect. Direct physical risk is the risk of damage or impairment to assets as a result of extreme weather events such as floods or hurricanes. Indirect physical risk is the risk of damage or impairment to assets as a result of second- or third-order impacts of climate change, such as disruption to trade due to an extreme weather event or the impact of prolonged drought on food prices.

As global economic activity is interconnected, a company can be affected through its supply chains, customers, availability of resources, markets where it operates, distribution networks, and many other secondary factors. Depending on the country of origin of raw materials, delays and overall exposure to supply shortages and high input costs could occur. Further, companies could experience varying climate change impacts depending on the markets where they sell their products. For instance, companies whose primary customers are in countries that are extremely exposed to climate change face higher physical risks. This suggests that the impact of physical risk on a company depends not only on where the company operates, but also on the rest of the company's activities and the exposure to

---

[46] Exposure consists of current and past emissions, as well as economic dependence on fossil fuel exports. Mitigation includes the share of renewables in the final energy mix, improvements in energy efficiency, and the commitment of each country to its National Determined Contribution (NDC).

climate risk of its various stakeholders. Obviously, the first-order effects are easier to predict (and mitigate) than these indirect impacts.

All scoring models[47] start with a framework of possible hazards derived from publicly available climate models, and try to predict climate-related variables (such as sea level, temperatures, and rain) in different parts of the world. The models then try to measure the company's level of exposure, based on its geographic footprint. Finally, they typically assess the company-level vulnerability, based on the preparedness of the company to tackle its exposure. The idea is that the consequences can be less serious if a company is well prepared for the exposures it faces. For example, the Four Twenty Seven (a provider of data on environmental risks) physical risk score has three key components: operations risk, supply chain risk, and market risk. Their model uses global climate data to provide asset-level risk assessments for each property/asset. The model assesses the risk of each property due to heat and water stress, sea level rise and flooding, exposure to hurricanes and typhoons, and other climate hazards. It has data on the locations of thousands of corporate facilities worldwide, which it uses together with climate evolution models to create a composite company-level risk score that incorporates each company's exposure to the physical risks across its value chain. The model includes both geographic exposure to climate hazards as well as business sensitivity to those hazards. Sustainalytics created the Physical Climate Risk Metrics (Sustainalytics, 2022), which measures a company's physical climate risks using three metrics: High Risk Assets, Asset Damage Risk, and Productivity Capacity Loss. The first metric is the degree of exposure of the assets of a company to physical hazards. The second metric is the relative vulnerability to direct infrastructural damage, and the third metric is productivity disruption.

Importantly, there are significant uncertainties around the different assessment models, and they often differ depending on the supplier of data (Hain et al., 2022). This implies that one cannot rely entirely on a single score or ranking (see also Section 5.1 on ESG ratings); instead, one should try to integrate the uncertainties into valuation and risk management processes.

KEY LEARNING POINT

Various scoring methodologies have been developed to measure physical risk, but there is no globally accepted standard yet. Well-prepared companies could mitigate some of the damage.

---

[47] Other providers of company-level risk scores include Trucost, Carbon4 Finance, and South Pole.

2.4   TRANSITION RISK

The physical impacts of climate change have tangible financial implications. However, perhaps even more important to investors than physical risks are the additional transition-related risks. Moving toward a low-carbon economy entails significant adjustment costs, such as the need to mobilize capital for low-carbon solutions such as renewable energy and sustainable solutions across almost all sectors of the economy.

Climate change also triggers changes in policies and regulations, spurs technological innovation, creates uncertainty around product availability, and exerts social pressures (that change consumer preferences), which may even translate into liability and reputational risks. The transition also involves changes in climate policy and awareness, which can impact consumer demand, prices, costs, and asset values.

Transition risk is thus related to the uncertain, but potentially large, impacts associated with the rapid decarbonization of our economies. The transition to a 1.5 °C or 2 °C (above pre-industrial levels) world would mean a shift away from carbon-intensive technologies and products/services/assets that depend on them. Transition risk affects all companies, even those that are not heavy polluters, but companies in some regions will be more seriously impacted.

The transition-related risks have also been identified by other stakeholders:

- o "The financial risks which could arise for insurance firms from the transition to a lower-carbon economy. For insurance firms, this risk factor is mainly about the potential re-pricing of carbon-intensive financial assets, and the speed at which any such re-pricing might occur." Prudential Regulation Authority
- o "What will happen to the 30-year mortgage – a key building block of finance – if lenders can't estimate the impact of climate risk over such a long timeline, and if there is no viable market for flood or fire insurance in impacted areas? What happens to inflation, and in turn interest rates, if the cost of food climbs from drought and flooding? How can we model economic growth if emerging markets see their productivity decline due to extreme heat and other climate impacts?" Larry Fink, Chairman of BlackRock.
- o "Transition risk refers to an institution's financial loss that can result, directly or indirectly, from the process of adjustment towards a lower-carbon and more environmentally sustainable economy. This could be triggered, for example, by a relatively abrupt adoption of climate and environmental policies, technological progress or changes in market sentiment and preferences." European Central Bank[48]

---

[48] https://www.ecb.europa.eu/pub/financial-stability/fsr/special/html/ecb.fsrart201905_1~47cf778cc1.en.html.

Emissions are a key focal point of policy, regulatory, market, and technological responses to climate change (see Chapter 6), and these global efforts to mitigate climate change, through emissions reductions and investment in various infrastructures and technologies, give rise to transition risks.

Decisions taken by governments to reshape energy and climate policies can reduce the profitability of assets in many industries. Heavy emitters will be the most challenged. Some of their assets can become stranded (reserves that will remain unutilized due to climate-change-related limitations) and will need to be written off. Carbon-intensive businesses may become less competitive, and many companies' business models may be challenged. Importantly, this often has community-level implications. An example of this is workers in the global coal industry. Several million workers will face job losses, which will obviously affect the regions where they live.[49] Finally, investors are increasingly demanding that companies show a credible transition path to a greener economy (see Chapter 5).

Transition risk is caused by a number of factors, including changes in climate policy/regulations regarding emissions, carbon taxes, restrictions on water and land use, reputational impacts, shifts in market preferences, and technological innovation. These factors impact companies differently. For instance, future constraints on emissions, either direct or indirect, will impact companies differently. This means that countries, sectors, and types of companies are differentially exposed to transition risk. Clearly, companies with significant emissions are more impacted by transition risk. However, the trajectory of the organization also matters. Some heavy polluters are already changing their business, whereas others are not.

However, the effects of transition risk are wide-ranging and extend beyond the energy sector. Climate change triggers regulatory risk as governments deal with the hazards from climate change. This can impact many sectors other than carbon-related sectors. For instance, changes to zoning laws[50] due to sea level rise could dramatically impact real estate prices. Even a company that does not appear to be directly affected could be financially impacted, for example, through a gradual increase in its operational expenses due to rising insurance costs, energy costs, or shifts in consumer behavior.

A company's transition risk depends on its supply chain, customers, partners, etc. For example, banks, which are not big emitters, are strongly affected by transition risk because they finance different companies, which has credit risk implications.[51]

---

[49] See Section 6.2 for a discussion of the concept of the *Just Transition*, and the political economy issues surrounding this topic.

[50] Zoning laws regulate buildings and structures, their mode of construction, and their usage.

[51] Section 3.3 discusses the banking-level implications of climate issues, and Section 6.6 focuses on the role of regulators and central banks.

KEY LEARNING POINT

Transition risk is related to changes in climate policy and regulations regarding emissions; carbon taxes; restrictions on land, water, and other resources; technological innovation; shifts in customer preference; and reputational impacts.

Exposure to transition risk means that a company is vulnerable to threats – or can exploit opportunities – from the transition to a lower-carbon economy. Under pressure from regulators, consumers, and investors, many companies are now proactively assessing their long-term risks and exposures. In Chapter 6, we discuss the evolving reporting requirements. In particular, the Task Force on Climate-related Financial Disclosures (TCFD) classifies four types of transition risk: policy and legal, technology, changing markets, and reputation.

The challenges associated with transition risk vary from country to country. On average, emerging markets are more exposed to fossil fuels, in terms of exports, GDP, and energy mix. No standardized measure has been globally adopted yet. HSBC (Paun et al. 2018), for example, aggregates transition risk as a function of the following:

1. Fossil rents: Countries that rely more on fossil fuel production to support fiscal budgets have higher risk.

2. Share of fossil fuels in exports: Significant net exports of fossil fuels increase a country's trade balance risk.

3. Share of fossil fuels in primary energy use: Countries heavily dependent on fossil fuels in their energy mix are less aligned with a 2 °C scenario, and will face greater challenges.

Table 2.2 Top and bottom countries in terms of transition risk

Higher transition risk	Lower transition risk
Bahrain	Switzerland
Kuwait	France
Qatar	Estonia
Oman	New Zealand
Saudi Arabia	Austria
Kazakhstan	Hungary
Malaysia	Kenya
Colombia	Denmark
Australia	Chile
UAE	Pakistan

Source: HSBC (Paun et al. 2018).

In all the measures, HSBC (Paun et al. 2018) looks at the current data, as well as the trajectory, that is, how it is changing over time. According to these criteria, HSBC deems

Bahrain the country with the highest transition risk (Table 2.2). The estimates assume that how each country is able to respond to this risk depends on several factors, including the government budget capacity to finance the climate transition, the quality of local governance, and the social environment (including education levels).

At the global level, different sectors face different exposures to transition risk, depending on their overall contribution to global CO_2 emissions. For instance, transportation and food production (which account for roughly 40% of global GHG emissions) are more affected than other sectors.

Lastly, at the corporate level, besides the country and industry, an assessment of the organization's own corporate resilience is crucial for understanding its risk. Companies can proactively try to manage their exposures and mitigate future risks. This includes investing in innovation to reduce their carbon footprint and changing the business mix, operations, markets served, etc. Whereas adaptation addresses the physical effects of climate change, mitigation focuses on the causes of climate change. Mitigation efforts are concrete actions to reduce GHG emissions. This includes the deployment of renewables in final energy consumption, as well as improved energy efficiency.

Transition risk obviously affects financial markets. Corporate fundamentals will change. The profitability change will vary from sector to sector. Some companies and industries are better positioned than others for a low-carbon economy. Repricing of assets is another way in which climate change impacts investments, collateral values, and balance sheets throughout the world. As a consequence of shifts in risk perceptions and societal preferences, the price that investors are willing to pay for different assets is changing, and so is the risk they attribute to them. The next sections cover these topics in further detail.

KEY LEARNING POINT

Adaptation plans and processes focus on the physical effects of climate change, whereas mitigation focuses on the causes of climate change.

2.5 STRANDED ASSETS

Stranded assets are assets that suffered premature write-downs, devaluations, or conversion into liabilities. They are particularly concentrated in some sectors, and they are important for countries that depend on commodity exports. However, the stranded assets problem can affect economies globally as economic and financial systems are interconnected.

2.5.1 The Impact of Stranded Assets

When climate risks materialize, one result can be stranded assets in many industries.

In the energy sector, given the global commitments to the reduction of CO_2 emissions, there is a real possibility that the value of oil and some other carbon-related assets may become zero. In fact, achieving the Paris Agreement's long-term temperature targets will certainly result in premature stranding of carbon-intensive assets. That is, several billion barrels of reserves will remain unutilized. Further, several investor campaigns seek to reduce emissions, and investors will tend to shift their capital away from carbon-intensive sectors (fossil fuel divestments or portfolio decarbonization) and direct them to carbon-efficient companies, projects, and technologies.

However, stranded assets are not restricted to the fossil fuel sector. For instance, in the agriculture sector, land degradation, extreme weather events, and wildfires can destroy crops, affect livestock farming, and transform these assets into stranded assets. Also, agricultural assets can become stranded because of the greening of the supply chain, shifts in consumer behavior or political changes, and environmental regulation. As an example, land erosion and the loss of forested land and habitat are serious risks in the palm oil supply chain. Moreover, biodiversity loss from habitat destruction also heightens the risks to palm oil companies' reputations (Morel et al., 2016).

Transition risks are associated with the uncertain financial impacts of a rapid low-carbon transition, including policy changes, reputational impacts, technological breakthroughs or limitations, and shifts in market preferences and social norms. The consequent financial impacts are multiple and include decreased revenues; increased operating costs; early closure of certain plants, especially those that exploit fossil resources (such as mines, oil pipelines, offshore platforms, and coal plants); and loss of reputation (Bolton et al., 2020).[52]

KEY LEARNING POINT

Stranded assets are assets that suffered premature write-downs, devaluations, or conversion into liabilities. They are concentrated in certain industries and regions.

---

[52] Byrd and Cooperman (2018) examined whether coal company shareholders perceive coal as a technologically stranded asset, by studying shareholder reactions to news about CCS (carbon capture and sequestration) technology breakthroughs and setbacks. The results showed significant positive reactions to CCS breakthroughs, but no reaction to setbacks. This suggests that investors have embedded expectations of stranded asset risk into their valuations, but also recognize the significance of successful CCS technology development and deployment for the economic prospects of the coal industry.

Peabody Energy

Peabody was the world largest private-sector coal producer and distributor. In 2008, it was nominated to the list of America's Most Admired Companies. In 2012, their revenue reached US$8 billion.

After being valued at US$20 billion in 2011, Peabody company filed for bankruptcy in 2016. After the bankruptcy announcement, Peabody renegotiated its debt. Mines in Queensland and Arizona closed years after, leaving the company with a high probability of facing lawsuits and impairment charges. Following the IEEFA update in 2020, Argonaut Insurance sued Peabody requesting US$128 million additional collateral. Other insurance companies also sued, for a total of US$800 million in additional collateral.

Peabody Energy is not a unique case. Since 2012, over 50 coal companies have declared bankruptcy, including some of the biggest companies in the United States (Sukhdev, 2016).

2.5.2 Macroeconomic and Financial Risks

In a study published in *Nature*, McGlade and Ekins (2015) estimated that if policymakers were to meet the goal of maintaining the global temperature rise "well below 2 °C above the pre-industrial levels" as stated in the Paris Agreement, half of the gas reserves, one-third of the oil reserves, and about 80% of the coal reserves would remain unutilized until 2050.[53]

In view of this possible scenario, the green transition poses serious risks to developing and middle-income economies, which are heavily reliant on commodity export. Some of these countries hold the largest share of fossil fuel reserves that are deemed to become unburnable or stranded.

Table 2.3 shows the reserves (also as a percentage of the current reserves of that region) that will be unburnable before 2050 under the 2 °C scenario. The importance of the various fuel types varies regionally. When looking at oil, 60% of the unburnable reserves (264 billion out of a total of 449 billion barrels) are in the Middle East, followed by Latin America, Canada, and Russia. In terms of gas, the Middle East once more accounts for the majority of the unburnable gas reserves, followed by Russia. In terms of coal, the picture is very different. The most affected countries are the United States, China, India, and Russia.

---

[53] Mercure et al. (2018) suggested a discounted global wealth loss of US$1–4 trillion. Also, there are clear distributional impacts, with winners (for example, net importers such as China and the EU) and losers (for example, Russia, the United States, and Canada, which could see their fossil fuel industries nearly shut down).

Table 2.3 Reserves unburnable under the 2 °C scenario

Country or region	Oil		Gas		Coal	
	Billions of barrels	%	Trillions of cubic meters	%	Billions of metric tons	%
Africa	28	26%	4.4	34%	30	90%
Canada	40	75%	0.3	24%	5.4	82%
China and India	9	25%	2.5	53%	207	77%
Countries of the erstwhile Soviet Union	28	19%	36	59%	209	97%
Europe	5.3	21%	0.3	6%	74	89%
Latin America	63	42%	5.0	56%	11	73%
Middle East	264	38%	47	61%	3.4	99%
OECD Pacific	2.7	46%	2	51%	85	95%
United States	4.6	9%	0.5	6%	245	95%
Global	449	35%	100	52%	887	88%

Source: McGlade and Ekins (2015). "%" represents the percentage of the stranded reserves within each region.

The regional aggregation in the table hides other realities. For instance, although the African continent has a small share of the overall reserves that will be unburnable, when we look in detail at African countries, a different picture emerges. Some countries, such as Angola, rely almost wholly on oil-related revenues to meet their government budget and service their foreign debt. Overall, the UNCTAD (2019) estimated that during 2013–2017, 102 out of 189 countries (54%) were commodity dependent.[54] Among these 102 commodity-dependent economies, 32 economies were dependent on energy export.

The distribution of commodity-dependent countries varies remarkably across regions. For example, 41% of the commodity-dependent countries are from Sub-Saharan Africa, followed by Latin America and the Caribbean (16%), and East Asia and the Pacific (16%).

Table 2.4 Commodity-dependent countries by region

Geographic region	Number of countries	% of commodity-dependent countries
Sub-Saharan Africa	42	41%
Latin America and the Caribbean	17	16%
East Asia and the Pacific	16	16%
Middle East and North Africa	13	13%
Europe and Central Asia	12	12%
South Asia	2	2%
Total	**102**	**100%**

Source: UNCTAD (2019), during the period 2013–2017.

---

[54] The United Nations Conference on Trade and Development (UNCTAD) classifies a country as "commodity-dependent" if commodity exports account for more than 60% of its total export revenue.

Vulnerability to external factors, and commodity prices in particular, has been a constant challenge for several developing economies. Climate-related risks exacerbate this problem. A sharp reduction in export revenues may therefore create difficulties for some of these commodity-dependent economies, and may lead to capital flight and currency devaluations. This in turn will create a currency mismatch in the balance sheets of banks and the government, which frequently borrow in foreign currency. Some of these economies may thus find themselves unable to service foreign debt, which represents a permanent risk for global financial and macroeconomic stability.

KEY LEARNING POINT

Decarbonization will seriously impact countries that are heavily dependent on carbon commodities.

The share of unburnable reserves of oil, gas, and coal in Europe does not account for more than 1% of the global unburnable reserves. Moreover, Europe's economic systems are much more resilient (in terms of exchange rate stability, economic structure, and industrial development) than those of commodity-export countries. This also holds true for the United States, Canada, and Japan. Further, unlike many commodity-dependent countries, advanced economies usually borrow in their own currency and not in foreign currency. However, this does not mean that advanced economies are immune to the stranded asset problem. Even in these economies, the risk connected with stranded assets is significant, due to the following:

- Their effective ownership of large stakes in integrated oil and gas companies, such as Shell, Exxon, BP, Repsol, or Total, which are large owners of these reserves: institutional investors (i.e., investment banks, insurances, pension funds, mutual funds, and other asset managers) worldwide (particularly in developed markets) hold stakes in companies operating in energy-intensive industries or energy companies.
- The investment activity of banks, and other investors, in emerging economies: if a large financial institution incurs losses due to a default that occurred in another country, it may trigger a financial crisis in its own home country.
- The interconnection in global economies: If there is a default in an emerging market, all industrial firms in Europe or the United States that have significant ties with that country will themselves face losses. An economic crisis occurring in a large emerging market economy is likely to reduce imports from other advanced economies. This, in turn, would also provoke economic (and job) losses in advanced economies.

Therefore, although stranded assets may hit commodity-dependent economies first, advanced economies can be affected "indirectly" through exposure of the financial sector to such assets, because their primary source of export revenues would be undermined.

Climate change mitigation is expected to seriously hit anyone holding a stake in companies whose assets become stranded. This includes investors, but also banks and other lenders, and even commodity-export-dependent countries. For instance, in a hypothetical scenario in which fossil fuels are suddenly prohibited, companies such as BP and Shell would suffer massive balance sheet write-offs, as they would not be able to exploit their oilfields. The inability of these oil giants to operate their assets and hence generate revenues to meet their pre-existing debt obligations would trigger cascading effects. Institutional investors that invested in stock or bonds issued by these companies would find themselves stuck with assets that are unable to generate the financial returns needed to support their liabilities. Commercial banks or bondholders that granted loans to these companies would stop receiving payments. Pension funds would no longer be able to pay the planned pensions to its retirees, due to their portfolio write-offs. Further, the export revenue from fossil fuels would drop in commodity-export-dependent countries, many of which would not be able to meet their sovereign debt obligations to foreign creditors. This catastrophic scenario, which has significant financial stability implications, was labeled the *green swan* by the Bank for International Settlements (Bolton et al., 2020).

KEY LEARNING POINT

Stranded assets can be a source of risk in all countries, through the impact on the value of companies, investment portfolios, bank loans, and collateral.

2.5.3 How Companies Are Responding to the Stranded Assets Problem

At the company level, assets on the balance sheets of companies operating in the fossil fuel industry (and others) are likely to become impaired. This means that companies will need to decrease the value of assets on the balance sheet, and recognize an extraordinary loss in the income statement in that period. For example, in the upstream energy sectors, stranded assets include reserves such as crude oil, gas, and coal, as well as production-related infrastructure assets and equipment associated with these reserves.

Erosion of assets from the balance sheet has capital structure implications, as the leverage ratios of the company will rise. If some highly leveraged firms were hit by losses due to stranded assets, they would be unable to service their debt obligations. For example, in early 2021, S&P downgraded the credit rating of three U.S. companies – Chevron Corporation, Exxon Mobil Corporation, and ConocoPhillips – mentioning "pressure to tackle climate change" among the causes.

Stranded assets represent an increasing source of credit risk for banks. Through direct or indirect exposure, if borrowers' ability to repay their debts is imperiled, additional financial risks may be created in banks' balance sheets. Borrowing costs for fossil fuel companies have risen since 2019 owing to lenders' increased perception of financial risks associated with fossil fuel assets. The possible impairment of assets, impact on capital ratios, and danger of disorderly transitions are further discussed in Section 3.3 (banking-level implications of climate issues) and Section 6.6 (the role of regulators and central banks).

KEY LEARNING POINT

Asset impairment can increase leverage ratios and lead to inability to service debt obligations.

Rapid changes in environmental policy might precipitate a radical repricing of carbon-intensive assets, including fossil fuel reserves and other related assets. This early obsolescence would translate into lower revenues and profits for the affected firms, and the stock price would react to the stranded assets. To protect the money they manage on the behalf of their clients, institutional and other types of investors have started, or committed to, divesting from fossil fuel assets. Other investors choose to engage with their portfolio companies to ensure a smooth transition (see Section 5.4).

Stranded assets concern both companies and investors. For a company, an asset that gets stranded cannot be used as a source of revenue. This inability to generate revenues in turn affects the company's ability to meet its debt obligations, generate a return of equity, and distribute dividends among shareholders. Companies operating in highly polluting industries can reduce their environmental risks and mitigate stranded asset risk in a variety of ways:

○ Divesting old/polluting assets: An oil company can sell off old and obsolete assets such as refineries or oil wells and diversify its portfolio to include renewable energy.
○ Not reinvesting into the old business: A company can choose not to reinvest in old (and polluting) assets and favor new investments in sustainable assets. This can be done by investing a gradually smaller proportion of the earnings into sectors/products that are "at risk."
○ Sourcing differently: A company can radically transform its supply chain and operating model, reduce its energy consumption, and switch to less carbon-intensive forms of energy supply.
○ Using M&As to transform their portfolio: By acquiring new technologies and pipelines of cleaner products, a company can sometimes transform its business faster than the organic rate of change.

Companies can also write down the assets, absorb the immediate shock, and assume the sunk costs related to these assets. For example, oil and gas companies worldwide wrote down about US$150 billion combined in the first two quarters of 2020.[55] Many of these companies are also making strategic moves to reshuffle their portfolio:

- o In November 2018, Exxon Mobil established a partnership with Ørsted's subsidiary Lincoln Clean Energy to acquire 500 MW of wind and solar power in Texas. This transaction represents one of the largest renewable power purchase agreements signed by an oil company.
- o In August 2020, BP announced its plan to cut its oil and gas output by 40% by 2030 and spend US$5 billion a year on low-carbon projects, with the objective of becoming one of the world's biggest green power producers.
- o In September 2020, Total announced its plan to convert its Grandpuits refinery (Seine-et-Marne) into a zero-crude platform. With an investment of more than €500 million, Total plans to convert the platform by 2024 to produce renewable diesel for the aviation industry and produce bioplastics, recycle plastics, and operate two photovoltaic solar power plants.

2.5.4 Summary of Stranded Assets

Stranded assets are assets that, despite being productive from a purely operational point of view, are no longer economically viable due to changing regulations and consumer tastes. Most of the stranded assets are concentrated in energy-related industries. For companies in this sector, stranded assets pose a challenge, as they have to write down significant amounts of assets from their balance sheets.

These assets are particularly concentrated in some regions of the world, which would have to weather potential macroeconomic challenges and financial instability in an abrupt-transition scenario. Under the 2 °C scenario, most of the economic adjustment burden will be borne by countries that are highly dependent on fossil fuel exports. However, it will also hit advanced economies through the interconnections of the global economy and through the financial system. Stranded assets are of utmost concern to shareholders, due to their consequences for capital structure, corporate ratings, and value. They also affect other institutions, including financial lenders, suppliers, and employees.

---

[55] https://www.wsj.com/articles/2020-was-one-of-the-worst-ever-years-for-oil-write-downs-11609077600.

2.6   OPPORTUNITIES

Climate change is not only about risks; it is also about opportunities. New mitigation and adaptation solutions will arise. New businesses and business models that are well adapted to a lower-carbon economy may profit significantly from the transition.

As technology, regulations, consumer expectations, and other social trends change, the capacity of companies to adapt their business model to the new landscape can be an important determinant of their success. This is especially true of the energy and transportation domains. The demand for energy and mobility will not decrease, and will need to be met by greener solutions. Section 2.1 gives some examples of the amount of investments needed over the next decades.

A reappraisal of climate issues, namely the transition risks, can be a fruitful way of generating business opportunities. Climate-related opportunities can be driven by the following:

- o   Resource efficiency: The use of more efficient transportation, production, and distribution processes; recycling; more efficient buildings; and lower water (and other raw materials) usage
- o   New products and services: The development of low-emissions goods and services, climate adaptation solutions, and better adaptation to shifts in consumer preferences
- o   New markets: Access to new markets and locations

Overall, apart from energy-related businesses, there will be opportunities to cater to new market needs. Examples are industries related to water efficiency, technology to keep buildings cooler, or crop seeds that are more suited to changes in precipitation and temperature. Many companies can experience increased revenues due to the greater demand for lower-carbon-footprint products and services.

Traditional companies will need to substantially overhaul their business model, from the procurement of raw materials and production to how they sell and market their products. In many industries, products, services, technologies, and processes will change, and new demand will arise that companies can profit from. These benefits can relate to additional sales and margins due to better alignment with consumer preferences, better recognition from stakeholders such as employees or suppliers, lower operational costs, better financing conditions, or deeper access to capital markets. For instance, in the automotive sector, novel technologies and government regulations create new competitive dynamics.[56]

Further, the need to adapt to climate risks may lead to innovations at the company level. For instance, Miao and Popp (2014) analyzed the adaptation to climate risk, and its effects on "risk-mitigating innovations." The results showed that natural disasters (flood, droughts,

---

[56] There will be winners and losers. Tighter emissions standards impact the mix of cars sold, which helps manufacturers with more fuel- or emissions-efficient cars.

and earthquake) are associated with innovation and an increase in the annual number of registered patents of risk-mitigating technologies. There are spillover effects. The data suggest that this happens not just in the affected country, but also in nearby countries. Others have shown that the innovators are not just new players with disruptive technologies; often, they are established players who feel the need for change. Cohen et al. (2020) documented that oil, gas, and energy-producing firms have dedicated a large and growing percentage of their innovation activity to green research. They found that these energy-producing firms are granted more patents – and of higher quality – than other firms.

The food industry and Nestlé

As the largest food company in the world (with more than US$90 billion in revenues in 2020), Nestlé made public its commitment to net zero emissions by 2050. To meet this objective, Nestlé committed itself to the following actions:

- "Speeding up the transformation of its products in line with consumer trends and choices"
- "Scaling up initiatives in agriculture to absorb more carbon"
- "Using 100% renewable electricity in Nestlé factories, warehouses, logistics and offices."

Nestlé has been able to reduce Scope 1 and Scope 2 emissions by 28% with respect to 2010 levels. In 2021, the company sourced 50% of its electricity from renewable sources. Another important environmental issue for Nestlé is the purchase of agricultural raw materials. Nestlé's Responsible Sourcing Traceability Programme promotes transparency in its extended supply chains back to the farm, implementing Nestlé's commitments on deforestation, responsible use of water, sustainable fisheries, and animal welfare, and addressing other specific environmental aspects. Another initiative is the Cocoa and Forests Initiative, an agreement to end deforestation and promote forest restoration and protection in the cocoa supply chain.

In a letter to *Fortune*, on February 21, 2021, Nestlé's CEO, Mark Schneider, wrote: "The global challenge of climate change is no longer the can that can be kicked down the road. Businesses like Nestlé, with a global footprint and vast supply chains, need to take the threat climate change poses to our civilization seriously to prosper in the long term [...] While our climate work is costly, it cannot be viewed as a giveaway or as corporate philanthropy. We are, after all, a business. We must deliver within the parameters of our society, and that means delivering for our environment and for our shareholders."

KEY LEARNING POINT

Climate change provides opportunities for new markets, products, and services in risk-mitigating innovations and resource-efficient solutions.

2.7 ASSET VALUATION AND CLIMATE EFFECTS

As discussed earlier in this chapter, climate effects have the potential to disrupt economic activities and thus the value of various assets.

Valuation is a key skill for managers who are considering spinning off part of their venture, looking to buy a new asset or company, or planning to sell a stake in the company to outside investors. Within companies, valuation techniques are relevant for capital budgeting and investment decisions. Valuation is also an important technique used by equity and debt investors (pension funds, other portfolio managers, family offices, banks, and other financial institutions). However, each of these investors uses valuation in a different way. Whereas asset managers (such as pension funds) may want to understand the value of a certain company, banks are more interested in its probability of default, and how much they can recover in case such a default occurs.[57] Many of the principles, however, are the same across assets.

There are two general methods of company valuation: discounted cash flow (DCF) or multiples analysis (also called relative valuation, as it is based on a comparison with other companies). In the DCF method, the value of a company (or asset) depends on the cash flows it provides to its investors and on the timing and risk of those cash flows. In the multiples analysis method, the key elements are an appropriate sample of benchmark companies and the correct computation of the chosen multiples.

In this section, we provide details on the valuation methods. Instead of talking about climate change in general, we must map the levels of physical risk, transition risk, and climate-related opportunities onto financial and economic inputs. The objective is to provide a valuation framework that facilitates the incorporation of climate change issues into valuation analysis.

2.7.1 Climate and Cash Flows

In this section, we outline a framework to incorporate climate change considerations into valuation of businesses and assets. The task ahead of us is complex, and we do not advocate a one-size-fits-all approach to factoring climate change into valuations.[58]

Climate risks (and their relative importance) vary substantially across assets, and must always be assessed on a case-by-case basis. For this, it is important to have a solid understanding of the company, as well as the significant impacts that climate change can have on its

---

[57] When talking about debt valuation, the key principle is to discount expected cash flows at a rate consistent with the risk. Alternatively, in a distress (or bankruptcy) scenario, one can focus on the expected value. In this case, we are interested in forecasting the probability of default (PD) and the loss given default (LGD).

[58] For instance, by relying on only secondary sources of data such as ESG ratings (discussed in detail in Section 5.1) to apply a black-box adjustment factor.

business. As explained further below, we need to identify the possible impacts across different parts of the firm's operations (revenues, costs, profitability, additional investments, financing mix, or risk profile), and think carefully about the timing of climate-related impacts and how to factor them into cash flow or multiple-based valuations.

The Discounted Cash Flow Method

The DCF method values a company from the cash flows it is expected to generate. The same method is used to value a proposed investment project, whether it is a capital expenditure, a new product launch, an entry into a new market, or a replacement of a machine.

The most common method of company valuation using discounted cash flows is free cash flow to the firm (FCFF). With this method, we attempt to determine the value of the company by discounting all the cash flows over the life of the company. The key steps of company valuation using the FCFF method are as follows:

- o Forecast future cash flows
- o Determine the appropriate cost of capital
- o Discount expected future cash flows at the cost of capital

The FCFF is defined for each year as

$$FCFF = EBITDA - (\Delta NWC - Taxes) - CAPEX \qquad (2.1)$$

Or

$$FCFF = EBIT \times (1 - Tax\,rate) + Depreciation - CAPEX - \Delta NWC \qquad (2.2)$$

where EBITDA is the earnings before interest, taxes, depreciation, and amortization generated by the company, EBIT is the earnings before interest and taxes, CAPEX is the capital expenditure, and ΔNWC is the annual change in the net working capital (NWC).

To compute the future FCFF, we need to forecast, for each year, each of the components of formulas (2.1) or (2.2). These cash flow forecasts should be based on sound industry and company analysis and should reflect industry trends, market research data, competitive pressures, and company strategy. Obviously, good-quality inputs are essential to generate accurate FCFF forecasts and, ultimately, a trustworthy company valuation.[59]

---

[59] See Fernandes (2017), Chapter 9, for more details on valuation in general.

Incorporating Climate Risks into Cash Flows

Climate risks and opportunities, as discussed earlier in this chapter, have economic consequences. There is significant evidence that extreme weather events affect businesses and that climate risks in general affect companies and can even lead to bankruptcies. Without a structured approach, these climate issues can also be too overwhelming to tackle.

Climate risks can be addressed using the DCF model. The mechanics of using a DCF model and valuing a business using discounted cash flows are always valid. Here, we focus on how to incorporate into the valuation the extra level of risk that climate change poses to companies and investments.

We propose a framework to reduce the number of inputs to manageable levels. In particular, the process requires us to translate physical and transition risks into financial modeling. Incorporating climate considerations into valuation should follow the following steps:

1. Identify the key value drivers of the company, and assess how climate impacts those value drivers

2. Prioritize the different effects by focusing on the materiality of each one

3. Identify actions that may either mitigate risks or use climate effects as opportunities

4. Integrate the impacts and the actions into the model

Key Value Drivers and Climate Impacts

We start by identifying the key drivers behind the company's value. This is a typical first step in any valuation, and requires a thorough competitive analysis and understanding of the company's value chain and business model. Ultimately, this culminates in a series of assumptions regarding the different elements underlying the forecasted free cash flows to the firm. Once we have these assumptions regarding sales and various costs, we can compute the projected EBITDA for each year, the net working capital needs, and the required amount of capital expenditures.

The next step is to think about how climate change may affect the valuation. This requires estimating the future cash flows that the company expects after factoring in whether and how climate change may affect their business. To follow this process, one must identify the ways in which climate change may affect the company's value, and assess where climate change can impact the assumptions of the financial model, namely, on revenues, growth, costs, margins, working capital levels, investments, etc.

Figure 2.2 Possible impacts of climate issues on cash flow drivers

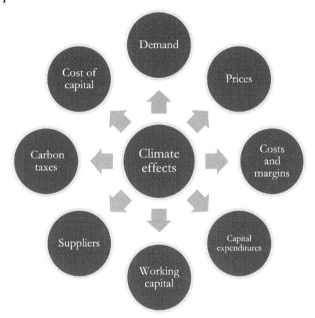

Ultimately, the cash flow projections should reflect the impact of climate-related issues (direct and indirect effects, as well as shifts in demand). This includes thinking about revenues and growth, which may change as customers move away from non-green products and services. It should also include a revision of the company's cost assumptions, as suppliers may pass on additional costs throughout the supply chain. In some industries, cash flows will be less impacted, as cost pressures can be passed on to customers, thereby maintaining profit margins. However, in other cases, there will be limited passing on of costs to consumers, and the margins will be significantly affected. Technological developments may affect the company's competitiveness in the market it operates in, necessitating higher capital investments to develop technological improvements.

As a result of climate effects and changes in its business model, the company may become more, or less, profitable in the future. For instance, the transition to a low-carbon economy may lead to significant carbon costs being passed on to its customers, which may reduce both sales and margins. Also, climate issues may affect the clients, employees, and suppliers of the company being valued, which can significantly affect future estimates of revenues, working capital levels, profitability, and so on.

Companies will experience different levels of vulnerability to climate hazards. When valuing a company using discounted cash flows, we must prioritize and translate the key impacts into detailed assumptions in our financial model. We provide the following examples of factors to consider for some of the most important line items of a financial valuation model.[60]

Customers and Revenues

- o Business interruptions due to extreme weather events can decrease company revenues.
- o Primary customers and markets could see a shift in preferences. This can lead to either opportunities or vulnerabilities and volatility in sales.
- o Changes in the competitive landscape can lead to better-positioned competitors attacking a company's business.
- o Lower availability of productive land and other raw materials forces production drops.
- o Demand for products and services provided by low-emissions providers and for products and services that ensure resiliency can increase.

Profitability and Costs

- o Higher temperatures will increase energy costs.
- o Higher insurance premiums will raise operational costs.
- o Heavy polluters may have to purchase carbon credits at more expensive prices, thus increasing their costs.
- o Changing input prices can increase operational costs.
- o Human productivity drops under heat stress, increasing the cost of labor.
- o Business interruptions due to extreme weather events can lower productivity.
- o Floods and heavy rainfall may affect a company's production capacity and increase distribution costs.
- o Heat waves, droughts, and water scarcity can lead to raw materials (such as food, for some industries) inflation.
- o Additional environmental requirements such as proper treatment of waste and residuals can increase production costs.
- o Supply chain risks can cause production disruptions, delays, shortages, and higher input costs.

---

[60] Results from academic research show a positive impact of ESG efforts on firm value and consumer behavior. Grimmer and Bingham (2013) showed a positive relationship between the perceived environmental performance of a company and consumers' purchasing intentions. Focusing on climate issues, Pankratz et al. (2019) documented that increasing exposure to high temperatures reduces companies' revenues and operating income. Eichholtz et al. (2010) analyzed a sample of 8,160 office buildings and found that buildings with a green rating—as certified by the U.S. Green Building Council—have 3% higher rental rates and a 16% higher selling price. Custódio et al. (2021) found that temperature increases lead to declines in supplier sales. Extreme heat and cold events can lower sales by more than 30% in some cases. They also found that changes in productivity and increases in operating costs lead to lower output. Pankratz and Schiller (2019) reported that heat waves and flooding at supplier locations generate losses across the global supply chain.

o The cost of transitioning to lower-emissions alternatives has to be considered.

o Reputational benefits can translate into higher margins.

Capital Expenditures

o Exposure of the company's assets to physical hazards can increase their maintenance costs.

o Assets that have shorter useful lives because of heat stress or other climate changes may need to be replaced.

o Sea level rise can change property values.

o Extreme weather events can damage capital equipment.

o The cost of preventive strategies can increase, as facilities may have to be moved away from weather-sensitive areas.

o Research and development expenditure on new alternative technologies may increase.

Supply Chain and Working Capital

o Climate issues may affect the clients and suppliers of the company being valued, which can significantly affect future estimates of profitability, working capital levels, etc.

o Supply shortages may lead to higher inventory costs and different terms of payment, thereby affecting working capital levels.

o Supply chain efficiencies can drop in some regions, changing the company's cash collection periods.

o Lower productivity of suppliers can decrease output.

Cost of Capital

o If the company is not considered attractive by some investors, its capital availability may decrease.

o On both the equity and debt sides of the balance sheet, companies significantly exposed to risks may face higher funding costs.

o As climate can affect many of the variables underlying credit ratings, the company's rating and capital structure may change.

Note that the above list is not exhaustive. When using the DCF method, we can incorporate the additional risks through a series of assumptions and adjustments. We must specify the economic drivers of the assets being valued, and then assess how climate can impact their performance. Importantly, the line items of a financial model to consider, in terms of their climate impacts, vary greatly by industry and geography. Also, many of the abovementioned issues may not be relevant in every case.

In Section 6.6.4, we describe several scenarios for physical and transition risks. Some of these can be used as inputs to valuation analysis; i.e., the impacts of various economic and financial variables on cash flows are considered.

KEY LEARNING POINT

Physical and transition risk pathways can affect the present value of future cash flows.

Priority, timing, actions

Underlying any valuation model are many assumptions, and climate change may exert multiple impacts. To remain practical, it is important to filter through the different climate change risks and opportunities, and focus on the most relevant ones, which will be evaluated in greater detail. Not all climate-related issues are equally important for all companies and industries. The materiality concept (further developed in Section 6.3) can also help focus our analysis on the most important issues that impact the financial condition of the company (which vary greatly across industries).

The timing of climate issues is also relevant. When thinking about translating assumptions into a financial model, it is important to consider the timing implications. Several of the abovementioned impacts may be spread out over time. This implies that when projecting cash flows, they do not all materialize in the same year.

For instance, higher carbon prices will likely be phased in globally. This implies that sectors with high carbon intensity will experience rising operating costs. BlackRock assumes a carbon tax of $125 (per metric ton of CO_2) in 20 years in one of their transition scenarios. In this case, the impact on each individual company's earnings and cash flows depends not only on its current level of emissions, but also on the expected abatement of emissions over time, and their ability to pass on the tax to consumers. Some companies, for instance, insurance companies, may face significant risks from physical climate damage, but may be able to pass on their increased costs to their customers; others may not. Similarly, capital expenditures have to be considered over a multiyear basis. Some will be repeated annually, whereas others will be one-off investments.

After this, one should think carefully about actions that may mitigate risks or use climate effects as opportunities, and include these actions into the model.

The above analysis should generate significant debate on the various assumptions that can be used. In fact, that is one of the benefits of this approach: to provide transparency regarding the assumptions underlying climate change, and where they can be expected to impact a company's activities.

KEY LEARNING POINT

Understand the business and how climate change can impact operations, and therefore valuations.

2.7.2 Terminal Value and Climate Effects

Because companies are usually assumed to have an infinite life, the valuation is usually split into two components: the explicit period (also called the forecast period) and the terminal value (also called perpetuity). For the explicit period, we compute forecasts of the FCFF for each year. The terminal value is estimated in the last year of the explicit cash flow period and represents the sum of all the future cash flows that the company is going to generate in the steady state thereafter. The formula for terminal value is

$$TV_t = \frac{FCFF_{t+1}}{WACC-g} = \frac{FCFF_t(1+g)}{WACC-g} \qquad (2.3)$$

where $FCFF_t$ represents the free cash flow to the firm at time t, $WACC$ is the weighted average cost of capital, and g is the constant growth rate that is expected in perpetuity.

Every company eventually reaches a mature stage. At this point, long-term growth is moderate, and is likely to be close to the inflation rate with some small adjustments for other factors. But in some sectors (such as fixed-line telecoms), where markets are mature and competitive pressures keep driving margins down, it is sometimes reasonable to assume negative long-term growth rates. As discussed below, climate risks may have a similar effect for some companies. It is important to remember that small changes in the growth rate produce large changes in the terminal value. Table 2.5 shows the terminal value in a valuation, using different discount rates and growth rates. In this example, the base scenario is a final year cash flow of 1,000, a base WACC of 7%, and a base terminal growth rate of 2%.

Table 2.5 Terminal value under different inputs

| | | Perpetuity growth rate | | | | |
		1.0%	1.5%	2.0%	2.5%	3.0%
WACC	**6.0%**	20,000	22,222	25,000	28,571	33,333
	6.5%	18,182	20,000	22,222	25,000	28,571
	7.0%	16,667	18,182	20,000	22,222	25,000
	7.5%	15,385	16,667	18,182	20,000	22,222
	8.0%	14,286	15,385	16,667	18,182	20,000

Under the base case scenario, where long-term growth is assumed to be 2% and the WACC is 7%, the terminal value equals US$20,000. However, if the long-term growth rate equals 1.5%, the terminal value goes down to US$18,182. Alternatively, if the long-term growth rate equals 2.5%, the terminal value grows to US$22,222 (a more than 11% increase).

In any valuation, it is important to carefully consider the long-term growth rate. As discussed above, climate change affects all the elements of forecasted cash flows and thus can significantly impact the terminal value, for instance, due to the following:

- o   Climate effects will drive demand (and margins) down, and it may be reasonable to assume negative long-term growth rates. Also, companies that are not prepared for the climate change transition may suffer negative perpetual growth rates.
- o   The final year of cash flow projections should indeed represent the company in the steady state. If the company has not reached steady state, in particular due to climate-related issues, it may be appropriate to extend the forecast until a steady state is reached.
- o   The forecast period (of say, 5 years) may be too short for climate effects to fully manifest. Above all, these effects can significantly impact the company's long-term competitiveness.
- o   It is possible that the company will not be able to operate in perpetuity as assumed (see Section 2.5 on stranded assets). In this case, the in-perpetuity assumption may be incorrect.

Overall, the terminal value is a very important component of a valuation, and often represents more than 50% of the final value. Small changes in the inputs to the formula can produce large changes in the terminal value. It is thus advisable to dedicate a substantial amount of time to understanding its key inputs, namely, the cost of capital and the steady-state growth rate, and how climate issues may impact these.

KEY LEARNING POINT

Perpetuity growth is very important in DCF valuations, and its inputs may be substantially impacted by climate effects.

2.7.3 Cost of Capital and Climate Effects

The cost of capital is not fixed internally; rather, it must be estimated by taking into account the rate of return required by the investors who finance the company. Investors who buy company bonds and stocks are looking for a return that compensates them for the risk in their investment, as well as for the time value of money. Thus, the cost of capital can be interpreted, from the investors' point of view, as the opportunity cost of funds and, of course, investors demand higher returns for riskier investments (risk-return principle).

At the company level, the most important concept is the weighted average cost of capital (WACC). The WACC reflects not only the business risk but also the financial risk of the company being valued. It is thus a market-value concept that the company's management needs to know to make good decisions for the company's owners.

The formula for the WACC is the weighted average of investors' required returns on equity and debt (opportunity cost of capital for them) and is given by

$$WACC = \frac{debt}{debt+equity}(1-t)r_{debt} + \frac{equity}{debt+equity}r_{equity} \qquad (2.4)$$

where r_{debt} is the cost of debt, r_{equity} is the cost of equity, and t is the tax rate. The term *debt* is the sum of the short- and long-term financial debts, and *equity* is the total value of the equity.

The WACC is the after-tax cost of funding for a company as a whole. It is computed as the weighted average of the cost of equity and the after-tax cost of debt, taking into account the appropriate mix of debt and equity.[61] To compute it, we need three key inputs:

1. The cost of equity (r_{equity})

2. The cost of debt (r_{debt}).

3. The appropriate capital structure, or target mix, of capital (debt and equity) of a company.

The costs of both equity and debt should be forward looking and reflect the cost demanded by the different sources of capital of a company (or the required return expected by investors given the risk of a company). Of course, these expectations depend on the level of risk.

The WACC combines the cost of debt, the cost of equity, and the capital structure. Climate risks can change each of these elements.

Risk-Free Rate

One of the key inputs in any valuation is the risk-free rate. As will be seen below, the risk-free rate influences both the cost of equity and the cost of debt. It is typically the yield to maturity of riskless government bonds.[62]

---

[61] Because interest payments are tax deductible, the after-tax cost of debt is lower than its before-tax cost. Thus, in the WACC formula, we include the term $1 - t$ (one minus the corporate tax rate) to represent the tax shield obtained through interest payments.

[62] In practice, it is common to use the yield to maturity of long-term government bonds (10 years or longer) as a measure of the risk-free rate.

For most advanced economies, environmental factors do not yet pose a significant credit risk. For many emerging markets, however, the situation is different (especially those in the Caribbean, Southeast Asia, and Sub-Saharan Africa). Particularly relevant is the situation of the so-called "vulnerable 20"[63] countries, which are already facing significant impacts arising from natural disasters and climate change.

When evaluating sovereign ratings, rating agencies include a potential adjustment for volatility in economic output due to exposure to natural disasters or adverse weather conditions. They also factor in the actual cost of natural disasters and how it affects the fiscal situation of the country (lower tax revenues and increased spending), and its external outlook (loss of exports). Economic activity concentrated in risky sectors is also assessed. For instance, a country that has high agricultural output is more vulnerable to weather-related events. Moreover, countries that depend on "brown" industries (such as mining) can suffer from limited budget inflows and future contingent liabilities. Studies suggest that the sovereign credit ratings of many countries can be significantly affected by climate risks.[64]

The results also suggest that natural disaster risk negatively affects the ability of governments to access financial markets and issue debt.

KEY LEARNING POINT

Climate risk can impact the sovereign ratings of the affected countries.

Cost of debt

The cost of debt is equal to the risk-free rate, plus a spread. Because a corporate has a certain probability of default, investors will always ask companies for interest rates that are higher than the risk-free rate. Naturally, for riskier borrowers, the spread (and thus the cost of debt) is higher than for safer ones.

Credit ratings play an important role in helping investors make better-informed decisions and judge the risk of lending money to a given company. These agencies, as well as other players in the bond and loan markets, may change their pricing due to climate risks. In turn, these will impact the cost of debt. See Section 3.3 for examples of the banking-level implications of climate issues.

Environmental risks can influence future revenues, costs, cash flows, profitability, etc. Rating agencies are beginning to incorporate these risks into their analysis when assessing a borrower's creditworthiness, if they consider them relevant. The relevance of different

---

[63] See Section 1.1.3.
[64] See also Sections 3.1.5 and 3.4.

factors varies from issuer to issuer. In general, rating agencies try to understand how a borrower's exposure to environmental factors can impact its revenues, earnings, cash flow generation, competitive position, and financial commitments (see Section 3.4 for examples of environmental factors used by rating agencies for different categories of bond issuers). When these factors significantly influence the borrower's capacity to meet financial commitments, the rating can change.

KEY LEARNING POINT

Environmental risks can affect a bond issuer's credit rating.

Cost of equity

The cost of equity (or the return required by equity investors) is proportional to the risk investors face and depends on the risk of the company (or project) being valued. The capital asset pricing model (CAPM) is the traditional model used by analysts, investment banks, and best-in-class world corporations to estimate the cost of equity. According to the CAPM, the cost of equity is equal to

$$r_{equity} = r_f + \beta \times (\text{Market Risk Premium}) \tag{2.5}$$

where r_f is the risk-free rate, and β is the beta of a company.

According to the CAPM, the main measure of risk is the beta coefficient. The beta is a measure of the systematic risk of a company's shares, which includes compensation for business and financial risks. It is important that this beta reflect an appropriate compensation for the business risk and also for the financial (capital structure) risk.[65] Two parameters are needed in addition to the beta to estimate the cost of equity: the risk-free rate and the market risk premium.

Equity investors are increasingly incorporating ESG and sustainability factors into their investment decisions. This can have implications for the cost of equity. It is possible that changes in the cost of capital will be related to carbon efficiency. Some suggest that the cost of capital will decrease for more efficient carbon companies, whereas it will increase for heavy polluters (as a penalty). However, there is no precise answer to the question of when these changes in the cost of capital will occur. This also depends on the transition period, and the duration over which long assets are being repriced (see also Section 5.3). There is no commonly accepted and robust asset pricing model that offers guidance on the proper

---

[65] For more details, see Fernandes, 2017, Chapter 9.

computation of discount rates to handle climate risks.[66] A detailed and rigorous association between returns, the cost of capital, and environmental performance is difficult to establish, as we still are within the transition period. Also, we lack long-term data series on risks and their impacts on companies around the world.

Capital structure

The final input to the WACC is the company's capital structure. Capital structure and the choices related to it are important decisions for a company. If a company's owners increase debt, less of their own capital needs to be invested in the company. However, they will incur additional financial risk, because the volatility of the company's returns will increase. Importantly, how a company balances its equity and debt financing impacts its cost of capital.

Climate risks can lead to changes in the capital structure of the company and, therefore, its cost of capital. It is well known that important factors determining the optimal capital structure are the need for financial flexibility and credit ratings,[67] and these (as well as other determinants of capital structure) can be affected by climate risks. Chapter 3 focuses on the effects of climate on the debt side of the balance sheet, including the effects on credit ratings. Also, in Chapter 5, we discuss how investors are changing their portfolios to account for climate-related risks. This means that climate risks can materially influence the investor base of the company and thus may impact how the company balances equity and debt financing.[68]

In general, climate risks may lead to changes in funding decisions and investor requirements. As discussed above, several of the variables commonly used to compute the WACC can change due to climate effects, which will have implications for the cost of capital of the company.

2.7.4 Risk in Cash Flows or Cost of Capital

In a DCF valuation, we have two options for incorporating the additional risks due to climate issues: (1) they can be included in the actual cash flows or (2) as an extra risk premium added to the cost of capital.

Some investors and managers may be tempted to account for these climate risks by adding an ad hoc risk premium to the discount rate (for instance, based on an ESG rating).

---

[66] This early research on a possible carbon factor in equity markets is discussed in Section 5.3. Other academic research suggests that investors should consider climate risks when making investment decisions (see Section 5.4).

[67] A full discussion on capital structure, its drivers, and its impacts on the cost of capital is beyond the scope of this book. The interested reader may consult Fernandes, 2017, Chapter 5.

[68] Ginglinger and Moreau (2019) found that greater climate risk leads to lower leverage, as lenders increase the spreads when lending to firms with the greatest risk.

Unfortunately, this can result in misleading valuations and opaque black box approaches. Finance theory is clear about the definition of the cost of capital and how it should compensate only systematic risk. Diversifiable risk can be eliminated by diversification. On the other hand, systemic risks cannot be avoided, as they affect all the companies in the economy.

Climate change has an element of systematic risk, as it will affect all economies to a certain extent. However, we have seen in the previous sections of this book that these risks (physical and transition) do not apply equally to all industries and countries. Even within a certain industry, some companies may be better prepared than others, and for some companies, climate change could even represent an opportunity. That is likely to be the case for companies that are further ahead and better prepared to handle transition risk. This suggests that applying the same extra risk premium to all companies in the country would be wrong. It would understate risk for some companies and overstate it for others.

When using a DCF model and thinking about risks, one of the most important pitfalls is double-counting. We must be careful not to include the same risks in the cash flows and in the discount rate. We also want to avoid double-counting risks that the market may already be pricing. For example, climate change risks may already have been considered and priced by the market. In this case, they are already implicitly accounted for in the different elements required to compute the cost of capital (for instance, risk-free rates, ratings, or betas), and thus require no additional changes in the methodology.

Whether to incorporate risks in the cash flows or discount rate also depends on our ability to determine the material likelihood and the impact of these risks. Risks whose effects are easier to quantify should preferably be included in the cash flows. This is also consistent with finance theory, whereby idiosyncratic risks are better handled in the cash flows.

There is a high degree of uncertainty in how a company will respond to the climate transition, and the precise impact of changing business models, consumer preferences, and regulations on its profitability. There is no historical precedent for the impact of climate change, both in terms of physical risk and transition risk.[69]

---

[69] The lack of good historical data complicates academic research studies. Indeed, there is mixed evidence in the literature on whether financial markets are already pricing climate risks for corporates. Some asset pricing models suggest the importance of climate risks as a long-run risk factor (Bansal et al. 2017; Bolton and Kacperczyk 2021; Hsu et al. 2022). Some, however, suggest that climate risks may be mispriced in financial markets (Hong et al. 2019; Daniel et al. 2016; Kumar et al. 2019). Kruttli et al. (2019) showed that extreme weather is reflected in option market prices, through additional uncertainty. They found that stock options on firms exposed to extreme weather (landfalls and hurricanes) exhibited increases in implied volatility of 5%–10%. In an analysis of municipal bonds issued by U.S. counties exposed to climate risk, Painter (2020) reported that these require higher yields compared to less exposed counties. Similar results were reported by Baker et al. (2018). However, Goldsmith and Pinkham (2021) found small differences in the yields of municipal bonds

The DCF method allows us to understand the economics of a business, and to explicitly incorporate different information on, and special insights into, climate change into a valuation. We can include in the valuation the expected impacts of climate risks on operating efficiency, the returns and useful life of different assets, profitability of different products, markets, inventory levels, distribution costs, and so on.

As described in Section 2.7.2, accounting for physical and transition risks in the cash flows, through several assumptions, can provide a more transparent and robust understanding of how valuations may change due to climate risks. Making the assumptions visible and thinking about how they affect the business model and translate into cash flows gives managers a much better understanding of the effects of climate on value than simply manipulating the discount rate.

Further, this is a very useful exercise that can generate a number of managerial insights. Thinking through specific risks and how they may impact value drivers allows investors and executives to make better plans to mitigate them. Companies have the ability to respond to climate risks. Climate risk management is possible, and companies can take many actions to prevent the emerging effects of climate change from hurting them more. These include modifying the business model, supply chain, operations, how they produce, how they source materials, and the products they bring to market.

With this model, one can test a variety of different business models for the company and assess the merits (and value) of several proposed managerial actions. For instance, if supply chain risk turns out to be a major concern for valuations, a company may decide to change its procurement practices (even if that may generate an initial cost) or implement sustainable supply chain finance solutions (Section 3.6).

Is the Model Right?

Even the best model cannot anticipate all the possible risks. That is why, in many settings, it is important to use scenarios to model the risks that the business may face. This is particularly relevant when discussing climate risks, due to the underlying uncertainty around many variables.

When constructing a transition risk scenario, we can specify how we believe carbon prices will evolve in the future. This requires specifying absolute amounts of carbon taxes and their phasing in over time. This in turn will affect several components of the projected cash flow: revenues, costs, and even investments and working capital levels.

---

exposed to sea level rise relative to other bonds. Baldauf et al. (2020) and Bernstein et al. (2019) documented that real estate valuations reflect the differential beliefs regarding the risk of future inundation, and that houses projected to be underwater sell for 7% less than unexposed houses. Murfin and Spiegel (2020) compared the prices of houses based on their inundation threshold (using projections of sea level rise) and found limited price effects.

It is possible for two parties to arrive at very different valuations, largely because of differing views about the impact of climate change on different inputs. However, this discrepancy in itself has significant utility, as it makes explicit the reason for the change in valuation.

We may come up with different what-if scenarios. Developing what-if scenarios and assumptions for different inputs requires careful business thinking about how the future may evolve, and how this evolution will affect the company's profitability and financial performance. Ultimately, after developing the what-if scenarios, we obtain a range of possible outcomes, each of which tries to quantify the company's existing risk from climate change issues. By highlighting specific risks, these what-if scenarios help executives make better decisions for their companies.[70]

Of course, even this tool is subject to a series of assumptions, which may turn out to be wrong. But the insights and transparency the ensuing discussions provide can enable a more structured approach to decision-making. It will allow managers to have a more meaningful dialogue about the trade-offs that different decisions, namely, mitigating efforts, may impose on value and its drivers.

Instead of a "plug-and-play" approach," where we simply use an ESG rating (see Section 5.1) to change the valuation, it is recommended to use judgment, and think about the underlying value drivers, and how these change cash flows over time.

In the case of capital investments with very long lead times, where the results may greatly depend on climate-related issues, developing scenarios can be a very useful exercise. It is also useful when companies regularly assess several investment projects. In this case, having a consistent approach to evaluating project profitability and their risks puts all projects on an equal footing. In doing so, we are transparent about the levels of risk and how they may affect the investment decision. We may be able to manage risks better once we understand how they can affect a project's economics.[71] That is, instead of trying to summarize each project with a single number, we will have a distribution of possible outcomes that depend on the risk. Managers can then discuss whether and how to mitigate risks. This is considerably easier when it is done from the start of a project, rather than fixing it later on.

KEY LEARNING POINT

Considering several scenarios and including the impact on cash flows (instead of on the discount rate) avoids double-counting and provides better visibility.

---

[70] See Section 6.6.4 for examples of different scenarios related to physical and transition risks.

[71] We may even use a probability-weighted scenario analysis. In this case, each scenario receives a weight that reflects the likelihood of occurrence. The final evaluation is the weighted average of the different valuations, taking into account their probabilities.

2.7.5 Using Comparable Companies as Benchmarks: Multiples

Up to now, we have been focusing on valuation by discounting cash flows. Alternatively, it is also common when valuing a company to analyze comparable companies' trading multiples as a benchmark.

A multiples-based valuation uses the valuations of a reference group of companies to infer the value of our target company. The rationale for a multiples analysis is to see how much the market is currently paying for an asset with similar characteristics as the one we are interested in valuing. Multiples are widely used when valuing small- and medium-sized companies, for which cash flow estimates are often not very reliable. In addition, multiples are frequently used to complement a DCF valuation in M&As and IPOs when it is important to know "how much the market is paying for similar companies."

When using multiples to value a company, we follow these steps:

1. Choose a multiple (price-earnings ratio (PER), enterprise value to EBITDA (EV/EBITDA), etc.).

2. Choose a curated list of comparable companies.

3. Compute the multiple for each of the comparable companies and average them.

4. Multiply the average (or median) multiple of the peer group by our company's relevant indicator (EBITDA, for instance, if the chosen multiple is the EV/EBITDA).

Some specific climate concerns must be taken into account when applying a multiples-based evaluation. First, it is important to establish whether the earnings (or EBITDA, or any other income variable) have been impacted by some extraordinary climate event. If so, one has to think about the financial impact on the earnings, as well as the probability that the event would recur in the future. Also, if the company has reported extraordinary, but unsustainable, earnings, then the current metrics may not be valid in the future.

Many factors contribute to a proper peer group selection, including geography, business model, growth, and profitability levels. It is therefore common to find, even in the same industry, very different multiples for companies with different business risk, costs, and growth potential. This is an important concern whenever a multiples-based approach to valuation is used. We should not blindly take the average of the multiples of all companies in a sector and use that as a benchmark.

Further, climate change and its risks can change valuation levels in markets. Accordingly, one has to also be careful in selecting appropriate peer group companies based on their exposure to climate risks. Some of the possible climate-related metrics (which obviously depend on the specificities of the sector) that can be used when selecting peer group companies with similar physical and transition risk exposures include the following:

o   Total annual GHG emissions (Scopes 1, 2, 3)[72]
o   Revenue carbon intensity, which is the amount of Scope 1, 2, and 3 GHG emissions divided by the revenues[73]
o   Scope 1, 2, 3 GHG/EBITDA
o   Scope 1, 2, 3 GHG/enterprise value
o   Scope 1, 2, 3 GHG/customers served
o   Scope 1, 2, 3 GHG/quantity delivered

Importantly, it is not only the current value that matters but also the trajectory. The transition path that a company is following, which is very different from its current value, is an important data item to take into consideration when choosing peers.

KEY LEARNING POINT

Various parameters can be used to consider physical and transition risk when choosing appropriate peer group companies.

2.7.6 Concluding Comments on Valuation

To make informed financial decisions, managers and investors need to understand how climate risks and opportunities can impact a company's future income statement, balance sheet, and cash flow statements.

Climate risk is a complex and multidimensional concept. We have to make it manageable by translating it to different economic and financial variables. The framework presented here provides a way to assess and value climate risks. Valuation entails assessing different inputs, which requires substantial knowledge of the business. Climate change brings a series of additional risks, the assessment of which can lead to differing valuations. We have provided a detailed description of the DCF method and discussed many practical issues regarding its implementation. We have also shown how the multiples method can be used to estimate the value of a company and discussed some practical issues and pitfalls that arise when it is applied.

In general, it is recommended to value companies using both the DCF and the multiples methods. When they give comparable results, it is reassuring for our estimates; and when they differ substantially, we can try to learn what is driving this difference, and refine our

---

[72] See Section 1.4.3 for a definition of the different scope levels of emissions.

[73] Focusing on absolute levels of emissions penalizes large companies. That is why most corporate/investment metrics divide emissions by a certain size metric, allowing the data to be comparable across companies, sectors, and countries.

analysis. Integrating climate risks into the valuation models can be challenging; the lack of established best practices, the uncertainty around its impacts, and the lack of disclosure by some companies[74] make this task even more complex.

It is not possible to provide a definite answer and a completely quantifiable result in all circumstances. Unfortunately, there is not a "one-size-fits-all" formula for factoring in climate issues into valuation. In reality, climate risks and opportunities vary greatly across industries and even across companies in the same sector. Rather, the objective here was to prevent mistakes when thinking about the valuation of different assets and to provide readers a framework that will allow them to think about how climate risks can be incorporated into the valuation.

Ultimately, this valuation should reflect the current (and future) position of the company, as well as its ability to implement its strategy and respond to new technologies, regulations, shifts in consumer behavior, and other issues that may arise because of climate change.

---

[74] See Section 6.3 for a detailed analysis of disclosure and its impacts.

REFERENCES: CHAPTER 2

Asian Development Bank. 2017. *A Region at Risk: The Human Dimensions of Climate Change in Asia and the Pacific*. Manila: Asian Development Bank.

Baker, M., D. Bergstresser, G. Serafeim, and J. Wurgler. 2018. "Financing the Response to Climate Change: The Pricing and Ownership of US Green Bonds." National Bureau of Economic Research.

Baldauf, M., L. Garlappi, and C. Yannelis. 2020. "Does Climate Change Affect Real Estate Prices? Only If You Believe in It." *The Review of Financial Studies* 33 (3): 1256–95.

Bansal, R., M. Ochoa, and D. Kiku. 2017. "Climate Change and Growth Risks." National Bureau of Economic Research.

Bernstein, A., M.T. Gustafson, and R. Lewis. 2019. "Disaster on the Horizon: The Price Effect of Sea Level Rise." *Journal of Financial Economics* 134 (2): 253–72.

BloombergNEF. 2021. "New Energy Outlook 2021." New Energy Outlook. https://www.irena.org/publications/2019/Sep/Transforming-the-energy-system.

Bolton, P., M. Despres, L.A.P. Da Silva, F. Samama, R. Svartzman, et al. 2020. *The Green Swan*. Bank for International Settlements.

Bolton, P., and M. Kacperczyk. 2021. "Do Investors Care about Carbon Risk?" *Journal of Financial Economics* 142 (2): 517–49.

Burke, M., S.M. Hsiang, and E. Miguel. 2015. "Global Non-Linear Effect of Temperature on Economic Production." *Nature* 527 (7577): 235–39.

Byrd, J., and E.S. Cooperman. 2018. "Investors and Stranded Asset Risk: Evidence from Shareholder Responses to Carbon Capture and Sequestration (CCS) Events." *Journal of Sustainable Finance & Investment* 8 (2): 185–202.

Chen, C., I. Noble, J. Hellmann, J. Coffee, M. Murillo, and N. Chawla. 2015. "University of Notre Dame Global Adaptation Index Country Index Technical Report," November.

Cohen, L., U.G. Gurun, and Q.H. Nguyen. 2020. "The ESG-Innovation Disconnect: Evidence from Green Patenting." National Bureau of Economic Research.

Custódio, C., M.A. Ferreira, E. Garcia-Appendini, and A. Lam. 2021. "Economic Impact of Climate Change." Working paper. Available at SSRN 3724940.

Daniel, K.D., R.B. Litterman, and G. Wagner. 2016. "Applying Asset Pricing Theory to Calibrate the Price of Climate Risk." National Bureau of Economic Research.

Dell, M., B.F. Jones, and B.A. Olken. 2012. "Temperature Shocks and Economic Growth: Evidence from the Last Half Century." *American Economic Journal: Macroeconomics* 4 (3): 66–95.

Diffenbaugh, N.S., and M. Burke. 2019. "Global Warming Has Increased Global Economic Inequality." *Proceedings of the National Academy of Sciences* 116 (20): 9808–13.

Doumbia, D., and M.L. Lauridsen. 2019. "Closing the SDG Financing Gap : Trends and Data." Washington, DC: International Finance Corporation. https://www.irena.org/publications/2019/Sep/Transforming-the-energy-system.

Eichholtz, P., N. Kok, and J.M. Quigley. 2010. "Doing Well by Doing Good? Green Office Buildings." *American Economic Review* 100 (5): 2492–2509.

Ferrazzi, M., F. Kalantzis, and S. Zwart. 2021. "EIB Working Paper 2021/03 - Assessing Climate Change Risks at the Country Level: The EIB Scoring Model." European Investment Bank. https://doi.org/10.2867/854649.

Fernandes, N. 2017. *Finance for Executives: A Practical Guide for Managers.* 2nd ed. London: NPV Publishing.

Fulton, M., and R. Capalino. 2014. "Investing in the Clean Trillion: Closing The Clean Energy Investment Gap." Ceres. https://www.ceres.org/resources/reports/investing-clean-trillion-closing-clean-energy-investment-gap.

Ginglinger, E., and Q. Moreau. 2019. "Climate Risk and Capital Structure." Université Paris-Dauphine Research Paper, no. 3327185.

Grimmer, M., and T. Bingham. 2013. "Company Environmental Performance and Consumer Purchase Intentions." *Journal of Business Research* 66 (10): 1945–53.

Goldsmith-Pinkham, P.S., M. Gustafson, R. Lewis, and M. Schwert. 2021. "Sea Level Rise Exposure and Municipal Bond Yields." Jacobs Levy Equity Management Center for Quantitative Financial Research Paper.

Hain, L.I., J.F. Kölbel, and M. Leippold. 2022. "Let's Get Physical: Comparing Metrics of Physical Climate Risk." *Finance Research Letters* 46: 102406.

Hong, H., F.W. Li, and J. Xu. 2019. "Climate Risks and Market Efficiency." *Journal of Econometrics* 208 (1): 265–81.

Hsiang, S., R. Kopp, A. Jina, J. Rising, M. Delgado, S. Mohan, D. Rasmussen, et al. 2017. "Estimating Economic Damage from Climate Change in the United States." *Science* 356 (6345): 1362–69.

Hsu, P.-H., K. Li, and C.-Y. Tsou. 2022. "The Pollution Premium." *Journal of Finance*, Forthcoming.

IEA and OECD. 2015. *World Energy Investment Outlook 2015.* World Energy Outlook. Paris: International Energy Association.

IMF. 2017. "The Effects of Weather Shocks on Economic Activity: How Can Low-Income Countries Cope?" In *World Economic Outlook, October 2017 Seeking Sustainable Growth: Short-Term Recovery, Long-Term Challenges.* World Economic Outlook.

IMF. 2019. *Fiscal Monitor, October 2019: How to Mitigate Climate Change.* Washington, D.C.: International Monetary Fund.

IMF. 2021. "Reaching Net Zero Emissions." https://www.irena.org/publications/2019/Sep/Transforming-the-energy-system.

IRENA. 2019. "Transforming the Energy System." Abu Dhabi: International Renewable Energy Agency. https://www.irena.org/publications/2019/Sep/Transforming-the-energy-system.

IRENA. 2020. "Global Landscape of Renewable Energy Finance 2020." Abu Dhabi: International Renewable Energy Agency. https://www.irena.org/publications/2020/Nov/Global-Landscape-of-Renewable-Energy-Finance-2020.

Kahn, M.E., K. Mohaddes, R.N. Ng, M.H. Pesaran, M. Raissi, and J.-C. Yang. 2019. "Long-Term Macroeconomic Effects of Climate Change: A Cross-Country Analysis." National Bureau of Economic Research.

Kruttli, M.S., B. Roth Tran, and S.W. Watugala. 2021. "Pricing Poseidon: Extreme Weather Uncertainty and Firm Return Dynamics." EBRD Working Paper.

Kumar, A., W. Xin, and C. Zhang. 2019. "Climate Sensitivity and Predictable Returns." Available at *SSRN* 3331872.

Kumra, G., and J. Woetzel. 2022. "What It Will Cost to Get to Net-Zero | McKinsey." January 29. https://www.mckinsey.com/mgi/overview/in-the-news/what-it-will-cost-to-get-to-net-zero.

OECD & IEA. (2015) World energy investment outlook.

McGlade, C., and P. Ekins. 2015. "The Geographical Distribution of Fossil Fuels Unused When Limiting Global Warming to 2 °C." *Nature* 517 (7533): 187–90.

Mercure, J.-F., H. Pollitt, J.E. Viñuales, N.R. Edwards, P.B. Holden, U. Chewpreecha, P. Salas, et al. 2018. "Macroeconomic Impact of Stranded Fossil Fuel Assets." *Nature Climate Change* 8 (7): 588–93.

Miao, Q., and D. Popp. 2014. "Necessity as the Mother of Invention: Innovative Responses to Natural Disasters." *Journal of Environmental Economics and Management* 68 (2): 280–95.

Morel, A., R. Friedman, D.J. Tulloch, and B. Caldecott. 2016. "Stranded Assets in Palm Oil Production: A Case Study of Indonesia." Sustainable Finance Programme, SSEE, University of Oxford, Working Paper.

Murfin, J., and M. Spiegel. 2020. "Is the Risk of Sea Level Rise Capitalized in Residential Real Estate?" *The Review of Financial Studies* 33 (3): 1217–55.

Painter, M. 2020. "An Inconvenient Cost: The Effects of Climate Change on Municipal Bonds." *Journal of Financial Economics* 135 (2): 468–82.

Pankratz, N., R. Bauer, and J. Derwall. 2019. "Climate Change, Firm Performance, and Investor Surprises." *Firm Performance, and Investor Surprises* (May 21).

Pankratz, N., and C. Schiller. 2021. "Climate Change and Adaptation in Global Supply-Chain Networks." In *Proceedings of Paris December 2019 Finance Meeting EUROFIDAI-ESSEC, European Corporate Governance Institute–Finance Working Paper*.

Paun, A., L. Acton, and W.-S. Chan. 2018. "Fragile Planet: Scoring Climate Risks around the World." HSBC Bank.

Seetharam, I. 2017. "Environmental Disasters and Stock Market Performance." Stanford University Working Paper.

Stern, N. 2007. *The Economics of Climate Change: The Stern Review*. Cambridge University Press.

Sukhdev, P. 2016. "Evolve or Perish: Lessons from Peabody Energy." Island Press. July 20, 2016. https://islandpress.org/blog/evolve-or-perish-lessons-peabody-energy.

"Physical Climate Risk Metrics by Sustainalytics." 2022. Sustainalytics.Com. 2022. https://www.sustainalytics.com/investor-solutions/esg-research/climate-solutions/physical-climate-risk-metrics.

UNCTAD. 2019. *The State of Commodity Dependence* 2019. UN. https://digitallibrary.un.org/record/3827206.

Chapter 3
Green Corporate Financing – Debt

This chapter covers the debt financing side of the balance sheet. The sustainable finance market has grown exponentially in recent years. First, we introduce the green bond as a debt-financing instrument that can be issued by some companies and issuers. We describe the requirements and evolution of the green bond market. Then we talk about sustainability-linked bonds, as well as the emerging market of transition bonds. These are financing instruments available to companies operating in "brown" industries or those that lack clear "green" projects for allocating bond proceeds. We then explore the market of green loans or sustainability-linked loans as an alternative green financing instrument available to companies, especially those that are not listed in the stock market or that cannot issue green bonds. We also describe how credit rating agencies incorporate climate risk in their creditworthiness assessments when assigning a security rating. In the last two sections, we discuss the role of project finance and supply chain financing as instruments to finance "green" infrastructures and reduce emissions across the whole supply chain.

3.1 GREEN BONDS

3.1.1 Yields and Bond Prices

A bond is a security that establishes a credit relationship between the purchaser of the bond and the issuer. The purchaser pays a certain amount of money up-front to the issuer, and in exchange expects to receive the principal at the end of the life of the bond, as well as coupon payments over the life of the bond.

Bond prices are computed as the present value of the cash flows the bond provides for its holder. The appropriate discount rate at which the cash flows are discounted is called the yield to maturity (YTM). It represents the rate of return that investors require before investing in a particular bond, given the alternatives available in the market. We can determine a bond's price based on its YTM. If investors demand a 4% yield, or rate of return, to lend money to the issuer for five years, then the price of a five-year zero-coupon bond with a face value of €1,000 is

$$Price = \frac{1000}{(1+4\%)^5} = \frac{1000}{1.04^5} = 821.93 \tag{3.1}$$

This means that if an investor buys the five-year zero-coupon bond now for €821.93, keeps it for five years, and then collects the final payment of €1,000, its annual return would be exactly equal to 4%. There is a negative relationship between bond prices and the YTM. If the investor were to demand a higher YTM, the price of the bond today would have to be lower for it to generate the required YTM. For instance, if investors demand a 6% yield, or rate of return, to lend money to the issuer for five years, then the price of the bond (with a face value of €1,000) will be €747.26.

The YTM on bonds includes a spread above the risk-free rate that varies according to the risk level of the issuer. Section 3.4 focuses on credit ratings and rating agencies, and the factors they use to assess the credit risk of issuers.

Buyers of bonds are mainly large institutional investors such as pension funds, insurance companies, mutual funds, and sovereign wealth funds. The bond market has traditionally not been designed for individual investors.[75] Trading small quantities of bonds entails high costs. Also, the average size of a bond trade is between €1 million and €2 million, and trades above €100 million are common.[76] In addition, the majority of bonds trade very infrequently, unlike equities, because there is not a constant supply of buyers and sellers looking to trade. This lack of liquidity is also important in determining which investors buy bonds. Most buyers tend to be long-term investors, who simply hold the bonds in their portfolios.[77]

---

[75] The exception is municipal bonds in the United States. In general, retail investors participate in the bond market by investing in mutual funds focused on bonds.

[76] International Capital Market Association.

[77] Mahanti et al. (2008) suggest that 50% of issued bonds do not trade at all in a certain year, and only 20% of the bonds trade more than 10 days in a year.

3.1.2 What Is a Green Bond?

Green bonds are debt securities issued by governments and private or public entities, whose proceeds are used to finance green projects and assets. A "green bond" differs from a regular bond only in its label, which commits the issuer to using the funds raised for financing (or re-financing) only "green" projects, assets, or business activities. For instance, green bonds are issued to finance specific projects that help reduce GHG emissions, such as renewable energy infrastructure, or that help countries and companies adapt to climate change, for example, by protecting coastal areas from sea level rise.

KEY LEARNING POINT

Green bonds are fixed income instruments that are subject to special restrictions governing how the capital raised is used.

The key question is what constitutes a green project or asset. The International Capital Market Association (ICMA) has issued voluntary guidelines known as the Green Bond Principles (GBP). These first guidelines for green bond issuers were developed in 2014 by ICMA, together with a group of leading international investment banks.[78] In particular, the GBPs identify four components that issuers have to comply with when issuing green bonds:

1. **Use of Proceeds:** The use of the proceeds raised through the bond should be described in the legal documentation of the security. The list of acceptable green projects includes (but is not limited to) the following:

   o Renewable energy
   o Energy efficiency
   o Pollution prevention and control
   o Biodiversity conservation
   o Clean transportation
   o Sustainable water and wastewater management
   o Climate change adaptation
   o Eco-efficient and/or circular economy products, production technologies, and processes
   o Green buildings

2. **Process for Project Evaluation and Selection:** The issuer of a green bond should clearly communicate the following to investors:

---

[78] Bank of America Merrill Lynch, Citi, Crédit Agricole, JP Morgan Chase, BNP Paribas, Daiwa, Deutsche Bank, Goldman Sachs, HSBC, Mizuho Securities, Morgan Stanley, Rabobank, and SEB.

- ○ The environmental sustainability objectives of the projects
- ○ The process by which the issuer determines that the projects are acceptable green projects as listed above
- ○ The eligibility criteria, including, if applicable, exclusion criteria or any other process applied to identify and manage potentially material environmental and social risks associated with the projects

3. **Management of Proceeds:** The proceeds of the green bond should be credited to a subaccount and tracked by the issuer separately from other projects or capital issues. This should be confirmed via a formal internal process linked to the issuer's lending and investment operations for green projects.

4. **Reporting:** Issuers should keep up-to-date information on the use of proceeds until full allocation. In particular, the annual report should include a list of the projects to which green bond proceeds have been allocated, as well as a brief description of the projects and their expected impact.

Before issuing a green bond, issuers build a green bond framework, which describes the abovementioned four components. Further, issuers typically obtain a second opinion on their green bond framework from an external reviewer.

The 2007 EIB bond: pioneering the market

The European Investment Bank (EIB) is the global development bank owned by the 27 member states of the European Union. The EIB is rated Aaa/AAA/AAA (Moody's/Standard and Poor/Fitch), Following the European Union's Energy Action Plan of March 2007, the EIB issued the world's first green bond—called a Climate Awareness Bond—with the aim of financing projects that proposed solutions to climate change.

The €600 million bond, which was issued in July 2007, was a zero-coupon bond with 5-year maturity. Bertrand de Mazières, Director General of Finance at the EIB, stated: "The EU has taken a leading role in tackling climate change. With this bond, the EIB is inviting investors and the banking community to join that endeavor, further highlighting EIB's commitment to promoting EU objectives."

Retail investors were significant buyers of this bond (particularly in Italy, Germany, Benelux, and Switzerland). In addition, many institutional investors, including pension funds, insurance companies, and some socially responsible investment funds, were also important to the deal. The €600 million were allocated to 14 green projects for renewable energy (83% of the funds) and energy efficiency (17%) in six countries in 2007 and 2008.

3.1.3 Green Bond Certification

The issuer of a bond can label it "green." To do so, the issuer must provide investors with details on the green eligibility criteria, namely, the stipulations regarding the use of the proceeds and reporting. These are typically disclosed in a green bond framework prepared by the issuer before launching a green bond. To increase transparency and accountability, issuers can ask for an independent external review of the green credentials of the planned bond.

The most common way to obtain an external review is through a second-party opinion (SPO). The purpose of an SPO is to give investors confidence that the issuer's green bond framework, or the actual debt issue, is aligned with a reputed international framework (typically the abovementioned ICMA Green Bond Principles).

A number of service providers offer this service to issuers, and a couple of the most popular ones are Sustainalytics and Vigeo Eiris. However, there are many others, including environmental consultants, scientific experts, and even auditing firms. As with credit rating agencies, these verifiers use an "issuer pays" business model; that is, the issuer of the green bond pays the green bond verifier in exchange for an opinion/rating. Also, similar to credit rating agencies, these verifiers rely on their reputation when providing an assessment to investors.

Specifically, most SPOs consist of an opinion that the issuer's framework is credible and aligns with the four core components of the GBP:

o   The "greenness" of eligible projects/assets: This depends on their alignment with market practices, and the credibility of the stated use of the proceeds for environmental purposes. The opinion addresses the likely impacts of the eligible projects expected to be financed/refinanced with the bond proceeds, but does not measure the actual impact.

o   Project selection and evaluation: This pertains to adequate disclosure and the suitability of the projects to be financed or refinanced.

o   Management of the proceeds: This deals with whether or not the proceeds will be fully dedicated to the projects; they should not be "lost" in the middle of all the organizational spending on various projects and costs.

o   Reporting: This pertains to assessment of the suitability of the planned reporting by the issuer, including its frequency, details of the allocation of funds to specific projects, as well as the reporting of quantitative and qualitative impact indicators.

KEY LEARNING POINT

Second-party opinions (SPOs), formulated by verifying agents, aim to assure investors that a green bond meets the defined global standards.

The case below summarizes an evaluation performed by Sustainalytics of the Corticeira Amorim Green Bond Framework.[79] Corticeira Amorim (Portugal) is the world's largest producer of cork products. In November 2020, the company published its Green Bond Framework and engaged Sustainalytics to review it. Sustainalytics released its evaluation report (November 27, 2020), after which the company issued a €40 million green bond.

Corticeira Amorim – second party opinion (excerpt from Sustainalytics report)

Sustainalytics is of the opinion that the Corticeira Amorim Green Bond Framework (the "Framework") is credible and impactful and aligns with the four core components of the Green Bond Principles 2018. This assessment is based on the following:

Use of Proceeds: The eligible categories for the use of proceeds—Environmentally Sustainable Management of Living Natural Resources and Land Use, Renewable, Low carbon, Eco-efficient and/or Circular Economy Adapted Products, Production Technologies and Processes, Waste Management and Resource Efficiency, Renewable Energy and Waste to Energy—are aligned with those recognized by the GBP. Sustainalytics considers that the eligible categories will lead to a positive environmental impact and advance the UN SDGs, specifically SDG 7, 8, 12, and 15.

Project evaluation/selection: The proceeds from the bond will be used to refinance existing projects that were undertaken by Corticeira Amorim over the past three and a half years and have been detailed in the Framework.

Management of the proceeds: The Finance Department of the company will manage the proceeds raised and allocate them to its existing projects held in various wholly owned subsidiaries. Sustainalytics considers this to be aligned with market practice.

Reporting: Amorim intends to report on the allocation of proceeds on an annual basis and publish such reports on its website. In addition, Amorim is committed to reporting on applicable quantitative and qualitative impact metrics. Sustainalytics views Amorim's allocation and impact reporting as aligned with market practice.

As part of this engagement, Sustainalytics held conversations with various members of Amorim's management team to understand the sustainability impact of their business processes and planned use of the proceeds, as well as management of the proceeds and reporting aspects of the Framework. Amorim representatives have confirmed that (1) they understand it is the sole responsibility of Amorim to ensure that the information provided is complete, accurate, and up to date; (2) that they have provided Sustainalytics with all relevant information; and (3) that any provided material information has been duly disclosed in a timely manner. Sustainalytics also reviewed the related public documents and non-public information.

---

[79] The full report is available at Corticeira Amorim's Investor Relations website: https://www.amorim.com/en/investors/investor-relations/.

3.1.4 Green Bond Market Development

The green bond market grows as more companies, governments, and multinationals try to raise funds to carry out environment-friendly projects. At the same time, a larger number of investors are attracted to these assets (see Section 5.5). Since the world's first green bond issuance operated by the European Investment Bank in 2007, the global green bond market has seen exponential growth. In particular, this market began to grow significantly from 2014 onward, following the publication of the Green Bond Principles.

Figure 3.1 World: annual green bond issuance

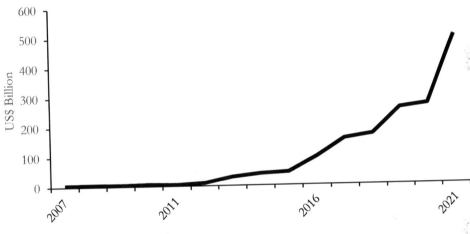

Source: Climate Bonds Initiative.

The annual issuance of green bonds increased from less than US$1 billion in 2007 to US$500 billion in 2021. Green bonds have been representing an increasing share of the total number of outstanding bonds and are now responsible for approximately 5% of all global issues (Amundi and International Financial Corporation, 2020).

The United States is the largest issuer of green bonds (over US$78 billion, issued in 2021 by the government, corporates, or regional issuers), followed by Germany (approximately US$62 billion) and China (approximately US$56 billion).

Green bonds are not exclusive to the Western world. China is one of the main issuers of green bonds. Between 2012 and 2019, China issued a total of US$142 billion of green bonds (which represents 76% of the total emerging market issuance during that period).[80]

---

[80] However, in China, there is no clear legislative definition of green bond classification comparable to the one set by the European Union with the European Green Bond Standard.

Figure 3.2 World: amount of green bonds issued in 2021 by country

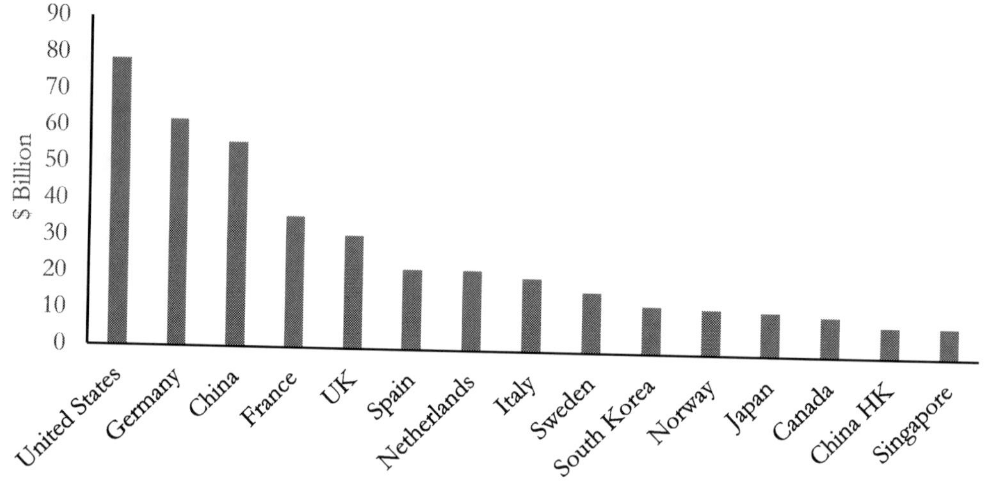

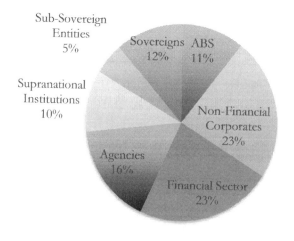

Source: Climate Bonds Initiative, via Statista (2021).

Different types of issuers issue green bonds. During the 2017–2021 period, non-financial corporates issued approximately US$300 billion (or 23% of the total volume), the financial sector issued approximately US$295 billion (23% of the total volume), and supranational institutions issued US$130 billion (10% of the total volume). More recently, sovereign issuers have also started to enter this market.

Figure 3.3 World: distribution of green issuance (2017–2021) by issuer type

Source: Climate Bond Initiative via UniCredit.

Regarding the use of the proceeds, in 2021, overall, Energy (energy efficiency, renewables, and others) and Buildings dominated (37% and 29% of the total, respectively).

Figure 3.4 Distribution of use of proceeds from green bonds worldwide

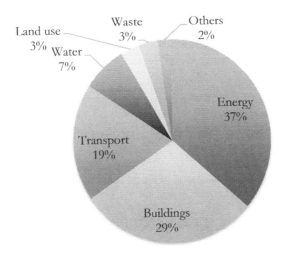

Source: Climate Bond Initiative.

The next sections outline examples, case studies, and specificities of each particular issuer type (sovereigns, corporates, and others).

KEY LEARNING POINT

The market is growing significantly. In 2019–2020, more green bonds were issued than the total issued in all the previous years.

3.1.5 Sovereign and Regional Issuers

Sovereign green bonds are debt obligations issued by national governments to directly finance projects aimed at the low-carbon transition, in line with the established national climate change targets (to comply with the Paris Agreement). The world's first certified sovereign bond was issued in December 2016 by Poland, followed by France (January 2017) and Fiji (October 2017). In 2020, the main issuer in Europe was France (€27.8 billion), followed by Germany (€11.5 billion) and the Netherlands (€8.9 billion).

The first sovereign green bond

On December 12, 2016, the Government of Poland issued its inaugural €750 million green bond, with a coupon rate of 0.5% and 5-year maturity. This inaugural sovereign green bond was hugely oversubscribed (demand from investors amounted to €3.25 billion). The main investors were from Germany and Austria (27%), Benelux (17%), the United Kingdom and Ireland (16%), and investors based in the Nordic countries (15%).

Most of the proceeds were allocated to projects related to sustainable agriculture operations (€292.1 million), clean transportation (€241.3 million), and renewable energy (€155.2 million).

The largest green sovereign bond issuer

France is the largest sovereign bond issuer worldwide. The French Treasury issued its first green bond in 2017 (called OAT). The amount issued was US$7 billion, with a coupon rate of 1.75% and maturity in 2039. Since then, France has issued more than €30 billion in green bonds. The bond proceeds were placed with asset managers, banks, insurance companies, pension funds, and hedge funds. Approximately one-third of green OATs issued were bought by investors located in France.

In compliance with the guidelines of the Framework for Green OAT, the proceeds from the issuance were disbursed to address the following objectives: combating (or mitigating) climate change, adapting to climate change, protecting biodiversity, and reducing pollution. According to the Agence France Tresor (2020), between 2017 and 2019, the most relevant fraction of the proceeds was allocated to projects related to sustainable reconversion of buildings, followed by projects in living resources and transportation.

Besides sovereigns, regional and local governments also raise funds through green bonds. A few examples include the following:

- Region Stockholm is the largest regional issuer of green bonds in Sweden. It issued its first green bond in 2014, and in 2020 it had 11 outstanding green bonds with a total volume of almost SEK 13.2 billion (approximately 1.3 billion euros). Almost 60% of Region Stockholm's debt is green financing.
- The Massachusetts Bay Transportation Authority operates mass transit in Greater Boston. In 2017, it issued a bond of US$370 million to fund projects related to energy and water savings, GHG reductions, recycling and improved materials management, and pollution control. The lead underwriter, Citibank, sold the bonds to high-net-worth individuals and family offices.
- The Canadian province of Ontario issued its first green bond (C$500 million) in October 2014. Since then, Ontario has become the largest issuer of Canadian-dollar-denominated green bonds, with seven green bond issues for a total of C$5.25 billion.
- Societe du Grand Paris, an infrastructure body wholly owned by the French state, has become one of the major green bond players, raising more than €8 billion. One of the largest issues was the June 2019 €1 billion bond, with a coupon of 1.70% and 30-year maturity. The bond received an AA2 rating from Moody's. Institutions

based in France purchased about 84% of the total amount issued. The proceeds were used to fund the Grand Paris Express metro expansion (68 new stations and 200 km of track).

3.1.6 Multilateral Institutions

Supranational (or multilateral) institutions are established by governments of several countries to pursue specified policy objectives. Among other objectives, they typically aim to promote economic development and regional integration (Section 6.5 covers the wider role and activities of supranational institutions. In this section, we focus on their role as issuers of green bonds).

The European Investment Bank (EIB) pioneered the market with its first green bond in July 2007. Since 2007, the EIB has become the largest supranational issuer of green bonds and accounts for approximately 50% of the issuance by multilateral institutions. At the end of 2019, the EIB had raised the equivalent of more than €25 billion across 13 different currencies (EIB April 2020 newsletter). The proceeds of these bonds are allocated to fund projects in renewable energy (67% of the total, in projects related to wind, hydro, solar, and geothermal energy production projects) and energy efficiency (33% of the total, in projects related to building insulation, energy loss reduction in transmission, and equipment replacement with significant energy efficiency improvements).

Figure 3.5 Outstanding supranational green bonds issued during 2007–2017

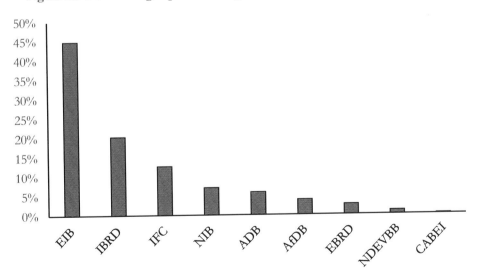

Source: European Investment Bank.

The World Bank issued its first green bond in November 2008 to raise funds for projects aimed at reducing the effects of climate change. The bond was denominated in Swedish krona (SEK 2.7 bn, approximately €260 million), with a coupon of 3.5% and 6-year maturity. During the period 2008–2019, the World Bank issued 158 green bonds in 21 currencies for a total of over US$13 billion. The proceeds were allocated to projects in 31 countries (International Finance Corporation, 2020). Renewable Energy & Energy Efficiency and Clean Transportation made up the largest portion (66%) of the eligible projects' portfolio. Table 3.2 shows some examples of projects co-financed by the World Bank for each type of eligible project.

Table 3.1 World Bank: sample of eligible projects

Sector	% of sector in portfolio	Example of an eligible project
Renewable Energy, Energy Efficiency	36%	Supporting intermediary loans for energy efficiency projects in medium- and large-sized Chinese manufacturing companies.
Clean Transportation	30%	Scale up the Colombian National Urban Transport projects by expanding trunk corridors and feeder routes to meet increased demand and improve the associated infrastructure.
Water, Wastewater	8%	Improve water resource management in Brazil, including improving coordination and capacities of key federal institutions in the water sector.
Waste Management	1%	Enhance the governance of the solid waste sector in Morocco.
Agriculture, Land, Forests	17%	Enhance reforestation in Belarus, increase the use of residues, and improve the public good contribution from forests in targeted forest areas.
Resilient Infrastructure	8%	Enhance the resilience of Belize road infrastructure against flood risks and the impacts of climate change.
Total	100%	

Source: The World Bank.

Besides global multilateral institutions, several countries have their own development banks. As an example, KFW (Kreditanstalt für Wiederaufbau, or Credit Institution for the Reconstruction) is the German state-owned development bank. KFW was established in 1948 to manage the funds of the Marshall Plan for the reconstruction of Germany after the Second World War. It issued the first green bond in 2014, and since then, it has issued a total of 18 green bonds denominated in different currencies. In 2019, proceeds from green bond issues amounted to €8.1 billion and were mostly (91%) allocated to German projects in the Residential Buildings (79%) and Wind Energy (15%) sectors.[81]

---

[81] KFW Annual Report 2020.

3.1.7   Corporate Financing through Green Bonds

In the case of corporate bonds, the rate required by investors is (for a given maturity) higher than the risk-free rate, and the spread varies according to the perceived credit risk (the spread is higher for riskier borrowers than for safer ones). Also, the spread tends to be higher for illiquid bonds than for liquid ones.

Credit ratings play an important role in helping investors make better-informed decisions and judge the risk of lending money to a given company. A credit rating is an opinion regarding the creditworthiness of an issuer (or of a specific bond). The role of credit rating agencies and how they incorporate sustainability issues are discussed in Section 3.4.

Green bonds have become a regular source of financing for the carbon transition across a range of industries, including automotive, telecommunications, energy, and agribusiness. In Europe, the corporate sector issued 24% of the global volume of green bonds issued in 2019 (approximately US$60 billion), followed by government-backed entities (22%) and financial institutions (21%).

Some companies issuing green bonds are in businesses related to sustainability and the environment (e.g., companies operating in the renewable energy industry, agriculture, and plantations). In this case, it is obvious that the company will use the funds to finance green projects, consistent with the main standards (see Section 6.3). However, many other companies are not in green sectors and find it difficult to access this market. In many cases, they use sustainability-linked bonds or transition bonds (see the next section).

Apple: the first U.S. green bond in the tech industry

In February 2016, Apple issued its first seven-year green bond, with a value of US$1.5 billion, as part of a larger US$12 billion bond issue. This bond had a coupon rate of 2.85%, and it was the largest green bond ever issued by a U.S. company. The lead managers were Goldman Sachs, Bank of America Merrill Lynch, and JP Morgan, and the proceeds were to be allocated to projects aimed at renewable energy sources, driving energy efficiency in the company's facilities, and the use of safer materials in the company's products and processes.

In June 2017, just after the announcement of the U.S. government's withdrawal from the Paris Agreement, Apple issued another bond with a value of US$1 billion and 10-year maturity. In November 2019, Apple issued the first green debt in Europe, with two bonds of €1 billion each (a total of US$2.2 billion) and 6- and 12-year maturity.

Proceeds from green bond issuance are allocated to support Apple's 2030 carbon neutrality roadmap, in projects such as reducing the waste and carbon intensity of products, developing new technologies to eliminate GHG from aluminum smelting processes, renewable energy for stores and data centers, and carbon sequestration. Lisa Jackson, Apple's vice president of Environment, Policy, and Social Initiatives, said: "We all have a responsibility to do everything we can to fight against the impacts of climate change, and our US$4.7 billion investment of the proceeds from our Green Bond sales is an important driver in our efforts. Ultimately, clean power is good business."

Telefónica S.A

Telefónica is one of the largest telecommunication companies in the world. The company operates in 16 countries in Europe and Latin America, and has more than 350 million customers. At the end of 2020, its market capitalization was approximately €21 billion.

In 2019, the Spanish company published its Sustainable Financing Framework, linked to the UN SDGs and aligned with the ICMA 2018 Green Bond Principles. Under Telefónica's Framework, the proceeds from green bond issuance are to be applied to ongoing or new projects in the energy efficiency of the network, renewable energy, and digital solutions for the environment.

In January 2019, Telefónica issued its inaugural green bond of €1 billion with five-year maturity. This was both the first green bond issued by a company in the telecommunications sector and the first issued by a Spanish company. The offer was well received by investors (mostly institutional) and was assigned a rating of Baa3/BBB/BBB (Moody's/Standard&Poor/Fitch). It was issued with a coupon rate of 1.069% (3 bps below the average issues during the year 2018). The proceeds from the green bond were allocated to the transformation of Telefónica's landline network in Spain from copper to fiber to the home (FTTH).

3.1.8   Challenges for Investors and Issuers

Despite significant growth over the last few years, several challenges still have to be overcome for the development of the green bond market.

One of the biggest dangers threatening green bonds, transition bonds, and other green products is greenwashing (see Section 1.5.3). We have seen cases of companies issuing "green" products while continuing to do what they were doing before (and not even allocating the proceeds to green projects). This has led some investors to be cautious with green bond offerings; they feel that such issues need further scrutiny.

Repsol – a problematic green bond

In 2017, Repsol issued €500 million in green bonds, intending to increase energy efficiency and promote carbon reduction projects that would reduce emissions. Repsol hired a second-party verification agent, Vigeo Eiris, which certified the green bond.

Although Repsol claimed that the bond proceeds would be allocated to a project aimed at saving 1.2 million metric tons of CO_2 per year, many investors declined to invest in this issue. Investors noted the incompatibility between the "label" of the bond and the industry in which the firm operated (petrochemicals). Several green bond index providers declined to include Repsol's bond in their index, and the Climate Bonds Initiative said that the bond did not deserve the green label because it did not represent a fundamental change in the oil company's business model.

Another important challenge is the lack of a common "green" definition and framework. Currently, the Green Bond Principles and the Climate Bond Standards are the main voluntary frameworks used to label green bonds, though other global regulations are being developed (see Section 6.4). Most investors want issuers to demonstrate the environmental impacts of their green bonds. However, there is no effective monitoring mechanism to ensure compliance with the standards, and it is not easy to legally enforce the green integrity of the bonds (and of the associated projects). There is also a lack of clarity regarding the definition of green and the green projects that are eligible for financing through this instrument. The existence of national, regional, and global definitions of green finance is a challenge for many investors. On the other hand, having a single definition based on a single global approach may not be adequate, as different markets and countries, at different stages of economic development, may have different priorities. If investors were to face significant costs arising from the lack of consistent disclosure of environmental information, that would pose an additional barrier to investment.

Green bond verifiers (or those entities that provide second-party opinions) play a crucial role in this market. Given the underlying business model, where the issuer pays for this verification, there is the potential for conflict of interest or self-serving behaviors. This is especially problematic if the verifiers also offer consulting services to companies, as conflicts of interest could arise. On the one hand, competition is good for the development of this market. On the other hand, having multiple service providers providing certifications allows issuers to shop around and eventually choose the entity that will provide a favorable recommendation.

Another problem is that sometimes the small scale of projects makes them unsuitable for green bond financing. Bond markets, in general, require large issues, and even traditional corporate bonds are only issued by companies of a certain size. In addition, many green projects involve innovative and less mature technologies where the risks and opportunities are more difficult to evaluate, and only a limited number of business cases are available as evidence. As a result, rating agencies and institutional investors often assess the technological risk to be higher for emerging green investments than for investments in mature sectors.

3.1.9 Empirical Evidence

The empirical literature has focused on two key areas. A large set of academic studies has focused on the comparison between green and non-green bonds to investigate whether a green premium exists in the bond market. Another set of academic studies has focused on the relationship between the issuance of green bonds and corporate performance.

Green Bonds and Non-Green Bonds

Practitioners talk about the concept of *greenium*, which refers to the situation in which issuers of green bonds benefit from lower borrowing costs. That is, the bonds are sold at a premium relative to conventional bonds, which is equivalent to a lower yield to maturity (or borrowing cost).[82] However, the greenium concept is hard to analyze. Issuers do not typically issue green and conventional bonds having the same characteristics on the same date. Nevertheless, a growing body of literature has investigated whether the green label of a bond is associated with a premium at issuance, or better performance in the secondary market, relative to a conventional bond issued by the same issuer. Some papers show that the yield of a green bond is lower than that of the equivalent conventional bond at issuance (also known as green premium or greenium), but the evidence is mixed because many confounding factors such as sample selection criteria, credit rating, bond maturity, investor preferences, the industry, and the macroeconomic framework influence the spread at which green bonds are issued and traded (MacAskill et al., 2021; Liaw, 2020; Horsch and Richter, 2017).

Larcker and Watts (2020) utilized a matching procedure in which they selected green and non-green issues that were identical in terms of structure and issued by the same issuer on the same day. The final sample contained 640 matched pairs of fixed-coupon securities issued by states and other governmental (non-sovereign) entities in the United States between 2013 and 2020. Empirical evidence showed that there was no green premium for issuers of green bonds.

These results contrast with ones obtained by Baker et al. (2018). They used a sample that includes 2,083 U.S. green municipal bonds[83] issued between 2010 and 2016 and 19 green corporate bonds issued between 2014 and 2016, and their results support the idea that green bonds are issued at a premium compared to otherwise similar ordinary bonds – that is, with lower yields – on an after-tax basis. Zerbib (2019) analyzed the yield of green bonds compared to that of equivalent synthetic non-green bonds through a matching method for bonds issued from July 2013 to December 2017. Empirical findings showed that investors' pro-environmental preferences have a low impact on green bond prices and that the main determinants of this premium are the rating and the issuer type. However, on average, a very thin yield premium of 2 bps is detected. Kapraun and Scheins (2019) found that only some green bonds trade at a premium (from governments, supranational entities, and large corporate issues). Further, the premium is higher when certification exists, or when the bond is listed on an exchange with a dedicated green bond segment and tight listing requirements.

---

[82] When the yield to maturity at the issuance date is lower, the price of the bond is higher, which in turn translates into higher proceeds to the issuer.
[83] These bonds are traditionally less liquid than other bonds.

Green Bonds and Corporate Performance

There is evidence of a positive relationship between the issuance of corporate green bonds and a firm's financial performance.[84]

Some studies have documented that stock prices respond positively to green bond issuance. Tang and Zhang (2020) used a sample of 1,510 green bonds issued worldwide from June 2007 to July 2017 and found that the issuers' stock prices increase significantly around the moment of announcement of the green bond issuance. They also found that institutional ownership, especially from domestic institutions, increases after the firm issues green bonds. Similarly, Wang et al. (2020) analyzed a sample of 159 corporate green bonds issued in China from January 2016 to June 2019 and found positive stock market returns for corporate green bond issues.

One of the most relevant pieces of empirical evidence of the impact of green bond issuance on firms' financial performance was provided by Flammer (2021), who analyzed a dataset that covered corporate green bonds issued by public and private companies across the world from 2013 to 2017. Using a methodology known as discontinuity analysis, she found that the results suggest that the issuance of green bonds has a positive effect on a company's stock price. The effects are stronger for first-time issuers and bonds certified by third parties. Moreover, the issuance of green bonds produces positive and statistically significant effects on the company's value, return on assets, and ownership by long-term investors.

3.1.10 Summary – Green Bonds

Green bonds are an important instrument for addressing climate change. They are used by issuers that want to finance environment-friendly projects such as renewables, infrastructures, or reduction of CO_2 emissions from operations. Various institutions can issue green bonds. We have reviewed the evolution of the markets and empirical evidence that includes sovereign issuers, multilateral institutions, municipalities/regions, and corporates.

These bonds are different from regular bonds, as the issuance process tries to assure their environmental end use. In particular, they are issued with provisions governing the use of the resources collected. Several countries have developed different regulatory structures for their green bond markets, but the most prominent guideline is the Green Bond Principles established by ICMA. However, some consistency across standards is required for the further development of this market.

---

[84] The hypothesis of a positive association between a firm's environmental performance and its financial performance has been widely investigated in the literature (see Chapter 5). In this section, we focus on the issuance of green bonds and corporate performance.

The certification process often uses third-party verifiers. Despite the additional credibility provided by these verifiers, doubts linger about the environmental integrity of green bond offerings by some issuers. Close attention to the role of certifiers and possible conflicts of interest is crucial.

Research has documented that green bond issues are related to tangible environmental results, and can therefore be seen a credible commitment to environmental issues. However, a significant threat to green bonds and other green products is greenwashing. If companies can issue green products and call their financing "green" without changing their operations, then the whole exercise is simply a deceptive marketing trick.

3.2   SUSTAINABILITY-LINKED BONDS AND TRANSITION BONDS

Green bonds have seen increasing demand from investors that want to align their investments with the Paris Agreement or the UN Sustainable Development Goals. Green-labeled securities can be issued by companies that want to finance green or environment-friendly projects such as renewables, infrastructures, or reduction of CO_2 emissions from operations.

In this section, we talk about sustainability-linked bonds and transition bonds. These are financing instruments available to companies operating in "brown" industries, or those that lack clear "green" projects for allocation of bond proceeds.

Green bonds are earmarked for specific projects. Sometimes companies want to issue bonds, but do not want to tie up the proceeds of the bond to a particular "green" purpose. Instead, they may want to use the proceeds for different purposes related to the company-wide transition and steps toward emissions reduction. In this case, issuers can use sustainability-linked bonds.

Also, green bond issuance is not suitable for highly polluting businesses and industries that want to become less brown and need to raise funding to finance projects related to these objectives. Sustainability-linked bonds and transition bonds meet those needs.

3.2.1   What Is a Sustainability-Linked Bond?

Most bonds offer investors a fixed coupon rate. Sustainability-linked bonds (SLBs) have coupon rates that are contingent on the accomplishment of some predefined ESG goals. The coupon rate is set at a base level; however, it goes down if the goals are achieved. On the other hand, if the goals are not met, the coupon rate goes up.

This sends a strong commitment signal from the company, as achieving some pre-specified sustainability goals[85] leads to lower financial costs. Also, the successful placement of these bonds would show that investors are willing to bear lower coupon rates if the sustainability goals are met, suggesting that investors believe that when sustainability risks are mitigated, the overall risk of the company goes down, thus making a lower coupon rate acceptable. However, if the goals are not met, the risks associated with the company increase; consequently, the rate paid to investors goes up to compensate them for the additional risk.

SLBs also differ from regular green bonds in how the proceeds are used. In the case of SLBs, the borrowed money is not earmarked for specific environmental and climate projects. Therefore, they can be used for general corporate purposes (such as funding working capital and investments). However, the cost of funding is performance based. That is, companies pay higher interest rates if they fall short of the committed ESG targets.

ICMA published the "Sustainability-Linked Bond Principles" in 2020, which is a set of voluntary guidelines for issuers and investors on this topic. It closely mirrors the sustainability-linked loans principles discussed in Section 3.3. These principles have five components:

1. Selection of key performance indicators (KPIs): This includes a clear rationale for these KPIs that should be material to the issuer. It also includes clear definitions of the KPIs, their calculations, and other methodological considerations.
2. Calibration of sustainability performance targets (SPTs): These targets should be ambitious, have a clear timeline, be comparable with external benchmarks, and be consistent with the issuer's ESG strategy.
3. Bond characteristics: This pertains to how the KPIs can affect the financial conditions of the bond, namely, the coupon payments.
4. Reporting: Issuers should keep readily available data on KPIs and publish, at least annually, their performance on the targets so that investors understand how it affects the bond conditions.
5. Verification: Post-issuance verification is necessary.

The incentive component is critical in SLBs. Enhanced sustainability lowers the interest rate paid on the bond (coupon), thus reducing the issuers' financing costs. SPTs are measurable KPIs that issuers commit to improving by a predefined amount over a certain timeline. They should be selected according to the materiality of the issues and the issuer's overall sustainability/ESG strategy. When setting the targets, it is important to establish the baseline. This baseline is a fixed point of reference that is used to measure the performance of the SPT.

---

[85] These are environmental, social, and governance-related objectives.

ENEL S.p.A – the world's first SDG-linked bond

ENEL S.p.A is an Italian multinational company operating in the sectors of electricity generation and distribution. With a market capitalization of approximately €81 billion, ENEL is the largest company in the Italian stock exchange by market capitalization and the largest company in the utility sector in Europe. Its debt obligations are rated BBB+ for S&P, Baa2 for Moody's, and BBB+ for Fitch.

In 2018, the company launched a US$1.25 billion green issuance to "finance green projects in the renewables field, in smart grid technology, in sustainable mobility, smart lighting, energy efficiency and demand response initiatives."

In September 2019, ENEL launched the first-ever SDG-linked bonds, whose coupon payments were linked to the environmental performance of the corporate. According to the terms of the US$1.5 billion bond, ENEL has set two objectives linked to SDGs 7 and 13. If the firm fails to increase its renewable power generation (from 45.9% to 55% by the end of 2021), the coupon rate of these bonds will rise by 25 bps.

SLBs are a growing segment within sustainable finance. Examples of issuers and targets include the following:

- In June 2021, ENI SpA issued the world's first SLB in the oil and gas sector, with a nominal amount of €1 billion and seven-year maturity. The SLB will be tied to the attainment of two sustainability targets: (1) a reduction of GHG emissions from upstream activities by 50% compared with 2018 levels in 2024 and (2) an increase in the renewable energy installed capacity to at least 5 GW by the end of 2025. Failure to achieve either one of these two targets will lead to an increase in the coupon rate by 0.25%.
- Pilgrim's Pride, a poultry company, sold US$1 billion of SLBs in March 2021. The interest rate on these bonds can increase by 0.25% if it fails to meet certain sustainability targets.
- New World Development, a Hong Kong conglomerate, issued an SLB committing to use 100% renewable energy by 2026 for all its rental properties. If it fails, it will pay a penalty worth 0.25%.
- In September 2020, Chanel, the luxury brand, issued a €600 million SLB linked to the company's climate strategy.
- In November 2020, LafargeHolcim issued a €850 million SLB. This was the first SLB issued in the building materials industry. LafargeHolcim committed to a target of 475 kg net CO_2 per ton of cementitious material by 2030 (versus 576 kg as a baseline in 2018). If the target is not met, the coupon rate will increase by 0.75%.

KEY LEARNING POINT

In sustainability-linked bonds, the interest paid varies according to predefined ESG targets.

3.2.2 Transition Bonds: Criteria and Use of Proceeds

SLBs are subject to a merit-based system characterized by step-up margins and penalties if targets are not met. However, not all issuers and investors want their coupons linked to sustainability objectives.

Transition bonds are debt securities issued from "brown industries" with high GHG emissions, to raise capital to fund the shift to greener activities and thereby become less brown. The first transition bond was issued in July 2017 by Hong-Kong-headquartered Castle Peak Power Co., which issued a US$500 million energy transition bond to pay for a natural gas plant that the company said was a critical contribution to Hong Kong's efforts to cut carbon emissions (Copley, 2019).

Transition bonds are designed to provide financing to companies that cannot issue green bonds because they are at the early stages of the transition and lack "sufficiently green" projects. According to Yo Takatsuki, AXA IM's Head of ESG Research and Engagement, "the establishment of a new asset class called Transition Bonds is vital for those issuers which do not have the capacity or capabilities to launch green bonds."

Snam S.p.A

Snam S.p.A is one of the world's leading energy infrastructure operators and one of the largest listed Italian companies in terms of market capitalization (rated Baa2 by Moody's, BBB+ by S&P, and BBB+ by Fitch). In June 2020, it published its new Transition Bond Framework, whose objective is "to ensure full alignment of the Company's financial strategy with the energy transition through its sustainability targets, and to further expand its investor base." In the same month, Snam issued their first transition bond: an €500 million bond with ten-year maturity and an annual coupon rate of 0.75%. The issuance was placed with institutional investors, and it was more than three times oversubscribed.

The first guidelines for transition bonds were developed by AXA IM (Takatsuki and Foll, 2019) and cover four different topics:

- o Use of proceeds: The proceeds can be used to finance new and/or existing eligible transition projects.
- o Project evaluation and selection process: The process should include details on the projects' environmental objectives, alongside the expected outcomes and impacts.
- o Management of proceeds: The proceeds should be tracked in a formal internal process, verified by an external audit.
- o Reporting: Companies should report on the environmental performance and outcome of the projects.

Transition bonds are to be used to finance projects within predefined climate transition-related activities. Some examples of sectors that can issue transition bonds are energy, mining, heavy industry, and transportation.

Table 3.2 Examples of transition-bond-eligible projects

Sectors	Examples of eligible projects
Energy	Cogeneration plants, carbon capture storage, gas transport infrastructure that can be switched to lower carbon intensity fuels, coal-to-gas fuel switch in defined geographical areas with defined carbon avoidance performance, waste-to-energy
Transportation	Gas-powered ships, alternative fuels for aircraft
Industry	Cement, metals, or glass energy efficiency investments, e.g., to reduce the clinker ratio, use of recycled raw materials, and smelting; achieve higher recycling

Source: AXA IM.

Cadent

Cadent is the largest U.K. gas distribution network with more than 80,000 pipelines delivering gas to 11 million customers. Cadent has committed to reducing its GHG emissions by 80% by 2050 (against a 1990 baseline). To achieve this goal, it needs to raise funds to support this transition. The company released the Cadent Transition Bond Framework, which describes the eligible projects, which include the following:

- Retrofit of gas transmission and distribution networks: Repair and replacement of pipelines to facilitate the integration of hydrogen and other low-carbon gases, and reduce methane leakage.
- Renewable energy: Developing the production and use of low-carbon energy, including biomethane and Bio-Synthetic Natural Gas (BioSNG) plants, with an emissions threshold of 100g CO_2e/KWh.
- Clean transportation: Developing new sustainable transport infrastructure, including a hydrogen fueling station, a high-pressure CNG refueling station, and electric-hybrid vehicles.
- Energy-efficient buildings: Reducing the energy consumption of buildings, offices, and depots.

On March 11, 2020, Cadent issued the United Kingdom's first transition bond. The €500 million bond was issued with a coupon rate of 0.75% and a maturity date of 2032. The bond was aligned with the EU Sustainable Finance Taxonomy and the United Kingdom's National Adaption Plan, and Cadent planned to invest the proceeds to replace pipelines for carrying hydrogen and other low-carbon gases and reduce methane leakage.

Transition bonds provide funding to corporations to help them transition to greener businesses and reduce GHG emissions. However, only US$7.3 billion of transition bonds have been sold since 2017 (Dealogic), partially due to the lack of clear standards. Indeed, definitions and standards are not universal. In Canada, the Council for Clean Capitalism has released its own Transition Bonds Guidelines, which should be "instrumental in enabling Canada's energy and other carbon-intensive industries to further reduce their emissions." In September 2019, the Climate Bond Initiative and Credit Suisse launched a partnership to "develop a framework that will underpin a scalable and robust Transition Bond market."

ICMA published the "Climate Transition Finance Handbook" in December 2020.[86] This handbook provides a framework for transition strategies and mentions that "transition" bonds should clearly show how the funding will be used to support the Paris goals. However, investors consider that there is a lack of clarity in the handbook about when a transition label can be applied. The handbook suggests that companies should support their transition by issuing use-of-proceeds bonds (where the proceeds are clearly earmarked for projects) or SLBs (subject to step-up margins and penalties if targets are not met) to create a merit-based funding system.

Transition bonds are not immune to controversies, as there are examples of companies with controversial business practices that have relabeled their debt issues as "transition" to make them more appealing to investors.

Marfrig – a controversial transition bond

Marfrig is the world's second-largest producer of beef. In its plants, it processes more than 33,000 cows every day, many of which come from deforested areas of the Amazon rainforest. Therefore, it was unlikely to meet the standards for most green investors.

When planning a bond issue, Marfrig's bankers suggested that they relabel the debt security for the transaction as a "sustainable transition bond" to meet the growing demand for "green" products from investors. In its Bond Framework, Marfrig indicated that transition bond proceeds would be used to purchase cattles from suppliers who committed to not taking part in further destruction of the Amazon rainforest.

This business case has sparked controversy and debate in the financial press and in the green investment community about the role of "transition bonds." Despite the new denomination for the bond, Marfrig would use the proceeds to finance what it had always been doing: purchasing cattle from suppliers based in the Amazonian region. In any case, the deal was more than three times oversubscribed, and the strong demand for the "sustainable transition bond" enabled the company to offer a coupon rate of 6.625%, its lowest ever, on a foreign-currency-denominated bond (Gore and Berrospi, 2019).

3.2.3 Concluding Comments and Challenges

Green bonds are not suitable for all issuers. We described sustainability-linked bonds (SLBs) as well as the still embryonic market of transition bonds. These financing instruments are available to companies operating in brown industries, or those that lack clear green projects for allocation of bond proceeds.

---

[86] The handbook was drafted by many financial entities—including Bank of America, BNP Paribas, the European Investment Bank, and the World Bank—under the overall coordination of AXA Investment Managers, JPMorgan Chase, and HSBC.

SLBs have variable terms that incentivize the issuer to improve on the predefined sustainability metrics. Enhanced sustainability lowers the issuers' financing costs. The terms are based on KPIs measured over a certain timeline. One key difference between SLBs and green bonds is that the issuer need not allocate the loan exclusively for green projects; the bond proceeds can be used for general purposes. Nevertheless, the borrower has an incentive to improve its sustainability performance, as the improvement lowers its financing costs.

Transition bonds aim to bridge the gap between brown and green companies and create a new source of finance for companies that want to initiate the green transition but cannot yet issue certified green bonds. There is not yet an active market for transition bonds, not any clear consensus on their scope and definition, which would be needed for the market to develop further.

3.3 GREEN LOANS AND SUSTAINABILITY-LINKED LOANS

Green bonds are vital instruments through which issuers can raise capital that is earmarked for specific environment-friendly projects. This often makes them unsuitable for highly polluting companies, or for those looking to use the proceeds for generic and diverse purposes. Further, most companies worldwide do not issue bonds. That is where novel forms of bank financing products come into play.

3.3.1 How Can Loans Promote Green Investment

A green loan is a loan that a financial institution grants to an individual or company for financing a green project. Green loans are especially suitable for the majority of companies that cannot raise capital by issuing corporate (green) bonds. Moreover, some large issuers of bonds have increasingly been using green loans in parts of their capital funding plans.

An embryonic green loan market started during the 1980s in the United States with the introduction of the program Energy Efficient Mortgages, supported by government-sponsored agencies such as Fannie Mae. A borrower could use an Energy Efficient Mortgage to purchase or refinance an energy-efficient home, and would benefit from more favorable financing conditions, depending on the value of the utility savings.

Many aspects, including the development of domestic financial markets, preclude most small and medium enterprises (SMEs) from raising funds from capital markets (bonds or equity issuance) to finance their business. OECD (2017a, 2017b) estimated that SMEs in the OECD area represented 99.7% of all enterprises and 60% of total employment, and they contributed between 60% and 70% of industrial pollution in Europe. Regardless of the geography and given their important contribution to global economic activity and CO_2

emissions, SMEs are fundamental stakeholders in the green transition. Given the predominance of bank financing in most national financial systems, in particular for SMEs, the development of a large market for green loans can encourage green investments.

The structure of the financial system varies across countries. For example, in Europe, unlike in the United States, bank loans dominate capital market financing. In 2020, the ratio of domestic banking system assets to GDP in the Euro Area was about double the ratio of domestic banking system assets to GDP in the United States (110% vs. 60%). Financing through equity or bond issuance is negligible for European SMEs.

The Loan Market Association (LMA), Asia Pacific Loan Market Association (APLMA), and Loan Syndications and Trading Association (LSTA) in collaboration with ICMA have developed a set of minimum green loan standards (Loan Market Association and Others, 2018). The Green Loan Principles are very much consistent with the Green Bond Principles. That is, if a loan is to be considered a green loan, it needs to be certified with respect to 1) Use of Proceeds; 2) Process for Project Evaluation and Selection; 3) Management of Proceeds; and 4) Reporting.

Porsche: green Schuldscheine

On August 9, 2019, Porsche issued its first "green Schuldschein," with a value of €1 billion. Schuldschein (Schuldscheindarlehen) are loan agreements unique to the German debt market. Schuldschein loans are typically senior unsecured instruments that pay a fixed or variable coupon rate.

The tranches of the "green Schuldschein" issued by Porsche offered maturities of five, seven, and ten years as well as fixed and variable interest rates. Porsche AG will be using the capital for researching, developing, and producing electric cars (Porsche Taycan) and to invest in efficient factories that manufacture battery-run vehicles only.

The transaction was arranged by Landesbank Baden-Württemberg, Bayern LB, and ING, with the latter providing support as a "green advisor"—an expert in green Schuldschein transactions. The fixed-rate notes were priced 105–120 bp and 130–145 bp over 6 month Euribor. The floating-rate notes were priced at 95-110 bp, 120-135 bp and 160 bp over 6 month Euribor. The green Schuldschein was issued within the Porsche Green Finance Framework under which the company can obtain green financing such as Green Schuldscheindarlehen (SSD) and/or green bonds and green loans to finance or refinance projects within the scope of clean transportation. The framework is aligned with the 2018 version of the ICMA Green Bond Principles (GBP) as well as the LMA Green Loan Principles (GLP). The independent agency ISS-oekom confirmed that the plans are aligned with the Green Bond Principles.

More than 100 institutional investors including banks, pension funds, and insurance companies participated in the Schuldschein transaction. Because of the huge demand, the original order book volume had to be increased.

However, the standards are not universally applied.[87] For instance, China has one of the world's largest green loan markets. The definition of green loans was introduced as early as 2013 by the China Banking and Insurance Regulatory Commission (CBIRC, formerly CBRC) in the Guidance on Green Loans. The Chinese system of labeling a loan green is different from that of the Green Loan Principles, or at least they are not easily comparable.

KEY LEARNING POINT

To be considered a green loan, several criteria have to be met, many of which are common to green bonds, including the use of the proceeds and reporting.

3.3.2 Sustainability-Linked Loans

Sustainability-linked loans (or ESG-linked loans), or SLLs, are loans whose terms are linked to the borrower's sustainability performance (measured by predefined ESG criteria). The rate of these loans is linked to sustainability performance targets. Enhanced sustainability performance lowers the interest rate, thereby reducing financing costs; if the targets are not met, the interest rate may increase.

SLLs align the cost of debt financing with a borrower's ESG performance (measured with specific sustainability performance targets). In contrast to green loans, the borrower is not restricted to using the loan proceeds to only green projects (they can therefore be used for general corporate purposes). However, the borrower is incentivized to improve its sustainability performance.

As in the case of green loans, in 2019, the LMA, APLMA, and LSTA in collaboration with ICMA developed a set of SLL minimum standards. According to these "Sustainability Linked Loan Principles," the bank loan agreement should cover the following components:

- o Relationship to borrower's overall CSR strategy: The borrower should clearly communicate to its lenders its sustainability objectives, as set out in its CSR strategy, and its proposed Sustainability Proposed Targets (SPTs).
- o Target setting (measuring the sustainability of the borrower): Appropriate SPTs should be negotiated and set between the borrower and lender group for each transaction.
- o Reporting: Borrowers should keep readily available up-to-date information relating to their SPTs (such as any external ESG ratings). They should also provide that

---

[87] See Section 6.4 for a discussion of various capital market regulations and taxonomies that classify economic activities.

information to the lenders at least once a year. Borrowers are also encouraged to report information relating to their SPTs in their annual report (or its separate sustainability report).

- o   Review: The need for external review is to be negotiated and agreed upon between the borrower and lenders on a transaction-by-transaction basis. For publicly traded companies, it may be sufficient for lenders to rely on the borrower's public disclosures to verify its performance against its SPTs. With respect to certain SPTs, even if data are publicly disclosed, the borrower's sustainability performance may be verified by independent external entities. For loans where information relating to SPTs is not made publicly available, this external review is even more important.

SLLs include an incentive component. That is, the spread (or margin) that the company pays depends on some predefined criteria. For borrowers, it clearly signals the company's commitment to sustainability performance. However, for lenders, there is currently no concrete benefit in terms of capital ratios, or supervisory requirements, that create a deeper incentive for this. This topic of banking supervision, and its impact on banks' activities, is further discussed in Section 6.6. Nevertheless, banks are willing to provide some interest rate reductions to companies, as often this fits their own internal strategy of being more visible in the sustainability area.[88] As an example, in the AB InBev case, one of the banks' consortium leaders, ING CEO Steven van Rijswijk, stated: "I'm proud that ING is supporting AB InBev toward their goals with this sustainable financing structure, and at the same time implementing our strategy to help our clients to address climate risks and steer towards a circular economy."

Some other targets commonly used in SLLs include the following:

- o   GHG emissions reduction
- o   Reduction in water usage
- o   Improvements in energy efficiency (of buildings and machinery)
- o   Diversion of waste from landfills
- o   Protection of biodiversity
- o   Circular economy: increases in recycling of materials and supplies
- o   Increases in renewable energy usage
- o   Increases in sourcing of sustainable raw materials

---

[88] Hoepner et al. (2016) studied the relationship between corporate and country sustainability on the cost of bank loans. They used a sample of 470 loan agreements signed between 2005 and 2012 with borrowers based in 28 countries. The results suggest that the country level of sustainability is more important than the firm-level sustainability performance in reducing the cost of debt.

AB InBev ESG-linked loan facility

AB InBev is the world leader in the beer market, with a global market share of over 20%. It is known for brands such as Budweiser, Stella Artois, Corona, Becks, Antarctica, and Brahma.

AB InBev decided to embed sustainability into its financing strategy to improve the internal and external alignment to its Sustainability Plan (Better World). AB InBev's 5-year revolving credit facility (implemented with more than 30 banks worldwide) was reaching its maturity, and the company decided to renew its credit facility through an ESG-linked loan.

In February 2021, it concluded the world's largest Sustainability Linked Loan Revolving Credit Facility (SLL RCF), for a total of more than US$10 billion. The SLL RCF has a five-year term (with a possible extension for two additional years). This new facility is provided by 26 global banks, and it includes a pricing mechanism that incentivizes improvement in the four climate-related areas (aligned with the company's 2025 Sustainability Goals, according to its inaugural 2020 sustainability report):

- Improving water efficiency in breweries globally
- Increasing PET recycled content in PET primary packaging
- Purchasing electricity from renewable sources
- Reducing GHG emissions

Under the new loan, these four climate-related factors can influence, upward or downward, the interest rate paid to banks. Under the new loan terms, there is an agreed margin grid whereby the actual interest rate charged depends on the credit rating of the company, the level of utilization of the credit facility, and four climate-related KPIs.

If the company achieves its targets (detailed numbers were agreed upon with its financiers), it will benefit from a lower interest rate on its loans. However, if none of the targets is achieved, the loan terms will become more expensive. Internally, the company traditionally has a performance-based evaluation scheme. Some managers do have KPIs related to climate issues, which ultimately determines their individual performance evaluation (and eventually bonuses).

"We are excited by the further integration of sustainable finance principles into the capital markets, and welcome the opportunity to embed these practices deeper into both our finance organization and the broader company," said AB InBev CFO, Fernando Tennenbaum.

These targets should be clearly defined, with a timeline and clear improvements relative to the baseline year. They are negotiated between the borrower and the lenders, based on the borrower's sustainability strategy. In contrast to bonds, whose terms are known because they are publicly traded, loans are often private, their terms being known only to the concerned parties.

KEY LEARNING POINT

SLLs are subject to a margin grid, with the actual rate varying according to predefined ESG targets.

SLLs are a growing segment within sustainable finance. Their aggregate volume totaled US$221 billion in 2019 and US$282 in 2020. In 2021, it expanded almost three times, reaching a total volume of US$843 billion.

Figure 3.6 Aggregate volume of sustainability-linked loans

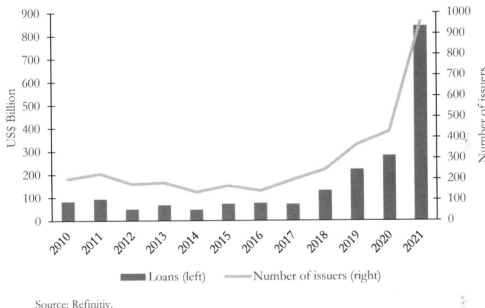

Source: Refinitiv.

Examples of borrowers that used SLLs and their targets include the following:

o Royal Dutch Shell received a US$10 billion revolving credit facility, signed in 2019 with a syndicate of 25 banks. The interest and fees to be paid will depend on the company's progress against a short-term net-carbon footprint intensity target.

o Total, the French energy company, announced in February 2021 that all new bonds would be linked to climate KPIs. The KPIs include Scope 1 and Scope 2 emissions from gas and oil, and also Scope 3 indirect emissions arising from customers' use of Total's energy products, and net carbon intensity objectives. The targets will be verified annually by a third-party auditor. [89]

o General Mills received a US$2.7 billion five-year revolving credit facility. The interest rate and fees depend on General Mills' GHG emissions reductions (Scope 1 and 2 emissions) and its use of renewable electricity for global operations.

o NRG Energy received a US$1.9 billion term loan. The targets include (1) total annual GHG emissions and (2) revenue carbon intensity (the amount of GHG emissions

---

[89] See Section 1.4.3 for a definition of the different scope levels of emissions.

divided by the revenues). Depending on the performance, the applicable margin can be adjusted up or down by 30 basis points.

o   UPM, the Finnish forest industry company, received an €750 million revolving credit facility linked to net positive biodiversity impact metrics and a 65% reduction in CO_2 emissions.

3.3.3 Banks and Sustainability Financing

Besides providing households with credit, banks play a prominent role in financing businesses, especially SMEs. Even for larger companies, banks remain an important source of funding.

As discussed in Chapter 1, most regions of the world are exposed to physical risk and transition risk to different extents. If physical risk materializes due to, for instance, a flood that damages industrial plants and real estate, borrowers may be unable to pay back their loans, as they would not be able to generate cash flows. If transition risk materializes due to changing financial regulations, environmental policy, technological advances, and consumer habits, firms operating in the industries or sectors subject to high transition risk would no longer be able to extract the expected cash flows from their operations to pay back the loans. In both cases, the lenders – namely, banks – would find a corresponding share of non-performing loans in their balance sheets.

The most extreme case of transition risk occurs when assets become stranded, that is, completely inoperable. Examples of stranded assets include abandoned oil platforms, refineries, and coal-fired power plants. Stranded assets represent an increasing source of credit risk for banks. Through direct or indirect exposure, the diminishing ability of borrowers to repay debts can create additional financial risks in banks' balance sheets.

Moreover, the potential impairment of assets used for collateral can also contribute to increasing credit risks. In a *green swan* scenario,[90] stranded assets would also hurt the capital ratios of banks. Stranded assets would certainly lower the capital adequacy ratio, which expresses a bank's available capital as a percentage of its risk-weighted credit exposures. This decrease can affect the financial stability of the banking system, as many banks would not have the capital cushion to absorb these losses from sudden asset price drops. As discussed in Section 2.5, stranded assets represent a systemic threat to financial stability in both commodity-dependent and advanced economies.

For example, in an extreme scenario in which the largest oil and gas companies became unable to operate profitably due to stricter regulations or a sharp drop in demand for their fossil-related products, the investors that financed them through bonds or bank loans would be forced to absorb significant losses too. When companies write off the stranded assets

---

[90] See Section 2.5.2.

from their balance sheet, lenders who have accepted them as collateral would find themselves at risk.

Further, a disorderly transition to a low-carbon economy would entail massive sales of the affected assets, which in turn may further increase risk premiums, reduce liquidity in the market, and precipitate an asset price collapse. The potential large-scale simultaneous sales of assets in response to a disorderly transition would be even larger if many investors' portfolios contain the same stranded assets. As in the case of the other financial crises such as the subprime mortgage crisis of 2007, panic could spread among market participants beyond the ones that hold the affected asset class, and then hit the whole financial system. Given the prevailing degree of financial integration, the crisis could freeze the interbank market and become global.

The former governor of Bank of England, Mervyn King, argued that "one of the conditions to consider carbon-intensive investments as a threat to financial stability is that exposure of financial institutions to carbon-intensive sectors be large relative to overall assets."

Sustainability financing can be an attractive opportunity for commercial and investment banks. Also, given stakeholders' pressure to incorporate ESG strategies and minimize climate risks, banks have been increasing their business in this area.

This includes loans with variable rates contingent on the achievement of a number of climate targets. If climate change does increase the risks to lenders, it is in their best interest to consider these risks when offering loans to customers.

Some of the biggest lenders include Bank of America (US$47.8 billion), J.P. Morgan (US$41.4 billion), and Citi (US$29.2 billion).

Table 3.3 World: Sustainable loan league table

Lender	Volume (billion US$)	Total deals
Bank of America	47.8	148
J.P. Morgan	41.4	125
Citi	29.2	96
BNP Paribas SA	28.9	128
Credit Agricole CIB	25.8	117
Mizuho Financial Group	24.5	100
Wells Fargo & Co	23.5	78
Mitsubishi UFJ Financial Group	21.4	100
Sumitomo Mitsui Finl Grp Inc	21.3	107
HSBC Holdings PLC	21.3	80
Societe Generale	16.4	82
Deutsche Bank	14.8	54

Note: EMEA = Europe, Middle East, and Africa.

Source: Refinitiv, 2021.

It follows from the foregoing discussion that how banks allocate resources to non-financial companies has cross-sectional implications. Research suggests[91] that banks decrease lending to brown companies and increase lending to companies with lower levels of emissions.

Financial institutions need to be able to assess and manage climate-related risks to their balance sheets (both physical and transition), which means making climate risk assessment a part of the screening, decision-making, and reporting aspects of their lending operations. To do this, banks need to assess the physical and transition risks associated with their lending operations (at the loan or counterparty level) and the future creditworthiness of these operations.

The European Investment Bank Climate Risk Scores

The European Investment Bank (EIB) has also developed a model for evaluating climate risk at the country level. The EIB computes the exposure of countries to physical and transition risks, and the scores are used to manage the exposure of the EIB portfolio to climate risk. EIB Climate Risk Country scores cover 184 countries. The physical risk scores are based on a large number of variables, aggregated to cover acute and chronic risks, as well as the adaptation capacity of each country. The transition risk scores are based on the country's exposure status and mitigation efforts. Exposure includes current and past emissions, as well as the economic dependence on fossil fuel exports. Mitigation includes the share of renewables in the country's final energy mix, improvements in its energy efficiency, and its commitment to its National Determined Contribution (NDC) and thus its efforts to reduce national emissions.

Regulators and central banks are taking various steps to promote the incorporation of climate issues in banking practices. Section 6.6.3 discusses the evolving role of banking regulation, namely, the possible adoption of a Green Supporting Factor in the EU financial regulatory framework. This factor envisions the reduction of capital requirements for green assets – i.e., loans and bonds – in the balance sheet of credit institutions. However, investors are asking for similar steps. Norway's sovereign wealth fund will start asking the banks in which it invests to disclose how their lending contributes to GHG reduction.

This also means that banks will have to assess evolving risks, in particular, environmental risks. Over the next few years, climate risks will change the models, risk management, and pricing of financial services. That is, banks will be asked to incorporate physical and transition climate risks into their models and businesses. Further, regulators are pushing banks to incorporate climate risks into their long-term planning and risk assessments, and to produce climate stress tests.

Sustainable supply chain financing (Section 3.6) represents another opportunity for financial service providers to "do well while doing good," that is, helping companies mitigate supply chain risks and reduce working capital while benefiting the environment. In other words,

---

[91] Kacperczyk and Peydro (2021) studied the links between firm-level carbon emissions and bank lending.

these financing schemes improve financial efficiency and enable companies to improve the environmental performance of their supply chain.

3.3.4 Summary – Green Loans

Most companies worldwide do not issue bonds. Instead, banks serve as intermediaries between depositors and borrowers. In this role, banks help companies secure the funds needed for their operations and growth. However, to protect their own balance sheet (and deposits), banks must estimate risk and price it appropriately.

Many banks are incorporating climate issues in their loans to facilitate the transition. At the same time, banks have been increasing the share of green loans on their balance sheet to reduce their exposure to climate risk (and fossil fuels).

Green loans and SLLs are two financial instruments that aid these objectives. Green loans are loan instruments that mandate that the proceeds be used for green projects. SLLs are loan instruments that incentivize borrowers to achieve green objectives. In this case, the terms are linked to the borrower's sustainability performance as measured by predefined ESG criteria. Enhanced sustainability performance lowers the interest rate, whereas unmet targets can lead to a rate spike.

One key difference between SLLs and green loans is that the borrower of the former is not required to allocate the loan exclusively for green projects. However, the borrower is incentivized to improve its sustainability performance, as the improvement lowers its financing costs.

3.4 CREDIT RATING AGENCIES

Credit rating agencies (CRAs) are important players in financial markets because they assess the creditworthiness of a debt issuer, that is, its ability to meet the principal and interest payments agreed upon in the bond agreement. Credit ratings play an important role in helping investors make better-informed decisions and judge the risk of lending money to a given company. A credit rating is an opinion regarding the creditworthiness of an issuer (or of a specific bond). This section describes how CRAs incorporate environmental factors into their credit ratings analysis, namely, how these factors influence the opinion regarding the creditworthiness of the rated entities. We also provide examples of the environmental factors used for different categories of issuers.

3.4.1 Credit Ratings and Credit Spreads

The main global rating agencies are Moody's Investor Services (Moody's), Standard & Poor's (S&P), and Fitch Ratings. They use the following rating categories:

	Moody's	S&P	Fitch
Investment grade	Aaa	AAA	AAA
	Aa	AA	AA
	A	A	A
	Baa	BBB	BBB
Junk bonds	Ba	BB	BB
	B	B	B
	Caa	CCC	CCC
	Ca	CC	CC
	C	C	C

An AAA rating suggests that the issuer is extremely likely to meet its financial obligations. A BBB rating suggests that the issuer has the resources to honor its financial obligations; however, in an adverse economic environment, its repayment capacity may be weakened. Major ongoing uncertainties around a company with a BB rating could undermine its capacity to meet its financial commitments.

Within each rating category, there are subcategories – also called *notches*. Moody's uses numbers (1 for the safest tier and 3 for the riskiest one), and S&P and Fitch use plus and minus signs. For instance, within the A category there are three different tiers/notches: Moody's has A1, A2, and A3; S&P and Fitch has A+, A, and A-. Bonds with a rating equal to or above Baa3 (Moody's) or BBB- (S&P and Fitch) are considered *investment grade* or *high quality*. Bonds with lower ratings are considered *speculative grade* – also called *junk bonds, sub-investment grade*, or *high-yield bonds*.

Rating agencies are concerned about two risks to bondholders: the risk that the intermediate coupons will not be paid, and the risk that the final principal will not be paid. Several financial factors are used to assess these two risks,[92] such as EBIT/interest expense, debt/EBITDA, operating margin, and debt/book capitalization.

Rating agencies use many other non-financial factors to determine a company's credit rating, for instance, cyclicality of sales, product differentiation, geographical diversification, and asset tangibility. These business profiles and geographic diversity factors are included because they indicate the capability of the company to pay its debts – the coupons and principal – in the future. Also, these factors take into account how differences in the

---

[92] See Fernandes (2017), Chapter 6, for more details.

company's operating model affect its ability to maintain its credit standing throughout the economic cycle.

Table 3.4 Examples of non-financial factors used by rating agencies

Oil	Software	Airlines	Retailers	Alcoholic beverages
Proven reserves	Product line diversity	Fleet age	Product range	Brand diversification
Development costs	Geographic diversity	Geographic diversity	Market concentration	Innovation and organic growth
Refining capacity	End-market diversity	Business profile	Geographic presence	Market position
Reserve replacement	Market share	Financial policy	Quality of execution	Geographic presence

Source: Fernandes (2017).

Different factors are used for different industries. In all cases, the CRAs define the factors and then apply them consistently to all the companies in a certain sector. For instance, proven reserves, replacement of reserves, and development costs are important factors in rating companies in the oil sector, as they signal future operating potential. In the airline sector, fleet age is a proxy indicator of operating efficiency and future investment needs.

KEY LEARNING POINT

Credit ratings depend on several company-specific factors, which include both financial and nonfinancial metrics.

Because ratings assess the potential default risk, lower ratings are associated with a higher cost of debt.

3.4.2 Do Environmental Factors Matter for Credit Ratings?

CRAs incorporate environmental factors into their analysis when they believe environmental risks can impact the capacity of a borrower to meet its financial commitments. For many issuers, environmental risks can decrease growth or profit margins and increase credit risk. Thus, a rating agency may consider that a borrower's exposure to environmental factors can endanger its revenues, earnings, cash flow generation, competitive position, or financial commitments.

Corporate Issuers

In other cases, borrowers are especially affected by environmental risks (for instance, extreme weather events). In these cases, the ratings can reflect an assessment of the cost and effectiveness of the measures taken to mitigate those risks. Also, public policy action and consumer behavior that affect companies may increase their exposure to environmental factors. In all these cases, the rating agency will change its models (and the estimated future financials) to reflect those factors and their impact on the creditworthiness of the borrower.[93]

When analyzing an issuer's credit rating, CRAs sometimes incorporate ESG factors, as they can influence the capacity and willingness of an issuer to meet its financial commitments, through impacts on revenues, operating performance, margins, liquidity, etc. The environmental risks considered by CRAs vary from situation to situation.

Given the multiple criteria used to assess different borrowers, according to their type and sector, there is no uniform way of assessing how environmental factors affect ratings. The following are some specific examples of environmental credit factors that have been drivers of historical rating changes for corporates:

- CO_2 and GHG emissions
- Physical climate risk, including weather events and other natural factors
- Types of pollution other than CO_2 and GHGs
- Water, land use, and biodiversity
- Environmental credit benefits that create profitable opportunities or reduce environmental risks

When some of the abovementioned environmental factors are sufficiently material to influence the borrower's capacity to meet its financial commitments, its rating may change. For instance, in 2020, S&P revised to negative the outlook of 36% of the North American regulated utilities. According to S&P: "The main causes of weakening credit quality reflected environment, social, and governance (ESG) risks, regulatory issues, and companies' practice of strategically managing financial measures close to their downgrade threshold with little or no cushion." Similarly, in January 2021, S&P announced that it was considering downgrading major oil and gas producers such as ExxonMobil, Shell, and Total. This reflected an increase in the perceived credit risk in the industry, arising from the challenges and uncertainties posed by regulation and the energy transition together with the expected growth of renewables.

---

[93] Seltzer et al. (2021) studied the bonds issued by U.S. public nonfinancial companies over the period 2009–2017 and found that both polluting firms and firms with poor environmental performance tended to have lower credit ratings and higher yield spreads, particularly when the firm was located in states with more stringent environmental regulation. Reznick and Viehs (2017) analyzed the relationship between CDS spread and ESG score in a sample of 365 companies over the period 2012–2016 and found that issuers with the lowest ESG scores tended to have the highest median CDS spreads.

As of 2022, the process of integrating climate risks into credit risk assessments is still mostly qualitative, and there is no clear quantitative methodology that applies across issuers (for example, see S&P (2019)). A recent report from the NGFS (2021) concludes that although rating agencies have improved the information they disclose, there is still a lack of clarity on how exactly climate-related risks (and, more generally, ESG risks) influence the final rating.

It is important to recall that CRAs monitor the creditworthiness of an issuer, that is, the borrower's capacity to meet future financial commitments. It is thus possible to find borrowers with strong creditworthiness and weak environmental credentials, that is, weak environmental factors, but strong and stable revenues, profitability, earnings, and cash flows. In this case, even considering the environmental risks, they may conclude that there is still a strong likelihood that the borrower will have the resources to meet its financial commitments. Similarly, a company that is viewed as environment-friendly, such as a renewable energy company, can have low ratings. This could occur when, despite a sound environmental stance, the company has weak creditworthiness (if, for instance, its revenues and profitability are low, and it has relatively high future financial commitments).

KEY LEARNING POINT

Strong environmental credentials do not imply a strong credit rating.

Banks and Insurance Companies

There are several ways in which a bank can suffer losses due to the impact of climate change: due to a lower valuation of assets that act as collateral for loans; due to climate-risk exposure; or from loan portfolio concentration in environment-unfriendly sectors, in which players may see their financial health deteriorating if the legal context changes rapidly. Another example is a bank that is heavily exposed to the agricultural sector, in a country vulnerable to climate change. Also, similar to insurers, some banks can be vulnerable to a sudden decrease in revenues and quality of loans triggered by a natural catastrophe. Thus, CRAs may consider environmental factors in their assessment of a bank's capital and risk positions. Some examples include the following:

- o In 2017, S&P changed the outlook of Lloyd's from A+/Stable to A+/Negative, because of the estimated losses of £3.3 billion due to the hurricanes Harvey and Irma, and it expected "further major losses from Hurricane Maria and other potential catastrophe events in the fourth quarter (Q4) 2017."
- o In 2017, S&P revised the outlook of Banco Agropecuario from BBB-/Stable to BBB-/Negative because of its exposure to the cyclicality of agribusiness and also climate change. After a severe drought, the bank's portfolio deteriorated, and the

nonperforming loans on its balance sheet increased to 7%, compared to an industry average of 3%.

In the case of insurance companies, environmental factors are taken into account in different ways. In this case, GHG emissions, climate change, natural resource contamination, and biodiversity can affect insurers' operating models, liabilities, and risk exposures. Populations living in areas affected by extreme heat, low water quality, or heavily polluted air can experience health problems. Thus, rising temperatures and droughts can pose health risks and lead to increased deaths, affecting the insurers that face these climate-related liability exposures.

For insurers, investments vulnerable to environmental issues may increase their operational costs. Weather-related phenomena are part of most insurance business models, and many are exposed to natural catastrophe risks across sectors (and insurers can partially diversify them, either directly, or through re-insurance). S&P models this by incorporating into their capital model the impact of one-in-250-year annual catastrophe losses. The uncertainty in an insurer's exposure to catastrophes can lead it to conclude that the risk is higher than earlier assessed and that the capital basis is not so high. In some cases, CRAs have considered that significant exposure to the impact of extreme weather events such as wildfires following droughts contributes to above-average volatility, and when capital levels are not increased, a lower debt rating follows.

Sovereigns

For most advanced economies, environmental factors do not yet pose a significant credit risk. For many emerging markets, however, the situation is different (especially those in the Caribbean, Southeast Asia, and Sub-Saharan Africa). Particularly relevant is the situation of the so-called "vulnerable 20"[94] countries, which already face significant impacts from natural disasters and climate change.

When evaluating sovereign ratings, CRAs include a potential adjustment for volatility in economic output due to exposure to natural disasters or adverse weather conditions. They also factor in the actual cost of natural disasters and how it affects the fiscal situation of the country (lower tax revenues and increased spending), and its external outlook (loss of exports). For instance, in 2018, S&P revised the rating outlook of Turks and Caicos Islands because of the huge losses, amounting to approximately 55% of the GDP, suffered by the small island state due to the hurricanes Irma and Maria.

Economic activity concentrated in risky sectors is also assessed. For instance, countries with high agricultural output are more vulnerable to weather-related events. Moreover, countries that depend on brown industries (such as mining) can suffer from limited budget inflows and future contingent liabilities. On the other hand, environment-friendly policies can

---

[94] See Section 1.1.3.

favorably impact sovereign creditworthiness, by reducing risk. Examples of these are investments in infrastructure that improve a country's resilience to natural disasters, investments in renewable energy that reduce input costs, lower imports, and improvements in a country's external terms of trade.

Studies suggest that the sovereign credit ratings of many countries can be significantly affected by climate risks. For instance, Klusak et al. (2021) used S&P's data and climate-adjusted macroeconomic indicators and found that, in a "business-as-usual" scenario (with no action to reduce carbon emissions), the sovereign ratings of 63 countries would be downgraded by an average of one notch[95] by 2030 (and 80 sovereigns would be downgraded by almost three notches by 2100). However, there is substantial cross-sectional variation. Similarly, Volz et al. (2020) studied the cost of sovereign borrowing in a sample of 40 developed and emerging market economies and provided evidence that climate risk affects the cost of sovereign borrowing. A higher Climate Vulnerability Index is associated with higher borrowing costs, whereas a higher Resilience Index is associated with lower borrowing costs.

The countries whose sovereign borrowing capacity will be significantly affected by the intensity and frequency of natural disasters are mainly emerging market economies, mostly located in Southeast Asia and the Caribbean. For example, Mallucci (2020) integrated natural disaster risk into a conventional standard sovereign default model to study borrowing capacity in a sample of seven Caribbean countries that are frequently hit by hurricanes. The results show that natural disaster risk negatively affects the ability of governments to access financial markets and issue debt.

KEY LEARNING POINT

Environmental risks, in particular physical risks, can affect an issuer's credit rating.

3.4.3 Summary – Environment and Credit Ratings

Environmental risks can influence future revenues, costs, cash flows, volatility, etc. CRAs are beginning to incorporate such risks into their analysis when they consider them relevant for the assessment of a borrower's creditworthiness.

---

[95] A notch is a subcategory within each rating category. For instance, within the A rating, there are three different notches: Moody's has A1, A2, and A3; S&P has A+, A, and A-.

Different factors are relevant for different issuers. Overall, CRAs try to understand how a borrower's exposure to environmental factors can impact its revenues, earnings, cash flow generation, competitive position, and financial commitments.

We have provided examples of environmental factors used for different categories of issuers. We have also shown that when these factors have influenced the borrower's capacity to meet their financial commitments, the rating has changed.

No comprehensive model that is applicable across sectors exists. Major rating agencies are currently working on this, as in several cases environmental factors have influenced rating changes.

3.5   PROJECT FINANCE

For much of the 20th century, large infrastructure projects were funded and operated by governments. Since the early 1980s, however, project finance has been increasingly used to fund infrastructure investments. Project finance dates back to the development of American railroads in the 19th century. Its use grew rapidly and was key to the development of oil and gas fields in the 1970s, and the transportation projects in the 1980s gave it a further boost. Project finance is today commonly used to fund long-term projects in infrastructure-related sectors such as highways, electricity production, and oil fields, and even for projects such as hospitals and prisons. It has emerged as an important way to finance large infrastructure projects (that might otherwise be too expensive or risky to be carried on a corporate balance sheet).

When a certain project is financed using traditional corporate finance, the investment appears on the balance sheet of the owner or sponsor of the project. In this case, the inability of the project owner to pay back the debt obligations entails the lender's claim on all of the assets of the borrower.

Alternatively, when a project is financed through project finance, the investment becomes an "off-balance sheet" item of the sponsor and shifted to a special purpose vehicle (SPV). This SPV is a separate legal entity, with its own management team and financial reporting, and can raise its own financial resources. A project finance contract defines the rights, duties, and responsibilities of the SPV for the life of the project. Traditionally, the features of project finance can be summarized as follows:

- A special purpose vehicle (SPV) is created by the sponsors using equity.
- The SPV borrows from different creditors so that it will have enough cash for the proposed projects.
- The debt payments are tailored to the cash flows of the project. That is, unlike a traditional loan, with constant payments, in the case of project finance the payments

vary on a yearly basis, depending on the forecasted cash flow generation of the project.

o Lenders consider the cash flow generated from the SPV as the major source of loan reimbursement. This implies that cash flows generated by the project must be sufficient to cover operating costs as well as to service the debt (capital repayment and interest payments).

o Creditors have priority on the cash flows from the project over any corporate claims. That means the priority use of cash flow (after operating costs) is to service the debt. Only funds remaining after this can be used to pay dividends to sponsors of the project.

o Assets and cash flows from the project serve as a guarantee to the lenders.

o Lenders have zero (or limited) recourse to the assets of the sponsor, as these are legally segregated from those of the project. That is, the creditors do not have a claim on the profit from other projects if the project fails. Also, the lenders have no claim over the project owner's assets (except those in the SPV) in case of a project default. This feature is also called non-recourse debt.

KEY LEARNING POINT

Project finance differs greatly from traditional corporate finance in the cash flows, covenants, collateral, and risk allocation.

3.5.1 The Importance of Project Finance for Renewable Energy Projects

Since the early 2000s, the share of renewable projects financed "off balance sheet" has been growing steadily, and in 2019 it accounted for US$81.1 billion, or approximately 35% of the total financing of renewable energy projects.

As an example, wind farms tend to be very large, and only a limited number of developers are able to finance the high capital investments with their balance sheets. Therefore, most investments in onshore or offshore wind projects are done through project finance. In 2019, the new financing of onshore wind farms totaled €13.1 billion, of which €7.5 billion was financed through project finance and €5.6 billion through corporate finance (Wind Europe, 2020).

Figure 3.7 Investments in renewables by mode of financing

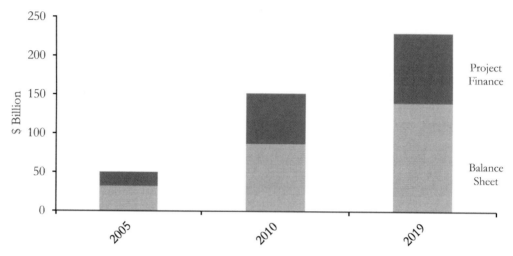

Source: UNEP, Frankfurt School-UNEP Center, Bloomberg.

Renewables are very suitable for project finance for the following reasons:

o   Their cash flows are long term and stable. Stability of cash flow is a precondition for the success of project financing. The stability of cash flows of renewable energy projects is further improved by government policies worldwide, such as tax credits, subsidized loans, guaranteed feed-in tariffs, and investment subsidies.

o   The low-carbon transition suggests stable (or growing) demand for the energy generated by renewable energy projects.

o   Renewable energy projects represent large investments, which are difficult to sustain in a normal corporate balance sheet. If these projects are financed through corporate finance, they become part of the risk-return of the developing company. In this latter case, the assets and cash flows from the existing business serve as a guarantee for additional lending used to finance the project; therefore, poor project performance can severely affect the existing business.

o   Assets in a renewable energy project are clearly separable from the other assets of the sponsor. Project finance allows shareholders to raise finance for a project without the lenders having a claim on their other assets (this is known as "non-recourse" financing).

KEY LEARNING POINT

Project finance is an important source of funds for renewables and other environmental-related projects

3.5.2 The Risks of Project Finance Projects

CRAs are vital for project finance because a significant portion of the funding is raised through debt, and thus the lenders need to ascertain the creditworthiness of the project and its ability to repay the principal and service the debt.

To calculate the debt rating of a project, the CRA analyzes the relevant risk factors and their effects on the ability of the project to operate and service its debts. CRAs and ratings are discussed in greater length in the previous section. In this section, we focus on the ratings of project finance projects. CRAs such as S&P and Moody's have specialized methodologies for project finance. These typically rely on a large set of variables and indicators, which can be grouped into four criteria that can affect (positively or negatively) the rating of a project:

- o Transaction structure criterion: This includes analysis of the structure of the contract and the legal framework of the country or region where the project is going to be developed.
- o Construction phase criterion: This concerns the analysis of the technical and construction feasibility aspects that may influence the budget planning of the project and the main potential risks that threaten the project's completion. First, the technology and design risk may affect the degree of reliability and predictability of the technology embedded in the project and the probability of its cost deviation from the budget laid down for the project. Second, the construction risk may affect the ability of the construction contractor to physically deliver the project in compliance with the contract terms. The third risk analyzed is the project management risk, which entails assessing the ability of the project management team to manage the financial and technical risks it is responsible for.
- o Operation phase criterion: This focuses on the financial and economic aspects of the project. First, the CRA assesses the performance risk, namely, the risk that the cash flows will fall short of expectations due to the project's inability to provide the services or products needed by the sector in which the asset operates. Second, the CRA assesses the market risk of the project, analyzing the market exposure and the competitive position, and how they can affect the revenues and operating expenses of the project. Third, the CRA assesses the country risk of the project. This consists of an analysis of the macroeconomic (inflation, interest rate, exchange rate, government default risk, etc.) and political (rule of law, enforcement of contracts, public administration transparency, government officials' integrity, expropriation risk, etc.) factors.
- o Counterparty risk criterion: This stage involves assessing the non-financial counterparties involved in the construction and operations of the project. At this

stage, the CRA assesses the exposure of the project in case of insolvency of one of the counterparties of the project finance contract.[96]

When outlining the rating of a class of debt obligation issued from a project finance structure, the main CRAs also incorporate ESG factors. Those factors are especially relevant for the construction and operation phases. Climate risk may materially affect the likelihood that a project is delivered on time and within the budget without exceeding its funding capacity. Climate risk may also affect the operation phase of a project, preventing the project itself from generating cash flows due to its inability to operate once it has been delivered. Therefore, if climate risks materially affect the construction or operation phase of a project, the rating agency could modify its evaluation of the credit risk of the project finance structure.

S&P (Forsgren and Kraemer, 2017) reported 20 cases involving project finance during 2015–17 in which environmental and climate issues directly resulted in a rating change. For example, in February 2017, S&P negatively revised the outlook of Scotland-based Aberdeen Roads Plc because of construction delays following flooding and uncertainty around the financial implications for the project.

S&P also evaluates the impact of the project on the local community and thus the likelihood that it can be completed on time within the budget (e.g., it assesses whether the project is likely to provoke social unrest).

KEY LEARNING POINT

Rating agencies have special methodologies to assess project finance deals, which includes ESG risks where applicable.

Project finance is sometimes perceived as riskier (compared to corporate finance) from a credit risk point of view. Some studies suggest that this is not necessarily true. In 2016, S&P published an extensive study on project finance defaults that occurred between 1980 and 2014. The agency collected data for 7,959 projects, of which 624 defaulted[97] and 377

---

[96] Multilateral insurance, or political risk insurance products, such as those offered by the Multilateral Investment Guarantee Agency (part of the World Bank Group) and other multilateral development banks (see Section 6.5), can help manage these risks.

[97] A project is in default if (1) a payment is past due for more than 90 days on any material credit obligation; (2) the lender takes a charge-off or an account-specific provision because of a perceived deterioration in the credit quality of the project exposure; (3) the lender sells the project instrument at a material credit-related loss; (4) the lender consents to a distressed restructuring likely to result in a diminished financial obligation caused by the material forgiveness of principal or interest; or (5) the obligor has sought or has been placed in bankruptcy protection.

emerged from the default and achieved resolution.[98] The data also show that almost 75% of the defaults occur within the first 5 years after closing, indicating that this is the critical "high-risk" period when a deal is most vulnerable. The 10-year cumulative default rate for project finance is in line with the 10-year cumulative default rate of BBB-rated corporates. Furthermore, project finance exhibits a strong average recovery rate of 77%, which is stronger compared to the average recoveries observed in the corporate bond market. Another analysis of project finance defaults has been provided by Moody's (2019) on a total of 8,583 project loans, with 587 project loan defaults and 289 ultimate recoveries.[99] The key findings are in line with the ones from S&P above.

3.6 SUPPLY CHAIN FINANCING

In this section, we examine the role of suppliers and supply chains in climate risk management. Climate issues are relevant at all levels throughout a supply chain, and many large companies are heavily dependent on their suppliers. These suppliers tend to be smaller companies, many of them SMEs, for whom working capital is critical. In particular, we focus on the financing aspects, and how they can be used to incorporate environmental issues.

3.6.1 The Different Scopes of Emissions

Carbon emissions from a company's operations and economic activity are typically grouped into three different categories[100]:

- o Scope 1: Direct emissions from production.
- o Scope 2: Indirect emissions from consumption of purchased electricity, heat, or steam.
- o Scope 3: Other indirect emissions from the production of purchased materials, product use, waste disposal, outsourced activities, etc.

Scope 3 CO_2 emissions are therefore defined end to end. That is, they include supplier-related emissions as well as the customers' emissions related to the use of the product/service. Thus, Scope 3 emissions are not directly controlled by the company and

---

[98] A project is resolved if (1) after default, a project loan(s) resumes scheduled payments on a regular basis (i.e., it starts performing again); (2) following the restructuring worked out, scheduled payments resume based on the restructured debt service; (3) the lender sells or transfers the defaulted debt instrument; (4) liquidation proceeds have been distributed to creditors; (5) the bankruptcy process is completed; and (6) the guarantor provides additional capital support covering a portion of the scheduled debt service.

[99] Based on the Basel definition of default.

[100] According to the Greenhouse Gas (GHG) Protocol: https://ghgprotocol.org/.

depend on its value chain. Moreover, as they depend on others (suppliers, customers, etc.), there is often lack of data, and they are more difficult to track.

When looking at major companies, the data show that most carbon emissions come from Scopes 2 and 3. For example, energy consumption due to raw material processing and component assembly results in significant volumes of emissions in the automotive industry.[101] Therefore, large firms such as Ford, Toyota, and Volkswagen face associated financial risks from their supply chain operations, through energy/carbon costs in intermediate products as well as through regulatory actions to curb climate change.

Other industries are not exempted:

- In 2017, Scope 3 emissions (indirect emissions) accounted for 85% of the total emissions of 15 major global food companies that disclosed their carbon footprints (Richards, 2018).[102]
- Annual Scope 3 emissions in the fashion industry add up to more than 2 billion metric tons of GHG emissions (the same as the total emissions of France, Germany, and the United Kingdom combined; Woetzel et al., 2020).[103]
- In 2019, the Scope 3 emissions of the world's leading tech companies by market capitalization exceeded 100 million metric tons of CO_2, with Amazon accounting for 40 million metric tons.[104] As a consequence, in recent years, tech giants such as Amazon, Apple, and Microsoft have also set targets for the reduction of their Scope 3 GHG emissions.
- Only 15% of global emissions are caused by the extraction, processing, and transportation of oil and gas. The remaining 85% of emissions are caused by using the oil and gas downstream of the supply chain (e.g., the end customer that buys the petrol to run a car and thus pollutes).[105]

---

[101] For example, at Toyota, 98.2% of Scope 3 emissions are generated by the company's consumers using its products.

[102] For example, Crippa et al. (2021) estimated that food-system emissions amount to 18 Gt CO_2 equivalent per year globally, representing 34% of the total GHG emissions, and that 71% of those emissions came from agriculture and land use/land-use-change activities. The remaining 29% came from upstream and downstream supply chain activities: retail, transport, consumption, fuel production, waste management, industrial processes, and packaging.

[103] In the fashion industry, Scope 3 emissions usually include those produced from fabric factories, dry cleaners, and cutting and sewing factories that are suppliers to the main brands.

[104] In the case of e-commerce companies such as Amazon, Scope 3 emissions include those arising from activities other than a firm's direct operations, such as the upstream production of goods and devices and their packaging. It also includes downstream emissions from product delivery, usage, waste, and end-of-life treatment.

[105] World Energy Outlook Report (2018).

This suggests that supply chain aspects are crucial to the green transition.[106] Increasingly, companies from all industries will be asked to report not only the emissions under their control but also Scope 3 emissions resulting from value chain activities.[107] As a consequence, decarbonization of the supply chain will become necessary for companies to fulfil their environmental commitments.

Supply chain decarbonization will also become necessary for companies to attract capital from investors, which traditionally have been concerned with Scope 1 and Scope 2 emissions. Given the increasing commitment to the net-zero transition, more and more investors are taking Scope 3 investment risks into account in their financial strategies. In addition, climate risks pose challenges to supply chains. For instance, extreme weather events may disrupt the supply chain of large multinational companies and thus affect their operations and profitability.

The interconnection of the global supply chains also means that environmental issues are no longer a matter of concern to just large, listed companies. SMEs around the world, who are suppliers of intermediate goods to large corporations, are also involved in supporting and speeding up the low-carbon transition. In addition, large corporations can put pressure on suppliers located in regions where government commitment to climate change is weak.

KEY LEARNING POINT

CO_2 emissions are classified into different levels of scope (Scopes 1, 2, 3). Scope 3 emissions are comprehensive and include suppliers' as well as customers' emissions related to the use of the product/service.

3.6.2 The Importance of Working Capital and Suppliers

A fundamental question in corporate finance is, how do firms choose their working capital levels? This question is at the heart of many CFO surveys and consulting reports. Analysts typically focus a significant part of their reports on understanding and evaluating a firm's usage of capital.

The importance of working capital can be understood by looking at its economic implications. For the median firm worldwide, the level of receivables is equivalent to 40%

---

[106] Meinrenken et al. (2020) analyzed 866 product carbon footprints (PCFs) from 145 companies, 30 industries, and 28 countries and found that, on average, 45% of the total value chain emissions arise upstream in the supply chain, 23% during the company's direct operations, and 32% downstream. This breakdown varies greatly by industry.

[107] For instance, in the new EU directive on Non-Financial Reporting. See Sections 6.3 and 6.4 for discussions on non-financial reporting and the evolving global standards.

of the total equity; inventories are at the same level as cash holdings, and payables are six times bigger than dividends. Working capital management is often cited among financial managers as one of the most critical issues defining firm financial performance over time, especially for firms facing both volatile and persistent changes in activity level (growth). The median CFO spends a significant part of her time on working-capital-related topics.

Given the interconnections of global economic activity, a company's physical risk also depends on its suppliers and their underlying exposure to environmental risks. Further, as environmental awareness is becoming increasingly relevant for consumer preferences and purchase decisions, corporates are attempting to minimize the impact of their business on the community.

Many global companies are incorporating ESG metrics in evaluating the performance of their supply chains.[108] For example, the supermarket chain Aldi has informed suppliers that by 2025, any supplier looking to sell in Aldi's stores must package their products in 100% recyclable, compostable, or reusable materials.

Supply chain and trade finance mechanisms are one of the ways to provide incentives for suppliers, and thus drive sustainable behaviors throughout global supply chains.

3.6.3 What Is Supply Chain Financing?

A supply chain finance (SCF) contract involves a supplier, a buyer, and a funder who set up a scheme to free up cash flows (for a supplier, buyer, or both). SCF (also called reverse factoring) is a financing program set up by a bank (or other private debt provider) that allows suppliers to be paid earlier and usually with better conditions than those the suppliers could get on their own.

If a buyer wants to extend supplier payment terms to optimize working capital, it can invite the supplier to participate in an SCF program. This enables the suppliers to be paid as soon as the invoice payment is approved and take advantage of the buyer's high credit rating to obtain financing at lower rates.[109] Once the supplier agrees to participate, the bank that operates the supply chain program credits the invoice payment to the bank account of the

---

[108] Eggert and Hartmann (2021) studied a sample of 260 companies from 2005 to 2017 and found that some companies had introduced environmental and supplier management programs to promote a significant reduction of the GHG emission intensity throughout their supply chains. Schiller (2018) studied a sample of 67,002 customer-supplier pair-year observations covering 52 countries from 2003 to 2016, and found that E&S policies propagated from customers to suppliers, especially when customers had more bargaining power and suppliers were in countries with lower ESG standards. This transmission mechanism matters: suppliers subsequently reduce their toxic emissions, litigation and reputation risks decrease, and financial performance improves.

[109] Other financial services that allow suppliers to be paid earlier include factoring and confirming.

supplier. That is, suppliers are offered the possibility of cashing in (or discounting) the receivables earlier than the planned payment date. They would thus benefit from a lower financing rate (as a result of the buyer's credit standing). SCF has grown remarkably since the financial crisis of 2008, and despite global disruptions to trade, the global factoring industry reached a volume of €2.7 billion in 2020 (source: Factors Chain International (FCI)[110]).

SCF is a liquidity tool for both buyers and suppliers. The "bridge financing" allows buyers to temporarily free up working capital, thus improving the company's liquidity position. At the same time, suppliers benefit from being able to get paid early, and they get access to better financing conditions than they could obtain on their own.

KEY LEARNING POINT

Supply chain finance is a financing program set up by a bank that allows suppliers to be paid earlier and usually with better conditions than those they could get on their own.

3.6.4 Sustainable Supply Chain Financing

Sustainable SCF consists of the incorporation of ESG considerations into SCF practices and techniques. The pressures arising from new environmental regulations, rising energy costs, workplace standards, and other consumer and government demands have prompted many corporates to incorporate sustainability requirements into both the eligibility of suppliers and the contractual relationship with them. Some companies are using novel SCF contracts, where the supplier's payment terms as well as the implied interest rate are linked to the achievement of agreed-upon sustainability standards and performance.

Sustainable SCF integrates ESG metrics into the SCF scheme. It requires a consistent methodology and data to assess suppliers' sustainability performance, and they can be financially rewarded for their performance.

Sustainable SCF schemes allow suppliers to access better financing conditions from banks, depending on their carbon footprint or environmental performance (or other prespecified ESG goals, or scores).

The environmental performance of the suppliers is evaluated using defined metrics, to assess how a supplier fits within the sustainability targets agreed upon in the financing scheme. As with sustainable loans and bonds, often the KPIs are audited by external providers.

---

[110] The global representative body for factoring and financing of domestic and international trade receivables.

KEY LEARNING POINT

Some companies are using novel supply chain finance contracts, where the supplier's payment terms and the implied interest rate are contingent on their sustainability standards.

Walmart's SCF program

In 2019, the U.S. retailer launched an SCF program in partnership with HSBC to improve suppliers' ESG performance and, in particular, to curb supply chain GHG emissions.

Under this financing agreement, HSBC committed to providing preferential credit rates to Walmart's suppliers based on their ESG performance. Suppliers' performance will be assessed against the two Walmart programs, the Sustainability Index program, launched in 2009, and Project Gigaton, launched in 2017. Therefore, suppliers that improve their sustainability credentials will have access to improved financing from HSBC.

Since its inception, more than 1,000 suppliers have joined Project Gigaton, which has resulted in the conservation of more than 93 million metric tons of emissions through the implementation of a set of projects that combine energy efficiency, renewable energy and sustainable packaging.

Bridgestone-JP Morgan SCF scheme

Bridgestone is the world's largest tire manufacturer, and the group owns 80 manufacturing plants and R&D facilities worldwide. Given its global reach, in 2018 the company established the Global Sustainable Procurement Policy in partnership with EcoVadis, a leading provider of sustainability, risk, and performance ratings for global supply chains.

Within the framework of the Global Sustainable Procurement Policy, in 2021, Bridgestone EMIA entered into a working capital financing scheme with the bank JP Morgan Chase in collaboration with the fintech firm Taulia.

The program—officially known as J.P. Morgan and Bridgestone EMIA Sustainable Supply Chain Finance—utilizes ESG-linked lending rates to provide preferential discounts to suppliers that receive high ESG ratings from the global sustainability rating platform EcoVadis. The choice of a third-party auditor such as EcoVadis was deliberate, both to enhance the transparency, and thus the credibility, of Bridgestone's ESG strategy and to incentivize suppliers to constantly improve their ESG performance. Therefore, this financing scheme allows Bridgestone to reduce the carbon footprint of its suppliers while providing them with early payments at favorable interest rates.

In 2021, the J.P. Morgan and Bridgestone EMIA Sustainable Supply Chain Finance program received the Adam Smith Award for the best supply chain finance solution.

3.6.5 Summary – Supply Chain Financing

Many companies are incorporating ESG issues into their supply chain and global trade networks. Increasingly, sustainable SCF is used to incorporate sustainability criteria into the funding financing conditions of suppliers.

Many large companies have started to introduce policies that foster change through the supply chain, in particular, by using SCF. These are financing program set up by a bank that allows suppliers to be paid earlier, and usually with better conditions than those they could get on their own.

In this way, corporate initiatives initiated by large multinational companies are expanded throughout their supply chains, namely, to SMEs worldwide, and incentives are used to drive behaviors. If suppliers perform well against certain ESG targets, they are rewarded with better conditions in financing programs.

Accordingly, when large companies implement ESG/climate targets and then pass them on to suppliers (for instance, through SCF contracts), these issues are shared by the entire economy instead of being confined to large publicly listed companies.

REFERENCES: CHAPTER 3

Agence France Trésor. 2020. "Green OAT: Allocation, Performance and Report for 2020." Paris: Agence France Trésor.

Amundi and International Financial Corporation. 2020. "Emerging Market Green Bonds Report 2019." Washington, D.C.: World Bank. https://www.ifc.org/wps/wcm/connect/Topics_Ext_Content/IFC_External_Corporate _Site/Climate+Business/Resources/EM-GB-Report-2019.

Baker, M., D. Bergstresser, G. Serafeim, and J. Wurgler. 2018. "Financing the Response to Climate Change: The Pricing and Ownership of US Green Bonds." Cambridge, Massachusetts, United States: National Bureau of Economic Research.

Copley, M. 2019. "Investors Eye 'transition Bonds' to Decarbonize Heavy Industry." *S&P Global Market Intelligence* (blog). July 5, 2019.

Crippa, M., E. Solazzo, D. Guizzardi, F. Monforti-Ferrario, F. Tubiello, and A. Leip. 2021. "Food Systems Are Responsible for a Third of Global Anthropogenic GHG Emissions." *Nature Food* 2 (3): 198–209.

Eggert, J., and J. Hartmann. 2021. "Purchasing's Contribution to Supply Chain Emission Reduction." *Journal of Purchasing and Supply Management* 27 (2): 100685.

Flammer, C. 2021. "Corporate Green Bonds." *Journal of Financial Economics* 142 (2): 499–516.

Forsgren, K.E., and M. Kraemer. 2017. "How Does S&P Global Ratings Incorporate Environmental, Social, and Governance Risks Into Its Ratings Analysis." S&P Global. November 21, 2017. https://www.spglobal.com/en/research-insights/articles/how-does-sp-global-ratings-incorporate-environmental-social-and-governance-risks-into-its-ratings-analysis-.

Gore, G., and M. Berrospi. 2019. "Rise of Controversial Transition Bonds Leads to Call for Industry Standards." *Reuters*, September 6, 2019, sec. Financials. https://www.reuters.com/article/idUSL5N25W2QT.

Hoepner, A., I. Oikonomou, B. Scholtens, and M. Schröder. 2016. "The Effects of Corporate and Country Sustainability Characteristics on the Cost of Debt: An International Investigation." *Journal of Business Finance & Accounting* 43 (1–2): 158–90.

Horsch, A., and S. Richter. 2017. "Climate Change Driving Financial Innovation: The Case of Green Bonds." *The Journal of Structured Finance* 23 (1): 79–90.

ICMA. 2015. "Green Bond Principles, 2015. Voluntary Process Guidelines for Issuing Green Bonds." Zürich: International Capital Market Association.

IEA. 2018. "World Energy Outlook 2018." Paris: International Energy Agency.

International Finance Corporation. 2020. "Green Bond Impact Report Financial Year 2020." Washington, D.C.: World Bank. https://www.ifc.org/wps/wcm/connect/Topics_Ext_Content/IFC_External_Co rporate_Site/Climate+Business/Resources/EM-GB-Report-2019.

Kacperczyk, M.T., and J.-L. Peydró. 2021. "Carbon Emissions and the Bank-Lending Channel." CEPR Discussion Paper No. DP16778.

Kapraun, J., C. Latino, C. Scheins, and C. Schlag. 2021. "(In)-Credibly Green: Which Bonds Trade at a Green Bond Premium?" In *Proceedings of Paris December 2019 Finance Meeting EUROFIDAI-ESSEC.*

Klusak, P., M. Agarwala, M. Burke, M. Kraemer, and K. Mohaddes. 2021. "Rising Temperatures, Falling Ratings: The Effect of Climate Change on Sovereign Creditworthiness." CAMA Working Paper.

Kuchtyak M. 2019. "2019 Global Green Bond Outlook." New York: Moody's Investor Services.

Larcker, D.F., and E.M. Watts. 2019. "Where's the Greenium?" Rock Center for Corporate Governance at Stanford University Working Paper, no. 239: 19–14.

Liaw, K.T. 2020. "Survey of Green Bond Pricing and Investment Performance." *Journal of Risk and Financial Management* 13 (9): 193.

Loan Market Association and Others. 2018. "Green Loan Principles: Supporting Environmentally Sustainable Economic Activity." London: Loan Market Association.

MacAskill, S., E. Roca, B. Liu, R.A. Stewart, and O. Sahin. 2021. "Is There a Green Premium in the Green Bond Market? Systematic Literature Review Revealing Premium Determinants." *Journal of Cleaner Production* 280: 124491.

Mahanti, S., A. Nashikkar, M. Subrahmanyam, G. Chacko, and G. Mallik. 2008. "Latent Liquidity: A New Measure of Liquidity, with an Application to Corporate Bonds." *Journal of Financial Economics* 88 (2): 272–98.

Mallucci, E. 2022. "Natural Disasters, Climate Change, and Sovereign Risk." *Journal of International Economics*, 103672.

Meinrenken, C.J., D. Chen, R.A. Esparza, V. Iyer, S.P. Paridis, Λ. Prasad, and E. Whillas. 2020. "Carbon Emissions Embodied in Product Value Chains and the Role of Life Cycle Assessment in Curbing Them." *Scientific Reports* 10 (1): 1–12.

NGFS. 2021. "Adapting Central Bank Operations to a Hotter World: Reviewing Some Options." Paris: Network for Greening the Financial System.

OECD. 2017a. "Enhancing the Contributions of SMEs in a Global and Digitalised Economy." Paris: Organisation for Economic Co-operation and Development.

OECD. 2017b. "Small, Medium, Strong: Trends in SME Performance and Business Conditions." Paris: Organisation for Economic Co-operation and Development.

Reznick, M., and M. Viehs. 2017. "Pricing ESG Risks in Credit Markets." Research paper. London: Hermes Credit and Hermes EOS.

Richards, M.B. 2018. "Measure the Chain: Tools for Assessing GHG Emissions in Agricultural Supply Chains." Boston: Ceres.

S&P. 2020. "The Role of Environmental, Social, and Governance Credit Factors in Our Ratings Analysis." S&P Global Ratings.

https://www.spglobal.com/ratings/en/research/articles/190912-the-role-of-environmental-social-and-governance-credit-factors-in-our-ratings-analysis-11135920.

Schiller, C. 2018. "Global Supply-Chain Networks and Corporate Social Responsibility." In 13th Annual Mid-Atlantic Research Conference in Finance (MARC) Paper.

Seltzer, L.H., L. Starks, and Q. Zhu. 2022. "Climate Regulatory Risk and Corporate Bonds." Cambridge, Massachusetts, United States: National Bureau of Economic Research.

Takatsuki, Y., and J. Foll. 2019. "Financing Brown to Green: Guidelines for Transition Bonds." AXA Investment Managers. June 10, 2019. https://qualified.axa-im.ch/content/-/asset_publisher/51B6S2lE4Ek1/content/financing-brown-to-green-guidelines-for-transition-bonds/23818.

Tang, D.Y., and Y. Zhang. 2020. "Do Shareholders Benefit from Green Bonds?" *Journal of Corporate Finance* 61: 101427.

Volz, U., J. Beirne, N. Ambrosio Preudhomme, A. Fenton, E. Mazzacurati, N. Renzhi, and J. Stampe. 2020. "Climate Change and Sovereign Risk." Tokyo: Asian Development Bank Institute.

Wang, J., X. Chen, X. Li, J. Yu, and R. Zhong. 2020. "The Market Reaction to Green Bond Issuance: Evidence from China." *Pacific-Basin Finance Journal* 60: 101294.

WindEurope. 2020. "Financing and Investment Trends 2019: The European Wind Industry in 2019." Brussels: WindEurope. https://windeurope.org/about-wind/reports/financing-and-investment-trends-2019/.

Woetzel, J., D. Pinner, H. Samandari, H. Engel, M. Krishnan, B. Boland, and C. Powis. 2020. "Climate Risk and Response: Physical Hazards and Socioeconomic Impacts." McKinsey Global Institute. January 16, 2020.

Zerbib, O.D. 2019. "The Effect of Pro-Environmental Preferences on Bond Prices: Evidence from Green Bonds." *Journal of Banking & Finance* 98: 39–60.

Chapter 4
Green Corporate Financing – Equity

This chapter covers the equity financing side of the balance sheet, and how it is affected by climate issues. We start with privately held companies, discussing topics such as private equity (PE) and family firms. We then analyze public capital markets, including initial public offerings and subsequent capital raises. The chapter also covers topics related to mergers and acquisitions, and the governance of companies. A discussion of other cutting-edge topics in corporate governance, such as shareholder voting on ESG issues, proxy advisory firms, shareholder activism, and the role of the board on ESG issues, rounds off the chapter.

4.1 PRIVATE EQUITY

PE is an alternative source of finance for a company. It consists of an investment made by a PE fund in the capital of a privately held company. In PE transactions, the PE fund supplies funds and can be an active shareholder. It can support the management and is also involved in the governance and monitoring of the invested company.

PE funds obtain capital from institutional investors (sovereign funds, pension funds, family offices, etc.) and invest it in private companies for a specific number of years. During the ownership stage, PE funds try to implement changes aimed at improving profitability, growth, and, ultimately, company value.

PE funds focus on specific target companies defined in terms of sectors, region, and also the life-cycle stage of the target. Some funds are interested in young firms that have not yet produced good results, but have high growth prospects and promising management teams (start-ups and venture capital).

Other funds target established companies with stable cash flows using leveraged buyout (LBO) acquisitions. In an LBO, a target company is acquired by a PE investment firm using a large portion of the debt (sometimes higher than 80%) as the main source of external finance.[111] By borrowing money from external lenders, PE firms aim to achieve a large return on equity (ROE) and internal rate of return (IRR) on their actual investment.

Another type of PE fund targets distressed publicly traded companies. In this case, the fund purchases all the shares of a distressed target company to delist it. After the company has improved its financial performance, the investor will exit the investment, either by selling off the shares to another PE investor or in the stock exchange (IPO).

4.1.1   PE Funds – Players and Stages

PE funds gather a pool of capital that is used to buy companies, strengthen their financial performance, and ultimately sell them. A PE fund is formed by a general partner (GP) and a pool of limited partners (LPs).

When a PE fund is launched, the GP – as the owner of the partnership – assumes the responsibility of managing the fund, targets investment opportunities, and provides post-investment advisories. A GP may have unlimited personal liability for the debt of the fund.

LPs are the investors that contribute most of the capital of the fund (GPs also invest their own capital in the fund), and they have limited liabilities (they can at most lose the money invested in the fund). However, LPs are mostly passive partners in the fund and are not involved in every investment. Ownership and investment decisions are taken by the GP, even if the investment policies and criteria are often defined by the ultimate investors (the LPs).

PE funds start by gathering financing from their LPs. They then invest that money in real operating companies. Finally, they divest their positions, hopefully with a substantial exit multiple and profit. Thus, the life cycle of a PE fund evolves in four stages:

- o **Fundraising**: At this stage, the PE firm tries to persuade investors (the LPs) to commit their money to the fund (this is also called the capital call).
- o **Deal sourcing**: During this phase, the PE fund tries to identify investment opportunities. It uses multiple screening processes and sources of information to find companies to invest in. When a prospect is identified, the GPs evaluate the target company to understand the financial and business aspects of the investment and possible returns. They also analyze the risks through due diligence – which can lead them to abandon the investment – and negotiate the terms and conditions of their stake in the investee company.

---

[111] This may include bank debt, high yield/subordinated debt, and mezzanine debt.

o **Ownership**: After the investment agreement has been closed, the PE fund becomes a shareholder of the company and focuses on managing and monitoring the company value. The GPs' typical interest is that the investee company boost sales, efficiency, improve margins, etc. They can do this through direct involvement (or nomination) to executive positions in the company or by sitting on a board that supervises the management.

o **Exit (or harvest period)**: After some years, the PE fund must return money to investors (typically 7–10 years). At this stage, the PE fund intends to sell its ownership stake in its portfolio companies. This can be done through a private sale to another PE fund (secondary buyout), a sale to a strategic buyer, or an IPO. The objective at this stage is to maximize the exit valuation, thus maximizing the returns of the fund (for GPs and LPs).

4.1.2 Incentives and Investors

After the market collapse of the Global Financial Crisis 2007-08, the value of PE-backed buyout deals worldwide increased from US$118 billion in 2009 to US$618 billion in 2015. During the global pandemic in 2020, the value of global PE-backed buyout deals stood at US$592 billion.

Figure 4.1 Value of private-equity-backed buyout deals worldwide

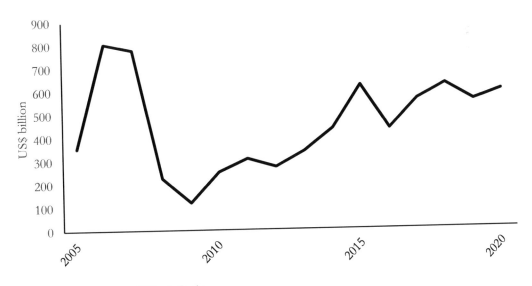

Source: Bureau van Dijk, via Statista.

Table 4.1 shows the rank of the largest PE firms by assets raised in the last five years (the ranking is not very different if one looks at the accumulated assets under management (AuM)).

Table 4.1 Largest private equity firms worldwide by assets under management

Private equity firm	Five-year fundraising total in 2021 (in US$ billions)
The Blackstone Group	93.2
KKR	79.9
CVC Partners	60.4
The Carlyle Group	50.8
Thoma Bravo	46.7
EQT	44.2
Vista Equity Partners	40.4
TPG Capital	40.3
Warburg Pincus LLC	37.6
Neuberger Berman Private Markets	37.5

Source: PEI 300 Ranking 2021.

PE funds typically have

- high-powered incentives (both for the PE portfolio managers and for the managers of the operating businesses),
- aggressive use of debt (financing and tax advantages),
- a focus on cash flow and margin improvements, and
- fewer constraints than publicly traded companies.

PE funds levy management and performance fees. Typically, GPs charge the partnership an annual management fee of 2% of the assets. They also levy a performance fee: when the PE firm sells the investee firms, they receive carried interest (or carry), which traditionally equals 20% of the profits. This is the so-called 2-20% compensation structure. These performance incentives aim to give the GP motivation for achieving strong performance, which, if achieved, will reward both the GP and the LPs with strong financial returns. In the partnership agreement, the parties can also establish a hurdle rate that specifies the minimum IRR that a PE must achieve before the GP receives the carried interest payment. This hurdle rate was conventionally set at 8%. However, the number of funds with a hurdle rate of 8% decreased from 71% in 2017 to 60% in 2019 (Mendoza, 2019).

PE funds are closed-end funds. They are considered an alternative investment class for many global investors. Investors in PE funds are mostly institutions (pension funds, endowments, foundations, sovereign funds, etc.). However, some family offices also invest in PE funds, as do some high-net-worth individuals. In 2019, the 10 largest PE investors were mainly pension and sovereign wealth funds, with more than US$350 billion allocations in PE.

Table 4.2 Largest investors in private equity globally in 2019

Rank	Investor	Allocation to private equity (US$ billion)	Investor type	Location
1	CPP Investment Board	61.3	Public Pension	Canada
2	Kuwait Investment Authority	59.2	Sovereign Wealth	Kuwait
3	GIC	43.8	Sovereign Wealth	Singapore
4	Abu Dhabi Investment Authority	34.2	Sovereign Wealth	UAE
5	CDPQ (Caisse de dépôt et placement du Québec)	28.1	Public Pension Fund	Canada
6	California Public Employees'	27.8	Public Pension	United
7	APG (All Pensions Group)	27.2	Asset Manager	Netherland
8	Ontario Teachers' Pension Plan	26.6	Public Pension	Canada
9	La Banque Postale	26.1	Bank	France
10	China Investment Corporation	23.2	Sovereign Wealth	China

Source: Preqin.

PE funds have other characteristics besides high fees and high-powered incentives. From the point of view of an investor, investing in a PE fund has the following implications:

- Liquidity: The LPs' capital is usually locked in for 7–10 years. This is to allow the fund to purchase, improve, and ultimately sell the assets. Therefore, if an investor (an LP) wants to exit this commitment, it can be done only by a personal sale of its commitments to other investors (a secondary sale). Although a public equity investor can easily sell off the share it owns in the stock market and exit the company's ownership, a PE investor must identify another investor willing to purchase its stake in the fund.
- Pricing: Whereas in a publicly traded company the share price is easily obtained in the stock market, in PE transactions the value of equity positions (or the whole fund) is not directly observable.
- Investor monitoring: In the stock market, investors' rights are safeguarded by financial regulation, supervisors, and the stock exchange, to protect minority investors. In the PE market, investors' ownership rights are negotiated case by case and vary according to the contract and the country under whose law it is signed.

Therefore, investing in PE funds has benefits, but it also entails risks, which investors must weigh before committing to invest.

4.1.3 Climate-Related Risks in Private Equity

Having a full-fledged climate strategy is important for the future viability of all businesses. Such a strategy is even more relevant for PE investments, given their long-term nature. Most

PE funds have maturities longer than 5 years, many last close to 10 years, and most of the returns are achieved with a successful exit. PE funds hold illiquid assets over many years. Climate risks and opportunities are difficult to predict, but can have a huge impact on the value at exit (and thus the PE fund's returns). Thus, modeling/forecasting the effects of, and changes in, regulatory developments, markets, and societal preferences is crucial.

A PE investor is typically interested in increasing the selling price of the portfolio company (the exit value), and thus has an incentive to engage with their invested companies to reduce climate risks. Having already identified and managed material environmental issues, the GP avoids the scenario where buyers raise unforeseen risks at the exit stage to negotiate a lower price.[112]

PE funds start by gathering financing from their LPs. They then invest that money in real operating companies. Finally, they divest their positions, hopefully with a substantial exit multiple and profit. Climate considerations arise in all these three stages. Moreover, these considerations should be properly integrated with the different phases of a PE fund. The underlying idea is that climate-related efforts during the investment cycle reduce risk and enhance company value (which will be realized upon exit). According to KKR, one of the world's largest PE players: "We believe responsibly governing a business is a part of achieving favorable investment outcomes."

The PE industry has two key ways to influence the climate transition: (1) through the choices the fund managers make for their portfolios (deal sourcing) and (2) by focusing on how the company operates (active ownership).

Since the United Nations Conference on Sustainable Development (UNCSD) in 2012, an ever-increasing number of investment firms have committed themselves to the UN Principles for Responsible Investment (PRI).[113]

KEY LEARNING POINT

Climate risks can have an impact on the exit return obtained by a PE fund. Because of this, PE managers should consider these risks in the different stages of their investment.

---

[112] Crifo et al. (2015) investigated the impact of ESG corporate practice disclosure on equity financing. Experimental evidence shows that entrepreneurs who do not manage ESG issues are likely to suffer limited access to PE, with a higher cost of capital, hence penalizing their shareholders by destroying firm value. Their results show that the disclosure of bad environmental policies by a company decreases valuations by approximately 11%, and PE investors are also 30% less likely to invest in it.

[113] The PRI Initiative in collaboration with the United Nations has published guidelines to be followed by investors during the different stages of a responsible PE investment (PRI, 2020). For more details about the PRI, see Section 5.4.3. Teti et al. (2012) investigated whether a fund's adherence to the PRI generates financial returns. They collected data for 135 U.S. PE funds during 2006–11, and found evidence that a fund's returns depend on the UN PRI compliance variable.

Climate Considerations in Deal Sourcing

Fund managers can screen deals against environmental criteria to identify critical issues. This could prompt further investigation during due diligence or lead to abandoning the investment. Then, during the due diligence phase, they can investigate material environmental issues[114] and how they are being managed. This involves investigating not only legacy issues but also the transition to a low-carbon economy. The scope of the investigation includes identifying opportunities to increase value and reduce risks through ESG initiatives, assessing the potential performance impact of climate change, and reviewing environmental permits and licenses.

Often, the critical issues identified at this stage become the focus of management efforts during the ownership period. During the investment agreement, the GP should clarify its expectations and goals regarding the portfolio company. The underlying idea is that proper consideration of climate issues will reduce risks (and sometimes offer new business opportunities). By limiting downside risk, it will also enhance the investment's future expected returns.

Lowercarbon Capital

In 2018, Chris and Crystal Sacca founded an impact investing firm called Lowercarbon Capital, which aims to supports technologies that help absorb CO_2 emissions from the atmosphere and thus "accelerate the capture of billions of tons of CO_2 via innovative technologies."

They raised a total of US$1.2 billion with two different funds, one of which was recently announced (April 2022) and raised US$350 million. They now have more than 50 investments. For instance, in a seed funding round, Lowercarbon Capital invested in Epoch Biodesign to develop the technology of plastic-eating enzymes, to reduce plastic waste. Another of Lowercarbon's investments is in Heart Aerospace, which plans to build a fully electric regional airliner with no emissions in its operations.

The criteria for an investment screening can come from the GP or LPs. It is important to have a strong alignment between the GP and the LPs. In practice, the GPs and LPs will generally agree on the criteria and screenings during the fundraising stage.[115] As leading global investors become more and more vocal about climate issues, GPs are increasingly integrating sustainability criteria into the running of their funds. Ultimately, investors place their capital with a PE fund to generate a return on their investment. This return can be measured in different ways. It is important to recognize that although some investors are willing to trade off financial returns for sustainability, most investors care only about their

---

114 For more details on materiality, see Sections 2.7.1 and 6.3.

115 Geczy et al. (2019) analyzed a set of 202 legal documents pertaining to impact funds' portfolio companies and investors. They reported that these contracts provide concrete and specific impact goals. However, most impact funds use the traditional financial incentives of other funds, and most tie the compensation of their managers to financial incentives; only very few funds tie compensation to impact.

financial returns.[116] Climate issues will be incorporated differently depending on the investors behind the fund.

Some PE funds start their analysis with the SDGs (and also the Paris Agreement) in mind, to identify areas of investment opportunity. Then, they specifically source companies whose business model addresses some environmental challenge and has possible social and financial returns.

Other PE funds focus on companies operating in the renewable energy and Greentech industries. An increasing number of small, innovative micro-companies are developing technologies that can be used to reduce emissions and address other climate challenges, and they often rely on PE funds for part of their financing.

Other funds invest in many different sectors and companies, and care about the environmental impact of their invested companies as they understand it can affect their fund's performance.

KEY LEARNING POINT

GPs and LPs should ensure that their climate change screening and investment criteria are aligned.

Active Ownership

Once the investment has been made, the GP will want to increase company value to ensure a successful exit. At this stage, through active ownership, PE funds can influence how the invested company operates, including how the business model of the company can incorporate climate issues.

There is not a one-size-fits-all approach to how active ownership can incorporate climate issues. The invested company could directly pursue business opportunities around climate issues, or the company's operations could be designed with environmental concerns in mind. In some other cases, it is about minimizing risk and avoiding future exposures to reputational risk, liability, and stranded assets.

There is some evidence that PE creates strong incentives to reduce pollution.[117] For instance, a PE acquisition can lead companies to invest in long-term projects that may negatively impact short-term results but maximizes long-term shareholder value (for instance, energy

---

[116] When investing in a company whose activities have a beneficial impact on the environment, 81% of respondents stated they would be unwilling to accept any reduction in returns, or would accept only a reduction of 100 bps or less (PwC, 2020).

[117] Bellon (2020) showed that PE ownership is associated with a 70% reduction in the use of toxic chemicals and a 50% reduction in CO_2 emissions.

abatement projects with high payback periods). This active ownership can involve asking portfolio companies to implement climate-related operational improvements and measure their impact. In terms of accountability, one good practice is to make the invested company's board accountable for environmental performance.[118] Also, setting KPIs at the beginning of the ownership period provides additional support for environmental issues.

KEY LEARNING POINT

Climate issues are relevant during the funding, investment, and exit stages of a private equity fund.

Summa and Sotera Garbage

Summa is a Swedish PE firm whose mission is to invest in companies engaged in fighting climate change while ensuring competitive returns to limited partners. In 2016, Summa invested in Sotera, the third-largest waste management company in the country.

Since the entry of Summa, Sotera has significantly increased its focus on sustainability and introduced innovative recycling processes that led to significant CO_2 reductions at the same time that it grew and became more productive.

In 2017, Sotera invested in a new electric recycling facility, which was the largest capital expenditure in its history. This investment increased profitability by reducing downstream costs as the recycling rate increased. The investment also generated social benefits, improving employees' health and safety, and reducing the odor, noise, and exposure to fire experienced by neighboring communities.

With its sustainability strategy, Sotera was able to significantly enhance the long-term attractiveness (and value) of the business. Under the new ownership, Sotera quadrupled the revenue to over one billion SEK, and also increased employment more than three times, from 95 to 350 employees (Indahl and Jacobsen, 2019).

4.1.4 Summary – Private Equity

Most PE funds have maturities longer than 5 years, and many last close to 10 years. Therefore, climate change and the physical risk it poses for certain assets, as well as the transition risk it poses for others, is a relevant topic in PE.

---

[118] In the Private Equity Responsible Investment Survey 2019, PwC (2019) surveyed 162 PE firms (general partners, or GPs) and investors (limited partners, or LPs) and highlighted the fact that 81% of the respondents reported that ESG matters to their Boards at least once a year, and 72% of respondents used or were developing KPIs to measure performance.

There is little academic work on PE and climate issues (or even on ESG). The little evidence that exists supports the notion that climate risks are priced, and are linked to investment decisions. The evidence also suggests that PE funds that properly incorporate this into their goals attract an increasingly large pool of investors.

Fund managers should have a consistent approach to identifying and managing climate (and other ESG issues) across the PE portfolio. A substantial number of PE funds are signatories to the Principles of Responsible Investment (PRI). Through this, funds commit that they will follow certain guidelines during the different phases of their investment, including through active ownership of the assets and their external reporting.

Proper consideration of climate risks through sound due diligence during the investment phase can prevent nasty surprises at the time of exit from a certain investment. In addition, many traditional companies will need to substantially overhaul their business model, from the procurement of raw materials and production to how they sell and market their products. Therefore, proper consideration of climate issues, namely, the transition risks, can also be a fruitful way to generate business opportunities.

4.2 RAISING CAPITAL: IPOs AND SEOs

In this section, we cover equity-raising activities in public markets. We describe the potential of climate-related initial public offerings (IPOs) and seasoned equity offerings (SEOs) – and actual cases as well. We also discuss how environmental issues can impact equity-raising activities.

4.2.1 Why Companies Go Public

Companies decide to go public, i.e., sell their shares on a stock exchange, for a variety of reasons. The most important reason is to raise investment capital. Besides the direct cash aspect (i.e., the company or its previous shareholders benefit from a cash infusion), there are other benefits of going public[119]:

- o Companies can use the market value of the stock as a metric for performance evaluation and compare the company's performance against that of its competitors.
- o Companies get an opportunity to reward management and employees with stocks or options, thus linking their rewards to the company's stock price.
- o Companies can diversify their sources of funding at a lower cost.
- o Companies that are publicly traded can use their stock rather than cash to pay for acquisitions, which facilitates growth.

---

[119] From Fernandes (2017).

o   Companies' shareholders will benefit from higher liquidity because they can dispose of their shares more easily if it becomes necessary.

An IPO is the process used by a company to sell stock to the public for the first time. Subsequent sales of shares are done through an SEO, also called a follow-on offering.

When a company issues new shares to investors and retains the proceeds from those issues, it is called a primary offering. The investors pay for the new shares, and the cash is injected into the company. This usually occurs when a company needs to finance additional growth opportunities, for which debt and current earnings are insufficient. Also, a company may be buying another company and therefore needs cash to pay for the purchase.

The company does not always gain cash when shares are sold. In secondary offerings, the shares sold belonged to previous shareholders. In this case, the "new" shareholders simply buy shares from the "old" shareholders, and does not increase the company's cash holdings.

IPOs (and SEOs) typically follow a standard process:

1. The financial advisor (which can be a single investment bank or a syndicate of several investment banks that manages the IPO) is appointed. The IPO mechanism and thus the arrangement with the bank is set; this includes an agreement on fees and possibly an underwriting agreement.[120]
2. The preliminary prospectus is prepared, and the company is registered with the securities regulator (e.g., in the United States, the regulator is the U.S. Securities Exchange Commission).
3. The company's shares are promoted through a roadshow.[121]
4. Following the roadshow, the company and financial advisor agree on the issue price.
5. The financial advisor allots the stock to investors.
6. Trading of the stock starts on the stock exchange.

Investment banks prepare the necessary filings, help market the IPO and sell the shares, and actively participate in determining the selling price. In addition, in most cases, the underwriters[122] also commit to undertake market-making activities (aimed at improving liquidity) for the stock during a certain period and generally dedicate a sell-side analyst[123] to

---

[120] When an IPO is underwritten, the underwriting firm or syndicate assumes the responsibility, and the risk, of selling a specific allotment of shares.

[121] During a roadshow, the company and its advisors meet with potential investors to promote the sale of the new share issue.

[122] Various decisions need to be made when a company decides to issue an IPO/SEO. One of these relates to whether or not a firm commitment (also called underwriting) is included by the financial advisors. When there is a firm commitment, the company's risk is lower, but it pays higher fees.

[123] Sell-side analysts issue research reports with recommendations to their clients, who typically are mutual funds, pension funds, and other institutional investors.

cover the new stock. The objective is to guarantee that the stock will be liquid in the post-IPO period.

4.2.2 Relevance of Climate-Related Risks for IPOs

Given the growing public interest in sustainable products and services, companies planning their IPO should integrate climate issues into the business model, regardless of the industry the company operates in.

Companies seeking to raise capital through IPOs need to be conscious of the recent trends in investors' climate awareness (see Sections 5.4 and 4.4.4). Before making investment decisions, investors consider a variety of factors associated with the financial deal at stake. These traditionally include a forecast of revenue growth and market share in the industry, and a trustworthy management team that can ensure profitability and assure investors they can handle ESG sustainability as well. That is, increasingly higher ESG standards are essential to pass (some) investor scrutiny in the due diligence phase of an IPO.

KEY LEARNING POINT

Increasingly, higher ESG standards are essential to pass investor scrutiny in the due diligence phase of an IPO.

A green IPO consists of the first-ever issuance of shares in the stock market from a formerly private company that seeks to raise capital to develop, make, or provide environment-friendly products and services.

Green IPOs are commonly launched by companies operating in the renewable energy and Greentech industries. However, a variety of sectors such as energy, buildings, and transport are growing rapidly. Besides large companies, an increasing number of small, innovative micro-companies are entering this sector to develop technologies that can be used to reduce emissions and address other climate challenges.

In the early stages of climate-related finance, green IPOs were scarce and investors were skeptical about them. Many IPOs launched to raise capital for sustainable investment were not successful. However, over recent years, the landscape has changed.[124] Investors have

---

[124] Anderloni and Tanda (2017) investigated European energy stock IPOs between 2000 and 2014. They found no significant performance difference (in the long run) between green and non-green IPOs. Diaz-Rainey (2020) analyzed 284 IPOs in Europe (2000–17) and found that green firms are less likely to withdraw their IPO. Further, results suggest greater PE and venture capital (VC) involvement for green firms and higher levels of retained ownership for green IPOs. On the other hand, green firms underperformed post IPO, producing significantly more negative buy-and-hold abnormal returns.

started becoming interested in projects with stable, long-term cash flows that minimize their exposure to climate risks. A few examples of green IPOs include the following:

- o   Italian Enel sold almost a third of its renewable energy business, Enel Green Power, and raised over 3.4 billion euros. This was Europe's biggest IPO in 2019.
- o   Array Technologies, a New-Mexico-based designer and manufacturer of solar ground monitoring systems, launched its IPO on the NASDAQ in 2020. At the IPO, 52 million shares were sold (7 million new shares and 45 million shares from a selling shareholder). With 127 million shares outstanding, the IPO valued the company at US$2.8 billion.
- o   Focus Energia, a Brazilian energy company, raised US$165 million in its 2020 IPO on the Brazilian stock exchange. The IPO involved a primary sale of 42 million shares and a secondary sale of 6.79 million shares by selling shareholders. The company used the proceeds to invest in 45 solar parks.

Beyond Meat IPO

As discussed in Chapter 1, agriculture is responsible for 15% of global GHG emissions, with 65% of those emissions coming from beef and dairy cattle. Beyond Meat is a Los-Angeles-based company, founded in 2009, that specializes in plant-based meat replacement products. The company began selling plant-based chicken products in U.S. Whole Foods supermarkets in April 2013, and it expanded to a simulated beef product in 2014. Its products are now sold in more than 6,000 stores across the United States.

In May 2019, the company went public on the NASDAQ by offering 9,600,000 shares at US$25 each. Through the IPO, the company raised US$240,000,000. Investor appetite was strong. The stock price more than doubled on its first trading day (to US$65), and Beyond Meat was considered the top-performing IPO of the year.

Between the IPO and the end of 2020, the company's share price increased by 840%. Beyond Meat is included in many climate indices, including the U.S. Vegan Climate Index. As of April 2021, there were more than 70 exchange-traded funds that held Beyond Meat shares (7% of the shares).

Sustainable and green stocks are subject to the same market laws as any other stock, and their valuation is based on their fundamentals, business model, and financial prospects. Besides the traditional considerations that apply to raising equity from capital markets, environmental topics are becoming increasingly important for investors' decisions. This means that companies planning to raise equity must consider climate risks as well as their climate transition strategy. Increasingly, these questions are raised during roadshow presentations to investors. Investors seek well-run companies with attractive financial prospects. They generally want to understand the company's exposure to ESG themes, the potential financial impact, and the management's strategy to mitigate risks and exploit opportunities. In addition, a coherent ESG strategy can be seen by investors as an indication of management quality.

NextEra Energy

NextEra Energy Partners (NEP) is a U.S. clean energy company that acquires and manages solar and wind energy projects. The company was established by NextEra Energy Inc (NYSE: NEE) as its wholly owned subsidiary in 2014, and NextEra Energy announced that NEP would be traded on the New York Stock Exchange.

In June 2014, NextEra Energy Partners went public through an IPO on the NYSE (under the ticker symbol NEP). 16,250,000 shares were sold at US$25.00 per share (at the top end of the expected US$23.00–US$25.00 range). The total offer was US$406,250,000, and the net IPO proceeds amounted to US$384,921,875 after subtracting US$21,328,125 in fees to the investment bankers. The joint book-running managers for the transaction were Goldman Sachs, Morgan Stanley, and Bank of America Merrill Lynch.

NextEra Energy Partners stock is traded on the New York Stock Exchange, and the company has been included in six stock market indices: S&P 100 Index, Dow Jones Composite Average, Dow Jones Utility Average, S&P 500 Utilities, S&P 500 Index, and PHLX Utility Sector. The company is also a constituent of climate indices such as the Nasdaq Clean Edge Green Energy Index, an index designed to track the performance of clean energy technology companies.

Investor demand for NEP stock drove the share price from US$25 in June 2014 up to US$82 in February 2021. Since the IPO in 2014, NextEra Energy Partners has been an attractive option for investors looking to invest their funds in the renewable power sector. As of February 2021, 85% of the shares were held by institutional investors, including many index funds and ETFs.

4.2.3 Summary – IPOs and SEOs

Issuing new capital in the stock exchange is a very important step in the life of a company. Companies can go public through their IPO by issuing new shares, which is called the primary offering. In this case, the proceeds from the issue enter the company's coffers. Companies can also go public by selling shares from current shareholders to the public, which is called the seasoned offering. SEOs are the sales of equity to investors subsequent to an IPO.

Besides the traditional considerations that apply to raising equity from capital markets, environmental topics are increasingly influencing investors' decisions. This means that companies planning to raise equity must take into account climate risks as well as their climate transition strategy. More and more questions related to this are being raised during roadshow presentations to investors.

4.3   CORPORATE GOVERNANCE

This section covers a number of topics related to corporate governance and climate issues. We start by reviewing the importance of voting.

We also talk about the increasing importance of the Big Three, and other passive investors. The rise of passive investors has important implications for voting behaviors, and it underlies the increasing importance of proxy advisors. Proxy advisors guide investors on how to vote in annual meetings. They do allow institutional investors to fulfil their fiduciary duties without having to hire analysts and other resources to investigate each proposal under vote in annual meetings. However, the rise of these advisors also poses some concrete challenges.

Finally, we discuss the role of the board of directors, which is responsible for supervising and advising the executive management of a company. Boards have an important role to play in the climate transition. We discuss how various boards are addressing this topic, for example, by setting up special committees and incorporating climate issues in executive compensation and overall performance assessment.

4.3.1 General Meetings and Voting

Shareholders typically have the right to vote at annual general meetings (AGMs) and extraordinary general meetings (EGMs). The exact points (or resolutions) on which they vote vary according to countries' legal frameworks. Some of the most typical ones include approval of annual accounts, voting on directors' appointments, management compensation, or mergers and acquisitions (M&As). Besides management-led proposals, there are also shareholder proposals. These are recommendations formally submitted by a shareholder advocating that the company take a specific course of action.

The rise of institutional investors radically changed the paradigm of shareholders' involvement with their companies. Nowadays, in most corporations, a significant portion of their shares is held by a small number of large shareholders with stronger bargaining power (Matos, 2020). During AGMs and EGMs, these large shareholders can coordinate and enforce their own petitions, or those from otherwise smaller and insignificant investors (see Section 4.4 on the role of activist shareholders).

During the decade 2010–20, a change in investors' attitudes toward environmental and social issues was observed. Many shareholders started to support environmental and social proposals by shareholders both in Europe and the United States. Also, companies (and therefore investors) started to feel the pressures from the public and regulators in the aftermath of the financial crisis, global policy initiatives, and major disaster events.

The increasing focus of shareholders on environmental issues is reflected in the growing number of environment-related proposals submitted by shareholders to be voted at annual meetings, and the increasing voting support these proposals attract.[125] In the United States, shareholder resolutions focusing on environmental and social issues have gradually increased, representing more than 60% of the shareholder proposals in 2020.

Many companies have introduced "Say on Climate" proposals into their annual meetings. These proposals focus on companies' climate strategies, goals, disclosures, and plans, and ask shareholders to vote on them.

Figure 4.2 Percentage of U.S. shareholder proposals relating to social and environmental issues

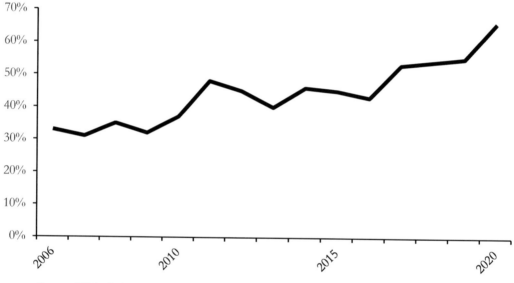

Source: ISS Analytics.

Nevertheless, consensus building through engagement (often through collective action or letter-writing campaigns) is the preferred approach – instead of more public and confrontational avenues such as media campaigns or shareholder resolutions. For most investors, filing a shareholder resolution marks an escalation of a failed direct engagement, not the beginning of the engagement process.[126]

There are legal and regulatory hurdles (including ownership requirements) to filing a shareholder resolution, and these restrictions are more onerous in most European than in

---

[125] Iliev et al. (2015) analyzed a sample of non-U.S. firms from 43 countries and found that around the world, shareholder voting is an effective mechanism for exercising governance.

[126] See Section 5.4 for a full discussion of institutional investors' approach to environmental issues, including engagement versus divestment. See also Section 4.4 for additional evidence on the impact of activist hedge funds.

U.S. markets. According to Rule 14a-8 of the Securities Exchange Act of 1934, in the United States, the ownership requirement to file a shareholder proposal is a holding of US$2,000 during the last three years or US$15,000 during the last two years. In most European countries, shareholders are required to own between 0.5% and 5% of a company to be able to file a proposal.[127]

Index Funds and the Big Three

The increased concentration in stock ownership due to the popularity of index funds has given them significant voting power over publicly traded companies worldwide. As a consequence, the Big Three index funds – Vanguard, BlackRock, and State Street – play an increasingly important role in proxy voting.[128] Together, the Big Three are the largest single shareholder in 96% of Fortune 250 companies, and Vanguard alone is the largest shareholder in 65.6% of such companies (Griffin, 2020).

Given their presence in almost all companies worldwide, these investors are called upon to vote on a huge number of proposals in shareholders' meetings:

- ○ BlackRock: In 2021, BlackRock participated in 17,000 meetings, voted on 164,000 shareholder proposals, and engaged 2,300 times on the themes of corporate governance related to environmental risks and opportunities.[129]
- ○ Vanguard: In 2021, Vanguard voted on more than 177,307 proposals, across 29 countries. It has engaged with nearly 1,074 companies on topics such as board composition, climate change, diversity, and executive compensation.[130]
- ○ State Street: In 2021, State Street Global Advisors voted on 125,286 proposals. It has engaged with 555 companies on a number of ESG topics.[131]

Investors who are dissatisfied with some aspect of a company's management can attempt to bring about change either by "voicing" their concerns (e.g., persuading management, intervening directly by voting their shares or engaging in confrontational proxy fights) or by threatening to "exit" (e.g., selling, also known as "governance by exit," "voting with their feet," or the "Wall Street walk" rule). A full discussion of these options, from the investors' standpoint, is provided in Section 5.4. However, it is clear that some investors cannot "exit" due to their index-tracking nature.

---

[127] For example, in Germany, proposals can be filed by shareholders representing 0.5% of the capital share (or with a capital holding of €500,000). In France, proposals can be filed by shareholders representing 5% of the capital. The ownership requirement established by Italian law is 0.025%, while it is set at 3% in Spain, where there is no provision for shareholders to band together to file a collective proposal.

[128] Under U.S. law, as well as that of many other jurisdictions, index funds have a legal right to vote their investors' shares in corporate elections.

[129] Blackrock (2021).

[130] Vanguard (2021).

[131] State Street (2021).

The Big Three are increasingly visible. By definition, they cannot "vote with their feet," given that their investments track a certain index. However, they are under increasing pressure to exercise their stewardship rights. They exercise their "behind-the-scenes" power in two ways: through private engagements with the managements and boards of invested companies, and through their voting activities.

Empirical Evidence on Voting

The research on voting patterns, effects, and the various monitoring roles of different investors is still underway. The effects of index funds on corporate governance are being vigorously debated. One view is that the presence of these passive investors shifts the control from investors to managers. Another view is that with their concentrated positions, they can bring about substantial changes. In some areas, the evidence is mixed. Some papers suggest that passive investors are passive monitors; others, that they improve the governance and monitoring of companies.

Some authors argue the Big Three might underinvest in stewardship, exhibit pro-management voting, and do not involve themselves in structural reforms. The reason is that their business model is based on matching the performance of indexes at low cost (because they compete on fees, they have no incentives to allocate resources to monitoring companies). Bebchuk and Hirst (2019) reviewed the arguments and suggested that the Big Three have relatively low engagement and limited governance personnel. Heath et al. (2020) showed that index funds (in the United States during 2004–18) are more likely to vote in accordance with management recommendations. Brav et al. (2018a) suggested that active funds exhibit stronger support for activist shareholders in proxy contests (compared with passive funds). However, Hshieh et al. (2021) compared the voting behavior of passive and active mutual funds and found that the latter are not more likely to vote for governance reforms than the former. These findings may suggest that passive mutual funds likely use a mixture of strategies, both overground and behind the scenes, to influence corporate governance.

Azar et al. (2020) studied the impact of Big Three ownership on corporate CO_2 emission around the world on a sample of approximately 8,000 companies for the period 2005–18. The results suggest that the Big Three engage with companies to try to reduce their emissions. Their findings show that higher ownership by the Big Three is followed by lower carbon emissions, especially in the later years of the sample period.

Adib and Zahra (2019) studied how index funds affect corporate governance, using a dataset that included all mutual fund votes on 159,262 proposals at 6,260 firms over the period 2005–16. The results show that (1) index fund ownership promotes good corporate governance, and value-creating proposals are more likely to pass; (2) managers of firms with higher index fund ownership present fewer value-reducing proposals; and (3) index funds optimally allocate resources to monitor proposals for which their votes are more likely to be crucial.

Briere et al. (2018) analyzed BlackRock and Norway's sovereign fund voting on ESG themes on 35,382 resolutions at 2,796 corporations across the world in 2014. They found that both investors opposed management significantly more often for shareholder resolutions on environmental and social issues than on financial issues.

He et al. (2020) collected voting data for U.S. companies for 2004–18 and built a dataset that included 1,196 firm-years with Environmental & Social (ES) proposals (400 unique firms). The results showed that proposals with higher investor support, but which management opposes and which do not pass, are informative about subsequent negative firm outcomes. They reported negative performance after ES-related negative incidents.

It seems that personal experiences and awareness matter, and when climate change intrudes into managers' lives, behaviors change. Di Giuli et al. (2022) studied how mutual fund managers changed their voting behavior on environmental proposals after being exposed to climate events. Their sample included 338,375 mutual fund votes on 1,728 ES proposals over the period 2006–18. The results suggested that there is significantly higher support for environmental proposals by funds whose managers were personally exposed to abnormally hot temperatures or were exposed to a major natural disaster.

KEY LEARNING POINT

Investors can influence companies on climate-related actions through many avenues. The Big Three have a particularly important role, given their increasing importance.

4.3.2 Proxy Advisors

Shareholders of public companies vote annually on board elections, management proposals, and shareholder proposals. The company's proxy statement and proxy card (ballot) must disclose all proposals anticipated to come before the shareholders at their annual meeting. A proxy vote is a delegation of voting authority to a representative of the original vote holder. The party that receives the authority to vote is known as the proxy, and the original vote holder is known as the principal. The concept is important in financial markets, and especially with public companies, as it allows groups of shareholders to exert greater influence by pooling their votes together.

Institutional investors invest in hundreds, and sometimes thousands, of companies. As most of them do not have dedicated teams that can adequately assess all the points to be voted in annual meetings, they rely on external help.[132] This is what is driving the rise of proxy voting advisors.

Proxy advisors are service providers that offer guidance to institutional investors on how to vote at the shareholder meetings. Some institutional investors mechanically follow a proxy advisor's voting recommendation, whereas others use it as just one input into the vote analysis process. Nowadays, there is an ongoing debate around the influence of proxy advisory firms on voting.

The two main voting advisors worldwide are Institutional Shareholder Services (ISS) and Glass Lewis. The clients of these two proxy advisory firms held approximately US$100 trillion worth of assets under management (AuM) worldwide in 2020. In the United States, these two firms controlled 97% of the market share as of 2019 (Mitchell and Tomson, 2020). ISS was founded in 1985 in Rockville. As of 2019, it had nearly 2,000 employees worldwide, advised more than 1,600 clients (i.e., asset managers, asset owners, and hedge funds), and covered more than 40,000 meetings each year (Herbst-Bayliss and Di Napoli, 2019). It generated more than US$280 million in net revenue in 2020. Glass Lewis is the second-largest provider of voting recommendations. It was founded in 2003 in San Francisco. It has approximately 400 employees worldwide, advises more than 1,300 investors, and covers more than 30,000 meetings each year.

The Role of Proxy Advisors

Active and passive investment funds use proxy advisors to guide their voting decisions at shareholder meetings. The rise in institutional investment is driving the increasing importance of these companies. Given the vast number of proposals to be examined and the scarcity of personnel in asset managers' corporate governance departments, the role of proxy advisors has become increasingly important. In particular, passive investment has gained significant importance in recent decades, through index funds or exchange-traded fund (ETFs). Given their low-cost structure, these funds have no time or resources to assess all the items being voted on an annual basis. Therefore, they increasingly rely on the recommendations of voting advisors. This is why it is important to understand how institutional voting advisors work, and how they arrive at their recommendations on climate-related issues.

Proxy advisors' recommendations carry a lot of weight, and so the management of a company typically likes to have advisors on its side. In particular, there is an alignment between proxy advisors' recommendations and the Big Three index funds' voting. That is, in most cases, institutional investors vote in line with proxy advisors' recommendations. In some cases, they blindly follow the proxy advisors and vote along with their

---

[132] Institutional investors have a stewardship responsibility to promote the interests of their clients and ultimate beneficiaries. Therefore, in pursuit of those goals, they typically vote in company shareholder meetings.

recommendations. For example, Rose (2021) documented the practice of "robovoting," a practice in which institutional investors automatically follow the advisors' voting recommendations. He showed that 114 institutional investors with more than $5 trillion of AuM voted with 99.5% alignment with ISS (or Glass Lewis) in 2020.

Table 4.3 Robovoting totals in 2020: "For" recommendations

Alignment with ISS	Number of institutional investors	AuM (US$ billion)	Number of resolutions
100.0%	44	1,184	43,466
99.9%	62	1,663	58,019
99.8%	87	4,421	82,875
99.7%	95	4,537	88,811
99.6%	105	4,722	94,880
99.5%	114	5,010	106,450

Source: Rose (2021).

Overall, it seems that the Big Three align more with the proxy advisors on "For" recommendations than on "Against" recommendations. For instance, BlackRock votes for recommendations provided by ISS 87.9% of the time, but the alignment with "Against" votes is lower (69.2%).

Table 4.4 Large institutions' alignment with ISS and Glass Lewis recommendations

Investor	"For" recommendations with ISS	"Against" recommendations with ISS	"For" recommendations with Glass Lewis	"Against" recommendations with Glass Lewis
BlackRock	87.9%	69.2%	83.0%	51.7%
State Street	88.2%	80.3%	80.2%	62.3%
Vanguard	86.4%	59.5%	82.4%	44.4%

Source: Council for Capital Formation, 2017–2018.

How They Assess Environmental Topics

Proxy advisors play an extremely influential role in shaping corporate governance by helping institutional investors decide how to vote for their shares. When assessing climate-related factors for proxy voting, ISS provides its view on a company's GHG emissions, climate strategy, and the impact of its activities on climate, putting these into context within its sector. In particular, ISS evaluates a company's climate-related performance on the following aspects:

- ○ Climate norm violations: Violations of globally recognized climate norms, including lobbying against climate actions.

- o Transparency: This includes many climate disclosure indicators aligned with the Task Force on Climate-related Financial Disclosures (TCFD) disclosure requirements, including Scopes 1–3 GHG emissions.
- o Current performance indicators: This includes GHG emissions data.
- o Future performance indicators: Climate targets, measures and strategies to reduce the carbon footprint, and the level of preparation for the carbon transition.

These ISS guidelines draw on the framework of the Task Force on Climate-related Financial Disclosures (see Section 6.3.3) and on other voluntary regulations at the global and regional levels. In cases of assessed underperformance on the key points listed above, ISS's Climate Policy will provide relevant information, flags, and voting recommendations.

The proxy voting guidelines also address corporate governance and its links with sustainability, in particular, the board of directors and executive compensation. When assessing the case for the election or reelection of the board of directors (or an individual director), ISS generally recommends voting for executive or non-executive nominees. However, if the company has not adequately addressed, managed, and reported climate-related risks, and/or failed to improve climate-related performance, ISS will typically recommend voting against an individual director or the entire board (see the example of the ISS recommendation after the Volkswagen's emissions scandal, Dieselgate).

KEY LEARNING POINT

Proxy advisors can recommend voting against individual directors, or even the full board, in the case of companies embroiled in environmental controversies or those that have no defined climate strategy.

Glass Lewis has its own Climate Policy Guidelines, which also draw on the TCFD and consider the size of the company and its industry. Each company's unique risk profile is informed by data from the Sustainability Accounting Standards Board (SASB) and whether it is included in the Climate Action 100+. In addition, Glass Lewis applies more rigorous standards for companies with significant GHG emissions and higher exposures to climate-related risks.

Below are some additional examples of proxy advisors' recommendations related to climate issues:

- o In 2017, ISS recommended voting for a shareholder resolution requesting Exxon to provide more information on the impact that climate change regulation could have on its business.
- o In 2019, ISS and Glass Lewis supported a resolution, filed by a group of more than 8,700 Amazon employees, asking Amazon to publish a report on plans to reduce

company-wide dependence on fossil fuels and prioritize climate impact in business decisions.

- o In 2021, ISS and Glass Lewis released their updated proxy voting guidelines on ESG resolutions. Glass Lewis will generally recommend (for all industries) voting for shareholder proposals that request enhanced disclosures on climate-related issues, such as (1) a scenario analysis or a report consistent with the recommendations of the TCFD and (2) climate-related lobbying.
- o In 2021, ISS and Glass Lewis recommended voting for a shareholder resolution that called for Berkshire Hathaway's board to report on how the company plans to manage climate-related risks and opportunities.

Proxy advisors, Dieselgate, and the board of directors

In September 2015, the U.S. Environmental Protection Agency (EPA) discovered that Volkswagen cars sold in the United States were equipped with a special device capable of manipulating CO_2 emissions when the car engine was being tested. This trick had allowed Volkswagen to circumvent the Clean Air Act (a federal law designed to curb carbon dioxide and other GHG emissions in U.S. territory). The EPA found that 482,000 Volkswagen cars were emitting up to 40 times more GHGs than permitted by federal law. The German company later admitted to having installed those devices in 11 million cars, cheating on GHG emissions worldwide. In 2018, Martin Winterkorn—former Volkswagen CEO—was charged by German prosecutors, and the Volkswagen Group and its two luxury brands, Audi and Porsche, were fined a total of €2.3 billion. Overall, since the scandal first broke in 2015, Volkswagen has been sentenced to pay out more than €30 billion in fines, compensation, and vehicle buyback schemes worldwide.

Electrification and board of directors' approval following Dieselgate were the two biggest topics discussed at the shareholder AGM held in May 2019. In light of the scandal, which also led to a cut in annual dividends, ISS and Glass Lewis recommended voting against the approval of all the executives and the members of the supervisory board directly involved in the scandal.

In its statement, ISS declared: "We believe they may be held responsible as board members for material failures of governance, stewardship, risk oversight, and fiduciary responsibilities at the company." Similarly, Glass Lewis recommended voting against all board members, with the exception of one, Stefan Sommer, who had joined the company only in July 2018.

Not all the voting recommendations were in favor of "climate-friendly" resolutions. For instance, in 2018, activist shareholder Follow-This filed a climate change proposal at Royal Dutch Shell. ISS and Glass Lewis recommended that shareholders vote against the resolution, and it received only 5.54% of the votes. Two years later, ISS supported Follow-This request that Shell set and publish their targets for GHG emissions. Also in 2018, ISS and Glass Lewis were heavily criticized for not supporting a resolution at Rio Tinto calling for increased transparency regarding its climate lobbying activities.

Similarly, in 2021, Glass Lewis backed Shell's climate plan and recommended to vote against a shareholder resolution filed by Follow-This asking the oil giant to set stricter targets for the reduction of GHG emissions.

These examples highlight the important role of their policies, which were only recently published (ISS, 2021; Glass Lewis, 2020). According to their policies on climate change, both ISS and Glass Lewis recommend "For" proposals that improve the disclosure of a company's climate change strategies. In the case of proposals for GHG emission reductions, or setting goals for GHG reductions (transition plan), they are determined on a case-by-case basis. Proxy advisors may recommend against proposals if they believe the existing climate policies sufficiently address the request or the proposal (see the Hello Fresh case in Section 4.3.4), or if they are inconsistent with long-term shareholder value creation.

The case-by-case analysis takes into account the materiality of the subject, as well as the feasibility of the proposed transition. If, for instance, at a bank's AGM, a shareholder proposal exists that aims to ban air travel by bank employees, this will most likely elicit a negative reaction from proxy advisors. Indeed, travel-related CO_2 emissions are not likely to be material for a bank. That is, there are much more relevant ways in which a bank contributes to the climate transition (see Section 6.3.2 for a discussion on materiality and the reporting of key climate risks).

Additional Research on Proxy Advisors

The increasing relevance of proxy advisory firms in shaping proxy voting and the controversies around them have been investigated in the academic literature.

McCahery et al. (2016) surveyed a sample of institutional investors and found that more than 60% used proxy advisors, and believed that their information improves the quality of their voting decisions.

Cai et al. (2009) analyzed director elections and found that ISS played a strong role in the outcome of elections. Iliev and Lowry (2015) showed that proxy advisory firms controlled a sizable share of voting power and exerted a large influence on governance practices. Larcker et al. (2015) found that proxy advisory firm recommendations significantly impacted say-on-pay voting outcomes. Malenko and Shen (2016) found that ISS exerted a strong effect on shareholder votes: relative to positive recommendations, negative ISS recommendations reduced the percentage of votes in favor of say-on-pay proposals by about 25 percentage points. Further, the influence of ISS was stronger in firms with large institutional ownership.

Shu (2022) raised concerns about mutual funds' practice of "robo-voting" in the United States during 2006–17, and reported two findings. On the one hand, proxy advisors' recommendations had a substantial impact on shareholders' voting in director elections and say-on-pay proposals. On the other hand, proxy advisors catered to investors' preferences, adjusting their recommendations to align with fund preferences independent of whether those adjustments led to recommendations that maximized firm value.

Due to the increasing influence of proxy advisory firms, questions have been raised about the accuracy and transparency of their recommendations, and possible conflicts of interest. This is particularly important when an advisor may sell services to both investors and issuers. Li (2018) showed that ISS favored management with which it had a consulting relationship. This biased advice by proxy advisors has real negative consequences that allow management to enjoy greater private benefits. The results also suggest that increasing competition could help alleviate these conflicts of interest.

Changing recommendations: Axcelis and ISS

In May 2012, ISS recommended that shareholders vote against the Equity Incentive Plan proposed by Axcelis Technologies, a manufacturer of capital equipment for the global semiconductor industry. A week after the meeting, Axcelis received a marketing call from an ISS representative, who suggested that the management could use their consulting services prior to filing a proxy proposal to have a certain degree of assurance about ISS's voting recommendation. By offering consulting products to an issuer, as the ISS representative attempted to do in the Axcelis case, a proxy advisor may encourage the company to "purchase consulting services from the proxy advisory firm in an effort to garner the firm's support for the issuer when the voting recommendations are made," and ultimately offer biased recommendations to its consulting clients.

KEY LEARNING POINT

Like other financial market intermediaries, proxy advisors are subject to potential conflict of interest problems.

In July 2020, the U.S. SEC adopted tighter regulation of proxy advisory firms. They will need to include additional conflict of interest disclosure in their recommendation materials. They will also provide their recommendation to the company no later than to the proxy advisory firms' clients. Further, proxy advisors should provide access to responses by the company to the recommendations.

4.3.3 The Role of the Board vis-à-vis Climate Change

The board of directors is responsible for defending the interests of shareholders and supervising the company's management. Charities, private companies, and nonprofit organizations may all have a board of directors. Only publicly traded companies, however, are legally required to set up a board of directors.

The exact structure of the board varies across countries, with two key models being used:

- o One-tier board: It is a single body of directors that makes the key decisions of a company. It is composed of both executive directors and non-executive directors.
- o Two-tier board: The company has two distinct boards: a management board and a supervisory board. The management board runs the day-to-day affairs of the company, has executive powers for operational decisions, and is accountable to the supervisory board. The supervisory board focuses on supervising the management, and also examines key long-term strategic decisions.

In what follows, we simply refer to the "Board," which denotes the entity that is responsible for overall supervision and long-term decisions, without distinguishing between the two types of board described above.

The board is typically tasked with a number of responsibilities, including the following:

- o Approving the annual accounts, dividend policies, and major changes to capital structure
- o Hiring and firing senior executives (especially the CEO)
- o Monitoring performance
- o Overseeing the management of risk
- o Establishing compensation for executives
- o Reviewing and approving major corporate objectives, budgets, and business plans
- o Protecting the rights of minority shareholders
- o Monitoring compliance with applicable laws and regulations

The Board's Role in Climate Issues

One of the board's most important responsibilities is the management of long-term risk. Climate change poses unique challenges for boards, as it affects the company in multiple ways: consumers, suppliers, financing and capital market changes, technological changes, business model disruption, regulatory risk, etc.

As concerns about climate risks have increased, investors and regulators are also demanding greater disclosure of these risks, and boards that ignore climate risks may be vulnerable to shareholder actions. Ultimately, neglecting climate change risks and opportunities can be considered a failure of fiduciary duty.

There are clear trends in company's agendas. PwC (2020) surveyed approximately 700 board members of large corporations, and 45% confirmed that climate and other ESG issues are a regular part of the board's agenda.

Many investors expect boards to be involved in their companies' climate transition and demonstrate a solid understanding of climate issues. For instance, a growing number of large institutional investors are submitting shareholder resolutions calling for companies to appoint a board member with environmental or climate expertise. In addition, boards are being pressured to be more climate-competent. Some of the issues relevant to this include the following:

- o Ensure that their composition (and that of the executive team) is sufficiently diverse to incorporate expertise on climate-related threats and opportunities.
- o Ensure that the executive team assesses climate risks and opportunities, and their materiality, on an ongoing basis.
- o Guarantee that material climate-related risks are transparently disclosed to all stakeholders.
- o Integrate climate change effectively into risk management, strategic planning, and internal decision-making processes.
- o Ensure that incentives are aligned with the long-term interests of the company.
- o Engage with shareholders and other stakeholders on climate issues.

BlackRock's Global Principles

In January 2020, BlackRock published the "Global Principles" that guide its investment stewardship. BlackRock supports boards that effectively manage strategic, operational, and material ESG factors. This includes the disclosure of material issues that affect the company's long-term value creation potential, and how the board is effectively identifying, managing, and mitigating risks. BlackRock assesses director performance taking into consideration the assessment of sustainable business practices and performance. For instance, BlackRock considers not supporting the re-election of directors if a company does not adequately disclose its strategy and commitment to sustainability, as they are considered accountable for this lapse.

Board Committees

Given the importance of climate-related concerns for their long-term future, some companies have also considered introducing a sustainability committee. Sustainability committees are generally set up within the board of directors with the aim of providing information and advising the company's management on sustainability-related issues.[133] A few examples of these committees are the following:

- o Shell: One of the four board committees is the Safety, Environment and Sustainability Committee. It reviews and advises on sustainability policies and practices to ensure that these are discussed, understood, and promoted at the board level. The committee is made up of a chairman and four members.
- o Nestlé: The Nomination and Sustainability Committee (NSC) periodically reviews the company's sustainability strategy. The board appoints the Chair (independent)

---

[133] The positive association between the presence of sustainability committees within the Board of Directors and the company's environmental performance is confirmed by Burke et al. (2019).

and the members of the NSC for a period of one year. The other members include the Chair of the Board and at least two independent non-executive board members.

o Unilever: The Corporate Responsibility Committee has oversight of Unilever's policies as a responsible corporate citizen, and comprises a minimum of two non-executive directors.

KEY LEARNING POINT

Some boards set up special environment-related committees, composed mostly of independent board members.

4.3.4 Executive Compensation

The board of directors is typically responsible for hiring and firing senior executives, monitoring their performance, and establishing compensation mechanisms. The overall idea is to ensure that the incentives are aligned with the long-term interests of the company.

Most boards have a special Compensation Committee, or a Compensation and Nominations Committee, made up of a subset of board members who define the key principles underlying executive compensation.

The important features of an effective executive compensation scheme include the following:

o Linked to long-term value creation
o Simple and transparent
o Linked to performance and promotes accountability
o Balances short- and long-run objectives

The structure of the executive compensation scheme is very important. Complex, opaque bonuses linked only to short-run targets can encourage misguided behaviors, such as cutting R&D or investment to meet short-term financial targets.

Paying a significant portion of executives' earnings as long-term equity is a simple and yet effective compensation mechanism. It helps align the incentives of managers with those of the shareholders (who care about long-term value).[134] In addition, in the long run, the value of a company captures the effects of the company on stakeholders as well (see Section 5.3).

---

[134] Fernandes et al. (2013) analyzed international executive pay for firms in 14 countries with mandated disclosure rules and found that the U.S. pay premium is mostly explained by differences in ownership and governance. In particular, the premium reflects the higher performance-based compensation demanded by institutional shareholders and independent boards of the more widely held U.S. firms.

Rejection of HelloFresh remuneration package

HelloFresh is a German publicly traded food retailer whose main service is a subscription-based plan involving the delivery of all the ingredients needed for a meal to customers (meal kits), who then cook the meal themselves (with the help of the provided recipe cards). In 2020, it delivered more than 600 million meals and had revenues of €3.8 billion and a market capitalization of €12 billion.

The company set internal goals of reducing its environmental impact by lowering carbon emissions by 60% (per euro of revenue) and reducing food waste by 50% (per euro of revenue) for 2019–22. Food waste in 2019 was 1,103 metric tons, and the company reported CO_2 emissions of 53,100 metric tons.

In the new proposed compensation plan presented to shareholders, HelloFresh would have three-year targets starting in 2021 in four areas: revenue, EBITDA, CO_2 emission reduction, and food waste reduction.

However, this inclusion of ESG elements in the compensation structure did not convince shareholders and voting advisors. Indeed, the ISS proxy promptly recommended against this package before the annual meeting. In its May 2021 AGM, shareholders rejected (55% against) the proposed management compensation package. Some of the key reasons for the shareholders' misgivings were the discretionary nature of the bonuses and targets, the lack of disclosure of the targets underlying the plan, and the possibility of giving bonuses if ESG targets were met without meeting the financial targets. The majority of shareholders did not like the fact that management could receive long-term rewards if not all targets had been met (for instance, if revenues and EBITDA fell, but the amount of food waste declined).

ESG incentives have become a critical issue for compensation committees around the world, and their adoption has more than doubled since 2018. There is increasing evidence that boards (and investors) are demanding changes in compensation metrics:

- Almost 20% of companies have at least one E&S incentive (ISS, 2021).
- Some activist funds (e.g., Cevian Capital) have announced that they will ask all investee companies to set out their ESG strategies and link them to compensation.
- Willis Tower Watson (2021) surveyed 338 board members in Europe and the United States on the use of ESG metrics in executive incentive plans. Energy, utilities, and materials are the sectors that more commonly use ESG metrics, and they typically account for 15%–20% of the total executive compensation.

These practices are still taking shape, as there is no universally agreed way of linking executive pay with sustainability considerations. Environmental metrics are more commonly employed in energy and materials businesses, but they are also starting to appear in other sectors that are increasingly concerned with the environment. When adopted, the specific KPIs that are used differ among firms:

- Apple: It introduced a 10% weight on executive bonuses related to "Apple Values," which include issues such as education, environment, diversity, privacy, and supplier responsibility.
- BP: It uses ESG measures in its annual bonus and long-term incentive plan (LTIP, also known as long-term share awards). The bonus has a 15% safety and emissions

reduction weight, and the LTIP has a 40% energy transition (renewables, car electrification, etc.) weight.

- o Danone: Twenty percent of its executives' annual variable compensation is linked to social (10%) and environmental (10%) targets. Further, its long-term share awards are based on climate scores over three consecutive years.
- o National Grid: It ties executive compensation to the company's GHG reductions.
- o Rio Tinto: It realigned its short-term incentive plan to include a 15% ESG weight.
- o Siemens: It links long-term stock awards to its "sustainability index," which is based on reduction of CO_2 emissions, training hours per employee, and customer satisfaction.

Shell: compensation tied to climate targets

In 2017, Shell announced its plan to reduce its carbon emissions by 20% by 2035 and by 50% by 2050. A group of institutional investors (led by Robeco and the Church of England Pensions Board) engaged with the board of directors to demand the incorporation of the carbon targets into the executive compensation schemes of the company.

In December 2018, Shell announced its intention to link the annual bonus for executive compensation to the reduction of carbon emissions. In 2020, the company confirmed the scorecard structure of bonus payments to executive directors based on the performance recorded in three managerial areas for the period 2020–23: financial performance (30%), operational excellence (50%), and sustainable development measures (20%). Thus, 20% of the annual bonus paid to executive directors was linked to the sustainability (10%) and safety (10%) performance of the company.

Financial performance is measured by the cash flow from operating activities. Operational excellence combines several output indicators, plant availability, and project delivery. The metrics are decided by the Safety, Environment and Sustainability Committee, which in 2019 replaced the Corporate and Social Responsibility Committee.

In 2021, Shell updated its annual bonus scoreboard, and "sustainability" was replaced with the more explicit measure "Progress in the Energy Transition," which accounted for 15% of the annual bonus. Progress in the Energy Transition includes two metrics: GHG abatement (carbon footprint) and management of the transition.

KEY LEARNING POINT

Executive compensation arrangements can include criteria related to the achievement of prespecified climate goals

Long-Term Goals and Sustainability Issues

Overall, it is clear that ESG should be linked to the company strategy and reported transparently (see Section 6.3). However, does it need to be separately measured for the purpose of executive pay?

Companies may respond to pressures from various stakeholders by taking ESG into consideration when determining executive compensation. However, linking ESG and compensation can be a tricky exercise. It could result in distorted incentives, in which executives are paid bonuses despite the lack of sustainable long-term performance. What in theory sounds interesting and natural can in practice prove to be very complex and even counterproductive.

Section 5.3 reviews the evidence underlying ESG and firm performance. Several papers have found that companies with strong ESG credentials typically have greater profitability and value, which is sometimes referred to as *"doing well by doing good."*

This has important implications for the design of compensation systems. If sustainability considerations do translate into better company performance and improved long-term value, it can be argued that traditional compensation systems that rely on stock awards can be good systems for ensuring that the interests of managers and shareholders will be in sync and that the right sustainability decisions will be made. That is, if ESG improves financial performance, executives will be indirectly rewarded for decisions that improve the company's sustainability.

It is important to remember that when managers have long-term equity incentives (long-dated vested stocks, for instance), they will obviously need to incorporate future-profitability considerations into their decision-making. This will require them to expand their thinking beyond short-run performance and embrace broader considerations. So, it should be clear why for any compensation plan that includes an ESG component in its long-term incentives, the goals would not be achieved by simply giving executives long-term vesting stock. Vesting stocks induce managers' to consider the long-run impact of their decisions on firm value, including how they promote innovation, environmental goals, and the likely reactions of customers, employees, society, etc.

In this case, boards are not required to include an ESG component in executives' compensation. Alternatively, what companies could do is to have a significant long-term incentive plan that is mostly composed of restricted share awards. In this case, executives could have a long-term holding requirement (or vesting) of at least 5 years, and that could actually go beyond the executive's tenure in the company. In this case, the executive would naturally have her compensation exposed to the long-term company performance.

Companies that want to include ESG metrics should clearly explain why they are relevant for their business and the rationale for linking them to executive pay. They should carefully consider and explain why a more traditional incentive plan based on shares would not suffice. That is why it is important to think about additionality, that is, what are possible reasons and likely benefits of having sustainability issues included in compensation design that cannot be achieved through long-term stock rewards. In certain cases, these could be the following:

- When top managers are compensated for sustainable goals, they could more easily cascade down throughout the company, thus leading to a more coherent strategy (Teti et al., 2012). Once managers have their own remuneration tied to ESG issues, they will have further incentives to integrate these factors at all levels within the company. At lower levels in the organization, the share price is a less relevant incentive metric.
- Priorities can be more easily communicated internally and externally. Companies can use ESG-linked compensation to signal commitment and improve their external credibility, while mobilizing the organization internally. As in the above example of Shell (see the box above titled "Shell: compensation tied to climate targets"), the new targets for executives are also a way to signal and mobilize the new priorities across the whole company.
- Sustainability actions and investments may take a very long time to be reflected in a company's performance and value, and thus a more reasonable time horizon for incentives is needed. For instance, in an oil company, the energy transition is a long-term initiative, and its success will take many decades to materialize. In this case, it may make sense to include some environment-related KPIs that capture the evolution of that transition in executive compensation.

Obviously, introducing ESG targets in compensation plans makes the targets more important for executives. It is key that the chosen ESG metrics be aligned with strategy and focus on the big material issues for the company.

First, setting the right target is important. To do this, the board must be aware of the ESG issues that are under the control of the management and, above all, their importance and materiality. For instance, a bank that introduces a compensation target related to its Level 1 emissions (that is, related to its own actual carbon footprint) is missing the point. The biggest difference that a bank can make is through its financing activities. A bank's sustainable financing policy affects the companies that use the loans obtained to emit (more or less) carbon.

Also, multi-factor executive compensation schemes risk distorting incentives. Focusing on a very narrow ESG issue can distract the board, and the management, from the broader objectives and capabilities.

In addition, the introduction of ESG factors in compensation must be aligned with the company's strategic goals.[135] But they must be realistic targets that are neither impossible to reach (e.g., an oil company that pays a CEO bonus if the company stops extracting oil the next year) nor too easy (e.g., stop producing oil in the most expensive extracting locations).

Some other important topics that must be considered are the following:

o Should ESG goals be measured using inputs or outputs? Input are activities that companies engage in internally (e.g., 60% of travel to be done by train). Outputs are related to external targets, which are relevant for stakeholders, such as the carbon footprint per employee. Decarbonization metrics can be output based (GHG reductions) or input based (% investments in renewables, or the adoption of a certain percentage of renewable energy sources).

o Soft targets, without clear-cut quantification, are not advisable (e.g., reduce our carbon footprint). Instead, companies should provide hard targets supported by clear quantification (e.g., a 15% reduction in CO_2 Level 3 emissions over the next three years). Hard targets, with clear time horizons and definition of milestones, are more effective for achieving ESG improvements than soft targets.

o Clarify why there is the need to link compensation to ESG targets and why the previous (or alternative) compensation mechanisms do not work. It seems logical that environmental issues are well suited for long-term incentives. However, having very vague long-term objectives (e.g., transformational objectives such as "Be Net Zero by 2040") has to be balanced with ambitious, yet realistic, annual targets (e.g., reduction in Scope 3 CO_2 as a percentage of sales).

o How to track and measure the progress of KPIs? Having a multidimensional scorecard that covers everything (employee satisfaction, customers, carbon emissions, diversity, supply chain, financial performance, etc.) can add complexity, and ultimately become unmanageable.

o Avoid gaming/greenwashing.[136] ESG targets are difficult to assess, and different ratings lead to different conclusions. There is no standardized set of ESG metrics. Therefore, it is important to be clear on the reason why a certain metric is used.

---

[135] Masulis and Reza (2015) suggested that we should be careful about possible sustainability-related agency problems. Their evidence suggests that some managers may use corporate donations to advance their personal interests and that the misuse of corporate resources reduces firm value.

[136] Berrone and Gomez-Mejia (2009) investigated the impact of linking executive compensation and environmental performance in polluting industries. They found that sometimes these executive compensation mechanisms are purely symbolic, and amount to greenwashing when firms signal that they are concerned with the environment but take no concrete steps in that direction.

    o   ESG targets should be part of LTIPs. Tackling sustainability issues typically requires long time horizons,[137] which is particularly true in the case of climate-related issues.

    o   Materiality is key. It is important to identify the key ESG value drivers that are relevant for each company. There is not a single set of universally applicable metrics; they differ by company and industry (see Section 6.3 for more details on the concept of materiality).

4.3.5 Summary – Governance

In this section, we have reviewed some governance topics that are influenced by climate issues.

We started by reviewing the importance of shareholder voting. An important aspect related to voting is the role of proxy advisors, which are organizations that provide recommendations to institutional investors on how to vote on different proposals at companies' general meetings. This is not a very competitive industry, similar to what is observed with credit rating agencies. The two major proxy advisory firms, Institutional Shareholder Services (ISS) and Glass Lewis, hold most of the industry market share.

Given the rising weight of passive investors in capital markets, we have observed the increasing influence of proxy advisory firms on corporate practices worldwide. Their recommendations influence the votes of many substantial asset managers, including most mutual funds and ETFs. The empirical evidence also shows that their recommendations are quite correlated.

Historically, proxy advisors focused on corporate governance topics, such as board independence and executive compensation. More recently, they have been focusing on environmental issues as well. The range of environmental issues upon which they provide recommendations is large: disclosure policies, lobbying activities, level of carbon emissions, the company's transition strategy, and how the board has been linking ESG to executive compensation.

In this section, we also discussed the board's role in climate and sustainability issues. This is increasingly becoming an important responsibility for corporate boards, but we still observe wide variation in how these issues are handled in different companies.

We have discussed some of the issues that a climate-competent board needs to be aware of to do its job properly. Risk management is a very traditional board role, and therefore

---

[137] Flammer et al. (2019) found that ESG metrics in compensation are associated with an increase in long-term orientation and undertaken ESG initiatives. However, this is just a correlation, and it can actually signal the reverse: companies that are long-term oriented are more focused on ESG activities, and thus more likely to include it in their compensation systems.

corporate boards need to understand climate-related threats and opportunities to prepare their companies for the long term.

Some important issues include the board's role in ensuring that the executive team properly discloses material climate-related risks to all stakeholders. In addition, the board plays an important role in fostering the integration of climate change into risk management, guaranteeing that climate issues are integrated into strategic planning, the business model, and internal decision-making.

There is wide variation in how companies structure their corporate boards. This applies to climate-related topics as well; some companies have special board committees that focus on sustainability topics.

Another typical role of a corporate board is to ensure that incentives are aligned with the long-term interests of the company, considering its various stakeholders. Executive compensation and sustainability are important discussions at the board level. However, what seems obvious and simple may actually be unsubstantiated and complex, with potential side effects or unintended consequences.

Compensation structures should focus on long-term value creation and avoid the unintended consequences associated with pay structures that are complex, lack transparency, and reduce the level of scrutiny. Introducing ESG into compensation can become a tick-the-box exercise, increasing complexity with no corresponding value addition. Board members must seriously consider the challenges associated with selecting proper targets, evaluate alternative compensation structures, and think clearly about not only the overall benefits but also the possible side effects.

4.4   SHAREHOLDER ACTIVISM AND ENGAGEMENT

In this section, we focus on activism related to environmental topics. The term *shareholder activism* refers to a range of activities undertaken by one or more shareholders in a publicly traded corporation, who use their equity stake to influence the target company's behavior. In general, shareholder activism refers to the activities of shareholders who seek a significant change in a company's strategy, financial structure, management, or board composition.

Over the past decade, activist shareholders have gained substantial importance. Despite owning typically small shareholding positions, their impact can be large. Activist investors engage with companies across a number of domains, including dividend policy and buybacks, executive compensation, portfolio management, and conglomerate underperformance. But increasingly, we are seeing the rise of activism focusing on environmental issues. This includes campaigns related to additional disclosure, capital expenditures, and portfolio management.

The role of activist shareholders in markets has increased. Most recently, activists have been targeting management on environmental topics, and policy priorities related to climate change have given rise to several shareholder campaigns. Overall, climate issues are becoming more relevant across the different corporate governance domains.

4.4.1 The Role of Activist Investors

The role of shareholders in corporate governance has evolved over time. The rise of public companies traded on Wall Street during the early 1900s was characterized by widespread ownership of individual investors. Therefore, the theoretical framework of corporate governance was represented by the theory of Berle and Means (1932) and was based on the separation between ownership and control. In this corporate management structure, the board of directors managed the company independently while a large number of small shareholders were simply the dividend-earner owners of the company. Today, corporate shareholders no longer fit this theoretical framework and have instead become empowered, largely because of the concentration of equity ownership, which has continued to increase since the 1990s (and the rise of institutional investors, who nowadays own more than 70% of the shares of most publicly traded companies).

Activist investors are relatively new – but very influential – players in international capital markets. They are shareholders of publicly traded companies who attempt to effect change in an organization either by directly appealing to, or putting heavy pressure on, the company's board of directors and management.

Shareholder activism has existed for a long time. Its concept originated in the United States during the 1970s and 1980s. Corporate raiders wanted to acquire businesses or take controlling positions with the aim of reshaping or dismantling those businesses. Famous activist investors such as T. Boone Pickens and Carl Icahn targeted well-known publicly listed U.S. companies such as Gulf Oil and TWA. The firms that activists targeted tended to underperform relative to their industry.

Due to their aggressive attitude toward management and hostile approaches to making short-term profits, they were often perceived negatively as "corporate raiders," "green mailers," or "asset strippers."

However, activism has beneficial effects. Academic research shows that share prices and the operating performance of the targeted companies often improved.

Today's shareholder activism is different. The goals are more often to unleash or create value without a change in control and do so by leveraging a small ownership percentage, generally 3% to 5%. Activist shareholders are usually fund managers (mainly hedge funds) who acquire minority stakes in publicly traded companies and then engage with the boards of the companies to influence corporate strategy while generating profits for themselves and other shareholders.

Table 4.5 World's 10 largest activist hedge funds in 2021

Company	Assets under management
Elliot Management	$41.8 billion
Third Point Partners	$21 billion
Cevian Capital	$13.5 billion
ValueAct Capital Partners	$12.3 billion
Starboard Value	$6.1 billion
Saba Capital Management	$3.3 billion
Sachem Head Capital Management	$2.8 billion
Amber Capital	$1.6 billion
Asset Value Investors	$1.3 billion
Oasis Management	$ 226 million

Source: Activist Investing Annual Review 2021, and funds' Web pages.

The motivations of activist investors are varied. Target firms usually have some of these characteristics:

○ Stock price underperformance
○ Non-transparent processes, especially in capital allocation
○ Undervalued stock prices compared to industry peers
○ Conglomerates misallocating capital
○ M&A transactions where synergies are difficult to find
○ Executive compensation not consistent with performance
○ Problems with corporate governance and management composition

Activist investors try to bring about change in several ways.[138] They often attempt to

○ bring in new management teams,
○ create operational efficiencies,
○ impose financial restructuring,
○ divest by selling off assets,
○ prevent value destruction through M&As,
○ break up conglomerates and focus on the core business, and
○ replace management and members of the board of directors.

Activist funds also engage with other shareholders, such as passive investors, to gain their support for the changes they advocate. Usually, their first step is to gather a coalition of like-

---

[138] Lazard (2020) surveyed global trends in shareholder activism and showed that, in 2020, the key objectives were M&A (34% of the campaigns), board change (34%), operational improvements (20%), and management change (7%).

minded investors, such as pension funds or other asset managers, who want to see greater returns on their investments.

Activist shareholders can conduct "voting-no" campaigns where they withhold their votes from one or more of the nominated director candidates. The most aggressive attacks can come in the form of loud media campaigns against management, attempting to force their hand through public pressure on specific issues.

KEY LEARNING POINT

Activist investors use various tactics to try to bring about concrete changes in the invested company.

Elliott Management and Evergy

In October 2019, the activist hedge fund Elliott Management Corp attempted to engage on a private basis with the board of the U.S. Midwest utility owner, Evergy, to demand changes in corporate strategy. In response to Elliott's demand, Evergy opted to make defensive changes in its corporate governance.

In January 2020, the New-York-based hedge fund disclosed a US$760 million stake in Evergy and pressed the firm to question its leadership or consider the possibility of a merger.

In its letter to the board, the hedge fund saw the possibility of rectifying the prolonged underperformance by implementing a new business strategy that might benefit shareholders, consumers, employees, and the whole community its utilities served. In particular, Elliott saw an opportunity to increase investment for deploying renewables and reducing its carbon footprint. As part of the settlement closed in March 2020, Elliott earned two seats on Evergy's board, giving shareholders the assurance that corporate strategy would be changed. In particular, under the influence of the directors appointed by Elliott, Evergy expects to increase capital spending by approximately US$9 billion through 2024 and expand clean energy power with the objective of slashing CO_2 emissions by 85% by 2030.

The ultimate objective is to achieve results and bring about the desired changes, and so they frequently prefer engagement with companies to public fights with them. Activist shareholders prefer not to have proxy fights, through which shareholders decide by voting and that are costly both in time and resources. They typically prefer to negotiate to achieve their objectives rather than subjecting them to a vote.

4.4.2 Empirical Evidence on Activists

The United States is the most developed market for activist hedge funds. Within Europe, the United Kingdom, whose corporate rules, governance, and political environment are closest to that of the United States, has accounted for around half of the activists' activity, but activism is also rising in France, Germany, and Switzerland (Deloitte, 2018).

Hundreds of companies worldwide, including very large ones such as General Motors, Dow Chemical, Nestlé, Apple, and Procter & Gamble, have been the target of activist investors in recent years:

- o   2013: Bill Ackman (Pershing Square Capital Management) forced Procter and Gamble CEO, Robert McDonald, to resign, by heavily criticizing his performance and promising higher stock prices under new management.
- o   2016: David Einhorn and Carl Icahn pressured Apple to return capital to shareholders (out of the company's cash reserves of more than US$150 billion).
- o   2017: Daniel Loeb (Third Point) targeted Nestlé's "strategic muddle." Third Point suggested several areas of improvement, including corporate restructuring, increased focus on efficiency, and divestiture of non-core assets.
- o   2020: Elliott ran a campaign to replace Twitter CEO, Jack Dorsey. Elliott argued that his double position as CEO of both Twitter and Square, as well as his plan to move to Africa, could divert his attention from managing Twitter properly.

These are just some examples. There is a large body of literature devoted to the study – with large samples – of how activist shareholders affect a firm's financial and operational performance.

The empirical evidence does not find substantial negative effects of shareholder activism. Rather, there is evidence that, in the most recent decades, activist involvement has had a significant positive impact on the targeted companies (Denes et al., 2017). The early research documented positive stock returns around the announcement of activism (Brav et al., 2008). Later, the body of evidence expanded from stock returns, and documented improvements in the target firms' values and operations (Bebchuk et al., 2015). Studies also found that activist hedge funds exert disciplinary pressure on management and boards, and that target firms experience increases in payout, operating performance, board restructurings, and higher CEO turnover after activism (Becht et al., 2008; Bebchuk et al., 2015; Becht et al., 2017). Others found that hedge fund intervention is associated with (1) higher labor productivity and profitability gains in the targeted companies (Brav et al., 2012, 2015); (2) improved monitoring of the management during M&As (Boyson et al., 2017); and (3) higher innovation output (Brav et al., 2018b; Tang, 2020).

Warren Buffet sums it up: "If every company were well managed, there would be no reason for activists. The truth is, at some companies, the managers forget who they're working for."

KEY LEARNING POINT

Despite the negative connotations, activist investors are typically associated with positive outcomes for the invested companies.

4.4.3 Collaboration – Active and Passive Investors

Activist investors typically hold small stakes in the company, and one of their first steps is to gain support from other investors and form a coalition of institutional investors. Examples are pension funds or other asset managers who want to see greater returns on their investments and share the activist's concerns. The rise of the big passive funds[139] gives activists a crucial advantage. The concentration of ownership in a few large passive funds means that an activist needs the support of just a few key voters to win a proxy contest. In this way, they can leverage their small positions and wield a much larger influence. Large-scale research supports this idea.

Engine No. 1 victory with Exxon Mobil

Engine No. 1 is an activist fund that aims to "create long-term value by driving positive impact through active ownership." In December 2020, Engine No. 1 announced that it proposed to change some top executives of Exxon Mobil. The Engine No. 1 campaign focused on Exxon's capital investments, lack of plans for the low-carbon transition, and the board's responsibility in this. They pointed out that Exxon was investing in new oil and gas reserves that would be profitable only at very high oil prices (much higher breakeven prices than those of their peers), which would lead to "reserves that could never be pumped out of the ground, as hydrocarbon demand shifted to clean energy alternatives." In addition, this fund complained that Exxon's peers were accelerating their investments in alternative energy technologies, whereas Exxon was taking only tentative steps. In particular, it stated that the Exxon's management's "refusal to accept that fossil fuel demand may decline in decades to come has led to a failure to take even initial steps towards evolution, and to obfuscating rather than addressing long-term business risk."

This fund was supported by prominent institutional investors, including large pension funds and the Big Three passive fund managers. Engine No. 1 succeeded in electing three (out of the four) candidates proposed for the board of Exxon.

---

[139] As discussed in Section 4.3.1, the largest index funds (the Big Three) are the largest single shareholder in almost all companies worldwide. However, despite the passive nature of their investment strategy, index funds have taken an active leading role in corporate governance, challenging management and voting against directors to make progress on different issues.

Appel et al. (2016) analyzed passive (mutual) funds holding shares in the companies in Russell 1000 and 2000 indices during 1998–2006 and showed that passive funds are not passive owners. Empirical evidence shows that ownership by passively managed mutual funds is associated with more independent directors on a board, fewer takeover defenses, and more equal voting rights (firms are less likely to have a dual-class share structure).

Appel et al. (2019) found that activists are more likely to seek board representation when a larger share of the target company's stock is held by passively managed mutual funds. Furthermore, higher passive ownership is associated with increased use of proxy fights, settlements, and a higher likelihood of the activist achieving board representation or the sale of the targeted company. On the other hand, Schmidt and Fahlenbrach (2017) found that increases in passive ownership are associated with fewer new independent director appointments.

> ### KEY LEARNING POINT
> *Activist investors frequently collaborate with passive investors to gain more support for their proposals.*

4.4.4 Environmental Activism

Up to now, we have discussed shareholder activism in general. Investors are increasingly embracing sustainability and becoming more active on climate issues. Since the Paris Agreement was signed, environmental activism aimed at influencing corporate strategies and minimizing climate risk exposures has been increasing.[140]

In the early days, environmental concerns were expressed only by climate activists such as Greenpeace. Nowadays, however, climate issues are increasingly relevant for institutional investors. From an investment perspective, ESG factors, especially those related to climate change, are seen as important drivers of portfolio risk and return. Further, institutional investors supported global agreements such as the Paris Agreement and the Sustainable Development Goals (Section 5.4).

Activist institutional investors increasingly ask portfolio companies to take action to reduce carbon dioxide emissions within the scope of the Paris Agreement, improve their disclosure around environmental topics, and properly integrate climate issues into their strategy and targets.

---

[140] See Dimson et al. (2015, 2021), Hong et al. (2020), and Krueger et al. (2020).

The early days: the battle between Shell and Greenpeace for the North Sea

In June 1995, Shell announced that it wanted to get rid of an oil platform, Brent Spar, by sinking it into the waters of the North Sea, for which Shell had received authorization from the British government. The platform weighed 1,450 metric tons and contained highly toxic and radioactive substances, which would seriously damage the flora and fauna of the North Sea. Shell justified the sinking economically, as dismantling the platform would cost £46 million, whereas the sinking into the sea would cost "only" £12 million.

Following Shell's declarations, the news spread in the European media. On June 11, Shell began to ferry the platform to the point established for its sinking, but Greenpeace used one of its boats to obstruct its plans. At the same time, Greenpeace Germany called on German motorists to boycott Shell gasoline stations. An opinion poll revealed that two out of three citizens in the country joined the boycott against Shell, and sales at gas stations dropped by 20% to 50%.

Despite the success of the boycott, Shell's management made it clear that it intended to complete the project, and also thanked the British government for its support. Meanwhile, Greenpeace reached the platform with a helicopter and, in front of the cameras, two men chained themselves to the platform.

After mid-June, the boycott spread to Sweden, Denmark, England, Spain, Luxembourg, and Belgium. Meanwhile, the Swedish Minister of the Environment, Anna Lindh, sent a letter to Shell in which she accused the corporation of being irresponsible. In an interview, the Swedish minister declared: "As a minister, I cannot tell citizens to boycott Shell but if I had a car, I would never fill up the tank on one of its stations and I don't think my collaborators would either." The Danish Minister of Environment asked his citizens directly to boycott Shell gasoline stations for refueling.

In the following days, Shell announced its decision to abandon the project of sinking the platform in the North Sea and requested permission from the British authorities to dismantle the platform on land. Andrew Viker—former Shell's vice-president for policy and external relations and at the time Shell's press officer—referring to this episode, which occurred in 1995, declared: "For Shell, it was about more than Brent Spar. Overplaying the legal card, underestimating the power of modern media tools and not seeing the deeper agenda are challenges that we work hard to address [...] The business model of the day was shown to have serious flaws, and many of the lessons remain applicable."

More than 140 climate-related shareholder proposals were filed during the 2020 U.S. proxy season.[141] Investors who filed or co-filed climate-related proposals include some of the largest U.S. public pension funds, state and city comptrollers' offices, labor pension funds, asset managers who specialize in ESG investing, religious investors, foundations, and individual investors. Some of these investors are also signatories to Climate Action 100+. A few other examples include the following:

  o BNP Paribas Asset Management requested Chevron's board of directors to conduct an evaluation and report if, and how, Chevron's lobbying activities align with the goal of limiting average global warming to well below 2 °C.
  o BNP Paribas Asset Management requested Delta Air Lines' board of directors to evaluate Delta's lobbying activities and its risks (and the plan to mitigate these risks).

---

[141] https://www.ceres.org/news-center/blog/how-climate-proposals-fared-during-2020-proxy-season.

o Mercy Investment Services requested United Airlines to assess the integration of concrete sustainability metrics into performance evaluation, goals, and vesting conditions, under United's incentive plans for its senior executives.

o Mercy Investment Services asked Pilgrim's Pride Corporation to report how the company plans to increase the scale, pace, and rigor of its efforts to reduce water pollution from its supply chain.

Climate Action 100+

Collaboration among institutional investors is increasingly common. Moreover, shareholders involved in campaigns are not only the activist shareholders; passive funds and institutional investors are also more willing to become involved in campaigns, whether publicly or privately.

Climate Action 100+ is an investor-led coalition of more than 450 international investors engaging with the world's largest corporate GHG emitters. In particular, they want to ensure that the world's largest GHG emitters implement the actions necessary to curb emissions and combat climate change.

Climate Action 100+ was informally founded in September 2016 during a meeting organized by the California Public Employees' Retirement System (CalPERS) at the French Mission to the UN. Then, following other meetings, Climate Action 100+ was officially launched at the One Planet Summit in Paris in December 2017. The list comprised 100 companies and 225 signatories.

Since then, more and more investors have joined Climate Action 100+. In January 2020, BlackRock—the world's largest asset manager—also joined the initiative, which now comprises 575 investors holding $55 trillion AuM. Companies that signed the initiative are estimated to account for more than 80% of global industrial emissions.

Figure 4.3 Climate-related shareholder resolutions in the United States

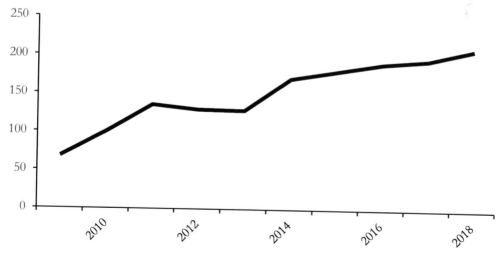

Source: Ceres.

KEY LEARNING POINT

Environmental activism campaigns are on the upswing globally, and many more institutional investors are getting involved in them.

Researchers have analyzed activist engagements that address ESG concerns. Barko et al. (2021) found that successful engagements are followed by positive stock returns. They also found that activists generally target large firms with large market shares, analyst coverage, stock returns, and liquidity. Dimson et al. (2015, 2021) also provided evidence that investor engagement in ESG issues is associated with positive abnormal returns, as well as improved accounting performance. Further, they documented that (1) success in engagements is more likely if the engaged firm has reputational concerns and greater capacity to implement changes; (2) collaboration among activists increases the success rate of environmental engagements; and (3) after successful engagements, institutional ownership goes up.

Others have studied the impact on firms' activities. Akey and Appel (2019) showed that hedge fund activism targeting companies' environmental behavior is associated with a 17% drop in chemical emissions at the plants of targeted firms. Naaraayanan et al. (2019) found similar results. Using plant-level data, they found that targeted firms reduce their total amount of toxic releases, production-related emissions, cancer-causing pollution, accidents, and legal risks through preventive efforts.

Importantly, research has shown that not all interventions are equally relevant. Grewal et al. (2016) found that the filing of shareholder proposals is related to subsequent improvements in the performance of the company on the more relevant (i.e., material) environmental or social issues, even if those proposals do not receive majority support. They also found that proposals on immaterial issues are associated with subsequent declines in firm valuation, whereas proposals on material issues are associated with subsequent increases in firm value.

KEY LEARNING POINT

Some activist investors focus specifically on environmental issues, including levels of emissions, disclosure, and transition strategies.

4.4.5 Summary – Shareholder Activism

An activist shareholder is a shareholder that uses its equity stake in a company to achieve certain goals. The scope of activist investors' actions is broad, and so is the set of tools used to influence a company's governance and strategy. Activist shareholders try to bring about changes within the company and influence its behavior by exercising their voting power, conducting campaigns, and influencing other shareholders.

Frequently, these activist funds engage with other shareholders, especially passive investors, to gain their support for the changes they advocate. Passive institutions can use their large voting blocks to channelize their voice and exert influence.

Key policy priorities related to climate change have further boosted shareholder campaigns that focus on climate issues. In environmental activism, shareholders try to engage with a company's management and push for a lower negative impact on the environment. Overall, the evidence suggests that firms with significant investment by activists are more likely to reduce their carbon emissions, and this reduction is not at the expense of shareholder value (whether based on stock returns or accounting performance).

4.5 MERGERS AND ACQUISITIONS

In this section, we cover the topic of mergers and acquisitions (M&As) and describe how environmental considerations have progressively become fundamental for the success of an M&A strategy. We will see that besides the conventional risks for the bidder associated with an M&A transaction, there are also risks associated with climate change, natural disasters, and company reputation. These risks can kill an M&A.

4.5.1 M&A as Part of Growth Strategies

Changes in the competitive environment fueled by the digitalization of the global economy require organizations to innovate at an increasingly faster pace just to survive. Unparalleled technological advances, disruptive new business models, the blurring of sectoral lines, and fast-changing consumer expectations are compelling many firms to rethink their strategies and reinvent themselves at lightning speed.

Executives have long pursued inorganic growth strategies to quickly boost corporate performance and acquire new product lines, business models, technologies, etc. In all business contexts, M&As will continue to play an important role in companies' growth and expansion efforts. There are several good reasons why organizations prefer to buy rather than build (Fernandes, 2019):

- o Speed: The ability to achieve strategic goals (and size) faster than through organic growth.
- o Access to new capabilities: Technologies, processes, business models, IP, and other resources (including human resources).
- o Increased product range: Combining two companies can improve the end offering to consumers, giving the merged entity a stronger product portfolio from which it can generate considerable gains.
- o Greater distribution range: Combining two companies can enlarge the distribution range and geographical scope of activities, allowing cross-selling of products and services.
- o Increased manufacturing and technological capabilities: This happens when the target company has a technological edge that can be better leveraged as part of a bigger combined organization.
- o Reduced operating and production costs: Often, deals are justified by the creation of cost synergies whereby the final costs of goods or services can be reduced if the two firms merge.
- o Greater pricing power: Deals can also be justified based on improvements in the competitive positioning if they enhance pricing power.

M&As are one of the biggest moves a company can make, and they often involve venturing into new territories (from either a geographical or a product standpoint). Much value can be created if they are well executed, but it requires hard work. The success of a merger depends on the deal structure and rigorous work. [142]

4.5.2 How Companies Can Use M&As to Improve Their Environmental Performance

Green M&As are used by some companies to diversify their investment into green sectors or activities. The relevance and relative importance of green M&As vary across industries. For instance, carbon-intensive businesses, such as oil and gas exploration and production, car manufacturers, electric utilities, chemical manufacturers, and other heavy emitters, face the need to reduce or eliminate their GHG emissions. Therefore, many have turned to M&As to mitigate the effects of climate risk on their portfolio of businesses. [143] For example:

---

[142] See Fernandes (2019) for more details. A full discussion of these generic M&A challenges, valuation, payment, and other topics is outside the scope of this chapter.

[143] Salvi et al. (2018) examined 84 M&A deals occurring from 2001 to 2013 and found that the bidders opting for "green" deals obtained better financial outcomes in terms of ROA compared to firms with deals in other sectors. Using a large sample of mergers in the United States, Deng et al. (2013) found that compared with low-CSR acquirers, high-CSR acquirers realized higher merger announcement returns, higher announcement

- In 2018, Shell acquired a 43.83% interest in Silicon Ranch Corporation, a developer, operator, and owner of solar energy plants. Shell is now the larger shareholder of the company.
- In 2021, Total acquired Fonroche Biogaz, a producer of renewable gas in France with nearly 500 gigawatt-hours of installed capacity. With this acquisition, the companies established a 50:50 joint venture of US$100 million.
- In 2021, Repsol acquired 40% of the U.S.-based solar and battery storage project developer Hecate Energy.
- In 2021, Lightsource BP acquired for US$220 million a pipeline of U.S. solar farms to generate electricity for 1.7 million homes.

But it is not only in these sectors that green M&As are relevant; many companies may benefit from pursuing green M&As to introduce innovation into business models and adapt to environmental challenges. Generically, companies can use M&As to[144]

- acquire new skills and processes to transform the production chain;
- acquire green technology, or resources, to be more environment-friendly;
- create less waste than conventional alternatives;
- become more energy efficient;
- green the company's portfolio of products to comply with standards (for instance, standards on CO_2 emissions in the car sector);
- obtain new customers and improve their reputation; and
- change their business model, by improving their environmental management experience and reducing climate-related risks.

KEY LEARNING POINT

Green mergers can be used to transform a company faster than is possible with organic portfolio changes.

---

returns on the value-weighted portfolio of the acquirer and the target, and larger increases in post-merger long-term operating performance. Similarly, Aktas et al. (2011) studied a large set of M&A data for 1997–2007 and suggested that the stock market rewarded the acquirer for making socially and environmentally responsible investments.

[144] Basse-Mama et al. (2013) analyzed 328 announcements of M&As, joint ventures, and asset disposals that occurred between 2001 and 2011 and provided strong evidence of significant wealth gains from cleantech deals. Indeed, on average, cleantech companies earned significantly higher abnormal returns than non-cleantech companies.

4.5.3 M&As and Environmental Risks

Environmental risks are relevant to M&As as they create financial and reputational risks. M&As are related to environmental risks through several channels. First, extreme weather events can physically damage or destroy assets (plants, infrastructures, crops, etc.), undermining the operational capacity of a company. Second, the increasing levels of investor awareness can initiate a process of divestment from industries and companies whose business operations are considered unsustainable. Buyers thus run the risk of bidding for assets that will become stranded (Section 2.5). In addition, companies whose business operations are considered unsustainable are also likely to face increasing shareholder activism (Section 4.4).

Several climate risk factors should be incorporated into valuations (Section 2.7), and can have a significant impact on potential deals. For instance, the merger of Fiat Chrysler with Peugeot helped the combined company avoid a potential US$2 billion in European carbon emission fines (Brownstein et al., 2020). In this case, the merger led to a reduction in carbon price exposure. However, in some other instances, companies can face, after the M&A, increased exposure to carbon pricing. This means that when assessing a potential target for acquisition, it is important to consider their exposure to potential climate risks, including increases in carbon pricing. In some cases, several assets of the target may be stranded (Section 2.5). Assessing the physical climate risks of the assets is also important.

Also, regulatory trends have to be considered. Several competition authorities (including the European Commission (EC), France, the United Kingdom, and the Netherlands) have acknowledged the importance of environmental factors in their competitive analyses, including for merger control. In the EU, environmental factors are becoming important in the merger control assessment. A few examples include the following:

- In the DEMB/Mondelez/Charger OPCO case, environmental considerations formed part of the EC's relevant product market analysis (organic, fair trade, and other certified coffees vs. conventional coffee).
- In the Aleris/Novelis M&A, environmental issues also formed a crucial part of the EC's market definition by framing the substantive assessment and influencing the remedies package.
- The EC's decision to open an in-depth probe into Aurubis/Metallo is another example. Among the EC's concerns was that the deal might reduce incentives for recyclers to collect and sort copper scrap.

M&As involve capital investment, and this is why sound due diligence is necessary to maximize the odds of success of an M&A transaction. The due diligence process gives bidders and purchasers the opportunity to identify the issues that have to be addressed in the definitive M&A transaction agreement. The main objectives of due diligence are the following:

○ Assessing whether the information obtained is reliable
○ Determining whether the risks associated with the transaction outweigh the potential benefits
○ Mitigating risks by identifying the issues that need to be addressed in the definitive merger agreement to protect the buyer from hidden liabilities

Besides these traditional goals, due diligence can also be helpful for developing a detailed integration plan and better identifying the team responsible for monitoring the progress of the integration efforts. Due diligence is also important for providing inputs to the communication and engagement plans for employees, customers, suppliers, and other stakeholders.

Due diligence is critical to preparing for M&As. Normally, the seller holds the majority of the information. Therefore, prior to closing the transaction, thoughtful bidders should obviously aim to learn as much as possible not only about the target's financials but also about its contracts, customers, suppliers, insurance, environmental risks, and other relevant information. A traditional due diligence process involves an in-depth screening of three main aspects of target corporate governance – financial, operation, and legal:

○ **Financial due diligence**: The acquirer needs to be assured of the financials and understand the risks associated with the target company. The acquirer needs to analyze historical financial statements to understand the margins, working capital, capital expenditures, and revenues and assess the current financial situation, and also whether future projections are reasonable.
○ **Operational due diligence**: It consists of a review of the operational and structural processes of the target company. It tries to identify whether serious operational risks are associated with the target's manufacturing operations, supply chain, information technology, and distribution channels. Of course, while doing this, the potential for performance improvements in different areas should also become clearer.
○ **Legal due diligence**: This is the detailed investigation of possible legal issues facing the target company as, after the deal, the acquirer will be responsible for the legal situation going forward.

KEY LEARNING POINT

Environmental issues pose significant risks to M&A transactions, including whether they are allowed by regulators.

4.5.4 Environmental Due Diligence

Besides the abovementioned normal business risks, environmental and climate-related risks are increasingly relevant to many M&As. Overall, ESG factors are becoming increasingly important in M&A activity because bidders need to incorporate the risks they could be inheriting when they acquire a target or merge with it.

For instance, companies worry about discovering large hidden liabilities (for instance, due to contamination or other environmental hazards) in their acquired assets. The discovery of critical environmental issues after the transaction has been closed is a clear case of value destruction. The company's owners can be considered responsible for reclaiming that contamination or cleaning that pollution, even if it was there before the purchase. This could also prove to be very expensive from the legal point of view.

Therefore, environmental due diligence is typically used. This consist of an environmental assessment to determine whether there is a link between a company's operations and potential contamination, pollution, or other environmental issues. Further, an ESG due diligence can focus on the material ESG issues (Section 6.3.2) of the target, its existing policies, structures, measures, and disclosure.

A sustainability assessment looks at tangible and quantifiable risks, such as emissions, land or subsurface contamination, and compliance with the laws related to waste management, or air and water pollution. However, it should go further and look harder to quantify risks and opportunities, including how the target company is managing the environmental impacts of its operations and how climate change could affect its business due to extreme weather events, water scarcity, or supply chain vulnerability.

Besides performing environmental due diligence, it is increasingly common for M&A transactions to use some of the following measures to mitigate environmental risks:

- Reduce the purchase price to compensate for potential hidden risks
- Indemnify the buyer for post-closing liabilities related to contamination and other environmental risks
- Use an escrow account to guarantee payment of any required environmental clean-up after closing the deal
- Purchase a pollution legal liability insurance policy to protect the buyer

---

KEY LEARNING POINT

The lack of environmental due diligence can backfire and destroy value.

General Battery Corporation and Exide Corporation

In 1966, General Battery acquired – for stock and cash from a single shareholder – Price Battery, a lead-acid battery manufacturer located in Pennsylvania. Consequently, Price Battery transferred all its properties (equipment, lands, and inventory) and legal obligations to General Battery. In 1992, the Environmental Protection Agency (EPA) discovered very high levels of lead contamination in two of General Battery's waste disposal sites and recommended its cleanup to protect human health. As a consequence of Price Battery's improper lead waste disposal, the EPA contended that General Battery was legally liable for the contamination. After General Battery merged with Exide Corporation in 2000, the United States filed an action against Exide as it was Price Battery's legal successor.

4.5.5 Summary – M&As

Climate considerations are becoming increasingly important in M&As. Mergers can be used by companies to "green" their portfolio quickly, acquire cleaner technology, and better comply with the expectations of stakeholders, including regulators. Large players have been using mergers to close technological and business model gaps in their portfolio, and quickly become more environmentally conscious.

M&As will be especially important in certain sectors such as oil and gas, as producers need to invest in the transition from fossil fuel to cleaner energy sources. In other cases, the goal can be to acquire energy-saving or emission-reducing technologies, or to move the business toward other low-pollution sectors.

However, M&As pose significant challenges. Some of the more important of these are paying attention to overpayment, accountability in the integration, and communication with different stakeholders, including employees.

Climate issues are becoming increasingly important for many M&As. There are many reasons for this development, which include pressure from outside investors, board of directors, regulators, and even external pressure from consumers.

Overall, climate-risk factors can affect the likelihood of a deal being closed, and environmental due diligence is necessary for most mergers. Poor performance on environmental issues can negatively impact the valuation, and it can be used to negotiate the price down. However, in some cases, value and efficiency can be increased after the deal, by bringing the target assets to the same level of ESG performance as the acquirer. This requires the integration to focus on improving the ESG factors of the target and thus bring its poor ESG performance on par with that of the acquirer.

4.6   FAMILY FIRMS

In a family firm, a single person or family enjoys a controlling interest (often 100%) in the company. Ownership and control of such companies changes through intergenerational succession. A common feature of family-owned firms is the intertwining of ownership and business needs. Family businesses, by definition, have a long-term orientation. Given this long-term nature, climate risks, which manifest themselves in the medium to long term, are very relevant for them.

The universe of family-owned firms is vast and spans small- and medium-sized companies with a local focus to large multinational corporations. According to the Family Firm Institute, family-owned companies account for two-thirds of all businesses worldwide, generating more than 70% of global GDP annually. In Europe, family firms are even more prevalent. According to Eurostat, more than 99% of companies in the EU are small- and medium-sized companies, most of which are family-owned companies.

4.6.1 Climate-Related Risks in Family Firms

Family-owned firms are vulnerable to the same climate change risks as any other firm. Therefore, physical risk and other risks associated with changing regulatory frameworks or consumer attitudes toward environmental issues are factors that the management of a private-owned company must take into account when formulating or adapting a business strategy.

Family firms, which differ from non-family firms, also vary from one another on various dimensions. Traditionally, the objective is to control the company over generations; therefore, family-owned businesses pursue a longer time horizon in their investment. Another important dimension is socioemotional wealth, which can be interpreted as the non-financial value (or emotional value) the family gains from the firm. [145] This socioemotional wealth links with goals common to family members, including maintaining family control and influence, passing the business to descendants, consolidating family identity, providing employment to family members, and raising the social status of the family in the community.

Decision-making is also different. Given the ownership structure, a family firm does not have to deal with shareholders or investor pressure to implement sustainability practices in the business model. Rather, decisions related to the implementation of sustainable practices – to reduce the impact of climate-related risks and benefit stakeholders – are at the discretion of the family.

---

[145] Berrone et al., 2012; Gómez-Mejía et al., 2014; Gómez-Mejía et al., 2007.

Overall, this suggests that climate-related risks and the lack of sustainability can undermine a family business. On the one hand, the materialization of climate risks can directly undermine a family's wealth. On the other hand, unsustainable practices in the family company's business model may undermine trust and reciprocity between the company and its stakeholders such as local communities, society, and customers. That is, for the majority of family businesses, besides the financial risks, there are also reputational risks associated with climate issues that can undermine the family's reputation.

Therefore, the emotional aspects, possible reputational risks, and the long-term horizon contribute to making the integration of ESG a critical factor for a family firm's success and long-term profitability.

4.6.2 Family Firms and ESG – Empirical Evidence

According to the Family 1000 report published by Credit Suisse (2020), family businesses are increasingly committed to ESG. The report analyzed ESG scores from the Refinitiv database[146] and found that family-owned companies have slightly better ESG scores than non-family-owned companies (See Figure 4.4). The report also showed that family businesses usually fare better in environmental and social areas. Further, it found that this relative performance is a recent phenomenon that has been strengthening over the past five years.

Academic studies have investigated the performance of family firms in terms of ESG, and in particular, environmental performance. Berrone et al. (2010) analyzed how family-controlled firms react to institutional pressures. They found that family firms have better environmental performance (pollute less) than non-family firms. However, the results also suggest that there is significant variation depending on the firm's controlling party. For example, Abeysekera and Fernando (2020) analyzed a sample of 232 firms from 2001 to 2009 to study the differences in policy toward corporate and social responsibility (CSR) between family and nonfamily firms in the United States. Their empirical evidence showed that (1) family firms were more responsible to shareholders than non-family firms; (2) when shareholder interests and societal interests coincided, family firms performed at least as well as non-family firms in protecting shareholder interests; and (3) when shareholder and societal interests diverged, family firms were significantly more on the side of shareholders.

---

[146] See Chapter 4 for a full discussion of ESG ratings.

Figure 4.4 Difference in ESG scores between family- and non-family-owned companies

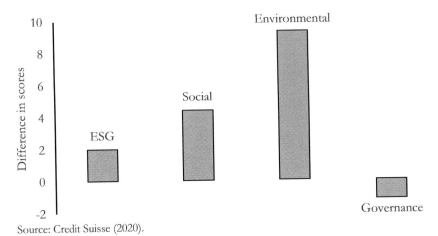

Source: Credit Suisse (2020).

Torres winery

Torres, a family-owned company, is the leading Spanish wine producer. Founded in 1870, it is now in the fifth generation of the family. Although great importance was always given to sustainability, nature, and climate, things changed substantially in 2006. Seeing Al Gore's 2006 documentary on climate change was a turning point for Miguel Torres, the company's president and CEO.

After that, he led the board to approve a stronger commitment to sustainability, through an investment of more than €10 million. To achieve that, 11% of the annual profits were to be dedicated to investments related to the environment and climate change. This included the conservation and replanting of forests in Spain and Chile, investing in renewable energies (solar panels and wind parks), and the use of hybrid cars. They are also considering the use of vineyards and forest biomass.

The Torres & Earth Program of this family business had two objectives: "adapting our activity to climate change and reducing our carbon footprint to help mitigate the effects of global warming." The goals were to reduce CO_2 emissions per bottle by 30% from 2008 to 2020, in carbon footprint Scopes 1, 2, and 3 (that is, from the vineyard to the consumer, including the entire supply chain). It achieved this target in 2019, one year ahead of schedule, and has now committed to reducing emissions by 55% in 2030 and 80% in 2045, compared to 2008.

These results can be explained by the lack of diversification by controlling families, which gives them strong incentives to act in the financial interests of all shareholders and dominates any noneconomic benefit families may derive from engaging in causes that do not benefit shareholders. Consistent with this, Gillan et al. (2020) used a sample of Swedish firms and found that family firms cater to investor demand for environmental (but not social) investment.

Ferrero

In 1942, Pietro Ferrero opened a small laboratory specializing in confectionery products in Alba (Piemonte). There he began to experiment and invent delicacies that, within a few years, would become among the best-selling products in the world. In 2011, Giovanni Ferrero—Pietro Ferrero's grandson—was appointed Executive Chairman of the group. In 2018, the group employed more than 33,000 workers, had 31 operating manufacturing plants worldwide, and sold its products in over 170 countries.

Ferrero has set itself two targets to reduce its carbon footprint. By 2030, the company aims to halve all emissions from its owned operations, which is consistent with the Paris Agreement goal to limit global warming to 1.5 °C. Across all scopes, Ferrero commits to reducing emissions by 43% for each metric ton of product produced. Both targets use 2018 as the base year.

In addition, some of Ferrero's flagship products, such as Nutella, are produced by blending palm oil. Therefore, since 2005, Ferrero has been an active member of the RSPO, an international organization whose focus is making sustainable palm oil sourcing a normal practice, and it has fundamentally changed its business practices. On January 17, 2020, the World Wildlife Fund for Nature (WWF)—the world's leading organization in wildlife conservation and protection of endangered species—declared: "Despite many long-standing commitments by brands and industry coalitions to eliminate the destruction of nature, including deforestation, from their palm oil supply chains, the scorecard shows that most companies still have a long way to go before they can prove to consumers that they are delivering on these promises. Meanwhile, only one company, the consumer goods manufacturer Ferrero, has scored over 20 points (out of the maximum 22), sending an encouraging signal to the rest of the industry that sustainable and deforestation-free palm oil is achievable."

KEY LEARNING POINT

Ownership of a family firm typically involves financial considerations as well as emotional attachment. Climate risks are especially relevant for family firms, which typically have a long-term orientation.

REFERENCES: CHAPTER 4

Abeysekera, A.P., and C.S. Fernando. 2020. "Corporate Social Responsibility versus Corporate Shareholder Responsibility: A Family Firm Perspective." *Journal of Corporate Finance* 61: 101370.

Adib, F., and F. Zahra. 2019. "Passive Aggressive: How Index Funds Vote on Corporate Governance Proposals." Working paper. Available at *SSRN 3480484*.

Akey, P., and I. Appel. 2019. "Environmental Externalities of Activism." Working paper. Available at *SSRN 3508808*.

Aktas, N., E. De Bodt, and J.-G. Cousin. 2011. "Do Financial Markets Care about SRI? Evidence from Mergers and Acquisitions." *Journal of Banking & Finance* 35 (7): 1753–61.

Anderloni, L., and A. Tanda. 2017. "Green Energy Companies: Stock Performance and IPO Returns." *Research in International Business and Finance* 39: 546–52.

Appel, I.R., T.A. Gormley, and D.B. Keim. 2016. "Passive Investors, Not Passive Owners." *Journal of Financial Economics* 121 (1): 111–41.

Appel, I.R., T.A. Gormley, and D.B. Keim. 2019. "Standing on the Shoulders of Giants: The Effect of Passive Investors on Activism." *The Review of Financial Studies* 32 (7): 2720–74.

Azar, J., M. Duro, I. Kadach, and G. Ormazabal. 2021. "The Big Three and Corporate Carbon Emissions around the World." Working paper. *Journal of Financial Economics* 142 (2): 674–96.

Barko, T., M. Cremers, and L. Renneboog. 2021. "Shareholder Engagement on Environmental, Social, and Governance Performance." Working paper. *Journal of Business Ethics*, 1–36.

Basse-Mama, H., N. Koch, A. Bassen, and T. Bank. 2013. "Valuation Effects of Corporate Strategic Transactions in the Cleantech Industry." *Journal of Business Economics* 83 (6): 605–30.

Bebchuk, L.A., A. Brav, and W. Jiang. 2015. "The Long-Term Effects of Shareholder Activism." *Columbia Law Review* 115 (5): 1085–1156.

Bebchuk, L.A., and S. Hirst. 2019. "The Specter of the Giant Three." No. w25914. National Bureau of Economic Research.

Becht, M., J. Franks, J. Grant, and H.F. Wagner. 2017. "Returns to Hedge Fund Activism: An International Study." *The Review of Financial Studies* 30 (9): 2933–71.

Becht, M., J. Franks, C. Mayer, and S. Rossi. 2008. "Returns to Shareholder Activism: Evidence from a Clinical Study of the Hermes UK Focus Fund." *The Review of Financial Studies* 22 (8): 3093–3129.

Bellon, A. 2020. "Does Private Equity Ownership Make Firms Cleaner? The Role of Environmental Liability Risks." May 18. European Corporate Governance Institute – Finance Working Paper No. 799/2021. Available at SSRN: https://ssrn.com/abstract=3604360 or http://dx.doi.org/10.2139/ssrn.3604360.

Berle, A., and G. Means. 1932. *The Modern Corporation and Private Property*. New York: Commerce Clearing House.

Berrone, P., C. Cruz, and L.R. Gomez-Mejia. 2012. "Socioemotional Wealth in Family Firms: Theoretical Dimensions, Assessment Approaches, and Agenda for Future Research." *Family Business Review* 25 (3): 258–79.

Berrone, P., C. Cruz, L.R. Gomez-Mejia, and M. Larraza-Kintana. 2010. "Socioemotional Wealth and Corporate Responses to Institutional Pressures: Do Family-Controlled Firms Pollute Less?" *Administrative Science Quarterly* 55 (1): 82–113.

Berrone, P., and L.R. Gomez-Mejia. 2009. "Environmental Performance and Executive Compensation: An Integrated Agency-Institutional Perspective." *Academy of Management Journal* 52 (1): 103–26.

BlackRock. 2021. "Investment Stewardship Annual Report (January 1–December 31, 2021)." New York: BlackRock.

Boyson, N.M., N. Gantchev, and A. Shivdasani. 2017. "Activism Mergers." *Journal of Financial Economics* 126 (1): 54–73.

Brav, A., W. Jiang, and H. Kim. 2012. "The Real Effects of Hedge Fund Activism: Productivity, Risk, and Product Market Competition." *US Census Bureau Center for Economic Studies Paper No. CES-WP-12-14, Johnson School Research Paper Series*, no. 33–2012.

Brav, A., W. Jiang, and H. Kim. 2015. "The Real Effects of Hedge Fund Activism: Productivity, Asset Allocation, and Labor Outcomes." *The Review of Financial Studies* 28 (10): 2723–69.

Brav, A., W. Jiang, T. Li, and J. Pinnington. 2018a. "Picking Friends before Picking (Proxy) Fights: How Mutual Fund Voting Shapes Proxy Contests." Working paper. European Corporate Governance Institute (ECGI).

Brav, A., W. Jiang, S. Ma, and X. Tian. 2018b. "How Does Hedge Fund Activism Reshape Corporate Innovation?" *Journal of Financial Economics* 130 (2): 237–64.

Brav, A., W. Jiang, F. Partnoy, and R. Thomas. 2008. "Hedge Fund Activism, Corporate Governance, and Firm Performance." *The Journal of Finance* 63 (4): 1729–75.

Brière, M., S. Pouget, and L. Ureche. 2018. "Blackrock vs Norway Fund at Shareholder Meetings: Institutional Investors' Votes on Corporate Externalities." Working paper. Available at *SSRN 3140043*.

Brownstein, A., D. Silk, and S. Niles. 2020. "The Coming Impact of ESG on M&A." New York: Wachtell Lipton.

Burke, J.J., R. Hoitash, and U. Hoitash. 2019. "The Heterogeneity of Board-Level Sustainability Committees and Corporate Social Performance." *Journal of Business Ethics* 154 (4): 1161–86.

Cai, J., J.L. Garner, and R.A. Walkling. 2009. "Electing Directors." *The Journal of Finance* 64 (5): 2389–2421.

Credit Suisse. 2020. "Family 1000: Post the Pandemic." New York: Credit Suisse Research Institute.

Crifo, P., V.D. Forget, and S. Teyssier. 2015. "The Price of Environmental, Social and Governance Practice Disclosure: An Experiment with Professional Private Equity Investors." *Journal of Corporate Finance* 30: 168–94.

Deloitte. 2018. "Sustainability and the Board: What Do Directors Need to Know in 2018?" London: Deloitte Touche Tohmatsu Limited.

Denes, M.R., J.M. Karpoff, and V.B. McWilliams. 2017. "Thirty Years of Shareholder Activism: A Survey of Empirical Research." *Journal of Corporate Finance* 44: 405–24.

Deng, X., J. Kang, and B.S. Low. 2013. "Corporate Social Responsibility and Stakeholder Value Maximization: Evidence from Mergers." *Journal of Financial Economics* 110 (1): 87–109.

Di Giuli, A., A. Garel, R. Michaely, and A. Petit-Romec. 2022. "Climate Change and Mutual Fund Voting on Environmental Proposals." Available at *SSRN 3997730*.

Diaz-Rainey, I. 2020. "The Role of Investors in Energy Transition." In *Energy in Transition, 7th IAEE Asian Conference, February 12-15, 2020*. International Association for Energy Economics.

Dimson, E., O. Karakaş, and X. Li. 2015. "Active Ownership." *The Review of Financial Studies* 28 (12): 3225–68.

Dimson, E., O. Karakaş, and X. Li. 2021. "Coordinated Engagements." European Corporate Governance Institute–Finance Working Paper, no. 721.

Fernandes, N. 2017. *Finance for Executives: A Practical Guide for Managers*. 2nd ed. London: NPV Publishing.

Fernandes, N. 2019. *The Value Killers: How Mergers and Acquisitions Cost Companies Billions—and How to Prevent It*. Springer.

Fernandes, N., M.A. Ferreira, P. Matos, and K.J. Murphy. 2013. "Are US CEOs Paid More? New International Evidence." *The Review of Financial Studies* 26 (2): 323–67.

Flammer, C., B. Hong, and D. Minor. 2019. "Corporate Governance and the Rise of Integrating Corporate Social Responsibility Criteria in Executive Compensation: Effectiveness and Implications for Firm Outcomes." *Strategic Management Journal* 40 (7): 1097–1122.

Geczy, C., J. Jeffers, D.K. Musto, and A.M. Tucker. 2019. "Contracts with Benefits: The Implementation of Impact Investing." Available at *SSRN 3159731*.

Gillan, S., N. S. Sekerci, and L. Starks. (2020) Do Firms Cater to Demand for Environmental and Social Performance? Working paper.

Glass Lewis. 2020. "2020 Voting Policies." https://www.glasslewis.com/voting-policies-2020/.

Gomez-Mejia, L., C. Cruz, and C. Imperatore. 2014. "Financial Reporting and the Protection of Socioemotional Wealth in Family-Controlled Firms." *European Accounting Review* 23 (3): 387–402.

Gómez-Mejía, L.R., K.T. Haynes, M. Núñez-Nickel, K.J. Jacobson, and J. Moyano-Fuentes. 2007. "Socioemotional Wealth and Business Risks in Family-Controlled Firms: Evidence from Spanish Olive Oil Mills." *Administrative Science Quarterly* 52 (1): 106–37.

Grewal, J., G. Serafeim, and A. Yoon. 2016. "Shareholder Activism on Sustainability Issues." Available at *SSRN 2805512*.

Griffin, C.N. 2020. "Margins: Estimating the Influence of the Big Three on Shareholder Proposals." *SMU Law Review*. 73: 409.

He, Y., B. Kahraman, and M. Lowry. 2021. "ES Risks and Shareholder Voice." *European Corporate Governance Institute–Finance Working Paper*, no. 786.

Heath, D., D. Macciocchi, R. Michaely, and M.C. Ringgenberg. 2022. "Do Index Funds Monitor?" Working paper. *The Review of Financial Studies* 35 (1): 91–131.

Herbst-Bayliss, S., and DiNapoli. 2019. "New Glass Lewis Chief to Expand Abroad amid U.S. Regulatory Clamp-Down." Reuters, October 4, 2019, sec. U.S. Markets. https://www.reuters.com/article/us-glasslewis-future-idUSKBN1WJ1J4.

Hong, H., G.A. Karolyi, and J.A. Scheinkman. 2020. "Climate Finance." *The Review of Financial Studies* 33 (3): 1011–23.

Hshieh, S., J. Li, and Y. Tang. 2021. "How Do Passive Funds Act as Active Owners? Evidence from Mutual Fund Voting Records." *Journal of Corporate Finance* 66: 101692.

Iliev, P., K.V. Lins, D.P. Miller, and L. Roth. 2015. "Shareholder Voting and Corporate Governance around the World." *The Review of Financial Studies* 28 (8): 2167–2202.

Iliev, P., and M. Lowry. 2015. "Are Mutual Funds Active Voters?" *The Review of Financial Studies* 28 (2): 446–85.

Indahl, R., and H.G. Jacobsen. 2019. "Private Equity 4.0: Using ESG to Create More Value with Less Risk." *Journal of Applied Corporate Finance* 31 (2): 34–41.

ISS. 2021. "Volatile Transition. Navigating ESG in 2021." Rockville, United States: Institutional Shareholder Services.

Krueger, P., Z. Sautner, and L.T. Starks. 2020. "The Importance of Climate Risks for Institutional Investors." *The Review of Financial Studies* 33 (3): 1067–1111.

Larcker, D.F., A.L. McCall, and G. Ormazabal. 2015. "Outsourcing Shareholder Voting to Proxy Advisory Firms." *The Journal of Law and Economics* 58 (1): 173–204.

Lazard. 2020. "2020 Review of Shareholder Activism." Hamilton, Bermuda: Lazard's Shareholder Advisory Group.

Li, T. 2018. "Outsourcing Corporate Governance: Conflicts of Interest within the Proxy Advisory Industry." *Management Science* 64 (6): 2951–71.

Malenko, N., and Y. Shen. 2016. "The Role of Proxy Advisory Firms: Evidence from a Regression-Discontinuity Design." *The Review of Financial Studies* 29 (12): 3394–3427.

Masulis, R.W., and S.W. Reza. 2015. "Agency Problems of Corporate Philanthropy." *The Review of Financial Studies* 28 (2): 592–636.

Matos, P. 2020. "ESG and Responsible Institutional Investing around the World: A Critical Review." SSRN Scholarly Paper. Rochester, NY. https://doi.org/10.2139/ssrn.3668998.

McCahery, J.A., Z. Sautner, and L.T. Starks. 2016. "Behind the Scenes: The Corporate Governance Preferences of Institutional Investors." *The Journal of Finance* 71 (6): 2905–32.

Mendoza, C. 2019. "Hurdle under Threat as Managers Question One-Size-Fits-All Approach." *Infrastructure Investor*, August 1. https://www.infrastructureinvestor.com/hurdle-under-threat-managers-question-one-size-fits-all/.

Mitchell, I., and L. Tomson. 2020. "Another Link in the Chain: Uncovering the Role of Proxy Advisors in Investor ESG Voting." *The Harvard Law School Forum on Corporate Governance* (blog). March 5, 2020. https://corpgov.law.harvard.edu/2020/03/05/another-link-in-the-chain-uncovering-the-role-of-proxy-advisors-in-investor-esg-voting/.

Naaraayanan, S.L., K. Sachdeva, and V. Sharma. 2021. "The Real Effects of Environmental Activist Investing." European Corporate Governance Institute–Finance Working Paper, no. 743.

PRI. 2020. "Guide for Limited Partners: Responsible Investment in Private Equity." Technical Guide. London: Principles for Responsible Investment. https://www.unpri.org/private-equity/guide-for-limited-partners-responsible-investment-in-private-equity/5657.article.

PwC. 2020. "Turning Crisis into Opportunity." Annual Corporate Directors Survey. London: PricewaterhouseCoopers.

Rose, P. 2021. "Proxy Advisors and Market Power: A Review of Institutional Investor Robovoting." New York: Manhattan Institute.

Salvi, A., F. Petruzzella, A. Giakoumelou, and others. 2018. "Green M&A Deals and Bidders' Value Creation: The Role of Sustainability in Post-Acquisition Performance." *International Business Research* 11 (7): 96–105.

Schmidt, C., and R. Fahlenbrach. 2017. "Do Exogenous Changes in Passive Institutional Ownership Affect Corporate Governance and Firm Value?" *Journal of Financial Economics* 124 (2): 285–306.

Shu, C. 2022. "The Proxy Advisory Industry: Influencing and Being Influenced." USC Marshall School of Business Research Paper.

State Street. 2021. "Stewardship Activity Report (Q4 2021)." Boston: State Street Corporation.

Tang, T. 2020. "Hedge Fund Activism and Corporate Innovation." *Economic Modelling* 85: 335–48.

Teti, E., A. Dell'Acqua, and F. Zocchi. 2012. "UN PRI and Private Equity Returns. Empirical Evidence from the US Market." *Investment Management and Financial Innovations*, 9 (3) : 60–67.

Vanguard. 2021. "Investment Stewardship (2021 Annual Report)." Pennsylvania: The Vanguard Group.

Willis Towers Watson. 2021. "ESG and Executive Compensation: Hearing from Board Members Globally." London: Willis Towers Watson Public Limited Company.

Chapter 5
Capital Markets – Green Investing

Capital markets play a key role in financing the transition to a green economy. Investors play an important role in lowering the carbon footprint and redirecting capital flows to environmentally sustainable projects and innovative technologies. Therefore, in this chapter, we discuss how ESG issues and climate risk considerations are being integrated into the business strategies of the key players in capital markets. We start with ESG rating agencies and the metrics applied to evaluate companies' climate risk vulnerability and sustainability footprint. As we will see, ESG rating agencies apply various metrics and methodologies, and therefore their ratings tend to be less homogeneous and predictable than the "conventional" credit rating. Therefore, we also look at the ESG stock market indices, providing practical examples to explain the methodology used to construct them. We discuss the performance of sustainable investment products in terms of risk, returns, flows, and other features. Finally, we discuss the implications of sustainability issues for institutional investors (insurance, pension funds, sovereign wealth funds, investment banks, etc.) and how they are incorporating ESG considerations into their investment decisions.

5.1   THE GROWING IMPORTANCE OF ESG RATINGS

Environmental, social, and governance (ESG) ratings help assess and identify financially material ESG risks in investment decisions.[147] The rise of ESG investing has led to a growing demand for ESG ratings, which has in turn rapidly increased the importance of ESG rating

---

[147] ESG ratings are sometimes also called sustainability ratings or corporate social responsibility (CSR) ratings. We use these terms interchangeably.

providers. Investors rely on these rating providers for scores that can help them assess and compare company performance on aspects other than finance.

Measuring ESG performance, and in particular climate-related efforts and risks, is a difficult task. Most international companies are being evaluated and rated on their ESG performance by various third-party institutions. Using teams of analysts, and a variety of company data, these institutions collect ESG information and convert it into different scores/outputs. Investors use ESG ratings to compare, screen, and rank companies.

5.1.1 What Are ESG Ratings?

ESG ratings aggregate a number of indicators into a composite score that measures a firm's ESG performance. They aim to capture information that is not part of standard financial statements, but that can be material from an ESG perspective. ESG scores can be used in many different ways. They

- o   help investors make investment decisions,
- o   are included in valuation models,
- o   help create portfolio ratings,
- o   help build investment products,
- o   help create sustainability indices that reflect the performance of a subset of companies based on their ESG profile, and
- o   guide companies in making changes in their operations and business model.

ESG ratings first appeared in the 1980s when the ESG rating agency Vigeo-Eiris commenced operations in France. This was followed by Kinder, Lydenberg & Domini (KLD) in the United States in 1988. The market for ESG ratings has expanded over the last decade, following the rise in importance of the Principles for Responsible Investing, and other initiatives, that led institutional investors to look for data on the ESG performance of their invested companies. The early ESG rating providers were acquired by large financial data providers (Eccles and Stroehle, 2018). For instance:

- o   2009: Thomson Reuters buys Asset 4.
- o   2010: MSCI (RiskMetrics) buys KLD.
- o   2015: ISS buys Ethix.
- o   2016: Standard & Poor's buys Trucost.
- o   2017: Morningstar buys Sustainalytics.
- o   2019: Moody's buys Vigeo-Eiris in 2019.
- o   2019: Standard & Poor's buys RobecoSAM in 2019.

Despite the substantial consolidation of providers over the last 30 years, over 70 different firms offer some sort of ESG ratings data, often with different focus areas. Some, such as MSCI, Sustainalytics, ISS, Asset 4 (Refinitiv, formerly Thomson Reuters) and Vigeo Eiris, rate companies globally, whereas others focus on a single country or region. Also, some have a domain focus (such as climate, governance, or human rights), whereas others cover the entire range of ESG issues. Most of the providers are for-profit organizations with a diverse product portfolio, including providing data, consulting services, and technology and management services for portfolio managers, and they have been substantially expanding their coverage. For instance, MSCI ESG coverage of the constituents of its MSCI World index was 34% in 2009, 58% in 2017,[148] and almost 100% in 2021.

ESG rating providers are increasingly influential institutions, in particular as investors with over US$100 trillion in combined assets have committed to integrating ESG information into their investment decisions (see PRI, in Section 5.4). Institutional investors, asset managers, financial institutions, and other stakeholders are increasingly using ESG ratings to evaluate and measure the performance of companies over time, and against their peers.

Some investors use ESG ratings to diversify their portfolios and reduce the impact of the low-carbon transition and climate-related risks, whereas others use them for portfolio screening/exclusion purposes. Activist shareholders also use the scores for voting or engagement purposes. Some investors specifically want to finance sustainable projects. Companies use the scores to determine where to focus their improvement efforts, particularly when they receive low scores compared to their industry peers.

KEY LEARNING POINT

ESG ratings vary from provider to provider, and have different focus and coverage areas. Investors use these ratings to evaluate performance and build their investment portfolios.

5.1.2 How ESG Ratings Are Constructed

ESG rating providers typically collect data once a year, and also regularly track pertinent news. Some of the data comes from companies' annual sustainability reports. They also use surveys, various datasets, analyses of company disclosures, interviews with employees and other stakeholders, and company-level analysis of incidents. Each provider has its own methodology, which generally involves three stages:

1. Defining attributes: Every provider chooses to assess different aspects of sustainability. That is, it defines the set of attributes that in its judgment describes a company's ESG performance.

---

[148] BlackRock, "Sustainability: The Future of Investing," February 2019.

2. Scoring each attribute: Data (qualitative and quantitative) from different sources are used to create a range of indicators, which are used to produce a numerical value for each attribute.

3. Weighting the attributes: The key issues are then aggregated using weights. That is, the individual scores are aggregated to create a key composite metric or overall score. This score be either absolute or relative to peers in the industry, and it is often also defined for each one of the key pillars of ESG (E, S, and G).

The final ESG score is thus a mix of different indicators that attempts to capture the exposure level of a company to ESG issues and its ability to manage that exposure. The final score aggregates different sub-metrics that measure specific aspects of how a company operates and uses its resources.

Each ESG rating provider has a different methodology. Some rely more on a "box-ticking approach,"[149] whereas others rely more on hard data, and yet others on interpretative analysis. Also, each provider contextualizes ESG through (1) its preferences for one category over another (e.g., more governance focus, less environmental focus) and (2) the specific measures used (e.g., stated intentions vs. hard data, qualitative factors vs. quantitative factors).

There is no list of agreed-upon ESG issues, and there is even less agreement on the metrics used. The number of attributes assessed for each company ranges from 30 to 300, depending on the provider.[150] Some attributes, such as carbon emissions, can be objectively measured (even if there is still disagreement regarding the scopes of emissions: 1, 2, and 3[151]). Others, such as "environmental harm," can be debated, and the evaluation depends on how different inputs are weighted. Social factors depend on societal norms, and many governance factors can also be debated (e.g., the appropriate structure for a board and the nature of compensation arrangements are widely discussed topics in academic and practitioner circles).

MSCI ESG Rating

MSCI is one of the world's biggest ESG rating providers. In 2020, MSCI ESG ratings were available for 8,700 companies. They are produced by a team of more than 200 analysts, who

---

[149] A "box ticking" approach consists of satisfying bureaucratic administrative requirements rather than actually dealing with the essence of something.

[150] Berg et al. (2019) studied six ESG rating providers, and categorized the 709 indicators provided by different data providers (Asset4 uses 282 indicators, Sustainalytics 163, RobecoSAM 80, KLD 78, MSCI 68, and Vigeo-Eiris 38).

[151] See the definitions in Section 3.6.1.

apply their methodology to measure a company's ESG performance. According to MSCI, their ESG ratings model seeks to answer the following questions[152]:

- What are the most significant ESG risks and opportunities facing a company and its industry?
- How exposed is the company to those key risks and/or opportunities?
- How well is the company managing its key risks and opportunities?
- What is the overall picture for the company and how does it compare to its global industry peers?

Some of the key characteristics of the MSCI ESG ratings include the following:

- The MSCI ESG rating scores companies on an AAA to CCC scale relative to their industry peers.
- The sources used to measure exposure and management response include datasets from various sources, company disclosures, and media searches.
- The sample of companies is based on the constituents of its flagship index, MSCI World, and some other indices.
- It focuses on 35 key ESG issues. Out of these, for each industry, a subset is chosen, as well as the weights that determine the contribution to the overall rating.
- Each key issue is scored on a 0–10 scale (0: very poor, 10: very good).
- It reviews controversies, as these may indicate structural problems with a company's risk management capabilities, and can signal future material risks. These can include events such as operations and/or products with negative environmental, social, and/or governance impact; spills; accidents; regulatory action; and health and safety fines.
- These scores are then aggregated for each pillar (Environment, Social, and Governance) with a set of weights.
- Finally, the scores of key issues are combined with weights to create an overall score that is then adjusted relative to industry peers, and presented as an ESG letter rating: AAA–CCC.

For each ESG pillar, MSCI defines a list of themes (10 in all). Each theme is based on several underlying key issues. However, as mentioned above, not all key issues are used for every industry, and the weight of each key issue also varies according to the sector.

For each key issue, MSCI measures risk exposure and risk management scores. That is, a highly exposed company with poor risk management will score worse than a company with the same management practices but lower exposure to the risk. For example, utilities are highly water dependent, but each company may be more or less exposed to water-related risks depending on the location of its plants. Companies operating in water-scarce regions must take measures to mitigate these risks, unlike those with adequate access to water.

---

[152] From MSCI ESG Ratings Methodology, December 2020

Similarly, heavy polluters are required to implement much stronger measures to mitigate their carbon risk, compared to low emitters.

Table 5.1 Rating sub-components

Pillar	Themes	Key ESG issues	
Environment	Climate change	Carbon emissions Carbon footprint	Financing environmental impact Climate change vulnerability
	Natural capital	Water, biodiversity, and land use	Raw material sourcing
	Pollution and waste	Toxic emissions and waste Packaging material and waste	Electronic waste
	Environmental opportunities	Opportunities in clean tech Opportunities in green building	Opportunities in renewable energy
Social	Human capital	Labor management Health and safety	Human capital development Supply chain labor standards
	Product liability	Product safety and quality Chemical safety Financial product safety	Privacy and data security Responsible investment Health and demographic risk
	Stakeholder opposition	Controversial sourcing	Community relations
	Social opportunities	Access to communications Access to finance	Access to health care Opportunities in nutrition and health
Governance	Corporate governance	Ownership and board	Compensation
	Corporate behavior	Business ethics	Tax transparency

Source: MSCI ESG Ratings.

Sustainalytics

Sustainalytics was formed in 2009, following the merger of several research and rating organizations. In 2016, Morningstar acquired 40% of Sustainalytics. Sustainalytics' ESG risk ratings are available for more than 12,000 firms worldwide, and are based on two dimensions: exposure and management. Some additional characteristics of its rating include the following (Sustainalytics, 2021):

- o The rating is based on three pillars: (1) idiosyncratic ESG issues, (2) material ESG issues (MEI), and (3) corporate governance.
- o An issue is considered "material" if its presence (or absence) in the financial reporting is likely to influence the investor's decisions on corporate equity or bonds.[153]
- o The rating assessment develops along two dimensions: (1) the company's exposure to material ESG risks and (2) its management of the exposure.
- o Sustainalytics ESG risk ratings classify companies into five risk categories: Negligible (0–9.99 points), Low (10–19.99 points), Medium (20–29.99 points), High (30–39.99 points), and Severe (40 and above).
- o The final ESG risk rating scores are a measure of unmanaged risk. They include two types of risk: (1) unmanageable risk, which cannot be addressed by company initiatives, and (2) the management gap, which represents risks that could potentially be managed by the company.

S&P DJI ESG Scores

Each year, S&P Global publishes an ESG analysis of more than 10,000 companies. Besides generating a company-level score, the S&P DJI ESG scores are also used to build the Dow Jones Sustainability Indices, the S&P 500 ESG Index, and other ESG indices. The following are some characteristics of the S&P ESG scores:

- o Companies are grouped into 61 industries, using the Global Industry Classification Standard (GICS®) to determine the industry classification.
- o Every year, in March, S&P Global issues a request to companies. It uses industry-specific questionnaires that evaluate a range of financially relevant sustainability criteria. If companies do not respond to the request, S&P analysts assess them using available data. In 2020, the S&P DJI ESG Score covered 11,556 companies. Among these, 1,436 responded to the questionnaire directly, and the remaining 10,120 companies were analyzed by S&P Global using available company disclosures.
- o Each of the 61 questionnaires (each per industry group) contains up to 120 general and industry-specific questions.
- o A company's final ESG score contains a separate assessment of each ESG factor (environmental, social, and governance). S&P ESG scores range from 0 to 100, with 0 representing the worst ESG performance and 100 the best ESG performance.

---

[153] See Section 6.3.2 for an overview of materiality, how it varies across industries, and its financial reporting implications.

5.1.3 Environment-Related Indicators

All ESG rating providers assess several environmental issues. The different environmental factors typically cover (1) natural resource use, (2) climate change and emissions, and (3) pollution and waste.

Many metrics can be used to analyze each factor, and, as described above, different providers use different metrics and criteria. Table 5.2 shows the number of category-wise indicators provided by various ESG rating providers.

Table 5.2 Number of indicators used per category by ESG rating providers

Topic	MSCI	Sustainalytics	Asset 4
Biodiversity	2	1	3
Climate Risk Management	2	0	1
Energy	1	3	5
Environmental Fines	1	1	1
Environmental Policy	0	4	4
GHG emissions	1	5	5
GHG policy	0	3	4
Green Buildings	1	5	1

Source: Berg et al. (2019).

5.1.4 Challenges with ESG Ratings

ESG ratings diverge considerably. Although credit ratings formulated by the three major rating agencies (S&P, Moody's, and Fitch) for securities issued by the same company tend to be very similar, ESG ratings tend to vary greatly.

Given their varying methodologies and focus, different ESG ratings providers can assign different ratings to the same company. This heterogeneity occurs for firms of all countries and sectors. A company with a high score from one rater can receive a middle or low score from another rater (Dimson et al., 2020). Gibson et al. (2021) analyzed the consistency in ratings produced by the different providers. Looking at ESG scores from Thomson Reuters, MSCI, Sustainalytics, KLD, Bloomberg, and Inrate for S&P 500 firms from 2013 to 2017, they found that the average correlation between overall ESG ratings of the six providers was close to 50%.[154] This means that the information users receive from ESG rating agencies is not uniform.

Unlike financial reporting, where there is a degree of global standardization across companies, industries, and jurisdictions, sustainability reporting still lacks adequate

---

[154] This number is substantially lower than that observed for credit ratings from Moody's and S&P, which have a 99% or higher correlation (Berg et al. 2019).

standardization (see Section 6.3), making sustainability assessment by rating agencies a subjective task. Given both the lack of standardization and the level of subjectivity of each provider, it is possible for a company operating in a "brown" industry to receive a higher ESG score than a company commonly considered more environmentally sustainable. Only digging into the details will reveal the truth.

Exxon vs. Tesla vs. BMW

In 2018, Exxon was assigned a higher overall ESG score than Tesla by two ESG rating agencies. An ESG rating divergence can also be observed within the same industry. For example, in 2018, Sustainalytics ranked BMW in a high percentile (93%), whereas Tesla achieved a much lower score (38%).

At first, this rating does not appear to make sense as BMW – similar to Volkswagen – was in legal trouble on account of the Diesel scandal, whereas Tesla is an electric car manufacturer whose goal is to reduce global CO_2 emissions.

However, the divergence of the ratings for Tesla, Exxon, and BMW is not completely devoid of logic, as the environmental impact of electric cars is still subject to debate. Although electric vehicles are powered with green energy, the energy used to produce them and the rare earth minerals used for their construction entail a high intensity of CO_2 emissions. In addition, there are governance concerns around Tesla, which also explain its lower ESG scores.

Why Are ESG Ratings Different?

There are several reasons, many of them technical, for the differences between ESG ratings across rating providers. An ESG rating involves judgment and subjective evaluations. All ESG ratings consider many different metrics, many of which are qualitative. As some metrics are included by one provider but not by another, the results obviously vary. Also, the conversion of qualitative metrics into a numerical score depends on the rating provider's algorithm. Different rating providers can assess a company's non-financial performance on the same issue differently. Also, the weighting scheme varies: different rating providers assign different weights to different metrics.

Facebook

In 2017, Facebook's environmental score was ranked in the top decile by one provider and below average by another provider. The rating divergence was essentially due to the different weights assigned by the two rating providers to the same single category used to assess a company's environmental performance. For example, Provider 1 assigned a weight of 33% to "Environmental Strategy," whereas Provider 2 assigned a weight of 3.3% to the comparable category, "Environmental Policy." Similarly, Provider 1 assigned a weight of 33% to the category "Minimizing Environmental Impacts from Energy Use," whereas Provider 2 assigned a weight of 3.3% to the comparable category, "Carbon Intensity."

Different rating agencies have different views on what are material risks, and thus on which issues to prioritize. Some tend to construct more quantitative, performance-based metrics, whereas others include more qualitative, policy-related information.[155]

Berg et al. (2019) decomposed the differences in ESG ratings into scope, measurement, and weights. They used data from six providers (KLD, Sustainalytics, Vigeo-Eiris, S&P Global, Asset4/Refinitiv, and MSCI) and decomposed the differences as follows:

- o Scope of categories: Each rating provider chooses a set of attributes that describes a company's ESG performance. Scope divergence can occur when one rater includes GHG emissions and employee turnover, whereas another rater does not consider these attributes in its score.
- o Measurement of categories: Different indicators can be used to produce a numerical value for each attribute. Measurement divergence occurs when providers measure the same attribute using different indicators. For instance, one rating provider might evaluate labor practices based on employee turnover, whereas another might count the number of labor cases against the firm.
- o Weights of categories: Combining multiple indicators into one rating requires weights. Weight divergence occurs because rating providers have varying views on the importance of different categories. For instance, one provider may value GHG emissions higher than human rights.

They found that scope and measurement divergence are the main reason why ESG ratings diverge across providers. That is, ratings differ mostly because two raters use a different set of attributes/criteria and also because different raters measure performance (in the same category) differently. They also found a "rater effect"; that is, the measurement is influenced by the raters' view of the analyzed company. When a company is above average in one category, it is more likely to be above average in the other categories.[156] They also found that weight divergence is less important.

Eccles and Stroehle (2018) also studied why ratings vary across providers. They focused on the dimensions used to define sustainability, the definition of materiality and the corresponding weights, and also the social origins of each rating company (founding members, legal status, geography etc.). The results suggest that the origin of each company influences its definition of sustainability, materiality, and, as a result, how ESG issues are measured and aggregated. Gibson et al. (2021) analyzed the legal origin of ESG rating firms.

---

[155] Chatterji et al. (2016) attributed the discrepancy in ESG ratings to the lack of a common view on what it means to be a socially responsible company, and also due to the lack of agreement on the specific metrics used to measure it.

[156] Some potential explanations for the rater effect include the following: rating agencies are mostly organized by firms rather than by indicators; the extent to which the firms answer specific questions is highly correlated across indicators; and firms' willingness to disclose information varies and is correlated across categories.

They found that civil-law-based[157] ESG data providers have stronger views on labor issues and social protection, whereas common-law ESG data providers emphasize investor protection and other governance issues. Kotsantonis and Serafeim (2019) documented inconsistencies in terms of how rating providers report data, define peer groups, and collect ESG data.

Overall, the research results highlight the fact that there is no consensus on both the list of ESG issues and their relative importance. This is normal. Sustainability is inherently subjective, as it depends on the interpretation of soft information. In the same way, the financial value of a company is subjective, as it depends on expectations of future growth, profitability, strategic outlook, and risk; therefore, it is normal for equity analysts and fund managers to have different views regarding the same company. It is one thing to have a historical sales number, and an altogether different thing to forecast sales over time. Depending on different views of the future, some analysts may believe the company is a "buy," whereas others may believe the company is a "sell."

Different opinions will always arise when considering the future outlook. We may expect companies to report accurate data on their CO_2 emissions, but an ESG rating attempts to reflect the future outlook as well as historical data. Most ESG rating providers state that they project the risks and opportunities of the firm into the future, and how its strategy, intended policies, and moves will position it in the climate transition.

Thus, it is reasonable that a single agreed-upon indicator cannot be used to determine the ratings. Different rating providers inject different preferences into their ratings through their methodological choices, data collection choices, and the type of issues analyzed and how they are weighted.

> ### KEY LEARNING POINT
> *ESG ratings differ due to varying attributes, metrics, and weights.*

5.1.5 Summary – ESG Ratings

ESG ratings are increasingly important, and many investors use them in their investment decisions. ESG rating providers assess companies across various sustainability metrics, including on climate issues.

---

[157] A civil-law system differs from the common-law system in several ways. The civil-law system is codified, and the main source of reference is the law, or the constitution. In contrast, the common law can be uncodified, and it relies on decisions made in the past in similar cases (precedents). In the common-law system, the judge has an important role in every case; in the civil-law system, the judge´s role is less crucial (The Robbins Collection, 2020).

The evidence suggests that different rating providers adopt different definitions of ESG performance. Also, their methodologies on how to measure (and weight) that performance differ. This is expected, as ESG ratings rely on hundreds of metrics, many of which are qualitative. Some metrics are included by one provider but not by others, and translating a concept into a numerical quantity depends on the provider's judgment and methodology. That is, each provider adopts an approach that determines the particular metrics used and how to assign them to the individual ESG criteria. Empirically, measurement differences have been found to be the main reason for discrepant ratings.

The fact that two rating providers can assign different ESG ratings to the same company is not a reason to ignore the ratings. In fact, the differences do not necessarily indicate flaws, but only imply that investors cannot simply expect to use any metric and achieve their objectives. Given the variety of ESG ratings and the subjective choices that underlie them, investors will need to exercise their own judgement when they use them. In Section 5.4, we cover ESG integration into investment strategies.

When assessing an ESG rating, investors must look beyond the scores, understand the methodology, and decide if it aligns with their own ESG preferences. Investors need to acknowledge that ESG ratings are different from credit ratings (where Moody's and S&P typically agree on the credit risk of a company, as their models are quite comparable). When using ESG rating data, users must exercise their judgment, understand the factors underlying each rating, and then form an independent assessment for their investment and business decisions.

5.2   ESG STOCK MARKET INDICES

A stock market index measures the performance of a basket of stocks. Each index uses its own methodology and construction criteria. Among these criteria, some of the more relevant ones are how to select stocks for the index (the list of constituent stocks), what weighting scheme is used, and how frequently the constituents (and their weights) are revised. Stock market indices are also defined according to their geographical characteristics. Indices such as the Dow Jones 30, the German DAX, the Nikkei, EURO STOXX 50, MSCI World, or S&P500 are used to measure general stock market performance in a certain region. In addition, they can be defined in terms of specific industries (consumer goods, biotech, energy, banking, etc.) or market segments (small stocks, high growth, dividend-paying, etc.). Given the increasing relevance of sustainability (and climate issues), nowadays most index providers have their own sustainability (and climate-related) indices.

5.2.1 What Are Indices Used For?

Stock indices measure the performance of a certain set of stocks over a period. Besides tracking the average performance of a certain market, stock indices can be used for the following:

o Benchmarking performance of individual stocks: Indices are used to measure the relative performance of individual stocks.
o Assessing the performance of active asset managers: By comparing the performance of a certain asset manager to the index, it is possible to evaluate whether or not it was able to deliver higher (or lower) returns than that benchmark (we should also adjust for risk).
o Passive investing: Investment vehicles such as index funds or exchange-traded funds (ETFs) replicate and track stock market indices with a passive investment portfolio's strategy.

DJTA: the first stock index

The first stock market index was created in July 1884 in New York by the journalist Charles Dow. It was named the Dow Jones Transportation Average (DJTA) because it was calculated as the price-weighted average of 11 transportation stocks traded in the U.S. market.

Each index has its own methodology and specific revision dates. For instance, the S&P 500 rebalances every quarter. That is, on the third Friday of March, June, September, and December, the weights of the index are revised, and new stocks replace the old ones in the index. Another important methodological definition is the weighting scheme. Stock market indices can be capitalization weighted, price weighted, or equal weighted:

o In a capitalization-weighted index, each constituent weight is computed based on market capitalizations. Thus, the larger the capitalization of a constituent, the larger is its weight in the index. S&P 500 and MSCI World are two examples of capital-weighted indices.
o A price-weighted index holds an equal number of shares for each stock, and the value of the index is given by the sum of all the securities' prices divided by the total number of stocks. Therefore, stock price changes (in absolute amounts) of a very small company have the same impact as those of a large company. The famous Dow Jones Industrial Average (DJIA) is an example of a price-weighted index.
o In an equal-weighted index, the performance of each company's stock carries equal importance in determining the total value of the index. All stocks carry the same weight regardless of the initial price and capitalization. The Dow Jones Industrial Average® Equal Weight is an example of an equal-weighted index.

Given the different coverage universes (geographic, industrial, etc.) and different methodologies, the number of indices is much higher than the overall number of stocks. For instance, in 2020 there were 3.05 million indices and more than 41,000 publicly traded companies worldwide.[158] That is, the number of stock indices worldwide was approximately 70 times the number of public companies.

5.2.2 The Rise of Passive Investing

Markowitz's (1952) diversification theory and Sharpe (1964) and Lintner's (1965) capital asset pricing model (CAPM) provide the fundamental theoretical basis for indexing and passive investment. Once the index criteria and the appropriate number of stocks that constitute a certain index are known, it is possible to replicate the index, and therefore to create a portfolio with the same returns as the selected benchmark. However, purchasing the shares of every company included in the index, weighted by market capitalization (or price), would be a very difficult, costly, and time-consuming strategy for an individual investor. For this reason, we have seen a rise in investment vehicles that replicate and track a stock market index: index funds and ETFs.

Index funds and ETFs are very similar investment vehicles that track stock indices at low cost to investors. The main differences between them relate to how they can be traded and the minimum investment requirements.[159] For simplicity, in the discussion that follows we simply refer to them as index funds.

Index funds use a passive investment strategy that aims to deliver returns similar to the index that is being tracked. The fund purchases the individual stocks in exactly the same proportions that they occur in that index. Additional trading (buying or selling additional stocks) occurs only when the index is revised. Index revision occurs when new stocks are introduced into the index (replacing old ones), or whenever the weights of the index across its different components change. Because index funds simply replicate and trade infrequently, they operate at lower costs than actively managed funds and charge much lower fees (the average actively managed fund charges fees above 1%, whereas index funds charge fees lower than 0.2%).

This rise in passive investing has led to the growing importance of indices. Individuals, as well as institutional investors, have been using more and more of these passive instruments that track index performance at a low cost.

---

[158] Sources: Index Industry Association, World Bank.
[159] Whereas an ETF can be traded throughout the day, an index fund can be bought and sold only for the price set at the end of the trading day. In general, ETFs have lower minimum investment requirements than an index fund. The role of passive (and active) shareholders is analyzed further in Sections 4.3, 4.4, and 5.4.

> **Vanguard: the first index fund**
>
> The first index fund was created by John Bogle, the founder of Vanguard, in 1976. Named "First Index Investment Trust," it collected only US$11 million during its initial underwriting. Many critics at the time considered it "un-American" and "a sure path to mediocrity." This first index fund was designed as a low-cost investing vehicle that simply tracked the market, and did not attempt to beat the average index. It is now called the Vanguard 500 Index Fund, and has more than $400 billion in assets. As of 2020, the fund had an expense ratio of 0.04%.

Since Vanguard started its first index fund in 1976, passive investing has grown exponentially. Today, index funds and ETFs represent almost 50% of the ownership in several stock markets,[160] and the Big Three (Blackrock, Vanguard, and State Street) are collectively the largest single shareholder in 96% of Fortune 250 companies, with Vanguard alone being the largest shareholder in 65.6% of such companies (Griffin, 2020).

KEY LEARNING POINT

Passive investors hold portfolios that replicate the index. These investors have gained increasing importance in financial markets.

5.2.3 Benefits of Being Included in an Index

Inclusion in an index can make a company more visible and appealing to portfolio managers. For example, in the United States, indices such as the S&P 500 are widely used as benchmarks, and both active and passive investors tend to own shares in the index that they use as benchmarks. For companies, this means that belonging to an index adds a new set of investors to the company shareholder records. Given also the increasing role of passive investing, being part of the main indices has become more important over time.

Research has shown that the share value of companies added to the S&P 500 increases, which is called the "inclusion effect." Inclusion in an index is associated with increases in institutional ownership, liquidity, analyst coverage, as well as some concrete changes in companies.[161] Bennett et al. (2020) showed that S&P 500 Index addition has significant effects on firms' decisions in areas such as investment, governance, dividend payouts,

---

[160] Bank for International Settlements (BIS) estimations suggest that the global share of passive equity funds was about 37% in 2017, up from 15% in 2007. See also "Owners of the World's Listed Companies," OECD Capital Market Series, Paris.

[161] Shleifer, 1986; Harris and Gurel, 1986; Jain, 1987; Dhillon and Johnson, 1991; Beneish and Whaley, 1996; Chen et al., 2004

financing, and managerial performance evaluation. Addition to a main index also thrusts the company in the limelight, as it attracts the attention of the media, analysts, and investors.

Overall, being part of an index is like being a member of a professional organization or club. On the one hand, it confers prestige and visibility. On the other hand, it enables additional comparisons with other members of that group.

KEY LEARNING POINT

Belonging to an index is like membership of a prestigious club. It confers prestige and visibility, but it also brings responsibilities.

5.2.4 The Main ESG Stock Market Indices

ESG indices are indices that show the performance of a basket of companies, selected according to an ESG assessment of each company. The purpose of ESG indices is the same as that of other indices: compare relative stock performance, benchmark fund managers, and provide a benchmark that can be replicated by index funds.

In 1990, MSCI created the first ESG index – the MSCI KLD 400 Social Index (originally called Domini 400) – to help ESG-aware investors get exposure to companies whose positive ESG impact had been assessed by KLD.[162] Thereafter, other ESG indices were launched, such as the Dow Jones Sustainability Index (1999), the FTSE4Good Indexes (2001), and the S&P 500 ESG Index (2019).

ESG index constituents are based on a parent index (that reflects the overall universe of stocks available). Then, different methodologies, including ESG scores, are used for deciding which stocks to choose from that specific ESG index. For instance, the S&P 500 ESG Index is based on the parent index, the S&P 500. Then, companies belonging to that index are selected according to their ESG scores. In addition, exclusion lists are often used (for instance, companies in specific industry sub-categories such as coal energy – the following examples further clarify the concept of exclusion lists).

The methodologies vary, and each index provider has specific features. Given all the possible combinations of geographies, industries, types of companies, and also specific ESG methodologies, there has been a proliferation of ESG indices (in 2019, there were more than 37,000 sustainable indices available worldwide). Table 5.3 reports some facts about selected relevant ESG indices.

---

[162] KLD was subsequently acquired by MSCI in 2010.

Table 5.3 Selected ESG indices

Index	Year	Parent index	Number of constituents	Region	Exclusion lists	ESG score used for deciding which stocks to include
S&P 500 ESG	2019	S&P 500	295	United States	Yes	S&P DJI ESG score
Dow Jones Sustainability	1999	S&P Global BMI	250	World	Yes	S&P DJI ESG score
FTSE4Good Developed	2001	FTSE Developed	2011	World	Yes	FTSE Russell's ESG Ratings
MSCI KLD 400 Social	1990	MSCI USA IM	404	United States	Yes	MSCI ESG Rating

Source: S&Ps, MSCI, FTSE, Dow Jones, as of January 2021.

The S&P ESG 500 Index

Constituents of the S&P ESG 500 Index must be part of the "parent" index, the S&P 500 Index. They are then selected according to their S&P DJI ESG Score (see Section 5.1) and business activities. First, companies from the S&P 500 Index involved in tobacco or controversial weapons, or those with a low UN Global Compact score, are excluded. The second screen is based on the company's ESG scores. In this step, companies with ESG scores in the bottom 25% of their industry are excluded. After these exclusions, the eligible stocks are sorted by their ESG score. S&P then selects companies, starting from the top-ranked companies, until it reaches 75% of the market capitalization of each industry.

As in the parent index, companies included in the S&P ESG 500 Index are weighted by float-adjusted market capitalization.

	Sector	Index (%)	Parent (%)
Apple	Info Tech	9.7	6.4
Microsoft	Info Tech	8.4	5.7
Amazon	Consumer Goods	4.3	2.9
Alphabet A	Info Tech	2.8	2.0
Alphabet C	Info Tech	2.6	1.9
Unitedhealth	Health Care	1.9	1.4
NVIDIA	Info Tech	1.9	1.2
Exxon Mobil	Energy	1.5	1.3
JP Morgan Chase	Financials	1.4	1.1
Procter & Gamble	Consumer Staples	1.4	1.0
Total		35.9	24.9

Table 5.4 shows the top 10 constituents of important U.S. ESG indices.

Table 5.4 Top 10 constituents of selected indices

	S&P 500 ESG Index	MSCI KLD 400 Social Index	FTSE4Good Developed Index
1	Apple	Microsoft	Apple
2	Microsoft	Alphabet C	Microsoft
3	Amazon	Alphabet A	Alphabet A
4	Alphabet A	Tesla	Alphabet C
5	Alphabet C	NVIDIA Corp	Johnson & Johnson
6	J.P. Morgan	Visa	Visa
7	Tesla	Home Depot	Nestlé
8	NVidia Corp	Procter & Gamble	NVidia Corp
9	UnitedHealth Group	Walt Disney	Home Depot
10	Visa	MasterCard	Procter & Gamble

Source: S&P, MSCI, FTSE.

Although there is certainly an overlap in the companies present in the top 10 of each index, the weights vary greatly, due to the differing index methodologies and ESG assessments.

KEY LEARNING POINT

ESG stock indices are created by different institutions, using widely varying methodologies. Typically, they rely on exclusion lists and an ESG score to select stocks and the appropriate weights in the index.

The Dow Jones Sustainability World Index

This index tracks the performance of the top 10% of the 2,500 largest companies in the S&P Global Index in terms of sustainability. As in the case of S&P ESG 500, the Dow Jones Sustainability World Index constituents are selected based on the company's S&P Global ESG Score.

First, the eligible universe excludes companies involved in controversies (this covers a range of issues such as corruption, fraud, human rights issues, workplace safety, catastrophic accidents, and environmental disasters). Then, companies with an ESG score less than 45% of the highest-scoring company's ESG score are also excluded. Next, for each industry, the top 10%–15% (depending on the industry and some rules to reduce turnover in the index) rated companies are selected to form part of the DJSI Index.

The index is rebalanced annually (in September), and it included 321 constituents as of January 2021. As of January 2021, the largest constituent was Microsoft Corp., which accounted for 10.8% of the index market capitalization.

5.2.5 Climate-Related Indices

Given the increasing relevance of climate issues, today most index providers have their own climate-related indices. To be included in a climate-related index, a company needs to be aligned to specific environmental criteria that are established by each index provider. Each index provider (S&P, MSCI, DJ, etc.) has developed its own methodology to assign a score/rating to each company operating in an eligible industry. However, the construction of ESG indices often entails complicated calculations and qualitative judgments, and some index methodologies are not completely transparent, which makes external verification through replication difficult.

Table 5.5 reports some facts about a selection of climate-related indices.

Table 5.5 Selected climate-related stock indices

Index	Inception year	Number of constituents	Region	Parent index	Number of constituents parent	Exclusion lists	ESG score used for deciding which stocks to include
MSCI ACWI Climate Change	2019	2,757	World	MSCI ACWI	2,975	Yes	MSCI ESG Rating
MSCI Global Environment	2009	257	World	MSCI ACWI IMI	9,287	Yes	MSCI ESG Rating
STOXX® Europe 600 Paris-Aligned Benchmark	2019	509	Europe	STOXX® Europe 600	601	Yes	MSCI ESG Research/ Low Carbon Transition score.
S&P 500 Paris-Aligned Climate	2020	349	United States	S&P 500	505	Yes	S&P DJI ESG score

Source: MSCI, EURO STOXX, S&P Dow Jones, Q1 2021.

As can be seen above, it is possible for the same provider to have different climate-related indices, each capturing a different set of aspects. Depending on the methodology and exclusion lists, the number of companies (relative to the parent index) varies. For instance, in the case of MSCI, approximately 95% of the firms in the parent index appear in the "climate index," whereas in the case of the S&P 500, approximately 70% of the firms in the parent index appear in the "climate index." In the case of the MSCI Global Environment Index, only 257 companies are selected (out of 9,287 of its parent's index).

MSCI Global Environment Index

The MSCI Global Environment Index focuses on companies whose primary source of revenues increases the efficient use of scarce natural resources, or mitigates the impact of environmental degradation. Its parent index is the MSCI ACWI IMI Index, a market cap-weighted index of 8,947 large-, mid-, and small-cap constituents from 50 countries (23 developed markets and 27 emerging market).

First, the methodology excludes companies operating in the fossil fuel and nuclear energy industries, in the controversial weapons business, and those that have been involved in serious ESG controversies. After this step, MSCI includes only companies that have at least 50% of their revenue from six environmental themes (aligned to the UN SDGs): Alternative Energy, Energy Efficiency, Green Building, Sustainable Water, Pollution Prevention and Control, and Sustainable Agriculture.

As of January 2021, MSCI Global Environment Index included 237 constituents (compared to the 8,947 constituents of the parent index). The market capitalization of the index was equal to US$1.576 billion, and the largest constituent was Tesla, with a market capitalization of US$591 billion.

The MSCI ACWI Climate Change Index

In 2019, MSCI launched the MSCI ACWI Climate Change Index. This index is based on its parent index, the MSCI ACWI (2,975 constituents from 50 countries as of June 2021).

The eligible universe excludes companies not rated by MSCI ESG Research and companies involved in controversial weapons. Companies in the eligible universe are over- or under-weighted according to their current risk exposure, and their management of the risks and opportunities presented by the low-carbon transition. MSCI first computes a "Carbon Intensity Profile." Then, it assesses a company's policies, commitments to mitigating the transition risk, governance structures, risk management programs and initiatives, targets and performance, and involvement in controversies.

The final weight of each stock in the index is obtained by multiplying its "Combined Score" by its weight in the parent index. In this index, companies with higher scores (better scores on their climate-related risk compared to their peers) have a greater weight in the index. As of January 2020, the MSCI ACWI Climate Change included 2,757 stocks. Below are the top 10 constituents in the index and its parent index as of 2021.

	Index (%)	Parent (%)
Microsoft Corp	5.30	3.92
Apple	3.91	3.46
Amazon	2.63	2.32
Tesla	2.55	0.78
Facebook	1.17	1.26
Alphabet C	1.04	1.11
Alphabet A	1.03	1.10
NVIDIA	0.90	0.74
Intel Corp	0.89	0.34
Taiwan Semicond.	0.84	0.79
Total	20.25	14.17

KEY LEARNING POINT

Most climate-related stock indices use exclusion rules and environmental scores to determine the weight of a certain stock in the index.

5.2.6 Company Implications

Stocks added to ESG indices can benefit from an improved commercial image, increased visibility, and larger media coverage. Furthermore, inclusion in ESG indices indicates a larger investor base, because the indices are replicated by passive investors (including index funds and ETFs).

Companies included in an ESG index are less likely to be subject to divestment or activist investor campaigns. McKenzie (2019) used 1,300 European companies' ESG ratings (from Refinitiv) and showed that 62% of activist targets in Europe since 2017 fall into the bottom two ESG quartiles, and that compared to industry peers, companies in these groups are on average 24% more likely to face an activist campaign.

The stock of companies included as constituents of an ESG/climate index is supposed to attract an increasing volume of equity investors, guided by both their appetite for "sustainable assets" and for diversification. However, the empirical evidence of positive stock market reactions to the inclusion of a company in a sustainability index is mixed. The early research has found that the impact of inclusion/exclusion is limited (Consolandi et al., 2008; Cheung, 2011). More recently, Hawn et al. (2018) investigated stock market reactions to the Dow Jones Sustainability Index. This global study covered 321 addition events and 215 deletion events in 27 countries from 1999 to 2015. The empirical results show that abnormal returns in event windows are not statistically significant.

Other sustainability index inclusion event studies have focused on visibility. Durand et al. (2019) showed that sustainability events provide added visibility. Inclusion events receive large media coverage, attract more attention from financial analysts, and lead to an increase in the percentage of shares held by long-term investors. Companies that are included in ESG indices tend to emphasize these inclusion events to attract the attention of sustainability-oriented investors. For example, on the occasion of the DJSI's acknowledgment of Enel's track record on tackling climate in November 2020, the company's CEO, Francesco Starace, declared: "By embedding innovation and sustainability into the Enel Group's business practices we are leading the energy transition towards a zero-carbon model, protecting the global environment while creating long term value for our stakeholders." Similarly, in 2020, after a positive evaluation of its ESG performance by the DJSI, AXA's CEO, Thomas Burbel, expressed his satisfaction by declaring: "I am very pleased that we are now ranked number 2 in the DJSI. This demonstrates that corporate responsibility is an important component of the Group's strategy and it illustrates the strength of our purpose: act for human progress to protect what matters."

5.2.7 Summary – ESG Stock Indices

Stock indices measure the performance of individual stocks in a certain country or region, or other common features (such as size, dividends, past growth, and other firm characteristics). There are several index providers, with varying methodologies (with respect to, e.g., the coverage, the list of constituents, and the weights of the different assets). Given the different methodologies, weighting schemes, and possible combinations of stocks, indices outnumber individual stocks.

Besides performance measurement, indices also allow performance to be benchmarked. That is, asset managers can use the indices to benchmark their own performance.

In addition, stock indices are a basis for passive investments. The evidence shows that over recent decades, passive investments, which merely track the performance of a certain stock index, have been increasing in importance. That is, as opposed to having individual retail investors or active managers investing in a company after a careful fundamental analysis, an increasingly large fraction of the ownership of a company is held by passive institutional owners, who replicate the index.

Research does not show a significant impact of additions to ESG indices on stock prices. However, addition to an ESG index has other effects: e.g., it demonstrates the company's commitment to environmental sustainability, attracts institutional investors, and increases visibility.

Given the growing relevance of climate investing, most index providers now have specific climate (or ESG) indices to track the performance of (what they consider to be) the most sustainable companies. Most environmental index providers use exclusion rules and environmental scores to determine the weights of each stock in the index. The methodology underlying sustainability varies greatly depending on the provider, the underlying ratings used to select companies, and their weights in the index.

5.3 PERFORMANCE OF "GREEN" PRODUCTS AND STRATEGIES

This section focuses on sustainable finance, environmental issues, and the relationship between risk and return. The traditional finance relationship, risk–return, is being redefined, as investors understand that ESG factors can be material to investment performance.

Several papers have examined whether companies with strong ESG credentials also have enhanced profitability and value, what is sometimes referred to as "doing well by doing good." Also, there is some empirical research on the implications of climate risk and ESG in general for investors. Overall, the evidence is mixed, and it is difficult to establish causality, especially for issues such as climate change risks, for which very limited data time series are available.

5.3.1 Company Performance – Do Well and Do Good

The topic of companies engaging in "socially responsible" behaviors has stimulated spirited debate for many decades, and dates back to Adam Smith. More recently, in 1970, Milton Friedman wrote a well-known article in the *New York Times Magazine* titled "The Social Responsibility of Business Is to Increase Its Profits" (Friedman, 2007).[163]

Friedman's controversial article claimed that a CEO should focus on maximizing profit and not on serving society. Despite being quoted thousands of times and being used by various organizations to emphasize the need for a new model of capitalism, the article has been ridiculed by people who never read past the title. Friedman says what he wrote applies "under certain conditions." These conditions are that companies do not have a comparative advantage in socially responsible actions (relative to individuals) and that governments are functioning well in their "responsibility to impose taxes and determine expenditures for such 'social' purposes as controlling pollution or training the hard-core unemployed." The first assumption means that €1 spent by a company on a social initiative creates the same value as €1 spent by someone else. Friedman recognized that individuals have social responsibilities, and that it is not the CEO's job to strip individuals of their flexibility by supporting, with the company's money, their own pet causes, instead of giving individuals the choices regarding which social responsibilities they wish to fulfil. A second key assumption in Friedman's article is that "there is one and only one social responsibility of business […] to increase its profits so long as it stays within the rules of the game." Governments should set regulations that represent the aggregate preferences of their voters. However, in reality, regulation is imperfect. For instance, governments decide on local taxes, but global issues require coordination. It is clear that pollution is an externality, but as there is no worldwide agreement, it is not yet taxed accordingly.[164]

Furthermore, Friedman never suggested that companies should exploit stakeholders. He actually wrote: "It may well be in the long-run interest of a corporation that is a major employer in a small community to devote resources to providing amenities to that

---

[163]   https://www.nytimes.com/1970/09/13/archives/a-friedman-doctrine-the-social-responsibility-of-business-is-to.html.

[164] See Section 6.1 for a further discussion of externalities and carbon pricing.

community or to improving its government. That may make it easier to attract desirable employees."

This means that it may be in a company's own best interests to adopt environmental and social objectives, as such objectives make good business sense. This is the value-enhancing role of ESG. Companies that protect the environment, treat employees fairly, and improve community relationships can do well by doing good. For instance, companies that improve their reputations and avoid getting mired in controversies can retain more customers and employees.

This does not mean companies should promote ESG/CSR at all costs. In fact, the agency view of CSR suggests that money spent on CSR initiatives is sometimes a reflection of agency problems inside the company and a waste of corporate resources. As an example, given that companies have no comparative advantage relative to individuals in giving money to charities, what they should do instead is pay dividends to shareholders, who decide on which charities to support.[165]

Many people misread Friedman's arguments, accusing him of promoting short-termism and suggesting that quick profits should dominate everything else. Friedman did not say this. The reality is more nuanced, and there are indeed sound business reasons for companies to take into account broader societal issues.

Several theoretical articles have addressed the topic of sustainability and the long-term value of firms. Bénabou and Tirole (2010) suggested that one motivation to consider ESG stems from the failure of policymakers to correct market failures and externalities.[166] They argue that stronger ESG performance can reduce short-term opportunistic behavior by executives that fails to take long-term value into consideration. Hart and Zingales (2017) incorporated possible negative externalities generated by companies in their analysis, and concluded that companies and asset managers must follow policies consistent with the preferences of their ultimate investors, to maximize their well-being (which includes not only monetary aspects, but also aspects related to the environment, democracy, and social well-being, among others). Heinkel et al. (2001) showed how firms excluded by socially responsible investors suffer a reduction in their investor base and have a higher cost of capital. Pástor et al. (2021) identified an "ESG risk factor" that captures investors' preferences for green holdings. When ESG concerns gain strength, "green stocks" outperform "brown stocks" over a

---

[165] Several papers show that firm participation in certain CSR issues, such as charity giving, is associated with higher agency costs and lower shareholder value (e.g., Di Giuli and Kostovetsky, 2014; Masulis and Reza, 2015; Cheng et al. 2013). This suggests that a part of the CSR expenditure can be a manifestation of managerial agency problems, which enable managers to engage in CSR that benefits themselves at the expense of shareholders.

[166] Externalities exist when an economic agent benefits from the production of a good but does not bear the external social costs associated with its production. See Section 6.1.

period of time, but have lower alphas in the long run. The short-term higher returns occur as the market transitions to the new set of ESG preferences.

The empirical literature has tried to assess whether companies with strong ESG performance enjoy enhanced profitability and value.[167] In an extensive review of the research published during the 1990s, Murphy (2002) highlighted that companies that score well according to objective environmental criteria achieve stronger financial returns than the overall market. In fact, better environmental performance is shown to be associated both with higher accounting performance (return on equity (ROE) and return on assets (ROA)) and with higher stock market returns. In a frequently cited study, Friede et al. (2015) analyzed the findings of 2,200 individual studies and showed that 90% of them found a nonnegative relationship between ESG and corporate financial performance, with the majority reporting positive findings. However, this evidence suffers from some drawbacks. First, the majority of these studies were not published in peer-reviewed journals, and therefore have not been subjected to significant scrutiny. For those that were published in peer-reviewed journals, very few were published in what are considered the top-ranked finance, economics, or business journals. Further, the methodology used different databases, including working papers, published journal papers, and articles written for a commercial audience, where the studies were chosen based on keyword searches; this can create a systematic bias toward articles that show positive results. Finally, the direction of causality was not analyzed. Do firms perform well because they "do good," or do firms invest in ESG issues because they are "doing well"?

Overall, the results in the early studies vary due to sample selection, definitions of ESG, the time horizon considered, the data comparison methods, and other factors.[168] Moreover, most papers struggle with the direction of causality. Is ESG driving firm performance, or do profitable firms have more resources to invest in areas that influence ESG? That is, is it "doing good by doing well" or "doing well by doing good"?

More recent research has attempted to tackle these issues. Flammer (2013, 2015) showed that companies reported to behave responsibly toward the environment experience significant stock price increases and have superior accounting performance. The positive effects of ESG are also confirmed by positive shareholder reactions to successful ESG engagements (Dimson et al. 2015, and others in Section 4.4). Deng et al. (2013) found that acquirers with high CSR scores achieve higher merger announcement returns, as well as larger increases in post-merger long-term operating performance. Edmans (2012) analyzed employee satisfaction and stock returns, and found that the "100 Best Companies to Work For in America" outperformed their peers. Khan et al. (2016) showed that firms with good

---

[167] Here we focus mostly on equities, as the evidence on bonds is covered in Chapter 2.
[168] As an example, Borgers et al. (2013) found that high-CSR stocks outperformed low-CSR stocks during 1992–2004, but not during 2004–2009. They concluded that this was related to investor expectations and temporary mispricing. As investors devote more attention to stakeholder issues, prior mispricing is eliminated.

performance on material sustainability issues (see Section 6.3.2 for a discussion on materiality) significantly outperform firms with poor performance on these issues. They also showed that having good ratings on immaterial CSR issues does not lead to a significant performance advantage.

Others have provided evidence that environmental policies lower risk. Sharfman and Fernando (2008) analyzed a sample of 276 publicly traded U.S. firms, and found that improved environmental risk management reduces the cost of equity capital. El Ghoul et al. (2011) also found that firms with higher ESG scores have a lower cost of equity. Dunn et al. (2018) found that firms with the worst ESG credentials have higher risk (stock-specific volatility is up to 10%–15% higher and betas up to 3% higher than stocks with the best ESG exposures). Hoepner et al. (2020) suggested that engagement with ESG issues can benefit shareholders by reducing firms' downside risk, measured using the lower partial moment and value at risk.

Another strand of research focuses on how investors react to sustainability-related news. Krueger (2015) found that investors respond very negatively to negative events for the company's stakeholders (environment, employees, communities, customers), and documented positive reactions from shareholders to the adoption of CSR policies that improve relations with stakeholders. Starks et al. (2017) found that investors in higher-ESG-rated companies are calmer (less likely to divest after negative earnings surprises). Lins et al. (2017) found that firms that invest in social capital benefit from an overall level of trust, which can provide downside protection in volatile markets. Amiraslani et al. (2022) reported that during a crisis, high-social-capital firms benefited from lower bond spreads and were able to raise more debt, and for longer maturities.

KEY LEARNING POINT

Companies can do well by doing good, and ESG can help them improve their reputations and retain customers and employees.

5.3.2 Risk and Performance of Climate-Related Investments

Besides the evidence at the firm level, there is a debate on whether ESG investment pays off for investors. Larry Fink, CEO of BlackRock, suggests that we typically do not include all risks when thinking about investments. But when we factor in all risks properly, portfolios that take sustainability and climate change into consideration should provide better risk-adjusted returns to investors. Some modern asset pricing models include climate risks as a long-run risk factor (Bansal et al., 2016), whereas others highlight the importance of environmental issues in the cross section of stock returns (Bolton and Kacperczyk 2021a; Hsu et al. 2022).

Industry research typically shows a positive correlation between ESG and financial performance. Some examples of this include the following:

- o S&P (2021) analyzed the performance of 26 large ESG investment funds (mutual funds and ETFs) with more than US$250 billion assets under management (AuM) and found that 19 of those funds outperformed the S&P 500 Index during the pandemic period, from March 2020 to March 2021.
- o MSCI (2020) showed that from May 31, 2013, to November 30, 2020, all MSCI ACWI ESG indices outperformed their parent index, the MSCI ACWI.
- o Bank of America-Merrill Lynch (2019) listed 10 reasons why investors should care about ESG in their investment decisions. These include the "evidence" that ESG can generate Alpha, ESG scores are a solid predictor of earnings risk, ESG could have helped avoid 90% of past bankruptcies, and companies with higher ESG scores have access to cheaper capital.
- o J.P. Morgan (Ward, 2021) ranked MSCI constituents by their ESG scores and showed that during the period December 31, 2012, to February 26, 2021, the stock of the companies in the top ESG quintile performed much better than that of the companies in the bottom quintile.
- o Alliance Global Investors (2017) showed that during the period September 2007 to February 2015, the MSCI Emerging Market ESG Index outperformed its parent index (MSCI EM) by more than 40%.

There are, however, some methodological problems with the above practitioners' studies. Some can even be considered self-serving and biased, as they were created by organizations that profit from its results (as it helps them to sell their services in those areas). Although there is some evidence that low-carbon portfolios have higher returns, the results are not robust. The reality is that significant methodological challenges stand in the way of obtaining a robust answer. Most of the studies have small sample sizes, are conducted in selected markets, and use specific time periods. Also, the evidence depends on the provider of ESG scores, benchmark selection, the time period, the scores used, and the analytical approaches employed.[169]

The academic evidence on the influence of socially responsible investing (SRI) and ESG on fund performance is also mixed. Renneboog et al. (2008) found little evidence that the performance of SRI-focused funds differs significantly from that of conventional funds. Henke (2016) analyzed the performance of 103 socially responsible bond funds in the United States and the Eurozone, comparing them with a matched sample of conventional funds in the period 2001–2014. The results suggest that responsible bond funds outperform

---

[169] Boffo and Patalano (2020).

their counterparts by 1.5% annually. Most of the better performance is related to the mitigation of ESG risks, achieved by the exclusion of corporate bond issuers with unsatisfactory CSR activity. Further, results suggest that the performance improvement is more likely to occur during crisis periods. Using a sample of 2,168 U.S. equity funds from 2003 to 2011, Engle et al. (2019) studied how to dynamically hedge climate change risk. They used a mimicking portfolio approach to build climate change hedge portfolios based on textual analysis of newspapers. This suggests that appropriate rebalancing can achieve industry-balanced portfolios that perform well in hedging innovations in climate news.

El Ghoul and Karoui (2017) documented the fact that higher-CSR funds have poorer performance (but stronger performance persistence and a weaker performance–flow relationship) than their low-CSR-scoring counterparts. Bannier et al. (2019) showed that a portfolio long in stocks with high ESG and that short in those with lower ESG scores has significant negative abnormal returns. However, the risk of the two portfolios is different. In particular, the evidence suggests that low-ESG portfolios also have a higher risk, and they seem to compensate their higher risk with higher returns.

Gibson, Glossner, et al. (2020) used data on PRI signatories and their portfolio returns. The results suggest that some ESG strategies reduce risks, but they failed to find superior performance for ESG strategies.

Overall, the mixed, and sometimes inconsistent, empirical evidence can be explained by problems related to different providers of ratings, investment strategies, methodologies, geographical selection, and time frames. In particular, in the next section, we will discuss the short- and long-term effects of sustainability on prices. Section 5.4.8 provides additional evidence on how institutional investors change their portfolios because of sustainability.

KEY LEARNING POINT

Low-ESG portfolios can bring higher returns, due to the need to compensate for higher risk.

5.3.3 Prices and Returns Are Correlated

"Buy low, sell high" is a famous investment principle. It seems simple, but is difficult to apply in practice. This simple phrase conceals deep investment ideas that are rather technical. For instance, one of finance's key concepts is the relation between risk and return. In the context of sustainability, this suggests that companies that are more sustainable should deliver lower returns to shareholders. That is, high-ESG companies should benefit from a lower cost of capital, consistent with their lower risk (as suggested by the theoretical papers reviewed earlier in this chapter). At the same time, as the firm is considered to have a lower risk, the market price should reflect that fact and its value should be higher than what it would otherwise be. This in turn suggests that, during a transition period, companies are rewarded for their good sustainability performance, and their share prices should outperform those of their counterparts. This occurs when the market is repricing shares. As companies with more sustainable practices generate higher cash flows and have lower risk than the market expects in the short run, they outperform their counterparts in terms of short-term stock returns. However, once the transition is over, greener companies should benefit from a lower cost of capital, which means a lower expected return on investors' capital.

Some suggest that investors should expect high returns from investing in high-ESG companies (see Section 5.3.2). This is not true, unless we use several dubious assumptions regarding the behavior of firms and investors. Consistently high stock returns and high valuation levels are incompatible. In fact, consistently high returns imply a high cost of capital for the company. That is, when a company carries a higher risk, investors are willing to bear these risks only if the expected returns are higher. However, when the expected returns are high (or when the cost of capital is high), the valuation levels are lower (Chapter 2).

The theoretical papers discussed earlier in this section suggest that more sustainable companies carry lower risk, and should thus deliver lower (not higher) returns to investors. A reduced cost of capital means stock prices should increase, as shareholders' expected rate of return is lower. In other words, if a company is responsible and the market knows it, the company's current value in the market should reflect this.

In summary, in the steady state, we should expect lower risk to be associated with lower returns. Accordingly, ESG-friendly companies have lower risk and a lower cost of capital. Conversely, low-ESG companies are punished with a higher cost of capital due to their additional risk.[170]

This means that saying you can both "do well and do good" is sometimes an exaggeration, and this sentiment can fuel exuberance in capital markets. For instance, sin stocks (Section 5.4.8) face a higher cost of capital, which is equivalent to higher investor expectations in terms of stock returns. The evidence suggests that the reduction in demand (due to investors being unwilling to hold companies with poor ESG performance) translates into lower stock prices today and higher returns in the future.

It is only during a transition period, when the market has not fully incorporated these differential risks and their consequences for companies, that high-sustainability companies

---

[170] As a parallel to this, it has been well known for many decades that small companies deliver higher returns relative to large companies (Fama and French, 1992). However, nobody says that the cost of capital of small companies is lower. It is well known why small companies have additional risks, and different asset pricing models have explained why their cost of capital is higher.

should enjoy higher returns.[171] Over time, these higher returns translate into higher valuation levels, and once the market is in the steady state, the alignment between risk and return should be back in place.

KEY LEARNING POINT

Risk and valuation levels are negatively correlated, and risk is correlated with expected returns.

5.3.4 Other Utility Functions Besides Wealth

Some studies have highlighted the importance of nonpecuniary motives when investing, and the investors' willingness to forego returns in exchange for achieving sustainability objectives. Some authors have examined impact funds, which are PE funds that have a dual objective: to generate both financial and social returns. Barber et al. (2021) documented that impact VC funds earn 4.7% lower internal rates of return (IRRs) ex-post compared to traditional VC funds. The authors suggest that the ultimate investors (LPs) derive nonpecuniary utility from investing in dual-objective funds. In particular, they found that some impact investors are willing to earn lower returns in exchange for impact. The results vary across investors. Development organizations, foundations, financial institutions, public pension funds, European investors, and United Nations Principles of Responsible Investment signatories are more willing to pay. Kovner and Lerner (2015) studied 28 community development VC funds in the United States, and found that they tend to invest in companies at an earlier stage, in industries outside the traditional VC areas, and overall have fewer successful exits.

Bauer et al. (2021) studied to what extent individual beneficiaries within the Dutch pension system preferred their pension savings to be used to promote sustainability and found that 68% of the surveyed participants preferred an approach that invests their pension savings in a sustainable manner – even if this comes at the expense of lower returns. Similarly, Riedl and Smeets (2017) surveyed 3,382 socially responsible investors and 35,000 randomly selected investors in the Netherlands and found that both social preferences and social

---

[171] Pástor et al. (2022) found that greener assets have lower expected returns in the future (and thus a lower cost of capital). They also showed that as investor tastes shift toward green assets and products, these greener assets realize higher returns. Their empirical tests support this. Thus, green stocks outperformed brown stocks in the 2010s. But this green performance was unexpected, and it was due to an increase in investor concerns about climate. Similar results were found with German government bonds. The green bonds trade at lower yields (and thus will generate, until maturity, lower expected returns compared to non-green bonds). But in the past few years, the green bond has outperformed its non-green twin, as their yield had decreased. This is also called *greenium*, which refers to the situation in which issuers of green bonds benefit from lower borrowing costs (i.e., green bonds are sold at a premium relative to conventional bonds). See Section 3.1.9.

signaling explain SRI decisions, whereas financial motives play less of a role. In particular, socially responsible investors expect to earn lower returns from SRI funds than from conventional funds.

These results suggest that responsible funds target a different subset of investors. That is, these investors derive nonpecuniary utility from investing in dual-objective funds, and are thus willing to sacrifice financial returns. This area of investors' willingness to pay is under-researched, and has to be assessed carefully. If taken to extremes, it can be used as an excuse by underperforming fund managers: *Forget about my returns, as I am doing good for the World. The stocks I bought underperform, but they are doing nice things.* This poses challenges to institutional investors, who can also have competing priorities. The association representing German occupational pension funds, in its response to the European Commission consultation on long-term and sustainable investment, stated that ESG factors were not a priority compared to pressing issues such as the low-interest-rate environment.[172]

Another strand of literature analyzes the drivers of investor flows and the role of client (end-investor) demand. Hartzmark and Sussman (2019) documented findings consistent with nonpecuniary motives in investment decisions. They documented reallocations of capital toward funds with high sustainability ratings. They found that after the introduction of Morningstar ESG ratings, U.S. funds with low ESG ratings experienced net outflows, whereas funds with high ESG ratings experienced net inflows. Ceccarelli et al. (2020) showed how funds compete for climate-conscious investors. They examined fund investor inflows following the introduction of an eco-labeling of "low carbon designation" funds (by Morningstar in the United States and Europe). The results suggest that fund managers adjust their holdings toward climate-friendlier stocks to retain their investors. Benson and Humphrey (2008) analyzed the link between current and past measures of performance and fund flows. The results suggest that SRI fund flows are less sensitive to returns than conventional funds. Starks et al. (2017) found that institutions with longer horizons tend to invest more in high-ESG-rated firms, and they are more patient, i.e., less likely to divest after negative earnings surprises. Renneboog et al. (2008), Riedl and Smeets (2017), and El Ghoul and Karoui (2017) also found a weak performance–flow relationship for sustainable funds. This suggests that socially and environmentally conscious investors are more committed to their investments than conventional investors. Their inflows are sensitive to past positive returns, but their outflows are less sensitive to past negative returns.

KEY LEARNING POINT

Some investors have motivations other than wealth maximization. These investors may invest in assets that align with their values, even if they are less profitable.

---

[172] https://www.ipe.com/esg-not-a-priority-says-german-pension-fund-association/10012461.article.

5.3.5 Summary – Risk and Return

In this section, we have discussed risk and return, and how sustainable products and strategies affect performance. We started by discussing the evidence on the impact of climate (and other ESG issues) on company performance.

ESG investment is gaining substantial attention from individual investors and, above all, from many institutional investors such as pension funds, sovereign wealth funds, and other asset managers. We have also discussed the performance of investment funds, or portfolio strategies, that take ESG and climate-related topics into account.

Despite anecdotal evidence provided by commentators, newspapers, and consultant reports, there is no scientific evidence suggesting superior performance by high-ESG funds in the long run.

This does not mean that investors should not consider climate issues and sustainability in their investment decisions. Importantly, prices and returns are correlated. Once we get to a steady state, firms with lower risk should have lower expected returns or cost of capital. However, during a transition period, we may observe high returns for sustainability-related strategies. It is important to be aware of one key investment principle: past returns do not predict future returns, and past average returns definitely do not necessarily imply strong expected returns in the future.

In the long run, it is reasonable to assume lower returns from assets with lower risk. Therefore, green assets (or sustainable investments) should have lower expected returns, as investors like holding them, and they also offer a hedge against climate risk. Conversely, brown stocks are riskier, and therefore they have to offer higher expected returns for investors to hold them.

Finally, it is sometimes assumed that everyone (investors in particular) seeks to maximize performance or shareholder value. Some investors, however, have different utility functions. If the values and goals of these investors align with sustainability considerations, then they pursue these strategies even if they do not promise superior performance. The evidence also suggests that these appear to be more "patient" investors.

In the following sections, we discuss the different strategies investors can use to pursue sustainability goals, and provide empirical evidence from various institutional investors.

5.4 THE IMPORTANCE OF CLIMATE RISKS FOR INSTITUTIONAL INVESTORS

Institutional investors are the largest holders of shares in publicly traded companies worldwide. They are also the majority holders of bonds (corporate and government).

Therefore, it is obvious that they are key players in the low-carbon transition. Most institutional investors believe that climate risks have financial implications for their portfolio firms, and that these risks, especially regulatory risks, already have begun to materialize. Besides being a scientific reality, climate change is also an economic reality (see Chapters 1 and 2), and thus, it is a relevant investment issue. This section analyzes the impact of climate risk for investors, in particular, institutional investors. We also discuss the main ways in which different types of investors use environmental data (and other ESG factors) in their investment decision process, and the resulting strategies.

5.4.1 The Rise of Institutional Investors

Institutional investors are professional investors that invest on behalf of their ultimate clients. They are now the largest group of shareholders in most publicly traded companies worldwide.

Figure 5.1 The relative ownership of each category of investors (% of market capitalization)

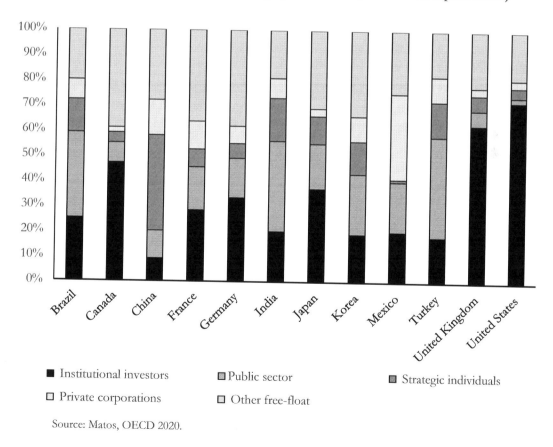

Source: Matos, OECD 2020.

Their relative importance varies across markets, but on average, they control more than 40% of the world's market capitalization. The most important institutional investors are mutual funds, pension funds, and insurance companies. U.S.-domiciled institutional investors account for 65% of global institutional investor holdings.

Several studies suggest that the increased role of institutional investors is impacting firms' behaviors. The evidence suggests that foreign institutional investors are agents of change, and play an important role worldwide in allocating capital efficiently in the long term and improving corporate governance practices.[173]

The rise of foreign institutional ownership is also related to the convergence of corporate governance and sustainability practices worldwide. (Section 4.4 discusses shareholder activism and Section 4.3 corporate governance practices.)

5.4.2 Why Institutional Investors Care about ESG

Broadly speaking, ESG investment is the incorporation of ESG factors into investment decisions.[174] Overall, investors want to better incorporate risks and opportunities into their decision-making, and improve their asset allocation and risk management decisions. Changing investor preferences can lead to changes in capital flows into different assets, and there could also be risk and repricing implications.

Several forces are driving the incorporation of ESG issues into investments. Increasingly, investors want to better incorporate long-term financial risks (and opportunities) into their decision-making processes. Some of the relevant issues include more investment regulations, asset owners' (or individual investors') preferences for sustainable allocation of their wealth, societal pressures, reputational risk concerns, or better risk management of the portfolio.

Most institutional investors are not the ultimate owners of capital. Instead, most institutional investors pool money from ultimate investors, and invest on their behalf. At the core of their fiduciary duty to their clients, institutional investors need to understand the risks and opportunities associated with their portfolio.[175] In his 2020 letter to CEOs, Larry Fink, founder and chairman of BlackRock, the world's largest asset manager, stated: "The money

---

[173] Among others, Gillan and Starks (2003), Ferreira and Matos (2008), Fernandes et al. (2013), Fernandes (2014), and Matos (2020) have provided a thorough review of the role of institutional investors worldwide, and also on their role in sustainable investing.

[174] Throughout this chapter, we will use the terms *sustainable investing, responsible investing, ESG investing,* and *climate investing* interchangeably.

[175] Amel-Zadeh and Serafeim (2018) conducted a comprehensive survey and documented that the vast majority of surveyed investors use ESG data for financial reasons rather than for ethical reasons. Also, the Schroders 2019 Global Investor Study (Schroders, 2019) confirmed that more than 60% of investors under the age of 71 believe that all investment funds should consider sustainability factors when making investments.

we manage is not our own. It belongs to people in dozens of countries trying to finance long-term goals like retirement. And we have a deep responsibility to these institutions and individuals – who are shareholders in your company and thousands of others – to promote long-term value." Similarly, the largest pension fund in the world, Japan's Government Pension Investment Fund (GPIF), is now incorporating ESG issues in its investments. According to its CIO: "Instead of trying to beat the market, our responsibility at GPIF is to make capital markets more sustainable."

Figure 5.2 Share of investors with an ESG policy worldwide, by organization type

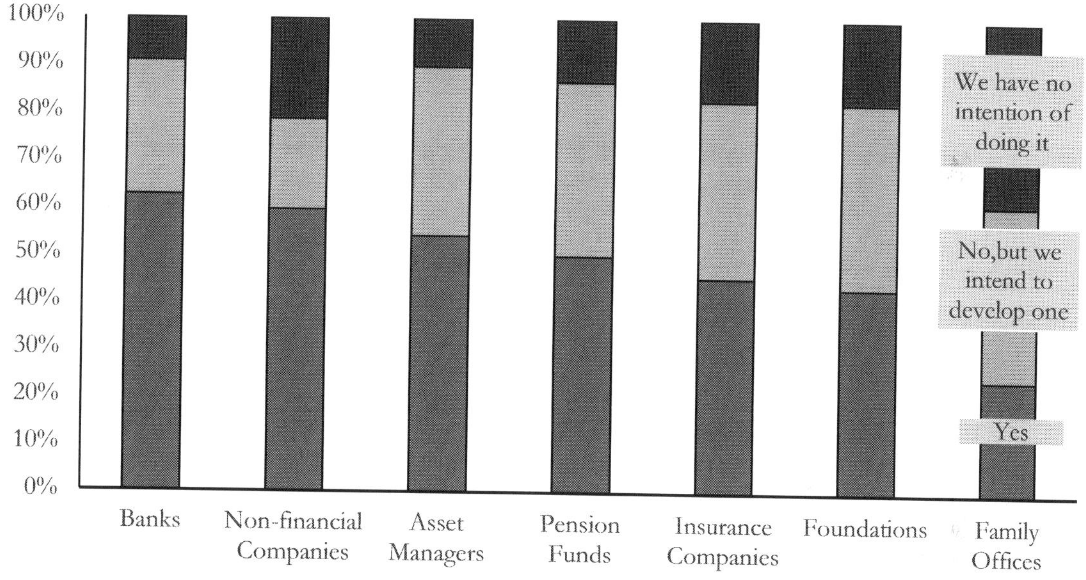

Source: HSBC (2020).

These are just a couple of examples, but they reflect a bigger reality. According to the BlackRock 2020 Global Sustainability Survey, investors plan to double their sustainable assets under management over the next 5 years, reaching almost 40% on average by 2025. The number of signatories to the UN-supported Principles for Responsible Investment has also grown significantly, and investors have committed to six principles governing the incorporation of ESG issues into their investments.

HSBC (2020) reported the results of a global survey of investors and capital markets issuers (See Figure 5.2). Among investors, there is widespread adoption of ESG policies. More than half of investors globally (51%) now have such policies, and a further third of investors intend to develop such policies. Banks and asset managers are the leaders in adopting ESG policies.

Although ESG overall has received plenty of attention in recent years, the focus is on climate-related issues. As discussed in Chapter 1, there is now a strong consensus around climate change and its long-term consequences for the planet. In economic terms, climate change results in different risks: physical and transition (see Chapter 2).

Climate change is a relevant factor in a company's long-term prospects. It can affect all asset classes, regions, and industries. Given the impact of climate change on firms' profitability and on the whole economy, climate issues have potentially significant long-term implications for investors' portfolios.

On the one hand, investors care about risk avoidance, and thus favor companies and projects that minimize downside risks and maximize opportunities. On the other hand, climate change also presents new business opportunities.

5.4.3 Principles for Responsible Investment (PRI)

The PRI is a United-Nations-supported network of institutional investors that helps its signatories incorporate ESG factors in their investment or ownership strategies.

The goal of this initiative is to develop a more sustainable global financial system by making investors understand the implications of sustainability in investments and so "better align their objectives with those of society at large."[176] It originated in 2005, and was an initiative of the then UN Secretary-General Kofi Annan, who convened investors, finance experts, international organizations, and civil society associations to formulate a series of principles on how to invest capital in a sustainable and responsible way.

Its signatories include asset owners (foundations, pension funds, etc.), asset managers (investment fund managers), and service providers (including some rating agencies) that voluntarily decided to join the PRI. By doing so, they committed themselves to integrating ESG issues into their decision-making and ownership practices

When the Principles were formerly launched in 2006 by the UNEP Finance Initiative and the UN Global Compact, there were around 200 signatories, and the total assets under management (AuM) were below US$5 trillion.

Since then, the annual number of new signatories has been steadily growing. At the end of 2021, the aggregate amount of AuM represented by PRI signatories totaled more than US$120 trillion. There were about 3,800 investors (voluntary) subscribers to the principles, from over 50 countries. European investors represent the greatest number of signatories, but in terms of AuM, North American investors lead.

---

[176] https://www.unglobalcompact.org/take-action/action/responsible-investment.

Figure 5.3 PRI signatories and assets under management

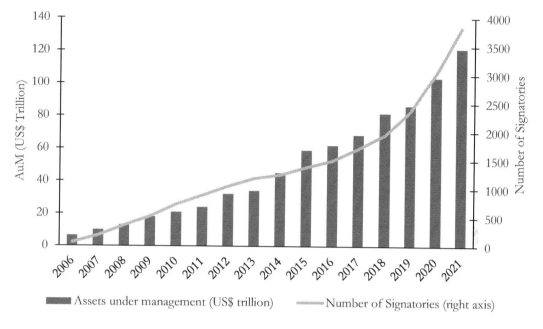

Source: Principles for Responsible Investments (PRI).

By joining the group, investors commit themselves to adhering to the following six principles:

o Principle 1: We will incorporate ESG issues into investment analysis and decision-making processes.

o Principle 2: We will be active owners and incorporate ESG issues into our ownership policies and practices.

o Principle 3: We will seek appropriate disclosure on ESG issues by the entities in which we invest.

o Principle 4: We will promote acceptance and implementation of the Principles within the investment industry.

o Principle 5: We will work together to enhance our effectiveness in implementing the Principles.

o Principle 6: We will each report on our activities and progress toward implementing the Principles.

These principles are voluntary, and can be adopted by asset owners, investment managers, and service providers. Asset owners include sovereign wealth funds, pension funds, insurance companies, endowments and foundations, and they have fiduciary duties/obligations toward their beneficiaries. Investment managers (or asset managers) are fund companies that manage asset owners' (or retail investors') money. Service providers includes ESG data providers, rating companies, auditors and verifiers, and others. PRI signatories commit to annually reporting their responsible investment considerations.

The principles can be implemented across different facets of the investment world. Principle 1 relates to the investment process. As explained in this chapter, there is not a one-size-fits-all approach, and investors integrate ESG factors in varied ways.

Principles 2 relates to engagement. By signing the PRI, investors commit to being active owners, and to engaging with climate change, for example, by engaging with companies on climate change and other relevant ESG issues, and exercising voting rights. One of the areas of engagement with companies is appropriate disclosure (Principle 3). The overall idea is that appropriate disclosure gives investors a better understanding of their invested companies' exposure to climate-related risks. In addition, Principle 5 relates to collaborating with other investors to promote relevant initiatives, and several collaborative action networks facilitate cooperation (Climate Action 100+, [177] The Transition Pathway Initiative,[178] and others). It is also common for different investors to work together and present a common proposal/viewpoint to the companies they invest in. Active ownership can also be exercised by engaging in policy making, and promoting policies and regulations that support the Paris Agreement objectives.

However, the PRI also imposes disclosure goals on investors themselves (Principle 6). Investors are both users and providers of climate-related disclosures. In particular, signatories of the PRI are required to report to the PRI several indicators regarding their management of risks and opportunities related to climate change. In the first stage, public disclosure of these indicators was optional. However, as of 2021, public disclosure of PRI signatories' reporting on these indicators is mandatory, and signatories' responses will be scored. The reporting is based on the disclosure framework of the Task Force for Climate-related Financial Disclosures (TCFD),[179] and includes the following topics:

o   Describing how ESG is integrated with investment practices
o   Disclosing active ownership activities (engagement, voting, etc.)
o   Publishing portfolio metrics, including the portfolio level of the carbon footprint
o   Assessing the financial implications of climate change for the portfolio (through a range of assumptions and scenarios)

As for companies, the TCFD recommendations for investment managers focus on governance, strategy, risk management, and metrics and targets. Some of the questions put to signatories of the PRI include the following:

---

[177] Climate Action 100+ is discussed in Section 4.4.4.
[178] TPI is an initiative created by asset owners from the United States and Europe. It provides research that help investors align their portfolios to the Paris Agreement. By May 2022, a total of 125 investors had committed to this initiative, representing over US$40 trillion AuM.
[179] For more details on the TCFD and its metrics, see Section 6.3.3.

Governance

- o   How is progress reviewed, and who is responsible for the review?
- o   Are climate-related risks part of the board's/management's responsibilities?

Strategy

- o   Is there a firm-wide strategy regarding the risks and opportunities associated with climate change?
- o   Are scenarios used to assess climate-related investment risks and opportunities across different outcomes?

Risk management

- o   Is there a process for monitoring, assessing, and integrating climate-related risks into investment decisions?
- o   How is climate scenario analysis used to test the resilience of your organization's investment strategy and inform investments in specific asset classes?

Metrics

- o   What are the climate metrics used, and how do they impact investment decisions?
- o   Is there disclosure of the investors' own climate commitments?

KEY LEARNING POINT

The number of PRI signatories has been increasing rapidly. By signing these principles, investors are committing themselves to including ESG issues in their activities.

5.4.4 The Different Investment Strategies

To integrate sustainability in their portfolio choices, investors can choose a number of strategies. There is not a one-size-fits-all approach, as investors follow sustainable investing strategies for different reasons. Some want to avoid or reduce exposure to companies that pose greater ESG risks, thus protecting their long-term value. Others want to enhance the profitability of their portfolio, by selecting stocks that are better suited to the carbon transition. In addition, some investors want to use their capital allocation to persuade companies to become more ESG friendly.

Although there is no official list of strategies, the following covers the most relevant approaches[180]:

1. **Negative/exclusionary screening**: The exclusion from a fund or portfolio of certain sectors, companies, or practices based on specific ESG criteria
2. **Positive/best-in-class screening**: Investment in sectors, companies, or projects selected for positive ESG performance relative to industry peers
3. **Norms-based screening**: Screening of investments against minimum standards of business practice based on international norms, such as those issued by the OECD, ILO, UN, and UNICEF
4. **ESG integration**: The systematic and explicit inclusion by investment managers of ESG factors into financial analysis
5. **Sustainability-themed investing**: Investment in themes or assets specifically related to sustainability (for example, clean energy, green technology, or sustainable agriculture)
6. **Impact/community investing**: Targeted investments aimed at solving social or environmental problems, and including community investing, where capital is specifically directed to traditionally underserved individuals or communities, as well as financing that is provided to businesses with a clear social or environmental purpose
7. **Corporate engagement and shareholder action**: The use of shareholder power to influence corporate behavior, including through direct corporate engagement (i.e., communicating with senior management and/or boards of companies), filing or co-filing shareholder proposals, and proxy voting that is guided by comprehensive ESG guidelines.

KEY LEARNING POINT

Investors can follow different strategies to integrate climate change and sustainability into their portfolios.

We follow the classification of Matos (2020), and aggregate these into three groups: screening, engagement, and integration. These groups are not mutually exclusive, and investors can apply more than one type of strategy simultaneously.

---

[180] This classification of strategies has also been used in the PRI (2013, 2016), Global Sustainable Investment Alliance (2019), and the CFA Institute, among others.

5.4.5 Screening

The first strategy is "screening" investment opportunities. This basically means using screens to identify candidate companies to invest in. In general, screens can be negative (exclude certain assets if some conditions are met) or positive (only consider certain types of assets).

Negative screening – This refers to the exclusion of assets from the investible universe, based on specific criteria or objectionable activities. The simplest form of negative exclusion is done by excluding certain sectors, or companies, based on their environmental (or other ESG factor) performance. Exclusion (and consequent divestment) are often the first steps investors take when implementing an ESG strategy. Also, as some sustainability stock indices themselves have exclusion lists (see Section 5.2), investors who track the index will be indirectly applying these exclusion rules as well.

Exclusion lists vary depending on the investor, and are defined according to some sustainability criteria. Some of the most frequently used lists exclude alcohol, tobacco, pornography, controversial weapons, or companies doing business with sanctioned countries. Exclusions can also be based on a more thorough analysis of the company's business (i.e., companies whose business contributes to deforestation, companies with more than 10% of revenue from oil, utilities with less than 40% of their power generated from renewable sources, companies having more than a certain level of pollution or CO_2 emissions, etc.).

Here are some examples of investors that have implemented exclusion lists:

- In December 2014, the Ministry of Finance of Norway made public a list of companies excluded from the Government Pension Fund Global. The Danish and Swedish pension funds followed suit.
- In 2015, Nordea Asset Management decided to exclude from its investment universe companies that derived more than 75% of their revenues from the sale of coal mining. Then, in 2017, Nordea lowered the threshold to 10%. In 2019, Nordea decided to also exclude companies with exposure to oil sand extraction, setting a revenue threshold of 10%.
- In 2020, the University of Oxford announced landmark plans to divest its endowment formally from the fossil fuel industry and asked its endowment managers to engage with fund managers to request evidence of net zero carbon business plans across their portfolios.
- In May 2020, BNP Paribas announced that it would no longer accept any new customers whose share of coal-related revenue was above 25%.
- In June 2020, HESTA – an Australian pension fund with A\$56 bn (US\$52 bn) AuM – announced its plan to exit fossil fuel over the following 10 years to meet the target of net zero emissions by 2050.

o In May 2021, the National Pension Service – the South Korea state pension fund with approximately US$800 billion AuM – announced plans to reduce investment in coal mines and businesses involved in coal power by adopting "negative screening."

o In September 2021, Harvard Management Co. – also driven by student activism – announced the goal of halting investments in fossil fuels. The endowment also announced plans to use its US$42 billion to support the transition to the green economy.

Norway Pension Fund in 2020

Norway has the largest sovereign wealth fund in the world (AuM of US$1.3 trillion). It is managed by Norges Bank (the central bank of Norway). The fund first excludes stock or debt from companies that produce weapons or sell weapons to states that are subject to investment restrictions. The fund also excludes sin stocks, such as companies that produce tobacco. Further, the fund excludes stock or debt from companies for the following:

- Serious human rights violations, such as murder, torture, forced labour, and the worst forms of child labor
- Serious violations of the rights of individuals in conflict situations
- Severe environmental damage
- Acts or omissions that lead to unacceptable GHG emissions
- Corruption
- Other serious violations of fundamental ethical norms

In May 2020, following recommendations by the Council on Ethics, the Norges Bank decided to exclude 12 companies due to environmental and human rights concerns:

- Canadian Natural Resources, Cenovus Energy, Suncor Energy, and Imperial Oil, due to "unacceptable climate gas emissions" linked to oil sand production
- Sasol, RWE, Glencore, Anglo American, and AGL Energy, who were above the new thresholds for product-based coal
- Eletrobras, due to "serious human rights violations"
- ElSewedy Electric and Vale, due to "severe environmental damage"

As of September 2020, 32% of institutions that had committed to divesting from fossil fuels globally were faith-based organizations, followed by philanthropic foundations and educational institutions.[181] Government and pension funds together represented 26% of the total.

---

[181] Bessembinder (2016) found that endowments incur significant costs to comply with divestment goals.

Figure 5.4 Distribution of institutions divesting from fossil fuels worldwide, by type

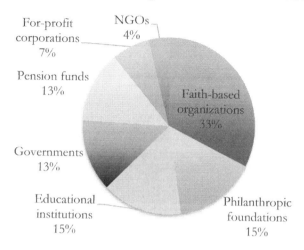

Source: Statista (September 2020).

Another form of negative screening is the so-called *norms-based screening* (or ethics-based screening). This strategy only includes in the investable universe companies that meet minimum standards of business practice based on some ethical considerations, or international norms or agreements (e.g., UN Global Compact, OECD, UNICEF, Paris Climate Agreement, ILO standards).

Positive screening – When using positive screening, investors only include in the investible universe sectors or companies that satisfy specific minimum ESG criteria. When using this strategy, investors should have a clear vision for the kind of changes they want their investment activity to bring about in society (so that they can focus on those criteria when selecting stocks). Screening can also be defined using relative performance. This is called *best in class*, as companies are selected on the basis of their strong performance relative to their industry peers on some criteria.

Thematic investing – This investment strategy is a form of positive screening that is based on sustainability-linked themes (climate change, labor conditions, education, health, etc.). Some thematic funds typically focus on specific environmental issues (e.g., green technology, biodiversity, renewable energy, and food and agriculture). Others use this strategy to select companies that develop solutions to global sustainability challenges, including the circular economy, sustainable food and agriculture, sustainable mobility, and social inclusion. Other examples of thematic investments are green bond funds, whereby investors allocate their fixed income portfolios exclusively to green bonds (see Chapter 3 for more details on green bonds).

When using any screening-based strategy, special attention should be paid to the actual ESG scores and data that support the screening. The top 20% highest-scoring companies in the energy sector have an average ESG score that is substantially above the world average. However, the top 20% tobacco companies also score higher than the world average. Conversely, the bottom 20% renewable energy firms score below the world average. This highlights the importance of correctly defining the peer groups against which firms are assessed. Also, it is important to appreciate that some institutional investors face objective investment-related constraints in trying to integrate ESG factors. For example, about 70% of Australian asset managers are signatories to the UN PRI, but the domestic equity index is very heavily weighted toward mining stocks. This significant concentration makes it hard for investors to diversify their local-currency portfolios while implementing a low-carbon screening strategy.

5.4.6 Engagement

Institutions that are dissatisfied with some aspect of a company's management can attempt to bring about change either through "voice" (e.g., persuading the management with quiet diplomacy, intervening directly by voting their shares or engaging in confrontational proxy fights) or by threatening to "exit" (e.g., selling, also known as "governance by exit"; or "voting with their feet," also known as the "Wall Street walk" rule).

Investors who are concerned with the environmental footprint of a company have two possibilities. One option is to exit these investments after conducting negative screening. This is what some investors do when they create exclusion lists based on predefined criteria such as the nature of the industry or the level of pollution or CO_2 emissions. Another alternative is to engage with the companies and try to bring about changes from within (also called active ownership, or stewardship).

Through engagement, investors use their ownership position to improve various aspects of sustainability performance. Some typical themes of engagement are disclosure of environmental performance, management of material ESG risks, metrics and performance measurement, lobbying activities, governance of climate change, and strategy.[182] The engagement could be individual (the investor engages with the board of directors to influence behaviors) or collaborative. In collaborative engagement, engagement with the board is typically led by a group of investors that share the same goals.

There is no exact definition of engagement, and it can take many forms:

---

[182] Section 4.3 covers investors' corporate governance practices, including voting. Section 4.4 discusses the evidence of engagement and the rising levels of shareholder activism on sustainability topics.

- o   Communicating with the board of directors
- o   Filing shareholder proposals
- o   Voting
- o   Running proxy campaigns
- o   Conducting public media campaigns

BlackRock and its ESG engagement

Recognizing the mounting threats arising from climate change, institutional investors have called for more robust disclosure of climate risk and corporate action on climate change. The Big Three passive investment managers (BlackRock, Vanguard, and State Street) invest in almost all publicly traded companies worldwide, and are often some of their largest shareholders.

In his 2020 letter to CEOs, BlackRock's Larry Fink recognized climate change as a "defining factor in companies' long-term prospects." Because climate risk is an investment risk, Fink explained that BlackRock will be placing "sustainability at the center of [its] investment approach." Other investors, asset managers, companies, and stakeholders have similarly pushed for standardized and accelerated sustainability disclosures and have indicated that this is a key focus area.

As a fiduciary investor, BlackRock undertakes engagements and proxy voting with the goal of protecting and enhancing the long-term value of its clients' assets. BlackRock emphasizes direct dialogue with companies on governance issues that have a material impact on sustainable long-term financial performance. For example, in January 2020, Blackrock formally asked investee companies to publish annual reports aligned with the recommendations of the Task Force on Climate-related Financial Disclosures (TCFD) and the Sustainability Accounting Standards Board (SASB) standards.

Between July 2018 and June 2019, BlackRock Investment Stewardship voted a total of 155,131 proposals during 16,124 shareholder meetings. In approximately 40% of the meetings, it voted against one or more management recommendations. Overall, it voted against 8% of all management proposals.

5.4.7 Integration

The third strategy is integration, which consists of a more comprehensive approach. In this case, the investment process incorporates ESG factors from the beginning.[183] In this section, we cover the structures, processes, and methods involved in integrating ESG factors into portfolio decisions. That is, ESG factors are incorporated into analysis and decision-making throughout the different phases of managing a portfolio (research, analysis, asset allocation, stock selection, performance measurement, risk management, and monitoring).

Sustainability factors can enter at different stages of the investment process, and there are different approaches to ESG integration. Integration can be done at the individual portfolio

---

[183] For many asset managers, the term *integration* includes also active ownership activities, which are covered in the previous section.

level (a single fund managed by the investment manager) or at the aggregate asset manager level. Also, integration approaches can be top-down or bottom-up.

Figure 5.5 ESG integration approaches

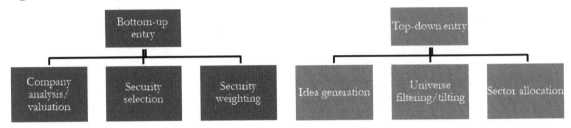

Source: Sustainalytics, Investor Responsibility Research Centre Inc (IRRCi).

Bottom-up integration means, for instance, explicitly including ESG factors in company-specific financial analysis, thinking about how sustainability topics impact cash flows and risks, and applying these factors to detailed forecasts of the company's business model. This requires the use of ESG indicators that are considered financially material for the company. This approach uses different ESG factors to adjust discount rates in valuation models, revenue growth rates, profit margins, costs, capital expenditures, etc. (Section 2.7). This bottom-up approach can also include a risk analysis of stranded assets in the context of valuing the reserves of oil and gas companies.

Top-down integration can be implemented in different ways:

o   Sector allocation: Using ESG factors to influence the target weightings of sectors within portfolios.
o   Overlay portfolio: Certain investment strategies aim to achieve, at the fund level, a certain specific aggregate ESG goal (for instance, a desired carbon footprint). This could be accomplished by overweighting green companies and underweighting companies with the worst climate exposures, while keeping the portfolio's return profile close to the benchmark.
o   Scenario analysis around key environmental issues: For instance, the analysis could focus on water constraints or the circular economy and attempt to understand the consequences for different asset classes and sectors.
o   Idea generation: Using ESG factors to generate investment ideas (e.g., how can they create revenue growth opportunities for some companies?)

Different investors, asset managers, and ESG ratings providers have their own views about the relative importance of issues to address and how to address them. Some investors may prefer low-carbon solutions, whereas others may prefer to tackle biodiversity or water usage. When designing investment strategies with those goals in mind, it is important to acknowledge the differences in ESG ratings. There is now an abundance of information (particularly for larger companies) on companies' ESG performance. However, as explained in Section 5.1, one has to analyze the quality and purpose of the data carefully.

5.4.8 Empirical Evidence on Institutional Investors

In recent years, institutional investors have increasingly incorporated environmental information into their financial analysis and investment decisions. Across all different players, there is a significant growth in the volume of managed assets that take ESG criteria into consideration. According to the Global Sustainable Investment Alliance, as of January 2020, ESG AuM accounted for over US$35 trillion worldwide.

Figure 5.6 Global ESG assets under management

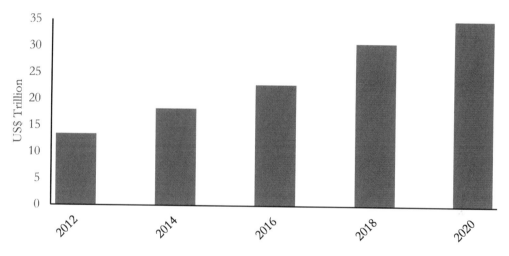

Source: Global Sustainable Investment Review.

Schroders (2021) surveyed 750 global institutional investors, with US$26 trillion of AuM, on their views on sustainability. Some of the results include the following:

- o 70% of the investors said they prefer to stay invested and use their power to effect change, rather than divest.
- o The environment and climate change were the key focus of engagement for 64% of the respondents, followed by employees (workforce diversity, for instance) for 61% of the respondents.
- o When asked about the motives driving their interest in sustainability, 54% mentioned that they were interested in "positively impacting society and the planet", 42% mentioned risk management, 36% the potential for higher returns, and 35% pressure from their clients.

Matos (2020) used data on PRI signatories' responses to the annual survey. He documented substantial heterogeneity in how investors implement sustainable investing. In terms of AuM, more than 80% of the assets were managed with one of these strategies: screening, integration, or engagement (investors can use more than one strategy). Within screening, 73% used negative screening, 44% used positive screening, and 40% used norms-based screening. In terms of engagement, 86% reported participating in individual engagement and 64% in collective engagement.

Figure 5.7 ESG incorporation: percentage of PRI signatories using a given approach

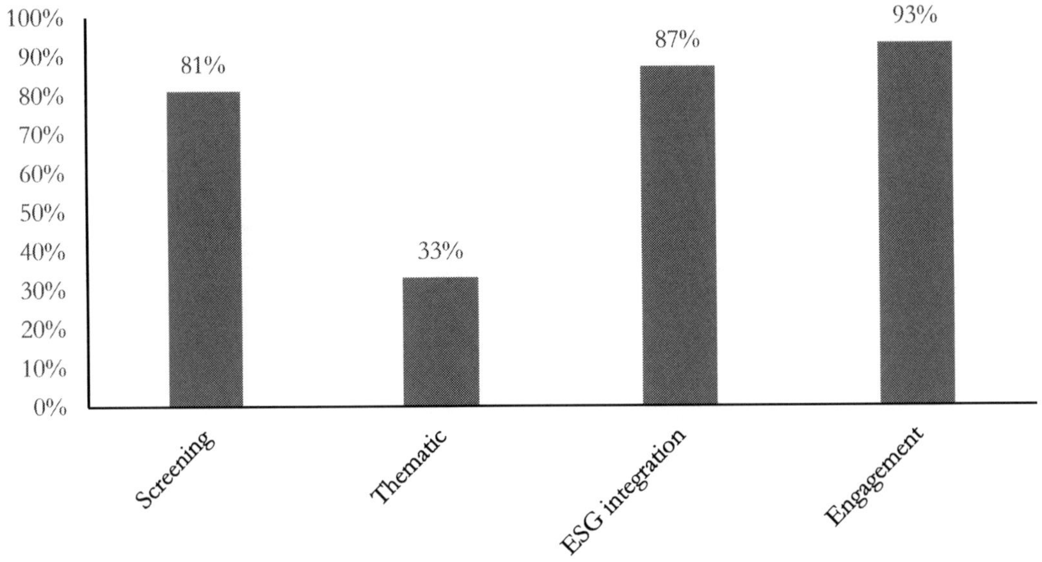

Source: Matos (2020).

Orsagh et al. (2018) and PRI conducted a survey on a large set of finance professionals, most of them CFA members, to understand how they use ESG scores/ratings in ESG integration. The findings show that

- o   the main drivers of ESG integration are risk management and client demand;
- o   there is no "one best way" to perform ESG integration;
- o   ESG integration is more developed in equity compared to fixed income;
- o   most portfolio managers integrate ESG into the investment process, but rarely adjust their quantitative models based on ESG data; and
- o   the main barriers to integration are the lack of comparable ESG data and a limited understanding of ESG issues.

Some academic research shows how sustainability issues motivate institutional investors to change their portfolios. Gibson, Glossner, et al. (2020) used data on PRI signatories to study whether they "walk the talk," that is, whether PRI signatories have a stronger ESG footprint than others (based on company-level ESG scores from Thomson Reuters ASSET4, MSCI, and Sustainalytics). They started by documenting that larger European investors are more likely to commit to responsible investing. Institutions that publicly commit to responsible investing exhibit better ESG portfolio-level scores in the EU, but not in the United States. Their results suggest that U.S. investors that commit to ESG strategies but only partially implement them (e.g., screening, integration, engagement) have worse ESG footprints than uncommitted investors. Finally, their results also show that responsible investing does not enhance portfolio returns but reduces risk.

Dyck et al. (2019) provided evidence that institutional investors push for stronger firm-level E&S performance around the world. Gibson, Krueger, et al. (2020) studied 13F [184] institutional investors in the United States during 2002–16 and showed that their sustainability footprint [185] increased remarkably during the period of analysis. Further, they provided evidence that measures of risk-adjusted returns are positively related to the sustainability footprint, with this link being particularly pronounced for institutions with longer investment horizons. Humphrey and Li (2021) found that mutual fund families that sign the PRI had significantly lower portfolio emissions after signing the initiative than did non-signatory families. Furthermore, fund families that reduced their emissions experience significantly increased fund flow.

Some authors have addressed the effects of negative screening on investments. Exclusion lists may reduce the diversification of portfolios (by limiting the range of available investible assets), and consequently increase risk. Various studies report that investing in "sin stocks" [186] has historically delivered significantly positive abnormal returns. Hong and Kacperczyk (2009) analyzed U.S. stocks over 1962–2006. Their results show that sin stocks have higher expected returns than otherwise comparable stocks. Also, sin stocks are less held by norms-constrained institutions such as pension funds (compared to mutual or hedge funds), receive less coverage from analysts, and face greater litigation risk. Similarly, Fabozzi et al. (2008) showed that a sin portfolio produced an annual return of 19% over the study period, outperforming other benchmarks. Bolton and Kacperczyk (2021b) showed that carbon risk is priced into markets. They analyzed Scope 1, 2, and 3 emissions of U.S. listed firms and documented a positive and significant effect on stock returns, volatility, and turnover. Firms with higher emissions have higher stock returns. Overall, this evidence suggests that negative screening based on social norms can involve a cost for investors.

Some authors have studied the impact of divestment/exit strategies, and also of engagement. The main idea behind a divesting strategy is that large divestment campaigns can exert

---

[184] Form 13F is the reporting form filed by institutional investment managers.
[185] Measured using environmental and social scores from Thomson Reuters and MSCI.
[186] Stocks of firms that earn money from human vice – such as firms in the alcohol, tobacco, gambling, and weapons industries – are typically referred to as "sin stocks."

downward pressures on a company stock price, increase capital costs, and thus induce the management and board of directors to change the company's sustainability strategy.[187] Other authors (see Section 4.4) focus on the effects of shareholder activism.

The 2010 Economics Nobel Prize winner, Oliver Hart, studied these two alternatives. In his paper "Exit versus Engagement," he concluded that engagement is more effective in achieving actual change. The main idea is that exiting a certain company achieves nothing in practice. Broccardo et al. (2020) also showed that in a competitive world, exiting is less effective than speaking up in pushing firms to act in a socially responsible manner.

The real impact of exiting/divesting at the company level is unclear. Many investors use divestment strategies, arguing that this will starve companies of capital. This is not necessarily true.[188] Whenever there is a seller, there needs to be a buyer for the transaction to be concluded. For a pension fund to divest its ownership position in a certain company, somebody else must buy those shares.[189] Even if the stock price goes down, many "brown" companies are not in need of additional capital, as they generate cash in traditional industries, and lack many new investment opportunities. Overall, for companies, an investor that divests due to an exclusion list is replaced by another investor that does not rely on exclusion lists for investment decisions.

Staying in the company, and remaining engaged with it, is more likely to bring about change. It is even possible to argue that if an investor stays in low-sustainability companies, and improves them, it can create more of an impact than investing in a company that already has high standards.[190]

The early literature on this topic suggests a positive relationship between investors' ESG engagement and financial performance.[191] Dimson et al. (2015) showed that successful ESG engagements are followed by positive abnormal returns and that after successful

---

[187] Heinkel et al. (2001) argued that investors' exclusionary strategies lead to lower share prices and, consequently, a higher cost of capital for polluting firms, as the exit of green investors leads to polluting firms being held by fewer investors. Results suggest that portfolio divestment of carbon-intensive holdings exerts downwards pressures on the stock prices of divested firms over several periods, and may improve managers' commitment toward ESG themes (Dordi and Weber, 2019; Rohleder et al., 2022).

[188] Ansar et al. (2013) showed that the direct impact of divestment on equity or debt of the affected companies is limited, as other investors can fill the gap relatively quickly. For example, political pressure and targeted investment policies to boycott companies operating in South Africa during the apartheid regime had little visible effect on the financial markets (Teoh et al., 1999). Davies and Van Wesep (2018) argued that divestment campaigns can be ineffective at best and perhaps counterproductive.

[189] See also "Fossil Fuel Divestment Has Zero Climate Impact, Says Bill Gates," *Financial Times*, September 17, 2019.

[190] Krueger et al. (2020) surveyed 439 large institutional investors. Most respondents stated that reputational risk is a key motivation to include climate issues in their investing decisions. They also found that the long-term, larger, and ESG-oriented investors considered engagement rather than divestment to be the better approach for addressing climate risks.

[191] For more on activist investors, see Section 4.4.

engagements, particularly with environmental/social issues, companies experience improved performance. ESG engagement can also have benefits such as valuable product differentiation, reduction in firms' downside risk, insurance against event risk, and lower regulatory risk (Albuquerque et al., 2019; Servaes and Tamayo, 2013; Hoepner et al., 2020).

KEY LEARNING POINT

It is not true that divestment campaigns lead to effective change in companies.

5.4.9 Summary – Institutional Investors

In this section, we discussed the importance of climate risks for institutional investors, which include asset managers, sovereign wealth funds, pension funds, and other types of investors. Many of these investors have a long-term orientation and are increasingly incorporating climate risks in their decision-making.

There is not a one-size-fits-all strategy; different investors follow different investment strategies. Some of the strategies rely on screening, which is based on identifying several observable firm characteristics (for instance, the sector, or the percentage of sales of a certain product) that qualify the firm for (or disqualify it from) inclusion in the investable universe. Other strategies focus on engagements with invested companies. By remaining engaged with the company, investors aim to achieve change from within. That is, they engage with the company's management and boards to influence their ESG corporate practices and business models, and promote various climate-aligned transformation strategies. Another strategy is integration, which is about incorporating a mix of financial and non-financial factors into decision-making. Integration can be achieved at all levels (company valuation, portfolio construction, reporting, performance measurement, and many different processes).

There is still limited empirical evidence on how different investors apply investment strategies, and the effectiveness and transparency of doing so. The little empirical evidence that exists suggests one has to be careful about greenwashing and initiatives on sustainability that are simply PR efforts without any concrete impact. The evidence also suggests that engagement seems to be more effective than divestment in achieving positive environmental results. The next section focuses on empirical evidence from different types of institutional investors.

5.5 EVIDENCE FROM DIFFERENT TYPES OF INVESTORS

In recent years, institutional investors have increasingly incorporated environmental information into their financial analysis and investment decisions. Many regulators are also increasingly focusing on sustainability/ESG and on the importance of incorporating it into fiduciary duties. Stricter requirements on considering climate change across the different phases of the investment process are being implemented. This section presents evidence from different kinds of institutional investors, in terms of incorporation of climate issues in their operations.

5.5.1 Mutual Funds

Mutual funds are actively managed financial instruments that collect money from a pool of investors and invest it, on their behalf, to generate a financial return. The type of assets selected by fund managers depends on the objective and the nature of the fund. There are different types of mutual funds. Some invest in equities, and others in fixed income securities (government bonds, corporate bonds, green bonds, etc.) and other assets.

Figure 5.8 Size of the mutual fund market over time

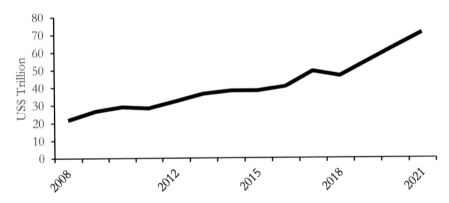

Source: Investment Company Institute (ICI), 2022.

Mutual funds can be active or passive. In the case of actively managed funds, the role of the portfolio manager is to define strategies and select stocks (and their weights in the portfolio), in order to outperform a certain benchmark. Passive funds replicate the behavior of the index (these are discussed in the next section). In 2021, mutual funds globally held more than US$71 trillion of AuM.

The largest asset manager in the world is BlackRock, which offers the iShares ETFs, with more than US$10 trillion under management. The pioneer of index funds, Vanguard, has US$8.1 trillion. The third largest player is Charles Schwab (almost US$8 trillion).

Figure 5.9 Leading global mutual fund groups

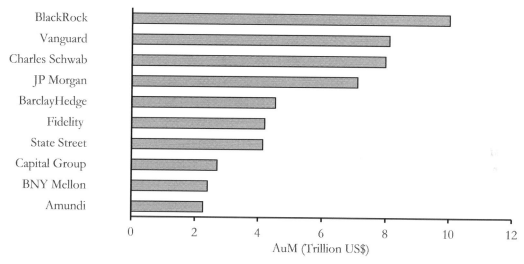

Source: Statista, March 2022.

ESG Funds

ESG funds differ from normal funds in that the pooled money from the fund is invested in assets that are supposedly more sustainable. For instance, green bond funds invest in bonds that have been labeled "green" as they comply with international standards (see Sections 3.1 and 3.2). Active ESG equity mutual funds conduct research to identify companies that meet their criteria, and often rely on ESG ratings (see Section 5.1) to implement different strategies (see Section 5.4).

Improved disclosure is crucial for investors to make informed choices. Regulators such as the Securities Exchange Commission (SEC) ask investment firms to be transparent about their ESG scoring systems, and how they affect investment decisions. The voting practices of these ESG funds are also important. These funds face a potential conflict between maximizing their investors' returns and incorporating environmental considerations. Their voting record can provide evidence on how they implement their sustainability mandate.

As of June 2021, with US$2 trillion of AuM, ESG mutual funds accounted for approximately 5% of the global assets in the mutual fund industry. Equity and bonds were the main asset class, totaling US$1.2 billion and US$400 million, respectively.

Figure 5.10 ESG mutual funds' AuM by asset class (in US$ billions)

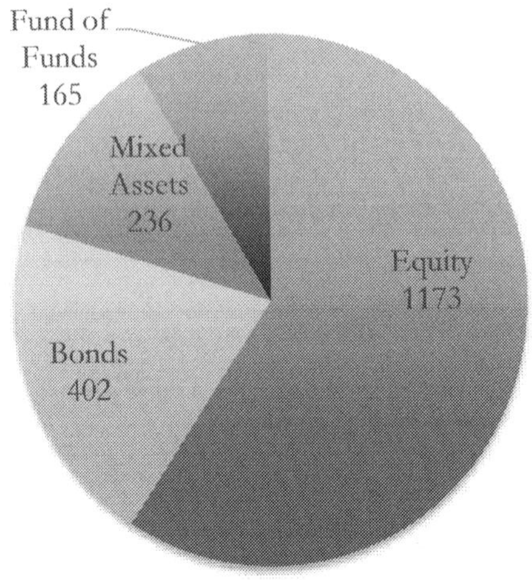

Source: MSCI.

The majority of the funds were actively managed (active funds = US$1884 billion AuM, index-based funds = US$274 billion AuM). Table 5.6 lists the largest ESG equity funds as of April 2021.

Table 5.6 Largest 10 ESG equity funds (AuM)

	Name	AuM ($bn)	Geographic focus	Fund type
1	Parnassus Core Equity Fund	22.9	United States	Active Fund
2	iShares ESG Aware MSCI USA EFT	13.0	United States	Index-based ETF
3	Vanguard FTSE Social Index Fund	10.9	United States	Index-based ETF
4	Stewart Investors Asia Pacific Leaders Sustainability	9.9	Pacific ex Japan	Active Fund
5	Vontobel Sustainable Emerging Market	9.6	Emerging Markets	Active Fund
6	Northern Trust World Custom ESG Equity Index	8.7	Global	Index-based ETF
7	Pictet – Global Environmental Opportunities	8.3	Global	Active Fund
8	Pictet Water	8.0	Global	Active Fund
9	KLP AksjeGlobal Indeks	7.7	Global	Index-based ETF
10	Nordea 1 – Global Climate and Environment	7.4	Global	Active Fund

Source: MSCI ESG Research, April 2021.

ESG investment strategies can be measured against general stock indices (such as the S&P 500) or against ESG benchmarks, depending on what investors are trying to measure. If the objective is to understand the value added by a certain portfolio manager (who is subject to ESG constraints), then a comparison with a similarly constrained ESG benchmark is the preferred option (see Section 5.2).

The world's largest green bond fund

Amundi Planet Emerging Green One (EGO) was launched in March 2016 as the world's largest green bond fund targeting emerging markets. The fund was co-launched in partnership with the International Financial Corporation (IFC), an agency of the World Bank Group, and aims to invest US$2 billion in green bonds issued in emerging markets by 2025. The fund was listed in the Luxembourg Stock Exchange and raised US$1.42 billion from a wide range of investors including the European Investment Bank and many institutional investors such as pension funds and insurance companies.

5.5.2 Passive Funds (Index Funds and ETFs)

Passive funds (index funds and ETFs) are investment vehicles that track the performance of a certain market index. Their goal is to deliver, at a low cost, returns that do not deviate from that index. Given their "passive" nature, index funds and passive ETFs incur lower operational costs than actively managed funds (for instance, they do not spend money on research and quantitative analysis to determine the securities to be included in their portfolios).

The main difference between the ETFs and index funds is that the former can be traded like stocks during the trading day, whereas the latter can be traded only at the price set at the end of the trading day. ETF shares are acquired (like any other stock or bond) in the stock exchange through a broker. Index funds, similar to mutual funds, are purchased directly from the fund manager (or a representative).

Figure 5.11 Global passive funds

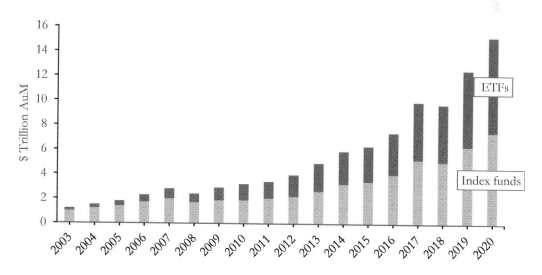

Source: Bloomberg, Deutsche Bank, Thomson Reuters, *The Financial Times*.

This is a trend toward the increasing use of passive, indexed investment strategies. AuM in passive strategies have grown significantly over the past decade. At the end of 2020, index funds and ETFs accounted for almost US$15 trillion of AuM (almost equally split between ETFs and index funds). For many companies, passive investors are their largest shareholders.[192]

Figure 5.12 Top ETF brands in the United States

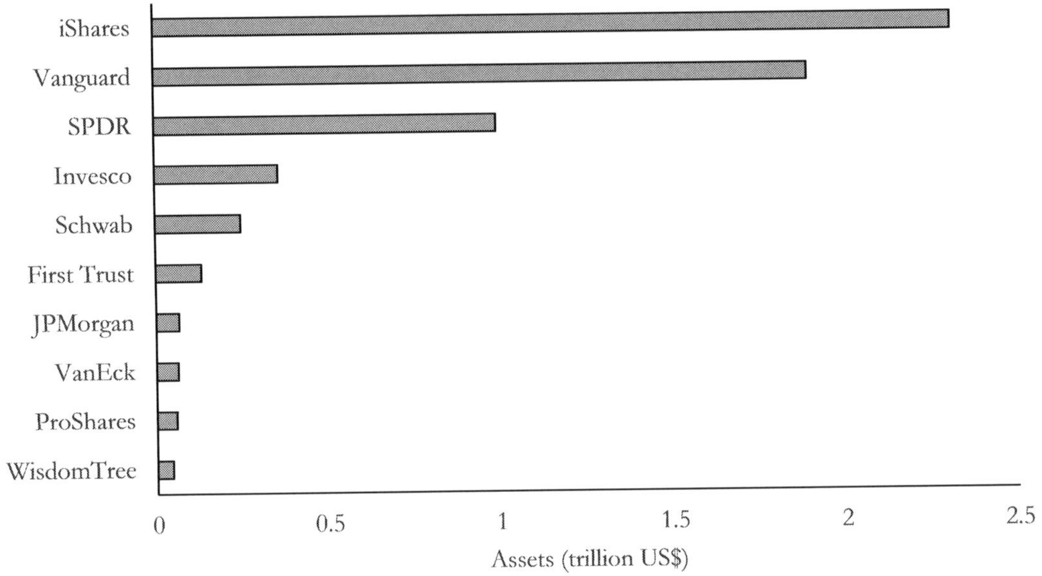

Assets (trillion US$)

Source: ETF.com, August 2021.

BlackRock, Vanguard, and State Street are some of the largest players offering indexed investments. These companies collectively hold about 80% of all indexed investments, and have become known as the Big Three.[193]

ESG and Environment-Related ETFs

Passive strategies can also take ESG issues into account. ESG index funds (or ETFs) are passive investment vehicles that track an ESG stock index. For index funds, ESG is incorporated by benchmarking the performance of special sustainability indices. That is,

---

[192] See Section 5.2.2 on the rise of passive investing.
[193] See Sections 4.3.1 and 4.4.3 for more information on the increasing importance of passive funds in capital markets, especially in governance and activism issues.

passive ESG funds rely on third-party indices to build their investment portfolio. The indices are built using various methodologies (see Section 5.2) that rely on ESG scores (Section 5.1). Therefore, the weighting schemes and the re-weighting toward higher sustainability shares depend on the methodology and the specific ESG scores that are used.

One of the key attractions of ESG passive funds is the low management fees (although ESG passive strategies have higher costs when compared with standard passive funds).

Some of the most widely used benchmarks include the following:

- o The S&P 500 ESG Index: It is a capital-weighted index that selects constituents from the parent index, the S&P 500. Its methodology excludes all companies involved in the tobacco or controversial weapons industries, or having a low UN Global Compact Score. It also excludes companies with lower ESG scores in their industry (the bottom 25%).
- o MSCI ACWI Low Carbon Target Index: It is a capital-weighted index that selects stocks across 23 developed markets and 27 emerging markets. The constituents come from the parent MSCI ACWI Index. This low-carbon index re-weights stocks to reduce carbon exposure.
- o FTSE Developed ESG Low Carbon Select Index: It is a capital-weighted index that selects constituents from its parent index, FTSE Developed (which covers 25 developed markets). The index is constructed using the FTSE Russell Target Exposure methodology[194] and also excludes sin stocks and stocks from companies operating in the fossil fuel industry or those involved in controversies related to the UN Global Compact principles.

Vanguard FTSE Social Index Fund

The Vanguard FTSE Social Index Fund was launched in 2003 to track the performance of the FTSE4Good U.S. Select Index, a capital-weighted index that offers exposure to large- and mid-cap stocks. Constituents are selected by applying negative screening criteria, and the index excludes from the investable universe sin stocks and stocks of companies that "own proved or probable reserves in coal, oil, or gas, or any company that FTSE determines has a primary business activity in the fossil fuel industry." The index also excludes the stock of companies that do not comply with the standards set by the United Nations Global Compact Principles for environmental protection, human and labor rights, and anti-corruption norms. As of June 2020, the fund held US$5.9 billion AuM, and its expense ratio was 0.12%. The top three holdings in terms of market capitalization were Apple, Microsoft, and Amazon.

---

[194] This methodology is designed to target specific factors, e.g., ESG or climate exposure, while maintaining a balanced exposure to other risk factors (market, size, momentum, etc.).

In recent years, retail investors have started investing in sustainability-related funds. This has led to significant growth, both in terms of active funds as well as passive investments such as ETFs.

Table 5.7 Top 10 ESG funds ranked by fund flows in 2020 (in US$ billions)

Fund	Flows US$ billion (12 mo.)	ESG rating	Type
iShares ESG Aware MISCI USA ETF	7.1	A	Index-based ETF
Pictet Environmental Opportunities	4.2	AA	Active Fund
iShares Global Clean Energy (US Listing)	4.0	A	Index-based ETF
iShares Global Clean Energy UCITS ETF	3.5	A	Index-based ETF
Handelsbanken Hållbar Energi	3.5	A	Active Fund
iShares ESG Aware MSCI EM ETF	3.4	A	Index-based ETF
Nordea 1 Glob Climate	3.0	AA	Active Fund
iShares MISCI USA SRI UCITS ETF	2.6	AA	Index-based ETF
Vontobel Fund mtx Sust EM Leaders	2.4	A	Active Fund
Northern Trust World Cst ESG	1.9	A	Index-based Fund

Source: MSCI ESG Research 2021.

Mainstream providers of ETFs have been creating more investible products that track ESG indices. For instance, BlackRock, the largest asset manager in the world, announced its strategic objectives of "making sustainability integral to portfolio construction and risk management; exiting investments that present a high sustainability-related risk, such as thermal coal producers; launching new investment products that screen fossil fuels; and strengthening our commitment to sustainability and transparency in our investment stewardship activities." For asset managers such as BlackRock, fiduciary duty is key to their business, and BlackRock has committed to including more and more sustainability-related factors into their portfolios and their operations. It considers the incorporation of material ESG factors to be part of its duty to clients when building its portfolios for long-term investors. Consistent with this, BlackRock has also expanded its offering of climate- and sustainability-related funds.

iShares MSCI World Paris-Aligned Climate ETF

This ETF was launched in April 2021 to passively track the performance of the MSCI World Climate Paris Aligned Benchmark Select Index, a capital-weighted index that offers exposure to large- and mid-cap stocks in 23 developed markets. The index includes stocks of companies that seek to reduce their carbon emissions in line with the Paris Agreement plan. This fund is designed for investors that want to reduce their exposure to climate risk. Index constituents are selected by applying negative screening criteria, and the index excludes from its investable universe sin stocks, stocks of companies in the fossil fuel industry, and stocks of companies that have been embroiled in serious environmental controversies. As of July 2021, the fund had US$15.6 billion AuM and an expense ratio of 0.20%. The top three holdings in terms of market capitalization are Apple, Microsoft, and Amazon.

As the number of ETFs and their AuM have been growing over the past decade, so has the number of environment-focused ETFs (from 39 in 2009 to 221 in 2019 (UNCTAD, 2019)). Environment-related ETFs offer equity and bond exposure to climate benchmarks such as the MSCI World Paris-Aligned Index, the MSCI ACWI Climate Change Index, S&P 500 Paris-Aligned Climate Index, and the STOXX Europe 600 Paris-Aligned Benchmark. Besides climate change and emissions, some of these ETFs focus on specific environmental topics such as biodiversity, water usage, and waste management.

> **Ossiam Food For Biodiversity ETF**
>
> The fund was launched at the end of 2020 on the Deutsche Börse to provide investors with exposure to large- and mid-cap equities operating in all the food sector areas such as agriculture, manufacturing, and restoration. The fund is actively managed, and it does not replicate any index. The index investment universe comprises 250 stocks, of which approximately 70 are selected. The selection criteria for the holdings are based on company-level biodiversity metrics developed by Iceberg Data Lab. As of June 2021, the fund held US$37.7 million AuM, and its expense ratio was equal to 0.75%. The top three holdings were Starbucks (7.13%), Costco Wholesale (6.72%), and Nestlé (6.72).

Although several ETFs have been targeting this climate space, investors need to assess if the underlying assets meet their goals, and the name of the ETF in and of itself is an insufficient criterion to determine this. For example, some ETFs include the words "Clean Energy" in their name, which suggests that the portfolio of the funds is representative of the clean energy infrastructure sector. However, digging deeper into the portfolio may reveal that a substantial part is invested in technology and IT companies (which have very low levels of emissions), which are unrelated to clean energy.

5.5.3 Pension Funds

A pension fund is a fund that aggregates monetary contributions from employers and employees, and invests them to provide for their members' retirement benefits. They are the largest type of institutional owner, with more than US$50 trillion of AuM in 2020. In addition, they are very large and concentrated players. By design, pension funds are long-term investors. They collect money from savers and invest it to pay their pensions in the future, typically after several decades.

Countries around the globe are engaged in intense pension reform efforts, often involving an increased use of pension funds managed by the private sector (OECD, 2020). As a consequence, the size of AuM in the pension fund industry has increased steadily over the last decade.

Figure 5.13 Global assets of pension funds

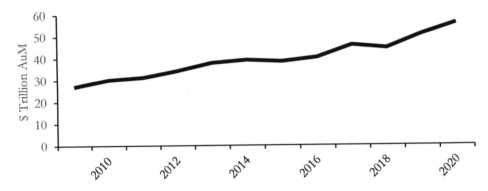

Source: The Financial Stability Board, via Statista.

In addition, pension funds are very large and concentrated players. In many markets, they are some of the largest investors. They can be government related (such as the GPIF from Japan, or the ABP from the Netherlands), corporate sponsored (such as The Boeing Company), or from a professional group (such as teachers).

Table 5.8 Top 10 pension funds worldwide

Rank	Fund	Market	Total assets (US$ billion)
1	Government Pension Investment	Japan	1,720
2	National Pension	South Korea	765
3	Federal Retirement Thrift	United States	651
4	ABP	Netherlands	607
5	National Social Security	China	448
6	California Public Employees	United States	426
7	Canada Pension	Canada	391
8	Central Provident Fund	Singapore	350
9	PFZW	Netherlands	307
10	California State Teachers	United States	259

Source: Willis Towers Watson, September 2021.

Pension funds invest most of their portfolio in equities and bonds. Increasingly, a significant part of their portfolio is passively managed. However, they can also invest in real assets (such as infrastructure assets and real estate), hedge funds, private equity, commodities, etc. These are the traditionally called alternative investments.

Given their size, long-term nature, and concentration, pension funds are an important voice in capital markets and have an important role to play in sustainable finance. They have been early adopters of sustainable finance principles, such as the PRI, and are nowadays adopting several climate change investment policies. They can then play a key role in combatting climate change by providing a significant amount of green financing for the low-carbon transition. At the same time, climate change is expected to negatively affect pension schemes' assets and returns worldwide, both due to the physical risk arising from extreme weather events and the transition risk related to the changing regulatory framework, stranded assets, and reputation.

The Boardroom Accountability Project (BAP)

In November 2014, The New York City Pension System (NYCPS), in collaboration with New York City Comptroller Scott Stringer, announced the establishment of the Boardroom Accountability Project (BAP). The objective of the project was to hold the boards of the portfolio companies accountable to long-term shareholders and give pensioners a voice in oversight concerning ESG governance-related aspects such as climate change risks, employee conditions, and board diversity.

Comptroller Stringer and the City's pension funds launched the initiative by submitting 75 proxy shareholder proposals in collaboration with other institutional investors in fall 2014. The group of 75 companies included mainly companies in the carbon-intensive industry, those with poor corporate governance, and those characterized by limited gender diversity in the board. These proposals produced excellent outcomes; indeed, two-thirds of the proposals that went to a vote achieved majority support.

Naaraayanan et al. (2019) analyzed the real effects on the air quality around the plants of firms targeted by the BAP. Using plant-level data, the authors estimated that the targeted firms reduced their toxic releases, GHG emissions, and cancer-causing pollution. Improvements in air quality within a one-mile radius of the targeted plants suggested potentially important externalities to local economies. These improvements came about through increased capital expenditures on new abatement initiatives.

The New York State Teachers Retirement System (NYSTRS)

With US$120.5 billion AuM as of June 2021, NYSTRS is one of the 10 largest public pension funds in the United States. In 2021, the divestment groups Divest NY and New Youth Climate Leaders targeted the NYSTRS to urge the fund to divest from fossil fuel stocks. Divest NY asserted that NYSTRS held more than US$300 million stakes in companies with substantial coal reserves, and many of those companies were still investing heavily in coal. However, in February 2021, the New York Senate passed a bill establishing the teachers' fossil fuel Divestment Act, which requires NYSTRS "to divest the retirement system of any stocks, securities, equities, assets, or other obligations of corporations or companies included in an exclusion list of coal producers and oil and gas producers."

Furthermore, because of the long-term nature of their business – providing retirement plans to employees who contribute to the pool of money managed by these investors – climate risk is very relevant for pension funds. Newer members of pension funds may still be drawing pensions after 2100, so these investors have to recognize the systemic risks posed by climate change, as well as the investment risks and opportunities driven by the transition to a low-carbon economy. Also driven by the increasing concerns of the newer members about climate risk, some large pension funds – such as the New York City Pension System

(NYCPS) – are engaging with the boards of the investee companies on climate-related issues, as we observed in Section 4.4.4.

An increasing number of regulatory authorities encourage pension funds to incorporate climate-related risks. California's Senate Bill 964 2018 requires the largest pension funds in the United States, CalSTRS and CalPERS, to assess their portfolios climate risks from 2020 onward.[195]

Some examples of climate considerations in pension funds include the following:

o CalPERS (California Public Employees Retirement System) and CalSTRS (California State Teachers' Retirement System) are the two largest U.S. public pension funds (US$484 billion and US$308 billion of AuM). Both funds have developed investment strategies that seek financial returns with social, human, and environmental impacts. They are signatories of the United-Nations–supported PRI. The CalPERS CEO is co-chair of CERES, and both pension funds supported the CERES initiative to lobby the SEC to issue a guidance to require climate change risk disclosure in corporate filings. This initiative led to the approval of the first U.S. guidance for climate change disclosure by the SEC in 2010. In the same year, CalPERS invested US$500 million in an internally managed public stock environmental index, while CalPERS allocated US$1.2 billion of its private equity portfolio to alternative energy and technology sectors. Both pension funds have also pursued engagement strategies to influence corporate governance on environmental issues. For example, since 2010, CalSTRS has targeted 100 companies in the Russell 1000 Index portfolio that have insufficient levels of disclosure of energy and water use management.

o Government Pension Investment Fund (GPIF) in Japan: With the equivalent of US$1.6 trillion of AuM, GPIF is the world's largest pension fund. In July 2018, the fund invested ¥1 trillion (approximately US$9 billion) into the three indices that track the stock of Japanese companies with high ESG credentials. During the same year, the fund also invested ¥1.2 trillion (approximately US$10 billion) in two carbon-efficient indices. In December 2020, the fund invested an additional amount ¥1 trillion (US$9.7 billion) in the MSCI ACWI ESG Universal Index. The fund also invested US$2.9 billion in a gender-diversity-themed index from Morningstar. GPIF president, Masataka Miyazono, said in a statement: "We consider these two indexes to be firmly in line with our objective of improving long-term returns through enhanced sustainability of individual issuers and the market as a whole."

o Ontario Teachers' Pension Plan (OTPP): OTPP is the largest pension scheme based in Canada, with C$205 billion (US$160 billion) AuM. The pension fund currently

---

[195] For example, under the UK Pension Schemes Act 2021, pension funds with at least GBP 5 billion of AuM will be asked to assess and publicly report climate change risks in their portfolios.

manages the pension schemes of 329,000 active or retired teachers in the federal state of Ontario. In January 2021, the pension fund announced its commitment to achieve net-zero GHG portfolio emissions by 2050. To achieve this goal, the fund will pursue different strategies: (1) integrate climate change considerations in its investment strategy; (2) engage with portfolio companies to request enhanced carbon footprint and voting policy disclosure; (3) improve the expertise of climate change solutions. Jo Taylor, President and CEO of the fund, said: "As a global pension plan, we will leverage our scale and influence to transition to a low-carbon economy and create a sustainable climate future."

o   The National Pension Service (NPS) in South Korea has planned to increase its ESG asset investment to approximately US$5 billion by 2024.

APG (Netherlands)

APG, the fund that manages the ABP pension scheme, has more than €500 billion AuM allocated for its clients in several business sectors including education, government, construction, housing associations, energy, and utility companies. Recognizing its important role as a large institutional investor, APB plans to achieve the goal of carbon neutrality by 2050.

This goal is part of the new sustainable and responsible investment policy established in February 2020. The policy also commits ABP to divest from coal mines and tar sands and reduce by 40% the CO_2 emissions of its equity portfolio between 2025 and 2030, compared to the 2015 levels.

Over 2014–19, the APG green bonds portfolio grew from approximately €1 billion to €9 billion. Further, in 2021, APG invested €250 million in ABP Dutch Energy Transition Fund (ANET), a fund established in 2019 by ABP to invest in companies that operate in the generation, storage, distribution, and conservation of energy. APG has also joined Climate Action 100+. In 2019, APG has engaged with 716 companies on ESG issues.

APG classifies companies as ESG leaders or laggards. Then it invests in "leaders" and decides whether to invest in and engage with laggards or add them to its exclusion list. APG automatically excludes sin stocks, stocks of companies involved in the production of prohibited weapons, and companies whose business does not comply with the principles of the UN Global Compact in terms of human rights, labor conditions, the environment, and combating corruption. In 2019, APG added 159 companies to its exclusion list because of the lack of a suitable ESG policy.

Around the world, regulatory initiatives are incorporating climate considerations. For instance, in 2015, the UK Law Commission considered that incorporation of ESG factors by pension trustees is entirely consistent with their fiduciary duty to beneficiaries. However, there are different opinions. In the United States, the Department of Labor guidance for pension plans stresses that fiduciaries must not put ESG goals ahead of financial ones. The conflicting goals, and sometimes competing priorities, are important for institutional investors. The association representing German occupational pension funds, in its response to the European Commission consultation on long-term and sustainable investment, stated that ESG factors were not a priority compared to pressing issues such as the low-interest-rate environment.

Canada Pension Plan (CPP)

CPP Investments manages the Canada Pension Plan, with total AuM of C$409.6 billion (US$295 bn; as of March 2020), and more than 20 million contributors and beneficiaries. CPP believes that "climate change was defined as a leading issue facing our organization as a long-term investor – one that must be considered and fully integrated into our investment decisions." Accordingly, CPP is implementing TCFD recommendations across different areas.

CPP believes that active ownership through constructive engagement can reduce investment risks and enhance and sustain returns over time. Therefore, the fund prefers to actively engage with, and attempt to influence, companies rather than simply selling their shares. According to them, "selling our shares and walking away is easy." Their active ownership activities consider the materiality, time horizon, resource implications, and likelihood of success and use various tools, including proxy voting, in-person meetings, formal correspondence with the company, and collaboration with other investors through networks. With a focus on improved disclosure, CPP has supported more than 130 climate-change-related shareholder resolutions.

CPP reports, on an annual basis, the carbon footprint of its portfolio. This includes metrics on total carbon emissions and carbon intensity. It bases the carbon footprint metrics on Scope 1 and Scope 2 GHG emissions. The specific measures reported are as follows:

- Total Carbon Emissions (million metric tons of CO_2e): The absolute GHG emissions associated with a portfolio. This figure would typically rise as the AuM grows.
- Carbon Footprint (metric tons of CO_2e/$ million invested): Total carbon emissions for a portfolio normalized by the market value of the portfolio.
- Carbon Intensity (metric tons of CO_2e/$ million revenue): Volume of carbon emissions per million dollars of revenue (carbon efficiency of a portfolio).
- Weighted Average Carbon Intensity (metric tons of CO_2e/$ million revenue): The portfolio's exposure to carbon-intensive companies.

It uses climate change scenarios to determine the risk of climate change for its portfolio. It also uses stress testing to assess the impact and resilience of investments under a range of scenarios, including extreme and tail events.

Pension funds have fiduciary duties to invest funds prudently and in the best interests of their beneficiaries. Therefore, integrating sustainability factors in investments depends on whether it is believed that these materially affect the long-run performance of the portfolios, and therefore, the well-being of the beneficiaries. Accordingly, they should not sacrifice the economic interests of their clients to promote vague sustainability goals. A key question for many pension fund trustees is how to integrate their investment beliefs regarding sustainability with a portfolio that needs to achieve long-term returns.

5.5.4 Sovereign Wealth Funds

Although definitions vary, sovereign wealth funds (SWFs) are essentially state-owned investment funds that invest in international financial markets. They are different from traditional large institutional investors in a number of other ways. Although the capital for SWFs comes mainly from national governments, the mission of such funds, and the incentives of the people who make the investment decisions, reflects a peculiar mix of public-sector goals and private-sector methods. They can also be used by governments to implement national "industrial policy" by channeling capital to favored industries (Fernandes, 2014).

In June 2022, the top 10 SWFs held approximately US$8 trillion AuM.

Table 5.9 Largest sovereign wealth funds

Rank	Name	AuM (US$ billion)
1	Norges Bank Investment Management	1,362
2	China Investment Corporation	1,222
3	State Administration of Foreign Exchanges	980
4	Abu Dhabi Investment Authority	829
5	Government of Singapore Investment Corporation	799
6	Kuwait Investment Authority	693
7	Public Investment Fund	620
8	Hong Kong Monetary Authority	587
9	National Council for Social Security Fund	452
10	Qatar Investment Authority	445

Source: Global SWF, June 2022.

A large portion of SWFs' portfolios is allocated to foreign markets. Given their long-term nature, where they are supposed to manage a country's wealth for current and future generations, they tend to invest in global diversified portfolios with low exchange rate risks and strong political stability.

As with other investors, SWFs' portfolios are not immune to the risks arising from climate change, and climate risk for SWFs may materialize in form of climate risk, transition risk, and liability risk.[196]

---

[196] Liang and Renneboog (2019) investigated whether and how SWFs incorporated ESG considerations in their investment decisions in publicly listed corporations, as well as the subsequent evolution of the target firms' ESG performance. The results show that SWF funds do consider the level of past ESG performance as well as recent ESG score improvement when taking ownership stakes in listed companies. These results are driven by the SWF funds that do have an explicit or implicit ESG policy and are most transparent, and by SWFs originating in developed countries and in countries with civil law systems. For a review of SWFs and

Many of the SWFs worldwide are capitalized with revenues from the extraction of oil and gas.[197] Therefore, the transition and liability risks are particularly high for these investors. The combination of climate risk and declining revenues from fossil fuels will significantly affect the risk-adjusted returns of SWFs in commodity-exporting countries.

One Planet: The SWF collaborative initiative

The One Planet Sovereign Wealth Funds Working Group was established within the framework of the One Planet Summit held in December 2017, following the 2015 Paris Agreement. The group was established as a collaborative initiative aimed at boosting SWFs' efforts to integrate climate change opportunities and risks in their portfolio investment decisions.

The six founding members of the group are ADIA, Kuwait Investment Authority, NZ Superannuation Fund, Norges Bank (Norway's pension fund), Saudi Arabia's Public Investment Fund, and Qatar Investment Authority. The six founding members of the One Planet SWF Working Group committed to:

- developing an ESG framework to address climate change issues, including the development of methods and indicators that can inform investors' priorities as shareholders and participants in financial markets and
- Publishing the framework, methods, and indicators in 2018.

In 2020, nine other SWFs joined the group: BpiFrance (France), CDP Equity (Italy), Cofides (Spain), Fonsis (France), National Treasury Management Agency (Ireland), and KIC (South Korea).

Despite the relevance of climate change for the finance industry, the participation of SWFs in green finance is still negligible, and most of the estimates in 2019 suggested that only 1% of their AuM were actually "green." For example, according to the Asset Owners Disclosure Project (AODP), which evaluates institutional investors' low-carbon performance, 5 of the 10 lowest-rated large investment funds were actually SWFs. However, some SWFs have already announced the implementation of actions aimed at reducing the impact of the transition to a low-carbon economy in their portfolios. For example:

o   In 2019, the Norwegian SWF announced its plan to divest from oil and gas exploration in an effort to diversify its exposure to fossil fuel assets.

o   In 2016, the NZ Superannuation Fund set a target of reducing portfolio emissions by 20% and its ownership of oil and coal by 40% by 2020. Having met its target, in 2020, the fund announced a more ambitious plan of reducing portfolio emissions by 40% and its ownership of oil and coal by 80% by 2025.

---

the impact of their investment choices, see Fernandes (2017), and for the impact on corporate value and performance, see Fernandes (2014). Using Chile's SWFs and pension funds as a case study, Hoffmann et al. (2020) contributed evidence indicating that ESG investments can deliver better ESG performance without sacrificing financial returns.

[197] The remaining SWFs are capitalized by non-commodity revenues, such as foreign exchange reserves and fiscal savings rules.

○ In 2020, the Abu Dhabi Investment Authority (ADIA) started to build a climate change equity portfolio with the objective of increasing its exposure to the green economy. ADIA's managing director, Hamed bin Zayed Al Nahyan, said: "We already routinely incorporate climate-change considerations into all of our investment proposals, and have been steadily expanding our exposure to renewable energy."

5.5.5 Endowments and Family Offices

A university endowment is a fund that receives money from charitable donations and private investors, and invests in assets to earn an income for future uses. This income is usually used to support the academic activity of the university, such as financing scholarships and research, upgrading campus facilities, and hiring professors. University endowments follow specific rules, and donors can indicate how they want their donations to be spent. U.S. academic institutions such as Harvard, Yale, and Stanford have the largest university endowments.

Table 5.10 Key endowments worldwide

Rank	Name	Endowment 2020 (US$ billion)
1	Harvard University	40.6
2	University of Texas System	32.0
3	Yale University	31.2
4	Stanford University	29.0
5	Trustees of Princeton University	26.6
6	Massachusetts Institute of Technology	18.5
7	Trustees of the University of Pennsylvania	14.9
8	The Texas A&M University System & Related Foundations	13.6
9	University of Michigan	12.5
10	Regents of the University of California	12.1

Source: National Association of College and University Business Officers (2021).

Endowments are feeling the pressure from students, faculty, alumni, and other stakeholders to respond to climate change through their endowments. Some endowments have responded to this demand and the changing dynamics of climate risks by integrating carbon footprint reduction into their portfolios.

University endowments are likely to incur substantial costs to implement their divestment strategies, but stewardship activities, such as proxy voting and engagement with portfolio companies, allow them to use their investor voice to emphasize climate risk concerns without incurring financial losses.[198] These actions aim to encourage companies to improve their reporting framework on climate risks, by offering more transparency and disclosure and even reduce their carbon footprint by setting GHG reduction targets. Climate Action 100+, a collaborative engagement initiative, allows investors to amplify their voice, exerting further pressure on companies to respond. This initiative was launched in 2017 and has demonstrated initial success. More than 40 U.S. universities[199] have responded to climate change by taking on a fossil fuel divestment approach, including the following:

- In 2014, Harvard University was the first U.S. endowment to become a signatory to the United-Nations-supported PRI. In September 2021, the President of Harvard University, Lawrence S. Bacow, announced that Harvard Management Company will completely divest from holdings in fossil fuels.
- In June 2020, the Stanford's Board of Trustees reported that Stanford Management Company (SMC) – under its program Ethical Investment Framework – had reduced fossil fuel holdings in its investment portfolio by more than 90%. With fossil fuel holdings equal to less than 1.5% of its investment portfolio, SMC had no direct holdings in the top 100 global oil and gas companies.
- In April 2021, the Yale Board of Trustees approved a set of ethical principles that would inform the university's decisions related to investee companies in the fossil fuel industry. This set of ethical principles led to the exclusion of 60 companies from the investment universe, as they did not comply with the principles.

Family Offices

Family offices are the institutions used by wealthy families to oversee and manage their wealth. The legal institution of the Family Office originates in the United States. Since the mid-19th century, wealthy families (such as the Rockefellers) have created such structures to invest their money, protect their family's assets, and distribute the returns among family members.

Family offices are classified as either single-family offices or multi-family offices. A single-family office supports the financial and investment needs of a specific family. A multi-family office provides family office services to more than one family group, and these multi-family offices sometimes also target high-net-worth individuals. In both cases, family offices provide services in areas such as investment, tax, estates, trusts, and lifestyle management.

The number of family offices has increased tenfold between 2008 and 2020 and now stands at around 10,000 (EIU, 2020), with more than US$6 trillion of AuM worldwide (UBS, 2020).

---

[198] Bessembinder (2016) estimated that the frictional costs of the divestment strategy may range between approximately 2% and 12% of the endowment's value.
[199] Lawrence and Zlatkova (2019).

Family offices are typically unrestricted by formal investment mandates and targets. They thus have freedom in determining their assets, maturity, risk, and return expectations. Family offices invest in many assets, including bonds, stocks, actively managed funds, index funds/ETFs, private equity, infrastructure funds, real estate, and others.

Table 5.11 Largest family offices

Rank	Family office	Total assets (US$ billion)
1	Cascade Investment	170.0
2	Walton Enterprises LLC	169.2
3	Bezos Expeditions	107.8
4	Mousse Partners	89.0
5	Dubai Holding	35.0
6	MSD Capital	31.0
7	Athos KG	30.7
8	Bayshore Global Management	30.1
9	Soros Family Office	30.0
10	Emerson Collective	26.0

Source: Sovereign Wealth Fund Institute (2021).

Sustainability has become attractive to wealthy families and the family office community. Many family offices are already playing a key role in helping families transition to sustainable and climate-friendly investment. Sustainable investing is an emerging trend within the family office space.

In its annual survey in partnership with Juniper Place, BlackRock Global Family Office Survey Report combined data aggregated from an extensive online survey completed by 185 Family Offices (Harvey and Needham, 2020) and suggested the following:

- o 80% of family offices now include some form of sustainable investing within their portfolio.
- o However, the size of commitments to sustainable investments is still relatively small.
- o Sustainable investing is more prominent in Europe, Middle East, and Africa (EMEA), with an average 22% invested in sustainable strategies, 14% in the United States, 7% in Asia, and 3% in Latin America.
- o 75% of family offices expect to increase their exposure in the coming years.

UBS (2020) reports that 39% of family offices intend to "allocate most of their portfolios sustainably over the next five years," and those that do are mainly using exclusion-based strategies.

5.5.6 Infrastructure Investment Funds

Historically, large investments in infrastructure used to be financed by public money. However, as government spending has been decreasing and the level of infrastructure investment has been increasing, governments around the world have been finding it increasingly difficult to fund all the infrastructure needed in their countries. This is why private sector funds, which invest in infrastructure assets, have a role to play in the transition.

The infrastructure investment gap is large. Also, it is not homogeneous across countries and regions (as described in Chapter 1, it is especially large for emerging market economies). One aspect of infrastructure is energy generation, where various steps are being taken to reduce the share of global power generation from fossil fuels. Despite the significant reduction that occurred after 2007, the global share of electricity generated by fossil fuels in 2019 was not far below the levels of 1985.

Figure 5.14 World: fossil fuels (% of electricity)

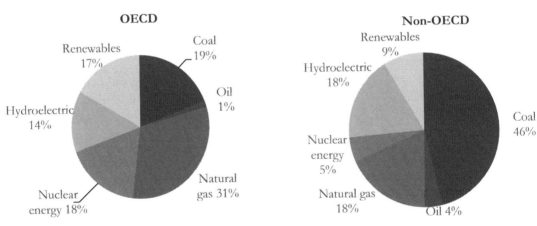

Source: BP Statistical Review of World Energy.

Between 2012 and 2020, global investment in renewable energy was close to US$300 billion per year. However, estimates suggest that global investment in renewables must increase to more than US$800 billion annually by 2050 if the international community wants to fulfil the climate and decarbonization goals (IRENA, 2020). This means that at current renewable investment levels, the gap will be approximately equal to US$15 trillion through 2050. Given the limited fiscal space available for direct investment by governments, the gap can be filled only by mobilizing private funds.

Infrastructure investing covers either capital-intensive projects with varying risk-return profiles in heavily regulated industries (e.g., utilities) or those under long-term concessions in collaboration with public sector entities through Public-Private partnerships (PPPs).

Infrastructure investment trusts (or investment funds) are collective investment schemes that enable institutional investors (and individuals) to invest financial resources in large infrastructure projects and earn a return. Infrastructure assets are attractive for investors as they

- o provide stable and predictable cash flows,
- o are non-cyclical and not strongly correlated with the economy, and
- o can take on high leverage, given the stable and predictable cash flows. Increasing leverage improves the returns on equity, and thus makes investments more attractive to investors.

Figure 5.15 World: investors in infrastructure by type

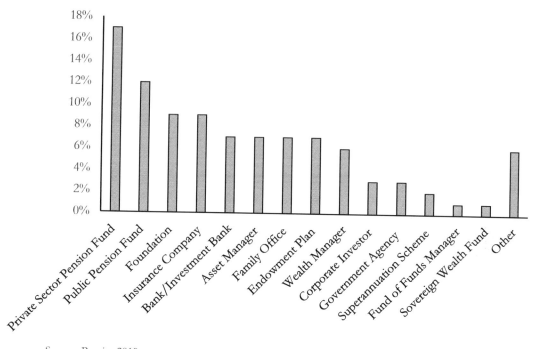

Source: Preqin, 2019.

Long-term investors are particularly interested in infrastructure assets. Investors such as SWFs, insurance companies, and pension funds tend to appreciate the stable and predictable cash flows of this asset class. As of the start of 2021, the global infrastructure investor pool consisted of 4,000 institutions, with US$655 billion of infrastructure AuM. Pension funds held 60% of the AuM and accounted for 32% of the investor base, followed by foundations, insurance companies, and banks.[200]

---

[200] Preqin (2020).

This asset class is concentrated in some very large investors. At the end of 2020, the 30 largest global institutional investors had committed US$321 billion to the infrastructure assets. Moreover, the top 10 infrastructure investors held approximately 35% of the total infrastructure AuM. The largest infrastructure investor was the Canadian CCP Investment Board with US$36.6 billion of AuM.

Table 5.12 The 10 largest institutional investors in infrastructure

Rank	Profile	Infra allocation (%)	Infra AuM (US$ billion)	Country
1	CPP Investment Board	10%	36.6	Canada
2	Abu Dhabi Investment Authority	5%	29.0	United Arab
3	Caisse de dépôt et placement du Québec	9%	25.2	Canada
4	Allianz Global Investors	3%	24.2	Germany
5	National Pension Service of Korea	3%	23.9	South Korea
6	APG	3%	19.9	Netherlands
7	Ontario Municipal Employees	20%	16.5	Canada
8	AustralianSuper	11%	16.4	Australia
9	BCI	10%	15.9	Canada
10	China Investment Corporation (CIC)	1%	15.0	China

Source: Infrastructure Investor, year-end 2021.

Despite several interesting characteristics, investing in the infrastructure asset class comes with a set of risks:

- o Macroeconomic and business risks: The profitability of an infrastructure project is subject to changes in macroeconomic variables such as exchange rates, interest rates, or inflation. Also, business risks are related to the asset's exposure to business cycles, especially shifts in consumer demand.
- o Technical risks: These risks are related to the complexity and feasibility of the project, construction, and technology.
- o Political and regulatory risks: Government actions, which include changes in policy or regulation, can negatively impact the returns of an infrastructure investment. These actions can affect a specific industry (e.g., utilities) or a specific contract (e.g., a PPP between a firm and a sub-sovereign or local institution).

Besides these traditional risks involved in infrastructure investments, there are additional risks due to climate issues. For instance, natural disasters can physically damage infrastructure. If a natural disaster limits the revenue-generating ability of an infrastructure, it affects the return on that asset, which can even become insolvent (given the traditional high leverage used).

Infrastructure funds typically have a long-term horizon, with the majority of them having an investment horizon of seven years or more. That is, a substantial amount of time can elapse from the moment the funds are funded until the exit. However, the underlying assets usually have a much longer useful life. That means that infrastructure funds frequently purchase assets, operate them for several years, and then sell them to another investor.

At the point of selling, the exit price can be maximized by de-risking the project. At this stage, the projects are fully operational and should have stable and predictable cash flows. These characteristics make them appealing to large institutional investors. Further, if the project poses a lower risk, then at the time of the exit investors will subsequently require a lower IRR of their investments, thus maximizing the exit valuation.

Given the long-term nature of these projects, investors must undertake due diligence and take into account both the climate risk considerations for different infrastructure assets and the time element. For instance, climate risks for property and infrastructure may materialize with different time horizons. Similarly, physical risks may be more relevant for some sectors, whereas transition and technological risks may be more relevant for other sectors (see Chapter 2). The growing awareness of this topic is reflected in the increasing number of PRI signatories that invest in infrastructure.

REFERENCES: CHAPTER 5

Albuquerque, R., Y. Koskinen, and C. Zhang. 2019. "Corporate Social Responsibility and Firm Risk: Theory and Empirical Evidence." *Management Science* 65 (10): 4451–69.

Amel-Zadeh, A., and G. Serafeim. 2018. "Why and How Investors Use ESG Information: Evidence from a Global Survey." *Financial Analysts Journal* 74 (3): 87–103.

Amiraslani, H., Lins, K. V., Servaes, H., & Tamayo, A. 2022. "Trust, Social Capital, and the Bond Market Benefits of ESG Performance." *Review of Accounting Studies*, 1-42.

Ansar, A., B. Caldecott, and J. Tilbury. 2013. "Stranded Assets and the Fossil Fuel Divestment Campaign: What Does Divestment Mean for the Valuation of Fossil Fuel Assets?" Smith School of Enterprise and the Environment, University of Oxford.

Bannier, C.E., Y. Bofinger, and B. Rock. 2019. "Doing Safe by Doing Good: ESG Investing and Corporate Social Responsibility in the US and Europe." CFS Working Paper Series.

Bansal, R., D. Kiku, and M. Ochoa. 2016. "Price of Long-Run Temperature Shifts in Capital Markets." National Bureau of Economic Research.

Barber, B.M., A. Morse, and A. Yasuda. 2021. "Impact Investing." *Journal of Financial Economics* 139 (1): 162–85.

Bauer, R., T. Ruof, and P. Smeets. 2021. "Get Real! Individuals Prefer More Sustainable Investments." *The Review of Financial Studies* 34 (8): 3976–4043.

Bénabou, R., and J. Tirole. 2010. "Individual and Corporate Social Responsibility." *Economica* 77 (305): 1–19.

Beneish, M.D., and R.E. Whaley. 1996. "An Anatomy of the 'S&P Game': The Effects of Changing the Rules." *The Journal of Finance* 51 (5): 1909–30.

Bennett, B., R.M. Stulz, and Z. Wang. 2020. "Does Joining the S&P 500 Index Hurt Firms?" National Bureau of Economic Research.

Benson, K.L., and J.E. Humphrey. 2008. "Socially Responsible Investment Funds: Investor Reaction to Current and Past Returns." *Journal of Banking & Finance* 32 (9): 1850–59.

Berg, F., J.F. Koelbel, and R. Rigobon. 2019. "Aggregate Confusion: The Divergence of ESG Ratings." *Forthcoming Review of Finance*.

Bessembinder, H. 2016. "Frictional Costs of Fossil Fuel Divestment." Available at *SSRN 2789878*.

Boffo, R., and R. Patalano. 2020. "ESG Investing: Practices, Progress and Challenges." Paris: OECD.

Bolton, P., and M. Kacperczyk. 2021a. "Do Investors Care about Carbon Risk?" *Journal of Financial Economics* 142 (2): 517–49.

Bolton, P., and M.T. Kacperczyk. 2021b. "Carbon Disclosure and the Cost of Capital." Available at *SSRN 3755613*.

Borgers, A., J. Derwall, K. Koedijk, and J. Ter Horst. 2013. "Stakeholder Relations and Stock Returns: On Errors in Investors' Expectations and Learning." *Journal of Empirical Finance* 22: 159–75.

Broccardo, E., O. Hart, and L. Zingales. 2020. "Exit vs. Voice." European Corporate Governance Institute – Finance Working Paper No. 694/2020, Finance Research Paper Series.

Ceccarelli, M., S. Ramelli, and A. Wagner. 2020. "Low-Carbon Mutual Funds." Research Paper (19–13). Zürich: Swiss Finance Institute.

Chatterji, A.K., R. Durand, D.I. Levine, and S. Touboul. 2016. "Do Ratings of Firms Converge? Implications for Managers, Investors and Strategy Researchers." *Strategic Management Journal* 37 (8): 1597–1614.

Chen, H., G. Noronha, and V. Singal. 2004. "The Price Response to S&P 500 Index Additions and Deletions: Evidence of Asymmetry and a New Explanation." *The Journal of Finance* 59 (4): 1901–30.

Cheng, I.-H., H. Hong, and K. Shue. 2013. "Do Managers Do Good with Other People's Money?" (No. W19432). NBER working paper. Cambridge, Massachusetts: National Bureau of Economic Research.

Cheung, A.W. 2011. "Do Stock Investors Value Corporate Sustainability? Evidence from an Event Study." *Journal of Business Ethics* 99 (2): 145–65.

Choi, J., D. Escalante, and M.L. Larsen. 2020. "Green Banking in China: Emerging Trends." CPI Discussion Brief. Climate Policy Initiative. www. climatepolicyinitiative. org/wp-content/uploads/2020/08/Green-Banking-in-China-Emerging-Trends-1. pdf.

Consolandi, C., A. Jaiswal-Dale, E. Poggiani, and A. Vercelli. 2009. "Global Standards and Ethical Stock Indexes: The Case of the Dow Jones Sustainability Stoxx Index." *Journal of Business Ethics* 87 (1): 185–97.

Davies, S.W., and E.D. Van Wesep. 2018. "The Unintended Consequences of Divestment." *Journal of Financial Economics* 128 (3): 558–75.

Deng, X., J. Kang, and B.S. Low. 2013. "Corporate Social Responsibility and Stakeholder Value Maximization: Evidence from Mergers." *Journal of Financial Economics* 110 (1): 87–109.

Dewi, J. 2020. "Family Office Boom: Contrasts Between East And West." London: Economist Intelligence Unit.

Dhillon, U., and H. Johnson. 1991. "Changes in the Standard and Poor's 500 List." *Journal of Business*, 75–85.

Di Giuli, A., and L. Kostovetsky. 2014. "Are Red or Blue Companies More Likely to Go Green? Politics and Corporate Social Responsibility." *Journal of Financial Economics* 111 (1): 158–80.

Dimson, E., O. Karakaş, and X. Li. 2015. "Active Ownership." *The Review of Financial Studies* 28 (12): 3225–68.

Dimson, E., P. Marsh, and M. Staunton. 2020. "Divergent ESG Ratings." *The Journal of Portfolio Management* 47 (1): 75–87.

Dordi, T., and O. Weber. 2019. "The Impact of Divestment Announcements on the Share Price of Fossil Fuel Stocks." *Sustainability* 11 (11): 3122.

Dunn, J., S. Fitzgibbons, and L. Pomorski. 2018. "Assessing Risk through Environmental, Social and Governance Exposures." *Journal of Investment Management* 16 (1): 4–17.

Durand, R., L. Paugam, and H. Stolowy. 2019. "Do Investors Actually Value Sustainability Indices? Replication, Development, and New Evidence on CSR Visibility." *Strategic Management Journal* 40 (9): 1471–90.

Dyck, A., K.V. Lins, L. Roth, and H.F. Wagner. 2019. "Do Institutional Investors Drive Corporate Social Responsibility? International Evidence." *Journal of Financial Economics* 131 (3): 693–714.

Eccles, R.G., and J.C. Stroehle. 2018. "Exploring Social Origins in the Construction of ESG Measures." *Available at SSRN 3212685*.

Edmans, A. 2012. "The Link between Job Satisfaction and Firm Value, with Implications for Corporate Social Responsibility." *Academy of Management Perspectives* 26 (4): 1–19.

El Ghoul, S., and A. Karoui. 2017. "Does Corporate Social Responsibility Affect Mutual Fund Performance and Flows?" *Journal of Banking & Finance* 77: 53–63.

Engle, R.F., S. Giglio, B. Kelly, H. Lee, and J. Stroebel. 2020. "Hedging Climate Change News." *The Review of Financial Studies* 33 (3): 1184–1216.

Fabozzi, F.J., K. Ma, and B.J. Oliphant. 2008. "Sin Stock Returns." *The Journal of Portfolio Management* 35 (1): 82–94.

Fama, E.F., and K.R. French. 1992. "The Cross-Section of Expected Stock Returns." *The Journal of Finance* 47 (2): 427–65.

Fernandes, N. 2014. "The Impact of Sovereign Wealth Funds on Corporate Value and Performance." *Journal of Applied Corporate Finance* 26 (1): 76–84.

Fernandes, N. 2017. "Sovereign Wealth Funds. Investment Choices and Implications Around the World." In *The Oxford Handbook of Sovereign Wealth Funds*, eds. Cumming, D.J., G. Wood, I. Filatotchev, and J. Reinecke, 322–49. Oxford, United Kingdom: Oxford University Press.

Fernandes, N., M.A. Ferreira, P. Matos, and K.J. Murphy. 2013. "Are US CEOs Paid More? New International Evidence." *The Review of Financial Studies* 26 (2): 323–67.

Ferreira, M.A., and P. Matos. 2008. "The Colors of Investors' Money: The Role of Institutional Investors around the World." *Journal of Financial Economics* 88 (3): 499–533.

Flammer, C. 2013. "Corporate Social Responsibility and Shareholder Reaction: The Environmental Awareness of Investors." *Academy of Management Journal* 56 (3): 758–81.

Flammer, C. 2015. "Does Corporate Social Responsibility Lead to Superior Financial Performance? A Regression Discontinuity Approach." *Management Science* 61 (11): 2549–68.

Friede, G., T. Busch, and A. Bassen. 2015. "ESG and Financial Performance: Aggregated Evidence from More than 2000 Empirical Studies." *Journal of Sustainable Finance & Investment* 5 (4): 210–33.

Friedman, M. 2007. "The Social Responsibility of Business Is to Increase Its Profits." In *Corporate Ethics and Corporate Governance*, edited by Zimmerli, W.C. and K. Richter, 173–78. Berlin, Heidelberg: Springer.

Gibson, R., S. Glossner, P. Krueger, P. Matos, T. Steffen, and others. 2020. "Responsible Institutional Investing around the World." Swiss Finance Institute.

Gibson, R., P. Krueger, and S.F. Mitali. 2020. "The Sustainability Footprint of Institutional Investors: ESG Driven Price Pressure and Performance." *Swiss Finance Institute Research Paper*, no. 17–05.

Gibson, R., P. Krueger, and P.S. Schmidt. 2021. "ESG Rating Disagreement and Stock Returns." *Financial Analysts Journal* 77 (4): 104–27.

Gillan, S., and L.T. Starks. 2003. "Corporate Governance, Corporate Ownership, and the Role of Institutional Investors: A Global Perspective." *Weinberg Center for Corporate Governance Working Paper*, no. 2003–01.

Griffin, C. 2020. "Margins: Estimating the Influence of the Big Three on Shareholder Proposals." *SMU Law Review* 73 (3): 409.

Harris, L., and E. Gurel. 1986. "Price and Volume Effects Associated with Changes in the S&P 500 List: New Evidence for the Existence of Price Pressures." *The Journal of Finance* 41 (4): 815–29.

Hart, O. and Zingales, L. 2017. "Companies Should Maximize Shareholder Welfare Not Market Value." *Journal of Law, Finance, and Accounting* 2: 247–274.

Harvey, P., and S. Needham. 2020. "Inside View." Global Family Office Survey. New York: BlackRock.

Hartzmark, S.M., and A.B. Sussman. 2019. "Do Investors Value Sustainability? A Natural Experiment Examining Ranking and Fund Flows." *The Journal of Finance* 74 (6): 2789–2837.

Hawn, O., A.K. Chatterji, and W. Mitchell. 2018. "Do Investors Actually Value Sustainability? New Evidence from Investor Reactions to the Dow Jones Sustainability Index (DJSI)." *Strategic Management Journal* 39 (4): 949–76.

Heinkel, R., A. Kraus, and J. Zechner. 2001. "The Effect of Green Investment on Corporate Behavior." *Journal of Financial and Quantitative Analysis* 36 (4): 431–49.

Henke, H.-M. 2016. "The Effect of Social Screening on Bond Mutual Fund Performance." *Journal of Banking & Finance* 67: 69–84.

Hoepner, A.G., I. Oikonomou, Z. Sautner, L.T. Starks, and X. Zhou. 2018. "ESG Shareholder Engagement and Downside Risk."

Hong, H., and M. Kacperczyk. 2009. "The Price of Sin: The Effects of Social Norms on Markets." *Journal of Financial Economics* 93 (1): 15–36.

Hoffmann, B., T. Armangue i Jubert, and E. Parrado. 2020. "The Business Case for ESG Investing for Pension and Sovereign Wealth Funds." Washington, D.C.: Inter-American Development Bank (IADB).

HSBC. 2020. "Commitment to ESG Financing and Investing Strengthens during Global Pandemic." News Release, October 14, 2020. https://www.hsbc.com/-/files/hsbc/media/media-release/2020/201013-hsbc-survey-of-issuers-and-investors-finds-largest-share-believe.pdf?download=1.

Hsu, P.-H., K. Li, and C.-Y. Tsou. 2022. "The Pollution Premium." *Journal of Finance*, Forthcoming.

Humphrey, J.E., and Y. Li. 2021. "Who Goes Green: Reducing Mutual Fund Emissions and Its Consequences." *Journal of Banking & Finance* 126: 106098.

IRENA. 2020. "Global Landscape of Renewable Energy Finance 2020." Abu Dhabi: International Renewable Energy Agency. https://www.irena.org/publications/2020/Nov/Global-Landscape-of-Renewable-Energy-Finance-2020.

Jain, P.C. 1987. "The Effect on Stock Price of Inclusion in or Exclusion from the S&P 500." *Financial Analysts Journal* 43 (1): 58–65.

Khan, M., G. Serafeim, and A. Yoon. 2016. "Corporate Sustainability: First Evidence on Materiality." *The Accounting Review* 91 (6): 1697–1724.

Kotsantonis, S., and G. Serafeim. 2019. "Four Things No One Will Tell You About ESG Data." *Journal of Applied Corporate Finance* 31 (2): 50–58.

Kovner, A., and J. Lerner. 2015. "Doing Well by Doing Good? Community Development Venture Capital." *Journal of Economics & Management Strategy* 24 (3): 643–63.

Krüger, P. 2015. "Corporate Goodness and Shareholder Wealth." *Journal of Financial Economics* 115 (2): 304–29.

Krueger, P., Z. Sautner, and L.T. Starks. 2020. "The Importance of Climate Risks for Institutional Investors." *The Review of Financial Studies* 33 (3): 1067–1111.

Lawrence, E., and S. Zlatkova. 2019. "3 Ways Endowments Can Adopt Sustainable Investing." Northern Trust Asset Management.

Liang, H., and L. Renneboog. 2020. "The Global Sustainability Footprint of Sovereign Wealth Funds." *Oxford Review of Economic Policy* 36 (2): 380–426.

Lins, K.V., H. Servaes, and A. Tamayo. 2017. "Social Capital, Trust, and Firm Performance: The Value of Corporate Social Responsibility during the Financial Crisis." *The Journal of Finance* 72 (4): 1785–1824.

Lintner, J. 1965. "The Valuation of Risk Assets and the Selection of Risky Investments in Stock. Portfolios and Capital Budgets." *The Review of Economics and Statistics* 47: 13–37.

Masulis, R.W., and S.W. Reza. 2015. "Agency Problems of Corporate Philanthropy." *The Review of Financial Studies* 28 (2): 592–636.

Markowitz, H. 1952. "Portfolio Selection." *The Journal of Finance* 7 (1): 77–91.

Matos, P. 2020. "ESG and Responsible Institutional Investing around the World: A Critical Review." SSRN Scholarly Paper. Rochester, NY. https://doi.org/10.2139/ssrn.3668998.

McKenzie, M. 2019. "Poor ESG Performance Increases Likelihood of Targeting by Activist Investors." Alvarez & Marsal | Management Consulting | Professional Services. December 2, 2019. https://www.alvarezandmarsal.com/insights/poor-esg-performance-increases-likelihood-targeting-activist-investors.

Murphy, C.J. 2002. "The Profitable Correlation between Environmental and Financial Performance: A Review of the Research." *Light Green Advisors*, 1–18.

Naaraayanan, S.L., K. Sachdeva, and V. Sharma. 2021. "The Real Effects of Environmental Activist Investing." *European Corporate Governance Institute–Finance Working Paper*, no. 743.

OECD. 2020. "Pension Markets in Figures." Paris: OECD.

Orsagh, M., J. Allen, J. Sloggett, A. Georgieva, S. Bartholdy, and K. Douma. 2018. "ESG Integration In The Americas: Markets, Practices, And Data." Charlottesville, United States: CFA Institute.

Pástor, L., R.F. Stambaugh, and L.A. Taylor. 2021. "Sustainable Investing in Equilibrium." *Journal of Financial Economics* 142 (2): 550–71.

Pástor, L., R.F. Stambaugh, and L.A. Taylor. 2022. "Dissecting Green Returns." *Journal of Financial Economics* 146 (2): 403–24.

Prequin. 2020. "2020 Preqin Global Infrastructure Report." London: Prequin.

Renneboog, L., J. Ter Horst, and C. Zhang. 2008. "The Price of Ethics and Stakeholder Governance: The Performance of Socially Responsible Mutual Funds." *Journal of Corporate Finance* 14 (3): 302–22.

Riedl, A., and P. Smeets. 2017. "Why Do Investors Hold Socially Responsible Mutual Funds?" *The Journal of Finance* 72 (6): 2505–50.

Rohleder, M., M. Wilkens, and J. Zink. 2022. "The Effects of Decarbonizing Institutional Portfolios on Stock Prices and Carbon Emissions." *Journal of Banking and Finance* 134: 106352.

Schroders. 2019. "Schroders Global Investor Study 2019." London.

Schroders. 2021. "Schroders Global Investor Study 2021." London.

Servaes, H., and A. Tamayo. 2013. "The Impact of Corporate Social Responsibility on Firm Value: The Role of Customer Awareness." *Management Science* 59 (5): 1045–61.

Sharfman, M.P., and C.S. Fernando. 2008. "Environmental Risk Management and the Cost of Capital." *Strategic Management Journal* 29 (6): 569–92.

Sharpe, W.F. 1964. "Capital Asset Prices: A Theory of Market Equilibrium under Conditions of Risk." *The Journal of Finance* 19 (3): 425–42.

Shleifer, A. 1986. "Do Demand Curves for Stocks Slope Down?" *The Journal of Finance* 41 (3): 579–90.

Starks, L.T., P. Venkat, and Q. Zhu. 2017. "Corporate ESG Profiles and Investor Horizons." *Available at SSRN 3049943.*

Sustainalytics. 2021. "ESG Risk Ratings Methodology." https://connect.sustainalytics.com/esg-risk-ratings-methodology.

Teoh, S.H., I. Welch, and C.P. Wazzan. 1999. "The Effect of Socially Activist Investment Policies on the Financial Markets: Evidence from the South African Boycott." *The Journal of Business* 72 (1): 35–89.

The Robbins Collection. 2020. "The Common Law and Civil Law Traditions." https://www. law. berkeley. edu/wp-content/uploads/2017/11/CommonLawCivilLawTraditions. pdf.

UBS. 2020. "Global Family Office Report 2020." Global Family Office Report. Zürich: UBS Group AG.

UNCTAD. 2019. "Leveraging the Potential of ESG ETFs for Sustainable Development." Geneva: The United Nations Conference on Trade and Development.

Ward, K. 2021. "The Impact of ESG Factors on Portfolio Returns." J.P. Morgan Asset Management. March   29,   2021.   https://am.jpmorgan.com/lu/en/asset-management/per/insights/market-insights/market-updates/on-the-minds-of-investors/the-impact-of-ESG-factors-on-portfolio-returns/.

Chapter 6
Global Public Sector Responses

Finance can play an important role in allocating capital to achieve sustainability goals, and ensure that long-term climate risks are understood and incorporated in business decisions. That was the subject of the previous chapters. However, additional policies and regulations are needed to provide markets with the right prices, signals, and incentives. This includes pricing externalities (such as pollution), phasing out subsidies to fossil fuels, and harmonizing regulations across countries.

It is important to recognize that political economy aspects are involved, and that each country has its own unique background. Some countries are more vulnerable to climate change. Also, some countries will face serious transition costs and social problems along the way.

This chapter also discusses the international framework for disclosure and transparency regulations, and other financial market regulations. We also analyze the role of central banks, and how they are integrating climate considerations into their monetary policy instruments and banking system regulatory frameworks.

6.1   PRICING EMISSIONS AND NEGATIVE EXTERNALITIES

In his book *The Economics of Welfare,* published in 1920, the British economist Arthur Cecil Pigou first developed the concept of negative externalities in economic theory. Negative externalities exist when an economic agent benefits from the production of a good but does not bear the external social costs associated with its production.

In public economics, cases where market mechanisms do not lead to social efficiency are commonly referred to as market failures, and pollution is a clear example of a market failure. As environmental quality (natural capital, clean air, climate, etc.) is a global public good, any local pollution produced by a single economic agent represents a cost to society as a whole, on account of the goods produced by it.

The typical economic solution to externalities is to provide agents with proper incentives to incorporate the full impact of their behaviors. In this section, we cover the main approaches used to address environmental externalities and emissions pricing.

6.1.1 Putting a Price on Carbon

As companies (and consumers) responsible for pollution do not necessarily bear the costs generated by their emissions, economists (and policymakers) argue that it is necessary to put a price on carbon emission.

Economic theory has developed two main approaches to tackle market failures due to negative externalities. One approach, based on Pigou (Pigou, 1932), favors government intervention through taxation and regulation to tackle negative externalities such as pollution. Pigou advocated taxes and subsidies (to incentivize sustainable behaviors), so that economic agents could internalize these externalities into their decision-making.

The second approach is based on the Coase theorem, which proposes market-based mechanisms to tackle externalities. Coase (1960) stated that if an externality can be traded, market mechanisms will lead to a Pareto-efficient outcome. The Coase theorem is the theoretical basis of non-interventionist policies in environmental issues.

Based on this, carbon pricing mechanisms follow two methods: (1) carbon taxes and (2) emissions trading systems. These are two policy tools that both government and companies can implement as part of their emissions reduction strategies. In this way, the costs of pollution are "internalized" by polluters, who will have incentives to reduce the stock of greenhouse gas (GHG) emissions to avoid higher tax burdens.

Carbon pricing can be a fundamental pillar of climate change mitigation measures. For example, the High-Level Commission on Carbon Prices[201] (2017) has estimated that a

---

[201] The Commission is chaired by the Nobel Laureate Joseph Stiglitz and Nicholas Stern, and comprises 10 academics from leading international universities. Its purpose is to assess "explicit carbon-pricing options and levels that would induce the change in behaviors – particularly in those driving the investments in infrastructure, technology, and equipment – needed to deliver on the temperature objective of the Paris Agreement, in a way that fosters economic growth and development, as expressed in the Sustainable Development Goals."

carbon price of at least US$50–100/tCO2 should be globally introduced by 2030 to cost-effectively reduce emissions in compliance with the Paris Agreement.

A carbon pricing mechanism would serve both as a deterrent to GHG emissions and as an indirect incentive to innovation. However, successful implementation of pricing schemes can be hindered by the resistance of local stakeholders. For instance, a typical argument against a carbon tax is that it would be difficult to get support for such a tax in many countries around the world. In Section 6.2, we address the political economy aspects of climate change, including ways in which governments can reduce resistance by eliminating elements of unfairness and promoting transparent communication.

KEY LEARNING POINT

There are two ways to put a price on carbon and GHG emissions: carbon taxes and emissions trading.

A carbon pricing mechanism – both internal and external – can also help companies incorporate climate-related risks and opportunities, for example, by investing in climate-friendly technologies that reduce GHG emissions. Investors – especially long-run investors such as pension funds – may use carbon pricing to analyze the potential impact of climate policies on the performance of their portfolios. This may represent an incentive to relocate capital toward low-carbon or climate-resilient securities.

To mitigate climate risks and prepare for the low-carbon transition, many corporates have started to introduce their own internal carbon pricing, which involves setting an internal charge on the amount of CO_2 released from business operations so that the organization can assess how, where, and when its emissions could affect its profit-and-loss (P&L) statements and investment choices (Fan et al., 2021). [202]

An increasing number of firms have adopted internal carbon pricing to inform strategic business decisions over the last five years. The CDP (Bartlett et al., 2021) conducted a survey on corporate use of internal carbon pricing globally, based on more than 5,900 corporate disclosures to the CDP in 2020, and found that more than 2,000 companies – with approximately US$27 trillion combined market capitalization – had adopted, or were planning to adopt, internal carbon pricing mechanisms.

---

[202] See also Abe et al. (2015) for a summary of the different ways in which companies apply internal carbon prices.

6.1.2 Carbon Taxes

A carbon tax is a penalty applied by the government on a market transaction that creates a negative externality. For instance, carbon taxes can be applied on the distribution, sale, or usage of fossil fuels (in a company's operations), because it is known that their use will create a negative externality on others (CO_2).

The basic rationale for environmental taxation is clear. Pollution imposes costs on society that (without any intervention) are not borne by the polluter, nor by the individual consumer of such products. Imposing a tax ensures that the polluter takes account of (or "internalizes") these wider costs when deciding how much to pollute.

Once the additional environmental costs are internalized through the carbon tax, the full costs of the good are paid by the consumers,[203] who are thus disincentivized from using carbon-intensive goods or services. At the same time, producers have incentives to innovate and find less polluting production processes to lower the cost of their products. In this way, both producers and consumers are disincentivized from using carbon-intensive goods, leading to lower carbon emissions.

Sweden's Carbon Tax 1991

In 1991, the Government of Sweden introduced a carbon tax alongside the already-existing energy tax. This application of the "polluter pays principle" represents a pillar of the Swedish climate policy.

The carbon tax was introduced at the rate of SEK 250 (EUR 24) per metric ton of fossil carbon dioxide emitted. Over time, the rate has gradually been increased to SEK 1,200 (EUR 116).

The gradual increase of the tax rates gave businesses and households time to adapt to the new tax regime, and thus the carbon tax does not seem to have harmed economic growth and business development. Since 1991, the size of emissions per capita has almost halved, while the GDP per capita has increased by more than 80%.

For governments, carbon pricing can represent an additional source of revenue that may be used to directly finance various projects, including climate-related ones.

Carbon taxes are typically applied to the units of emissions generated by carbon-generating activities. At the right level, the tax can serve as an incentive for consumers (and producers) to switch to cleaner production methods.

Table 6.1 shows data on carbon tax rates and the percentages of emissions in European countries that are covered by this policy instrument.

---

[203] In a Pigouvian taxation scheme, the tax rate equals the marginal costs (or social damage) associated with the negative externality.

Table 6.1 Carbon tax rates and share of covered GHG emissions

Country	Carbon tax rate (per metric ton of CO2e)	Share of GHG emissions covered	Inception year
Denmark	€23.8	35%	1992
Estonia	€ 2.0	6%	2000
Finland	€62.0	36%	1990
France	€45.0	35%	2014
Iceland	€29.7	55%	2010
Ireland	€33.5	49%	2010
Latvia	€12.0	3%	2004
Liechtenstein	€85.8	26%	2008
Luxembourg	€20.0	65%	2021
Netherlands	€30.0	12%	2021
Norway	€58.6	66%	1991
Poland	€0.1	4%	1990
Portugal	€24.0	29%	2015
Slovenia	€17.3	50%	1996
Spain	€15.0	3%	2014
Sweden	€116.3	40%	1991
Switzerland	€85.8	33%	2008
Ukraine	€0.3	71%	2011
United Kingdom	€21.2	23%	2013

Source: Tax Foundation.

At the international level, an additional problem is that of coordination, which has given rise to the concept of carbon border tax. This tax addresses the problem of the competitive disadvantage of companies located in countries that adopt carbon taxes versus competitors located in countries without any such taxes, or with substantially different levels of enforcement capacity. The carbon border tax could allow the importing country to adjust the prices of products from countries without carbon taxes. In particular, an assessment of imported goods' carbon content would be done at the border, and the products (or services) would be taxed appropriately. This mechanism could also provide an incentive to countries that have not set a price on carbon to consider implementing one in order to stop paying the tax at the border.

KEY LEARNING POINT

Carbon taxes affect all parties involved in the business transaction: polluters, consumers, and governments.

6.1.3 Emissions Trading Systems

Following the Coase theorem, the pollution problem originates from poorly defined property rights. If resources such as clean air and water were clearly defined as a form of property whose corresponding rights could be traded in a market, individuals and companies could allocate the use of this property in a cost-effective way (Hahn and Stavins, 2011).

An Emission Trading System (ETS), also called a cap-and-trade system, is a market mechanism introduced by the government. Under this system, the total amount of emissions released cannot exceed a certain set level. Further, the overall level of emissions can be lowered every year to foster technological development and the search for less carbon-intensive processes.

This system was popularized by the Kyoto Protocol in 1997, which introduced a cap-and-trade system mechanism for advanced economies to tackle global emissions that came into force in 2005.

The regulatory authority sets a maximum level (cap) of authorized emissions for plants included in the program. The authority then splits this cap into individual authorizations to emit a specific amount of a pollutant (for example, one metric ton of CO_2). The licenses to pollute can initially be distributed in different ways, by granting them freely (based on certain criteria), selling in auctions, or trading in exchanges. To comply with the regulatory framework, at the end of each period, each company must demonstrate that it has authorizations that match its current emissions.

Within a country (or region), each company decides its own strategy to achieve compliance, either by obtaining emissions permits, reducing emissions, or acquiring new permits, but the system guarantees that the total amount of emissions will not exceed the set level (or carbon budget) for the market.

Companies participating in the system can trade their permits (or emission allowances). The permits can be traded on the secondary market, whereby low emitters can sell their credits to high emitters. In this way, companies that expect to emit more carbon than allowed can purchase permits to emit more carbon from companies that have reduced their carbon emissions. For example, emissions trading, as set out in Article 17 of the Kyoto Protocol, allows countries that "consume" fewer emissions than agreed to sell the excess emissions to other countries that could not meet the reduction target.

Market participants are therefore given incentives to save carbon, as they can sell their unused emission quotas, and the system ensures that emissions are used in the most productive manner (Nordhaus, 2015). This policy allows companies to respond to technological or market changes without requiring government intervention or approval.

The EU-ETS

The emissions trading system set up in 2005 in Europe, the EU-ETS, is one of the key pillars of the EU energy policy and the world's first trading system for emissions. Since its inception, companies located in 31 countries (EU-27, Iceland, Liechtenstein, Norway, and the United Kingdom) have participated in the EU-ETS.

The EU sets a "cap" for the total amount of GHGs that can be emitted and distributes emission allowances to 12,000 energy, manufacturing, and aviation companies. Within the cap set by the EU, companies can sell or purchase emission allowances. Every year the cap decreases, which ensures that the total GHG emissions will decrease as well. Between 2005 and 2019, EU facilities covered by the ETS reduced emissions by about 35% (Source: EU Commission).

Many countries and regions have adopted ETS policies that cover different typologies of emitters:

- The EU Emission Trading System, set up in 2005 in Europe.
- The Tokyo Cap-and-Trade Program was launched in 2010 by the Tokyo Metropolitan Government as the first mandatory ETS. Under this scheme, allowances are assigned to large buildings, heat suppliers, factories, and other fossil-fuel-consuming facilities. The participants in the program are required to reduce carbon emissions under specific assigned targets (annual reductions in the allowances), and can trade such emissions allowances.
- The U.S. ETS includes manufacturing industries and large energy producers.
- Under the Ontario ETS, all electricity importers, facilities, or natural gas distributors that emit 25,000 metric tons or more of GHG emissions per year and all fuel suppliers are required to participate by law. The Quebec ETS cover emissions in power, buildings, transport, and industry. [204]
- China's ETS covers only the power sector. [205]

When establishing an ETS, the government can give emission allowances for free or auction them. Table 6.2 summarizes the commonly proposed approaches to allowance distribution, and their implications.

---

[204] In 2019, the Canadian federal government implemented a federal-level emissions target that applies to all the territories and provinces.

[205] China's ETS started operating in 2021, and its scope is expected to be gradually extended to petrochemical, chemical, building materials, steel, nonferrous metals, paper, and domestic aviation. However, there is no specific timeline for these extensions.

Table 6.2 Main allocation criteria with their interpretations and operational rules

Criterion	Interpretation	Operation rule
Sovereignty/Grandfathering	All nations (firms) have an equal right to pollute and to be protected from pollution	Distribute permits in proportion to historical emissions (energy)
Egalitarianism	All people have an equal right to pollute and to be protected from pollution	Distribute permits in proportion to population
Ability to pay	Mitigation costs vary directly with national economic well-being	Distribute permits inversely to GDP or per capita GDP
Economic activity	All nations should be allowed to maintain their standard of living	Distribute permits in proportion to GDP
Horizontal equity	All countries should be treated equally in terms of changes in welfare	Distribute permits to equalize net welfare change (net loss as proportion of GDP equal for each nation)
Vertical equity	Welfare gains vary inversely with national economic well-being, and welfare losses vary directly with GDP	Progressively distribute permits (net gain/loss proportions inversely/directly correlated with per capita GDP)
Polluter pays/historical responsibility	Nations with more historical emissions need to take a larger abatement burden	Distribute reduction responsibility in proportion to accumulated emissions
Merit (efficiency)	Nations should be compensated for emission reduction efforts	Distribute permits inversely to emissions intensity

Source: Zhou and Wang (2016).

The political economy aspects that shape the design of an ETS pose challenges to the global coordination of the carbon market. The ETSs around the world differ in terms of sectoral coverage (industries and sectors), types of target (caps and metrics), and permit allocation methods (auctions or free allocation). In the EU-ETS, a very large share of emission allowances is auctioned. On the other hand, China's ETS covers only the power sector, and emissions allowances are granted for free. The CDP (Bartlett et al., 2021) reported that, as of April 2021, there were 40 regional, national, and subnational ETSs, each with its own sectoral coverage, type of target, and emissions allowances allocation methods. Gulbrandsen et al. (2019) examined the political economy of the diffusion of nine ETS designs around the world, and found substantial divergence in design and implementation. They found that the "architects" of the different ETSs adapt their ETS to the local economic system situation, and to local and administrative goals.

Table 6.3 Emissions trading systems across the world

Name of the initiative	Coverage	Jurisdiction covered	Year of implementation
Alberta TIER	Subnational	Alberta	2007
BC GGIRCA	Subnational	British Columbia	2016
Beijing pilot ETS	Subnational	Beijing	2013
California CaT	Subnational	California	2012
Canada federal OBPS	National	Canada	2019
Chongqing pilot ETS	Subnational	Chongqing	2014
EU ETS	Regional	EU, Norway, Iceland,	2005
Fujian pilot ETS	Subnational	Fujian	2016
Guangdong pilot ETS	Subnational	Guangdong (except Shenzhen)	2013
Hubei pilot ETS	Subnational	Hubei	2014
Kazakhstan ETS	National	Kazakhstan	2013
Korea ETS	National	Korea, Republic of	2015
Massachusetts ETS	Subnational	Commonwealth of	2018
Mexico pilot ETS	National	Mexico	2020
New Zealand ETS	National	New Zealand	2008
Newfoundland and	Subnational	Newfoundland and Labrador	2019
Nova Scotia CaT	Subnational	Nova Scotia	2019
Quebec CaT	Subnational	Quebec	2013
RGGI	Subnational	RGGI	2009
Saitama ETS	Subnational	Saitama	2011
Saskatchewan OBPS	Subnational	Saskatchewan	2019
Shanghai pilot ETS	Subnational	Shanghai	2013
Shenzhen pilot ETS	Subnational	Shenzhen	2013
Switzerland ETS	National	Switzerland	2008
Tianjin pilot ETS	Subnational	Tianjin	2013
Tokyo CaT	Subnational	Tokyo	2010
Virginia ETS	Subnational	Virginia	2020

Source: CDP (April 2021).

Most of these carbon schemes were introduced in advanced economies, both at the national and regional levels (e.g., the province of Tokyo, Canadian provinces, and territories in the European Union). More recently, carbon pricing initiatives have also taken off in emerging markets and low-income countries or regions. For example, after the East African Alliance on Carbon Markets and Climate Finance was launched in June 2019, more African countries – under the guidance of the UNFCCC and other international initiatives – began exploring the possibility of implementing carbon pricing mechanisms. In 2021, China launched its national ETS market, which could become the world's largest ETS market.

> **KEY LEARNING POINT**
>
> *An ETS is a market trading mechanism that is prevalent in many countries at the national and subnational levels.*

6.1.4 Summary and Challenges

There are two main methods of carbon pricing: carbon taxes and emissions trading systems. A carbon tax imposes a fee on each emissions unit. In a trading system, regulators place a limit on the overall carbon budget for the market, allowing participants to trade permits among themselves and thereby arrive at a market-based price.

Climate change is a global problem. As a metric ton of CO_2 produces similar environmental damage across the globe regardless of the region in which it is emitted, a uniform worldwide carbon price would be an ideal solution. Uniform global carbon pricing would be an ideal tool to tackle GHG emissions efficiently without creating competitive imbalances and arbitrage due to different tax regimes. A single price for carbon that reflects the cost of the externalities would also help fight "pollution havens" (jurisdictions where the lack of environmental regulation allows business to keep polluting freely).

However, carbon pricing schemes set in place across the world are far from uniform. According to the World Bank's Carbon Pricing Dashboard, in 2021 there were 64 carbon pricing initiatives (carbon taxes and ETSs) across the world, in 45 jurisdictions, covering 11.7 $GtCO_2e$ (21% of the global GHG emissions).

6.2 JUST TRANSITION, SUBSIDIES, AND POLITICAL ECONOMY

It is important to recognize the political aspects of introducing new climate change policies. Even well-intended policymakers have a hard time translating words to actions. Actions often face resistance, and several policy rollbacks have occurred. For example, the United States returned to the Paris Climate Accords with the election of Joe Biden (after Donald Trump abandoned them).

Electoral cycles are also important. Most politicians want to be reelected, and so they carefully consider climate-related policies that are controversial, albeit important, in light of their political support and their chances of reelection. Special interest groups engage in organized lobbying[206] around climate policies. Also, many governments provide subsidies to fossil fuels in different ways. When a government provides subsidies, consumers pay energy prices below the costs incurred by companies to supply the energy. Fossil fuel subsidies represent an obstacle to the low-carbon transition because they essentially work as a "negative" Pigou tax that incentivizes companies to pollute.

6.2.1 Socioeconomic Consequences

In the low-carbon-economy world, hydrocarbons will gradually be phased out, and alternative sources of power will develop further. However, this will not only affect the environment and influence climate change, but it will also have wider consequences for many industries. Some industrial activities will come to a halt, and others will commence. This in turn will affect employment rates and wealth in different countries and regions.

Dealing with climate change requires balancing competing interests and recognizing that there are winners and losers. Some of the losers could be coal mine or fossil fuel companies and workers. For example, territories heavily reliant on carbon-intensive industries for employment face the risk of rising structural unemployment rates and stagnating growth. As many countries shift their energy systems away from fossil fuels, coal mines and refineries are likely to shut down across the world over the next decade (Cameron et al., 2020). Competing interests must be reconciled for successful change to occur. Change can also be beneficial. For instance, when whale catching was prohibited, many of these regions turned to whale watching, with significant tourism-related benefits and the creation of a totally new set of economic activities.

According to the European Commission, in 2015, there were 128 coal mines in 12 member states (41 regions at the NUTS-2 level) and 207 coal power plants in 21 member states (103 NUTS-2 regions). Poland had the largest number of coal mines (35), followed by Spain (26), Germany (12), and Bulgaria (12) (Widuto, 2019). The European coal sector employs nearly 340,000 people in direct and indirect activities, and it is estimated that between 54,000 and 112,000 direct jobs may be lost by 2030 due to the phasing out of coal mines (Alves Dias et al., 2018). Similarly, Diski et al. (2021) estimated that the British region of Yorkshire and the Humber relies excessively on carbon-intensive industries such as steel, cement, chemicals, and energy generation; approximately 360,000 jobs will be affected by a low-carbon-economy transition. In May 2021, thousands of miners and power workers protested in front of the European Commission office in Wroclaw against the decision of the Court of Justice of the European Union to close the Turów lignite mine that used to employ 1,250 people.

---

[206] Brulle (2018) estimated that in the United States, between 2000 and 2016, more than US$2 billion was spent on lobbying around climate issues.

On the other hand, some territories surrounding large metropolitan areas with significant technological resources and skilled workers will benefit from the low-carbon transition, which is expected to create green job opportunities and power the post-COVID-2019 recovery.

An important concept is the *Just Transition*. This societal movement argues that "no one should be left behind when we reconstruct our world into one driven by clean energy." Originated by unions in the 1990s to support workers who lost their jobs due to environmental protection policies, it has grown in importance.[207] For instance, as mentioned above, the transition away from coal will significantly impact workers in the coal industry and their communities.

To maintain socioeconomic cohesion in regions that will be negatively affected by the low-carbon-economy transition, governments and supranational organizations such as the EU have implemented measures to support innovation, investment in green technologies, and labor force training.

A common policy tool used by governments is the creation of special economic zones (SEZs) to accelerate the development of regions affected by economic decline and high unemployment rates. The main aim of this policy tool is to attract foreign direct investment by offering tax rebates for corporate income tax and regional and local taxes to support small- and medium-sized enterprises (Kustova et al., 2021). According to the UNCTAD's World Investment Report, in 2019 there were more than 5,000 SEZs worldwide, with 26 located in advanced economies (Europe and North America) and 103 in developing and transition economies (Asia, Africa, and Latin America).

Another policy tool to support socioeconomic stability during the transition is the use of cohesion funds[208] or regional investment banks to finance infrastructure and renewable energy projects, as in the case of the European Union, and the European Investment Bank.

KEY LEARNING POINT

The transition to a low-carbon world will have significant socioeconomic consequences if it is not well managed.

---

[207] In 2015, the UN's International Labor Organization produced "guidelines for a just transition towards environmentally sustainable economies and societies for all" that incorporated contributions from unions, employers' organizations, and governments. The final text of the Paris Agreement also mentions "taking into account the imperatives of a just transition of the workforce and the creation of decent work and quality jobs in accordance with nationally defined development priorities."

[208] These funds were created to provide social and economic support to EU countries with a gross national income (GNI) per capita below 90% EU-27 average.

6.2.2 Fossil Fuel Subsidies

Fossil fuel subsidies can take the form of direct and indirect subsidies to companies that produce and distribute fossil fuel for energy purposes, or to their consumers. Subsidies are incentives to keep consumer prices below market levels (or above market levels, if the incentives are for producers). Different sectors, such as energy, agriculture, and many others, have their own type of subsidy.

Fossil fuel subsidies can be direct producer subsidies or consumer subsidies. Producer subsidies target companies with the aim of reducing the costs of exploring, transporting, capturing and storing carbon, and refining fuel.

Consumer fossil fuel subsidies are commonly adopted to reduce the price of energy for consumers. In particular, in emerging market economies, such subsidies help households afford energy prices and access electricity services. In this case, consumers pay energy prices below the costs incurred to supply the energy.

Fossil fuels are subsidized by governments in different regions of the world. Most subsidies take the form of direct funding and tax breaks, but they can also involve land allowances for pipelines and refineries, or loans and guarantees at favorable rates for fossil fuel companies.

Governments worldwide subsidize fossil fuels for both political and economic reasons. In countries with a large fossil fuel sector such as Russia, Mexico, and the United States, fossil fuel subsidies also support employment, especially when the international oil price drops. In transition or emerging market economies, fossil fuel subsidies are also used to make energy more affordable, allowing more people to access electricity services. Subsidies also have international implications. For instance, Russia – the second-largest provider of government support to fossil fuels by at US$80.9 billion annually (2017–19 average) – is the largest supplier of energy products to the European Union.

Because fossil fuel subsidies reduce energy prices, they are often used to stimulate specific economic sectors and indirectly support companies that use energy extensively to operate their business.

Besides some positive effects (employment, affordable energy prices for firms and households), fossil fuel subsidies also produce negative effects related to environmental degradation (negative externalities). Moreover, they contribute to inefficiencies (market distortions) and inequality.

Artificially lowering energy prices leads to overconsumption of energy in capital-intensive industries such as transport and steel. Further, fossil fuel subsidies distort competition. By making electricity from fossil fuels cheaper, subsidies discourage companies from investing in energy efficiency projects or obtaining cleaner energy from renewables. Last but not least, fossil fuel subsidies often end up being regressive, an undesired effect being greater inequality. Del Granado et al. (2012) estimated that in developing countries, the wealthiest 20% of the population benefits from 43% of fossil fuel subsidies, whereas the poorest 20% of the population receives only 7% of the subsidies.

The OECD, in collaboration with the International Energy Agency (IEA), estimated that support provided to fossil fuels increased by 50% worldwide in 2019 (OECD and IEA, 2021). In particular, the largest increases in fossil fuel support were observed in the United States (+28% between 2017 and 2019) and in Mexico, where the government tripled fossil fuel support between 2017 and 2019, mainly in the form of producer support.

According to the IEA, in 2019, the amount of fossil fuel subsidies (oil, coal, gas) granted in 40 emerging market and developing economies totaled approximately US$312 billion. The figure was lower in 2020, due to the economic recession that followed the COVID-19 pandemic.

Figure 6.1 Total government support to fossil fuel

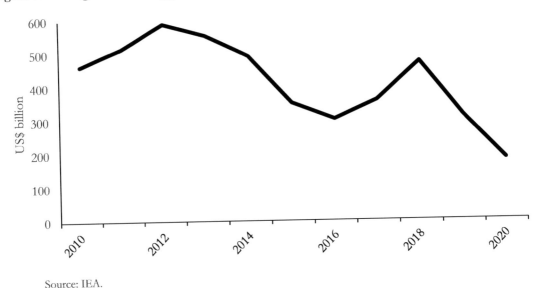

Source: IEA.

KEY LEARNING POINT

Despite the introduction of ETS and carbon taxes, substantial subsidies continue to drive the extensive use of fossil fuels.

6.2.3 Political Economy Considerations

Climate change has intergenerational implications, as the costs of mitigating climate change are borne by some individuals and companies, but everyone will benefit in the future. Here is another way to see this: preventing further climate change requires the elimination of some jobs in specific locations/sectors (for instance, in coal mines). In exchange, global emissions will decrease, and climate change will potentially be reversed, or mitigated, benefiting future generations worldwide.

That is why political economy considerations are relevant. Political economists examine political forces and institutional arrangements, and how they affect choices of economic policies. The political economy of climate change involves an analysis of the social, distributional, and political processes that can affect decision-making on climate change.

Several authors have analyzed the political processes that influence how public economic decisions, especially those pertaining to environmental policies, are made. Oates and Portney (2003) reviewed the early literature on the political determination of environmental regulation, the role of political interaction of the government with various interest groups, and the effectiveness of different types of regulatory measures. Others have studied why some countries adopt climate change policies whereas others do not (Brandt and Svenson, 2003; Steves and Teytelboym, 2013; Furceri et al., 2021). These studies shed light on why many well-intended policies failed to gain traction. Some of the findings are as follows:

○ Public knowledge of climate change matters. Countries where the population better understands the implications of climate change have more effective policies.
○ A higher concentration of carbon-intensive companies in a country hinders the adoption of climate change   policies.
○ The presence of democratic   institutions is not the main determinant. That is, successful mitigation policies are not associated with the type of political regime of the country.
○ Competitiveness in the global economy matters. Lack of economic diversification and global competition concerns can hinder the adoption of policies.

Some of the actions that can mitigate the resistance to climate change policies include the following:

○ *Mitigate inequality:* For instance, a gasoline tax that raises the price of gasoline by 50% will affect all drivers. For the median household (and even more so for poorer ones), gasoline costs are often a significant percentage of their income. However, for very wealthy households, gasoline costs are a small proportion of their disposable income. Such a gasoline tax would compound the inequality problem.
○ *Incorporate the cost of negative externalities in the mitigation plan/budget:* For instance, provide social protection to the poor and those affected by job losses. Social welfare

programs can help provide a reasonable living standard to those who lose their jobs, and policy initiatives may help reduce resistance to the transition. Reskilling programs will enable workers from the affected industries to successfully reorient their careers.

o   *Carefully select the timing*: For instance, an increase in carbon taxes that affects fuel prices is easier to implement when the oil price is low, and so are the gas prices for retail consumers. Also, during economic recessions or downturns, it is more difficult push through changes that will impose significant costs today to a large number of voters.

o   *Consider how global policies will address climate change at the local level, and how they will impact the local economy*: Different mitigating policies have unequal consequences. For instance, if a green factor is introduced in banking regulation, banks lending to "brown" firms will have to raise more capital. This regulation is likely to be opposed, at a global level, by governments from countries that have more brown firms, if no mitigating, or phasing, measures are planned ahead.

o   *Pay attention to the structure of the industrial base of the country*: If companies in the country are exposed to international competition, imposing domestic carbon taxes can lead to concerns about their global economic competitiveness. It can also create unfair competition, as foreign producers could be producing in environments where there are no carbon taxes. One possible way to address this is to impose a carbon border tax (see Section 6.1.2), such as the one that is being discussed right now in the European Union.

If the transition is left unmanaged, the risk of creating winners and losers is high, and those most affected could mount significant resistance. Policy initiatives and regulations are products of political compromises. To take credible steps forward, policymakers must consider different political economy elements, and think about the abovementioned ways of mitigating them.

KEY LEARNING POINT

Political economy elements matter in bringing about the required policy changes.

6.2.4 Summary and Challenges

Fossil fuel subsidies are commonly applied worldwide. They can take different forms, but ultimately, they keep consumer prices below market levels. Another way of seeing this is that subsidies represent negative taxes on carbon, when we know that externalities should be priced into the goods and services.

Governments use subsidies to achieve a number of objectives such as controlling unemployment and inflation. However, fossil fuel subsidies produce significantly negative effects and contribute to market distortions and inequality. By making electricity from fossil fuel cheaper, subsidies discourage companies from investing in energy efficiency projects or obtaining cleaner energy from renewables.

Climate change is a global crisis. However, global policies ultimately must be translated into specific national policy contexts. The implication is that climate change mitigation policies are not separable from social and political tensions.

Global policies must be flexible enough to accommodate specific national conditions. If they do not factor in national environmental–economic trade-offs, the one-size-fits-all transition policies will produce unintended (negative) consequences.

Political economy elements matter if the required changes are to be achieved through policies. The concept of *Just Transition* is an important element in this discussion. It is not reasonable to assume that policymakers will ignore local issues and act for the global common good without factoring in the concerns of their domestic constituents. Many initiatives may fail to achieve the desired outcomes if key stakeholders are not taken into consideration.

6.3 NON-FINANCIAL REPORTING AND CLIMATE DISCLOSURES

In response to the challenges posed by climate change, governments, central banks, and regulators identified the need to have reliable climate-related financial information, so that financial markets can properly price climate-related risks and opportunities.

In this section, we discuss the ways in which climate risk is being reported within organizations. This is especially important for institutional investors. It is clear that there is a growing demand for sustainability reporting and that some significant steps on sustainability reporting have already been taken, but there are also substantial challenges. We will also discuss the emergence of non-financial reporting, its benefits and limitations, the metrics used, and the role of the evolving global regulations underlying it.

6.3.1 Regulating Non-Financial Reporting

For decades, financial reporting was the common language used by companies and investors to talk about performance. However, traditional accounting was developed in a period when tangible assets comprised most of the companies' assets and explained most of the companies' market valuation.

Today, long-term trends, stakeholders, and sustainability issues are relevant business issues, as they impact the operating and financial performance of a company. It is clear that serious reputational and environmental risks do often surface, and these can have very real impacts on the company's bottom line. Effectively managing these issues can therefore improve business performance.

Also, driving the transition to a low-carbon economy requires whole industries to change toward climate-conscious operations. That is another reason for the introduction of additional reporting metrics that go beyond traditional financial metrics.

Regulating financial reporting is a complex topic, and needs to consider what non-financial information firms should be required to disclose, as well as how these reporting standards should be enforced. Before laying down rules, regulators should also consider the impact of these sustainability reporting requirements on company behavior.

To do so successfully, it is important to understand the relationship between financial and non-financial factors, how they influence a company's performance, and how a company creates and captures value in the long term. It is also important to remember that value is not created by the company in a vacuum; it is influenced by the external environment, through relationships with other stakeholders, and through the use of various (natural) resources. Therefore, some guiding principles govern the preparation of an integrated report: the strategic focus and future orientation, consideration of stakeholder relationships, and materiality.

Non-financial reporting, or integrated reporting, is about communicating non-financial measures of performance that go beyond the traditional financial statements (income statement, balance sheet, cash flow statement). The idea is that non-financial reporting (which provides information on the company's sustainability risks, metrics, and impacts) allows the company's shareholders and other stakeholders to make informed investment and active ownership decisions (see Sections 4.4 and 5.4).

The International Integrated Reporting Council (IIRC) defines integrated reporting as "a process founded on integrated thinking that results in a periodic integrated report by an organization about value creation over time and related communications regarding aspects of value creation." The IIRC produced the International Integrated Reporting Framework (also called the International <IR> Framework). According to the IIRC, integrated reporting aims to

- o improve the quality of information available to providers of capital;
- o enable a more efficient and productive allocation of capital;
- o promote a more cohesive and efficient approach to corporate reporting;
- o communicate the full range of factors that materially affect the ability to create value over time;

- o enhance accountability and stewardship for the broad base of capitals (financial, manufactured, intellectual, human, social and relationship, and natural) and promote an understanding of their interdependencies; and
- o support integrated thinking, decision-making, and actions that focus on the creation of value over the short, medium, and long term.

The <IR> Framework takes a principles-based approach. This means it recognizes a wide variation in individual circumstances,[209] and so it does not prescribe specific key performance indicators, measurement methods, or specific items to be disclosed. However, it does include some requirements so that an integrated report can conform to the <IR> Framework. An integrated report typically includes eight key topics,[210] which are posed in terms of questions to be answered:

1. Organizational overview and external environment: What does the organization do and what are the circumstances under which it operates?
2. Governance: How does the organization's governance structure support its ability to create value in the short, medium, and long term?
3. Business model: What is the organization's business model?
4. Risks and opportunities: What are the specific risks and opportunities that affect the organization's ability to create value over the short, medium, and long term, and how is the organization dealing with them?
5. Strategy and resource allocation: Where does the organization want to go and how does it intend to get there?
6. Performance: To what extent has the organization achieved its strategic objectives for the period and what are its outcomes in terms of effects on capital?
7. Outlook: What challenges and uncertainties are the organization likely to encounter in pursuing its strategy, and what are the potential implications for its business model and future performance?
8. Basis of preparation and presentation: How does the organization determine what to include in the integrated report and how are such decisions quantified or evaluated?

Globally, besides the IIRC, a range of organizations have weighed in on the debate around integrated reporting. Some of the main ones include the Sustainability Accounting Standards Board (SASB), the Global Reporting Initiative (GRI), the Climate Disclosure Sustainability Board (CDSB), and the Task Force on Climate-related Financial Disclosures (TCFD, established by the Financial Stability Board). The need for global coordination is ongoing, and a convergence and merging of entities is occurring. For example, in June 2021, the IIRC and the SASB announced their merger to form the Value Reporting Foundation (VRF).

---

[209] Christensen et al. (2019) show a substantial variation in ESG disclosures, depending on the company's activities.

[210] However, the detailed content of a company's integrated report will depend on the specific circumstances (International <IR> Framework, January 2021).

Later, in August 2022, the VRF was absorbed in the IFRS Foundation. According to Erkki Liikanen, Chair of the IFRS Foundation: "These consolidations help us to respond to the demand from stakeholders and deliver on the commitment we made at COP26 – to harmonise the sustainability disclosure landscape and build on the work of existing reporting initiatives."[211]

In the EU, Directive 2014/95/EU – also called the non-financial reporting directive (NFRD) – laid out the rules on disclosure of non-financial and diversity information by large companies (more than 500 employees). Under the NFRD, 6,000 of the largest EU companies were required to disclose non-financial information. However, the Directive allowed companies to disclose information in the way they considered most useful, and did not specify any requirements or standards. In June 2019, the European Commission published guidelines on reporting climate-related information, supplementing the prior guidelines on non-financial reporting. Also, the new European Union Sustainable Finance Action Plan includes different features (see Section 6.4). One of the most important steps is a Taxonomy, or common language, to define green activities. Further, new guidelines on reporting climate-related information were introduced.

KEY LEARNING POINT

Different types of non-financial reporting requirements are being introduced. The diversity of these requirements may be confusing or lead to nonconformity. Coordination of standards is key to ensuring that companies report on the same metrics, allowing better comparisons of company performance.

6.3.2 Materiality

Materiality is a principle which states that items that matter most to a business and its stakeholders must be defined, and publicly disclosed/reported.

Companies must publicly disclose to current and prospective investors any information that is significant (or material) to making an informed investment (or voting) decision. As ESG information becomes integrated in companies' disclosures, a key question is how what is financially material should be determined. The Financial Accounting Standards Board defines materiality as "any information which would be considered decision-relevant to an investor." The U.S. Securities and Exchange Commission (SEC) defines a material requirement to disclose by the following criterion: "there must be a substantial likelihood

---

[211]   https://www.ifrs.org/news-and-events/news/2022/08/ifrs-foundation-completes-consolidation-with-value-reporting-foundation/.

that the disclosure of the omitted fact would have been viewed by a reasonable investor as having significantly altered the total mix of information made available."

The Sustainability Accounting Standards Board (SASB) is an organization (in August 2022, it joined the IFRS Foundation) that sets standards related to the disclosure of financially material sustainability information by companies to their investors. In particular, the SASB Standards identify the subset of ESG issues that are most relevant for financial performance and value, across 77 industries. The main tool produced is the SASB Materiality Map. This map focuses on the issues (out of a list of 26 sustainability-related business issues) that are considered financially material, that is, likely to affect the financial condition and operating performance of a company. In terms of the environmental dimension, the SASB Materiality Map considers six different categories of environmental issues: emissions, air quality, energy management, water and wastewater management, waste and hazardous materials, and ecological impacts.

The SASB Standards are industry specific to account for industrial heterogeneity. They define 11 broad sectors: Consumer Goods, Extractives and Mineral Processing, Financials, Food and Beverage, Healthcare, Infrastructure, Renewable Resources & Alternative Energy, Resource Transformation, Services, Technology and Telecommunication, and Transportation. Each of these sectors is further decomposed into industries (covering a total of 77 industries). For instance, within Health Care, they consider six specific industries: Biotechnology & Pharmaceuticals, Drug Retailers, Health Care Delivery, Health Care Distributors, Managed Care, and Medical Equipment & Supplies.

One of the key uses of this map is for a company in a certain sector to understand whether or not an issue is likely to be material for it, and which are the critical items that must be disclosed. However, some sustainability issues may be immaterial for a company in a given sector.

For each industry, it shows how material an issue is and how the materiality of the same issue varies from industry to industry. For example, the issues "GHG Emissions" and "Air Quality" are material to the Metals & Mining industry, but are not material to the Financial industry. This means that a bank need not provide non-financial disclosures on the "Air Quality" item. That is, this lack of reporting, in the case of a bank, would not directly influence managers' and investors' decisions. However, if a mining company does not disclose this information, the outcome would be very different, as the information is very material to investors.

Here is an extract of the SASB Materiality Map:

Dimension	Issue	Financials	Food & Beverage	Health Care	Metals & Mining
Environment	GHG Emissions				
	Air Quality				
	Energy Management				
	Water & Wastewater Management				
	Waste & Hazardous Materials Management				
	Ecological Impacts				
Social Capital	Human Rights & Community Relations				
	Customer Privacy				
	Data Security				
	Access & Affordability				
	Product Quality & Safety				
	Customer Welfare				
	Selling Practices & Product Labeling				
Human Capital	Labor Practices				
	Employee Health & Safety				
	Employee Engagement, Diversity & Inclusion				
Business Model & Innovation	Product Design & Lifecycle Management				
	Business Model Resilience				
	Supply Chain Management				
	Materials Sourcing & Efficiency				
	Physical Impacts of Climate Change				
Leadership & Governance	Business Ethics				
	Competitive Behavior				
	Management of the Legal & Regulatory Environment				
	Critical Incident Risk Management				
	Systemic Risk Management				

Legend:
- ■ Issue is likely to be material for more than 50% of industries in the broad sector
- ▨ Issue is likely to be material for fewer than 50% of industries in the broad sector
- ☐ Issue is not likely to be material for any of the industries in the broad sector

Source: SASB.

KEY LEARNING POINT

The Materiality principle suggests that sustainability topics (including environmental topics) that matter most to a business must be defined and publicly disclosed.

6.3.3 Climate Reporting and the TCFD

Investors and other users of companies' disclosures are interested in assessing the climate risks to which they may be exposed by investing in a certain company, as well as the financial impact of the most material risks. Effective climate-related disclosures clarify the concentrations of carbon-related assets (and assets exposed to physical risks) in the financial sector, and the financial system's exposures to climate-related risks.

In 2015, the G20 finance ministers and central bank governors asked the Financial Stability Board (FSB) to "review how the financial sector can take account of climate-related issues." The Task Force for Climate-related Financial Disclosures (TCFD) was created under former Chair and Bank of England Governor, Mark Carney. It aims to identify the information needed by investors, lenders, and insurance underwriters to appropriately assess and price climate-related risks and opportunities. The TCFD defines climate risk as "a combination of physical and transition risks which may potentially pose financial and reputational damage to financial and non-financial services firms." After a consultation period, in 2017 the TCFD released its final climate-related financial disclosure recommendations.

The TCFD (2017) developed several recommendations (on a voluntary basis) on climate-related financial disclosures[212] applicable to organizations across sectors and jurisdictions, centered around four themes:

- Governance: This pertains to the organization's governance of climate-related risks and opportunities, which includes the board's oversight role, as well as the management's role in assessing and managing climate-related risks and opportunities.
- Strategy: This pertains to the actual and potential impacts of climate-related risks and opportunities on the organization's businesses, strategy, and financial planning. It includes risks and opportunities in the short, medium, and long term. It also involves analyzing the resilience of the organization's strategy, taking into consideration different climate-related scenarios, including a 2°C or lower scenario.
- Risk Management: This pertains to the processes used by the organization to identify, assess, and manage climate-related risks. Besides describing the processes, the organization should explain how they are integrated into its overall risk management.

---

[212] According to the TCFD, in general, disclosure should (1) present relevant information; (2) be specific and complete; (3) be clear and understandable; (4) be consistent over time; (5) be comparable across companies; (6) be reliable and verifiable; and (7) be provided on a timely basis.

o   Metrics and Targets: These pertain to the metrics used to assess and manage relevant climate-related risks and opportunities, in line with its strategy and risk management processes.

One of the TCFD's recommendations relates to forward-looking disclosure, through scenario analysis. This allows different stakeholders to understand not only how a company is faring under current conditions, physical exposures, and risks of extreme weather events, but also how it is planning for a future in a low-carbon economy (transition risk).

The materiality concept discussed above is still relevant. In fact, the SASB Standards facilitate TCFD disclosure by providing industry-specific metrics to evaluate a company's exposure to, and management of, climate-related risks and opportunities.

In 2017, the TCFD issued three recommendations for the disclosure of climate-related metrics and targets by financial and non-financial corporations:

1. Disclose the metrics used to assess climate-related risks and opportunities. This comprises, among others, the metrics for the disclosure of "Internal carbon/methane price," "Monetary value of methane emissions," "Expenditures on methane emissions mitigation," and "Returns from methane reducing investments."[213]
2. Disclose Scopes 1 and 2, and, if appropriate, Scope 3 GHG emissions.[214]
3. Describe the targets used by the organization to manage climate-related risks and opportunities, and its performance against those targets. Companies should set their emissions reduction target, and disclose their performance against it. The reduction target should specify relevant information such as "Scope," "Form," "Stringency," and "Timeline."[215]

Besides metrics and targets, the Task Force has also recommended disclosure of climate-related risks and opportunities in three other domains: corporate governance, strategy, and risk management. For instance, it recommends that companies describe whether and how the performance metrics are incorporated into remuneration policies.

---

[213] The internal carbon price is an internal shadow price a company applies to its operations, or when considering investment decisions. The disclosure of "Expenditures on methane emissions mitigation" helps investors understand how a company is addressing the challenge of climate-related risks. The disclosure of "Returns from methane reducing investments" implies that companies should provide investors metrics about the internal rate of return and payback periods from the reduction of methane investment.

[214] Scope 1 emissions arise from a company's direct operations, Scope 2 emissions arise from a company's indirect emissions associated with the purchase of energy, and Scope 3 emissions are a company's indirect emissions arising from the whole value chain.

[215] To summarize, when describing their targets, companies should specify whether the target is absolute or intensity-based, the time frame to achieve that target, the base year to measure the progress, and the KPIs used to evaluate progress toward achievement of the target.

In 2021, the TCFD published a proposed cross-industry list of climate-related metrics that organizations should disclose. The metrics include the following[216]:

- GHG emissions (absolute Scope 1 and Scope 2, and relevant Scope 3 emissions), as well as carbon intensity (emissions divided by revenues)
- External and shadow/internal carbon prices in the local currency, per metric ton of CO2e
- Proportion of assets, operating, investing, or financing activities materially exposed to physical risks
- Proportion of assets, operating, investing, or financing activities materially exposed to transition risks
- Proportion of assets and operating, investing, or financing activities aligned toward climate-related opportunities
- Amount of management compensation impacted by climate considerations
- Amount of costs and capital investment deployed toward climate risks

The TCFD recommendations, although not legally binding, are becoming a clear worldwide benchmark for information disclosure by companies on their governance and risk management of climate-related risks. In addition, the support for the TCFD comes from different stakeholders:

- Nearly 60% of the world's 100 largest public companies support the TCFD, provide reports in line with the TCFD recommendations, or both.
- More than 1,000 organizations have become TCFD supporters since the Task Force issued its 2017 recommendations (TCFD, 2020), including investors managing over US$138 trillion in assets.
- The European Commission's "Guidelines on Non-financial Reporting: Supplement on Reporting Climate-related Information" issued in June 2019 integrates the TCFD recommendations.
- Financial regulators in many countries have endorsed the recommendations and have incorporated them into existing codes, standards, and reporting requirements.
- The European Central Bank (ECB, 2020) adhered to the TCFD recommendations when drafting policies for financial institutions in Europe.
- Investors are supporting global standards. As an example, BlackRock, the world's biggest asset manager, supports harmonizing sustainability accounting rules and standards globally (including mandatory TCFD reporting) so that investors can track how companies are transitioning to a lower-carbon economy.
- The Principles for Responsible Investment (PRI) launched its own recommendations for climate risk reporting for institutional investors, in line with

---

[216] Source: TCFD (2021).

the TCFD. In particular, the strategy and governance indicators became mandatory for PRI signatories from 2020.

KEY LEARNING POINT

TCFD recommendations are becoming more prevalent worldwide. They focus on how organizations can measure and monitor their climate risks and opportunities, and also strategize for the future through scenario analysis.

Standard metrics provide a basis that investors can use to compare companies within a sector. Improved disclosure will also likely reduce "greenwashing," where some companies publicize their commitment to ESG goals to attract investors, but fail to act accordingly. Increasing the quality (and quantity) of disclosures can significantly benefit capital markets and therefore issuers (lower cost of capital, higher liquidity, and better capital allocation).

6.3.4 Future Outlook and Research Evidence

Academic research has found that non-financial reporting has important effects. The value of disclosure, as well as its effects on investors and other stakeholders, has been studied. Research has also studied the differences between mandatory and voluntary disclosures, and their potential side effects.

Ilhan et al. (2021) surveyed institutional investors' preferences for companies' climate risk disclosures. Their results show that a majority of the respondents believed climate risk reporting to be an important factor in their investment decisions. However, they stressed the need for improved reporting both in terms of quantity as well as quality. This echoes Mark Carney´s call "to develop consistent, comparable, reliable and clear disclosure around the carbon intensity of different assets."

In general, the situation is improving. Recent data suggest that among the largest 5,200 companies by revenue worldwide, 80% report on sustainability (Threlfall et al., 2020). This survey shows that high rates of sustainability reporting prevail all over the world, and in 14 (out of 52) countries, more than 90% of companies report on sustainability.

Khan et al. (2016) studied the concept of materiality, focusing on the relevance of investments in material versus immaterial sustainability issues. They found that firms with good performance on material sustainability issues significantly outperform firms with poor performance on these issues.

Bucaro et al. (2020) examined the effect on investors' reactions to CSR measures when they were integrated with financial information in a single report, compared with when they were presented in a separate CSR report. Their experimental evidence suggests that CSR measures have greater influence on investors' views when presented in a separate report. Also, investors incorporate less CSR information when it is integrated with financial information.

Bolton and Kacperczyk (2021) estimated the effects of voluntary and mandatory disclosure of carbon emissions on stock returns, volatility, and turnover. They found that voluntary disclosure of Scope 1 emissions lowers both the cost of capital and stock-level uncertainty. Badia et al. (CAR 2021) documented that after mandatory disclosure rules are introduced, stock price informativeness and stock liquidity increase. Heflin and Wallace (2017) analyzed the motivation for environmental disclosures. They analyzed oil and gas firms drilling in U.S. waters, in the context of the 2010 BP Macondo incident. Their findings suggest that firms with greater environmental disclosure suffered smaller negative shareholder wealth effects following the spill. They also found that increased disclosure by poor (pre-spill) environmental performers led to later improvements in their environmental performance.

Barth et al. (2017) found that improved information to outside investors is also associated with better internal decision-making. Christensen et al. (2019) showed that ESG disclosures vary substantially depending on a company's activities. They surveyed the literature on corporate disclosures and found that increasing the quantity and quality of information has positive effects on markets. It generates higher liquidity, better capital allocation, and lower cost of capital. They also discussed the economic effects of standards for disclosure and reporting, potential firm responses, and real effects on firm behavior. Krueger et al. (2021) studied a global sample of 37,129 firms, across 52 countries, and showed that mandatory ESG disclosure increases the accuracy of analysts' earnings forecasts, lowers forecast dispersion, reduces negative ESG incidents, and lowers the likelihood of stock price crashes.

Another strand of research reveals the role of institutional investors. Lyon and Maxwell (2011) developed an economic model of "greenwashing" in which firms strategically disclose environmental information. They found that the presence of activist shareholders deters greenwashing, but also induces some firms to disclose less information about their environmental performance. Moreover, environmental management systems deter firms with a poor expected environmental performance from practicing greenwashing, which may justify public policies encouraging firms to adopt such systems. Consistent with this, Flammer et al. (2021) found that environmental shareholder activism increases voluntary disclosure of climate change risks, especially if initiated by institutional investors. The results also suggest that investors value transparency with respect to firms' exposure to climate change risks. Ilhan et al. (2021) showed that greater institutional ownership, particularly in high-social-norm countries, is associated with a greater tendency by firms to voluntarily disclose their carbon emissions and to provide higher-quality information.

6.3.5 Summary and Challenges

Historically, companies disclosed only financial information. However, there is a growing demand for sustainability reporting, and it is even becoming mandatory in several settings. A key question is what kind of (non-financial) information firms should be required to disclose. The principle of materiality (defining the key topics that matter to a business) is crucial here.

Standards and frameworks play a role by substantially increasing the quality of published reports. Several organizations have issued standards and recommendations for sustainability reporting, each with its own purpose and rationale. A convergence is occurring, and it seems that the TCFD has emerged as a key disclosure recommendation. It is supported by many government organizations, and several regulators are mandating its adoption. The TCFD gives companies a framework for how to think about climate change and disclose their efforts along four dimensions: Strategy, Governance, Risk Management, and Metrics & Targets.

Overall, the research evidence suggests that disclosure is valued by investors, and leads to actual changes in companies' behaviors. Voluntary disclosure of emissions is associated with a lower cost of capital and lower stock-level uncertainty. Also, non-financial reporting is associated with better internal decision-making. Greater institutional ownership, especially investors from high-social-norm countries, is associated with a greater tendency by firms to voluntarily disclose their carbon emissions and to provide higher-quality information.

Standardization of terminology would constitute a significant market development. Consistent corporate reporting will allow investors to better assess the financial materiality of different risks. Some other developments to expect going forward include the following:

o   Improved consistency of disclosures and a clearer focus on materiality
o   Standardized reporting at a basic level, complemented by more customized reporting on material items
o   Improvements in comparability within an industry and also across countries

6.4   GLOBAL   REGULATIONS: THE   NEED   FOR CONVERGENCE

Globally, several regulations can either promote or hinder the development of green finance markets. Various institutions, such as the securities and exchange commissions, stock exchanges, regulators, and also banking-related entities (e.g., the European Banking Authority (EBA), European Central Bank (ECB), Federal Deposit Insurance Corporation (FDIC), and Bank for International Settlements (BIS)), as well as IMF and others, set standards on different aspects of green finance.

In Section 6.3, we focused on disclosure. However, other regulatory policies help slow down climate change. Many of these policies are global in nature, as capital markets and finance flows are increasingly globally integrated.

6.4.1 Different Capital Markets Initiatives

One of the first priorities in capital markets regulation is to clarify definitions related to sustainable finance. A lack of clarity as to what constitutes a green loan, green bond, and other green activities hinders banks, companies, and investors and increases the potential for greenwashing activities.

Major markets have witnessed various policy initiatives and guidelines related to sustainable finance. These cover many topics such as disclosure (for both corporates and financial institutions):

o In the EU, the European Commission launched its Action Plan on Financing Sustainable Growth to meet the 2030 targets that it has committed to, in line with the Paris Agreement. This includes several policy initiatives to direct capital toward low-carbon projects, allow better management of the financial risks associated with climate change, and to foster transparency in financial and economic activities.

o In the United States too, the regulatory environment is evolving. The U.S. SEC is considering ESG investing across different areas such as labeling of funds, corporate disclosures (TCFD), and standards for pension plans. The SEC created a Climate and ESG Task Force to identify important ESG-related topics as well as misconduct.

o The U.K. Prudential Regulation Authority wrote to the CEOs of listed companies, stressing the importance of incorporating climate risks into their business model, strategy, and governance. In 2017, the London Stock Exchange Group issued "Your Guide to ESG Reporting" to help listed companies understand what information they have to provide to investors and how to provide it. Furthermore, the United Kingdom has made climate risk reporting mandatory for most publicly traded firms and financial companies.

o The Tokyo Stock Exchange and Japan's Financial Services Agency published a "Practical Handbook for ESG Disclosure" that focuses on voluntary disclosures.

o China's guidelines for ESG disclosure were established by the China Securities Regulatory Commission (CSRC) in 2021. The rules apply to companies listed in the stock markets of the People's Republic of China, Hong Kong, and Taiwan. Under this set of rules, listed companies are required to disclose procedures for preventing pollution of air, water, and soil, as well as methods for managing waste. Companies are also required to report environmental incidents, and any penalties associated with them.

o   In August 2020, the Toronto Stock Exchange (TSX) published the updated version of the "Primer for Environmental & Social Disclosure," first published in 2014 by TSX and CPA Canada (TMX and CPA, 2020).[217] Under the country's securities regulations, all issuers have to provide investors with all the information related to material environmental and social issues.[218]

o   The three European supervisory authorities (EBA, the European Insurance and Occupational Pensions Authority (EIOPA), and the European Securities and Markets Authority (ESMA)) develop ESG disclosures under the EU regulation on sustainability-related disclosures in the financial services sector (Sustainable Finance Disclosure Regulation (SFDR)), which aims to strengthen protection for investors and improve the disclosures that they receive from financial market participants regarding financial products.

Policies, however, are not yet consistent and comparable at the global level. There is a need for further consolidation of guidelines regarding corporate disclosure, materiality, fund reporting, benchmarking, data consistency, and product labeling (what is a "green" fund, for instance). Investors note that the lack of consistent international disclosure frameworks makes it difficult for them to compare companies around the world and manage their portfolios. Although progress is being made (SASB, GRI, TCFD, EU Action Plan, and others), there is still no universally accepted global set of guidelines on climate (or ESG) reporting.

Global convergence on critical regulatory issues is important to achieve the following:

o   Help finance the low-carbon transition, and allocate capital appropriately.

o   Avoid market fragmentation and a "race to the bottom," which can occur if varying standards exist.

o   Promote comparability in disclosures (especially on material issues) so that global investors can act appropriately. This also includes comparability of methodologies across different ESG rating providers. Currently, several ratings are heterogeneous, and even biased (Section 5.1).

o   Establish clear benchmarks. Indices are used as a benchmark to assess performance, and they are also used as the basis of passive investment strategies. How indices are created, and used as benchmarks, has clear implications for markets (Section 5.2).

o   Ensure transparency of ESG products so that investors can determine how these align with their objectives.

o   Reduce the risks of greenwashing.

---

[217] Canadian Institute of Chartered Accountants.

[218] The list of environmental issues include GHG emissions, Air Quality, Climate Change Impact, Water and Wastewater Management, Energy Management, and Supply Chain Environmental Issues.

KEY LEARNING POINT

Lack of consistency hinders comparability among companies worldwide.

6.4.2 European Union Action Plan

The EU, similar to most regions in the world, is examining how to integrate sustainability into its financial frameworks. To promote green finance, the European Commission drafted an Action Plan on Financing Sustainable Growth that aims to integrate sustainability considerations into economic activities and the investment process in a consistent way.

In May 2018, the European Commission appointed a Technical Expert Group (TEG) on Sustainable Finance with the task of developing a European framework of taxonomy, recommendations, and standards for companies. In March 2020, it published the Final Report, which details the following:

- An EU classification system of sustainable activities (the EU Taxonomy)
- An EU Green Bond Standard
- Methodologies for EU climate benchmarks and disclosures for benchmarks
- Consistent labeling and disclosure of funds to enable investors to make informed choices
- Guidance for institutional investors on their disclosures, including how to factor in investor preferences and integrate ESG into their investment processes
- Guidance to improve corporate disclosure of climate-related information

The EU Taxonomy

The EU Taxonomy provides a classification framework for sustainable economic activities. It was developed by a group of technical experts set up by the European Commission. The main outcome is a technical document that was developed after consultations with over 200 industry specialists and scientists. Its objective is to provide a common language and uniform criteria that corporates and investors can use to describe environment-friendly activities.

The Taxonomy is based on an extensive analysis of activities across a range of sectors, including energy, agriculture, manufacturing, and technology. Across more than 60 sectors (covering more than 93% of the European GHG emissions) it identifies

- low-carbon activities compatible with a 2050 net zero carbon economy (such as zero-emissions transport or forestation);

- activities that support the transition to a net zero economy, but have no technologically and economically feasible low-carbon alternatives (such as manufacturing of aluminum and cement); and
- enabling activities that support the above two activities (for instance, manufacturing wind turbines).

To claim alignment with the Taxonomy, economic activities need to substantially contribute to one of six environmental objectives:

1. Climate change mitigation
2. Climate change adaptation
3. Sustainable use and protection of water and marine resources
4. Transition to a circular economy, waste prevention, and recycling
5. Pollution prevention and control
6. Protection and restoration of biodiversity and ecosystems

The Taxonomy includes "technical screening criteria" that set quantitative thresholds to classify activities. Also, economic activities must not significantly harm others (Do No Significant Harm, DNSH), and must comply with some minimum social standards.

The EU Taxonomy applies to financial market participants offering products in the EU. Further, large companies (i.e., those under the scope of the Non-Financial Reporting EU Directive[219]) will need to disclose in their annual accounts the percentage of sales, operating costs, and capital expenditures associated with Taxonomy-aligned activities.

The underlying documents that describe the technical screening criteria are complex, and have attracted criticisms such as the following[220]:

- It includes controversial energy sources such as nuclear, and others such as natural gas that release CO_2.
- Imprecise criteria for some projects and sectors.
- It does not sufficiently account for the positive contributions of sustainable agriculture.
- It imposes too many requirements on smaller companies.
- It focuses only on sectors that are directly responsible for GHG emissions, but does not include activities related to energy efficiency and energy savings.
- Sourcing and matching data are imprecisely defined, and there are many possible data suppliers.

---

[219] According to the Non-Financial Reporting Directive, companies are required to disclose information on environmental, social, and employee matters when that information is necessary for understanding the company's development, risk, and performance. The new rules explicitly include climate-related information as a key matter to be reported.
[220] PRI (2020), Pfaf and Altun (2022), and Crêpy (2021).

The EU Green Bond Standard

Another feature of the EU Action Plan is the development of an EU Green Bond Standard, which aims to promote transparency and comparability in the green bond market, as well as support its growth. As with other possible new eco-labels and standards, the alignment with the Taxonomy will determine whether or not a certain product can be considered "green" or "sustainable."

The EU Green Bond Standard represents the European guideline for green bond issuers, and complements the Green Bond Principles (by the International Capital Market Association). The EU Green Bond Standard is designed for all EU and non-EU issuers that want to conform to these standards. Some of its features include the following:

o   It is a voluntary standard that issuers can choose to follow when issuing green bonds.
o   Issuers must explain how their strategy aligns with the six EU environmental objectives.
o   Issuers must provide details on their use of proceeds and their reporting on green bonds.
o   Pre- and post-issuance verifications are mandatory, and need to be made by an accredited verifier.
o   The EU Green Bond Standard uses the Taxonomy. This standard clarifies how the proceeds should be used and reported on. At the same time, it will provide investors with data on Taxonomy-related issues that they themselves will need for their own reporting requirements.

An important difference from other standards is the mandatory features. For instance, in the case of the ICMA Green Bond Principles, most of the principles are couched as recommendations. However, in the EU Green Bond Standard, these are framed as requirements.

EU Climate Benchmarks

The European Commission also created measures to enhance the transparency of the methodologies used by ESG financial indices (benchmarks) and standards for low-carbon benchmarks in the EU.[221]

A climate benchmark is an investment index (or benchmark) that incorporates specific objectives related to GHG emission reductions and the transition to a low-carbon economy. Climate benchmarks are aligned with the Paris Agreement goal of limiting the increase in global average temperatures to well below 2 °C, and ideally below 1.5 °C, above pre-industrial levels. The benchmarks should fulfil these objectives, with an appropriate selection and weighting of the constituent investible assets.

---

[221] https://ec.europa.eu/info/business-economy-euro/banking-and-finance/sustainable-finance_en

The EU Action Plan includes a reform of the EU Benchmarks regulation. In particular, it introduces two new types of climate benchmark:

- o   The EU Climate Transition Benchmark (EU CTB)
- o   The EU Paris-Aligned Benchmark (EU PAB)

These benchmarks are supposed to be used by institutional investors, such as pension funds and insurance companies, in their efforts to protect assets against climate change and the transition to a low-carbon economy. Both benchmarks have decarbonization objectives, but with different thresholds. The minimum standards for these climate benchmarks require the following:

- o   The GHG intensity or absolute GHG emissions must be at least 30% lower than the emissions of the investable universe.
- o   Emissions must include Scopes 1, 2, and 3 GHG emissions (Scope 3 with up to a four-year phase-in period).
- o   The yearly decarbonization trajectory must show a reduction in GHG emissions of at least 7%.

The EU Paris-Aligned Benchmark is more stringent. It requires emissions to be at least 50% lower than those of the investable universe. It also imposes additional exclusionary restrictions on fossil fuel and electricity producers with high GHG emissions.

KEY LEARNING POINT

The EU Action Plan on Financing Sustainable Growth aims to establish a common language (EU Taxonomy) for the creation of standards and labels in order to promote transparency and comparability in the green market.

6.4.3 Summary and Challenges

Various regulations and requirements are being introduced for companies worldwide, and even if some of them are not yet mandatory in many environments, the trend is clear.

The development of capital markets, and their ability to properly allocate risk and fund projects, requires some degree of convergence in regulations. In particular, encouraging further mitigation of risks and improved allocation of capital requires standardization in terminologies, including product definitions and labels. Further developments in this area also address greenwashing concerns and the associated reputational risk problems.

Policies, however, are not yet consistent and comparable at the global level. However, significant steps are being taken, and progress is being made on some critical regulatory issues. Some doubts remain about whether voluntary initiatives will suffice or whether regulators will take a more active role. Also, will regulation be effective? Will it be able to avoid perverse incentives and negative implications?

6.5 MULTILATERAL DEVELOPMENT BANKS

Supranational institutions are owned by governments of several countries. Supranationals are also called multilateral lending institutions (MLIs) or multilateral development banks (MDBs). They are usually created to promote economic development in their respective region, expand global trade, and promote global economic integration.

6.5.1 The Role of Supranational Institutions

Supranationals are large lending institutions that differ from regular banks in several ways:

o They are established by a group of sovereign states and charged with a public policy mandate.
o They engage primarily in lending (or guaranteeing) operations, and do not engage in other banking activities such as underwriting, asset management, and retail deposits.
o They have a high earnings retention, as distribution of dividends is low or nonexistent.
o They have a special status, are governed by international treaties, and are not subject to national banking regulations or commercial law.
o They enjoy preferred creditor treatment in regard to sovereign exposure. Historically, supranationals have enjoyed preferred creditor treatment whenever a sovereign state has defaulted on its debt. They have also been exempted from haircuts applied during sovereign debt rescheduling, and they are typically repaid ahead of commercial banks. This feature of supranationals has enabled them to operate with low credit losses, and is one of the important determinants of their credit rating.

As they do not have deposits, they rely on market funding. Their high ratings make supranationals strong players in bond markets, and they typically issue with long-dated maturities. In many instances, these are some of the longest dated bonds available.

These large players in capital markets can also play a critical role in the climate transition. Through their lending and other business activities, they can direct significant amounts of funding into climate finance around the world, thus reducing the infrastructure investment gap.

Table 6.4 The main multilateral banks in the world

Bank	Assets (billions)	Credit rating	Founded
European Investment Bank	€ 565	AAA	1958
World Bank	US$317	AAA	1944
Asian Development Bank	US$272	AAA	1966
European Bank for Reconstruction and Development	€ 69	AAA	1991
Asian Infrastructure Investment Bank	US$40	AAA	2016
Nordic Investment Bank	€ 39	AAA	1975
Caribbean Development Bank	US$21	AA+/Stable	1969
African Development Bank	US$18	AAA	1964
Inter-American Development Bank	US$17	AAA	1959

Source: Banks' investor relations materials.

As discussed in Chapter 1, the world's poorest countries are not heavy emitters, but they are the countries most impacted by climate change. Therefore, several international agreements have been signed to direct international funding for mitigation action and adaptation to climate change to the least developed countries. Examples of these are the Copenhagen Accord (2009) and the Cancun Agreements (2010), according to which developed countries agreed to provide additional resources for climate action in developing countries.

Similarly, Article 2 of the Paris Agreement talks about "making finance flows consistent with a pathway towards low greenhouse gas emissions and climate-resilient development." In this context, multilateral institutions have been aligning their financing and investment portfolios with the goals of the Paris Agreement. Given their capability of attracting large volumes of long-term funding at low rates, they can help address some gaps in financing, especially in developing markets. The main multilateral institutions have made significant pledges to scale up financing for climate action.

Moreover, multilateral organizations can also be helpful on the capital market side. In fact, multilateral lending institutions were early adopters of green bond issuance, and are today major players in the global green bond market. As discussed in Section 3.1, the European Investment Bank launched the world's first green bond on July 2007, calling it a "Climate Awareness Bond." This was followed by a World Bank green bond in December 2008.

In addition, they can mobilize private sector funds. Historically, every dollar invested by MLIs has attracted a significant amount of private capital. Several reasons can be given for this inflow. Some of the more important ones are the credibility provided by MLIs (they monitor their investments vigilantly to ensure compliance with different risk assessments) and the additional guarantees that they can bring to projects.

Supranationals are promoting alignment with the Paris Agreement on climate change. In 2011, the biggest multilateral institutions developed a joint methodology to track their climate finance flows in a consistent manner. In 2015, some of the world's leading financial institutions signed the "Voluntary Principles to Mainstreaming Climate Action in Financial Institutions." By signing these principles, MLIs have committed to scale up their efforts to address climate change through their operations.

MLIs classify their actions as adaptation and mitigation. Mitigation activities reduce GHG emissions. These activities include moving from fossil-fuel-based energy production to renewable energy sources, improving manufacturing standards and energy efficiency, and promoting low-carbon business solutions. Adaptation activities are related to preparation for negative climate effects, for instance, investments to make regions more resilient to extreme weather events.

Overall, supranational institutions have been working on the following:

- o Incorporating climate targets into their operations
- o Improving climate risk screenings, GHG accounting, and climate-focused country and sector assessments
- o Helping least-developed countries include climate issues in their development plans
- o Mobilizing their own funds, as well as private sector funds, into lower-carbon investments
- o Promoting the standardization of green finance practices and disclosure standards

6.5.2 How Supranational Institutions Are Supporting Climate Finance

According to the Joint Report on Multilateral Development Banks' Climate Finance, in 2020, MDBs committed US$66 billion to climate finance (76% for climate change mitigation and 24% for adaptation). They have also managed to gather additional public and private funding totaling more than US$85 billion along with their investments. Overall, MDB and private sector co-financing partners directed US$151 billion to climate action.

Figure 6.2 Total multilateral development banks' climate finance commitments

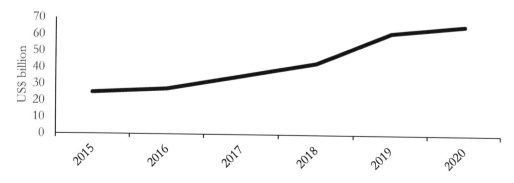

Source: 2020 Joint Report on Multilateral Development Banks' Climate Finance.

Figure 6.3 Multilateral development banks' climate finance commitments by bank

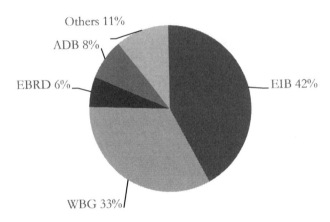

Note: ADB = Asian Development Bank, EBRD = European Bank for Reconstruction and Development, EIB = European Investment Bank, WBG = World Bank Group.

Source: 2020 Joint Report on Multilateral Development Banks' Climate Finance.

In addition to regular loans, MDBs offer several instruments[222]:

o   Equity: Ownership interest in an enterprise that represents a claim on the assets of the entity in proportion to the number and class of shares owned.

o   Grants: Transfers made in cash, goods, or services for which no repayment is required. Grants are provided for investment support, policy-based support, and/or technical assistance and advice.

o   Guarantees: Guarantees are instruments provided by an MDB to cover commercial and non-commercial risk. Guarantees are extended for eligible projects that enable financing partners to transfer certain risks that they cannot easily absorb or manage on their own. Guarantees cover equity and a wide variety of debt instruments, and support financial sector projects (including projects related to capital market investments and trade finance, and non-financial-sector business activities corresponding to activities across sectors).

o   Lines of credit: Lines of credit provide a guarantee that funds will be made available, but no financial asset exists until funds have been advanced.

o   Policy-based financing (PBF): Financing for a public borrower that helps it address actual or anticipated requirements for development finance of domestic or external origin. PBF supports a program of policy and institutional actions for a particular theme or sector of national policy. Disbursements of PBF are conditional on the borrower fulfilling their policy commitments in the lending agreement.

---

[222] Definitions based on the "2020 Joint Report on Multilateral Development Banks' Climate Finance."

o Results-based financing (RBF): RBF directly links the disbursement of funds to measurable results in a government-owned program. RBF aims to increase accountability and incentives for delivering and sustaining results, improve the effectiveness and efficiency of government-owned sector programs, promote institutional development, and enhance the effectiveness of development.

Out of the total MDB climate finance in 2020, US$38 billion (58% of the total) was directed to low-income and middle-income economies, and US$28 billion targeted high-income economies. 76% of the total climate finance was committed through investment loans, and the rest through other instruments (equity, grants, guarantee, etc.).

PUMA and International Finance Corporation (IFC)

Puma, the sportswear manufacturer, traced 94% of its environmental impact to its supply chain. In 2016, BNP and IFC (part of the World Bank Group) partnered with Puma to reduce GHG emissions in the supply chain operations of the company.

Under this sustainable working capital initiative, the lenders offered Puma's global suppliers (most of whom were in emerging markets, with restricted access to finance) access to discounted financing, based on their CSR rating (assigned by an external auditor). This rating ranges from 1 to 5 and "suppliers get a significant discount every time the rating goes up, or an increase in their financing costs if it goes down," explained Jacques Levet, Head of Transaction Banking EMEA at BNP Paribas.

Often, MDBs play a role in deals that commercial banks typically do not get involved in, especially in emerging markets. For instance, MDBs play an important role in SCF programs in emerging markets (such as IFC in the PUMA example). They provide working capital solutions (typically through local financial institutions) to suppliers that normal commercial banks would not favor.

European Investment Bank

The European Investment Bank (EIB) is the global development bank owned by the Member States of the European Union. The EIB is the largest multilateral financial institution in the world (with total assets in 2021 of €565 billion), and its main activities consist of granting loans and providing technical assistance to projects that contribute to EU policy objectives.

The EIB is currently one of the largest providers of climate finance in the world, and it is rated Aaa/AAA/AAA (Moody's/Standard & Poor's/Fitch, December 2021). More than 90% of its activities are concentrated in Europe, but it also promotes external cooperation and development assistance outside Europe.

As discussed in Section 3.1, the EIB issued the world's first green bond in 2007. Since then, its activity has expanded significantly. In 2021, EIB green bonds accounted for about 15%

of its total funding needs. It has more than €36 billion of bonds outstanding, across more than 20 currencies.

The EIB uses the proceeds of its bond issuance to finance projects. According to its future roadmap, an increasing portion of its proceeds will be directed to climate action. Here are some examples of EIB finance projects:

- o In July 2020, Iberdrola signed a financing agreement worth €800 million with the EIB and ICO[223] to drive green recovery by improving renewable energy capacity in Spain. The EIB has granted €600 million, and ICO has granted €200 million. The funds will be used to finance the construction of 20 renewable energy facilities (photovoltaic plants and wind farms) with a total power of over 2,000 megawatts (MW), a volume equivalent to the average annual energy consumption of about one million people.
- o In July 2020, the EIB agreed to support Edison's energy efficiency and renewable energy programs in Italy with two loans of €300 million and €150 million, each with a duration of 15 years. The loan was granted to help Edison considerably reduce CO_2 emissions and double the percentage of electricity produced from renewable sources from 20% to 40% by 2030.
- o In July 2018, the EIB agreed to provide Zumtobel, an Austrian manufacturer of integral lighting solutions, a loan of €80 million to support its R&D on the production of more efficient lighting systems. Connecting the systems to digital services can ensure more sustainable light management in the buildings where Zumtobel technology is installed.
- o In 2018, the EIB granted Endesa the first EIB Green Loan (€335 million) to finance investments in energy efficiency and energy production from renewable sources (15 wind farms and 3 photovoltaic solar plants). Although the EIB has financed numerous renewable energy projects, this was the first time that the Bank granted a loan officially labeled "green." As a consequence, the loan is treated as a green bond, and the operations fully comply with the requirements defined in its Climate Awareness Bond program.

In November 2020, the EIB Board established the EIB as the "EU Climate Bank," and developed the Climate Bank Roadmap 2021-2025, with commitments to

- o increase climate action and environmental sustainability to above 50% of the new lending activity by 2025,
- o support more than €1 trillion of investments in climate action,
- o align project tracking and green lending targets with the EU Taxonomy,
- o align bond issues with the EU Green Bond Standard, and
- o align activities with the Paris Agreements goals, targeting carbon neutrality by 2050.

---

[223] ICO (Instituto de Crédito Oficial) is the Spanish state development bank.

The EIB group also operates, through the European Investment Fund (EIF), in venture capital as well as in private equity funds that finance SMEs. The EIF was established in 1994 as a subsidiary of the EIB in a public-private partnership with the European Union and a group of private financial institutions. As of 2021, the shareholders of the EIF are as follows:

- o The European Investment Bank (EIB) (60.24%)
- o The European Union, represented by the European Commission (30.42%)
- o Financial institutions from EU member states, the United Kingdom, and Turkey (9.34%)

The EIF targets the environment in at least 10% of its activity. It targets investee funds that operate capex-related investments (greenfield, expansion, refurbishment, etc.) in projects on the energy transition, energy efficiency, the digital economy, sustainable mobility, the circular economy, urban development, and social infrastructure.

KCM and the European Investment Bank

In December 2019, the European Investment Bank agreed to provide a €65 million loan to KCM AD, a Bulgarian producer of lead and zinc that employs more than 1,500 people. KCM is the main producer of lead and zinc in the country and the leader in the production of non-ferrous and precious metals in Southeastern Europe and the Black Sea region.

The objective of the loan is to help KCM meet the target of increasing production output by 25% while improving its environmental performance. The project includes replacing the outdated lead refining plant and zinc electrolysis unit, and refurbishing the zinc recycling unit to lower production costs and improve the company's environmental performance.

The World Bank Group

The World Bank Group was established in 1944 during the Conference of Bretton Woods, and it currently consists of five institutions: the International Finance Corporation (IFC), the International Bank for Reconstruction and Development (IBRD), the International Development Association (IDA), the Multilateral Investment Guarantee Agency (MIGA), and the International Centre for Settlement of Investment Disputes (ICISD). Overall, the World Bank Group (WBG) is the largest multilateral funder of climate investments in developing countries, having committed US$83 billion to this end during 2016–20.

The IFC is the agency of the World Bank Group that focuses exclusively on the private sector in developing countries. Since its inception in 1956, the IFC has provided more than US$285 billion finance for businesses in developing countries in the form of loans and equity. As of June 2021, the IFC's assets totaled US$105 billion, with US$74 billion liabilities and US$31 billion of capital.

The IFC can either lend money directly, or help mobilize private capital to finance investments and projects. It also provides advisory services to businesses and governments. The areas of expertise of the IFC include Agribusiness and Forestry, Financial Institutions, Private Equity Funds, Education, Health, Infrastructure, Manufacturing, Public-Private Partnership, Tourism, Retail & Property, and Venture Capital.

The IFC is a leading global provider of climate finance among development banks, in particular those financing green projects in developing countries. In these countries, fiscally constrained governments often use private-market-based schemes to finance the environmental transition.

In its direct lending operations, the IFC provides finance mainly to companies and projects, but it also provides finance to intermediary banks, leasing companies, and other financial institutions to stimulate domestic lending activity to the real sector. In March 2019, the IFC announced its plan to help accelerate the development of the green loan market by offering green loan products in accordance with the Green Loan Principles.

IFC green loan to Latin American Agribusiness Development Corporation (LAAD)

In August 2021, the IFC announced a green loan to LAAD, a private investment and development company that provides finance to SMEs for agribusiness projects targeting the adoption and improvement of water use efficiency, sustainable practices, and renewable energy generation. The financing package includes a seven-year US$50 million loan disbursed directly from the IFC account and a seven-year US$50 million loan from Symbiotics S.A, a leading Swiss market access platform for impact investing that targets MSMEs. The loan was granted to help LAAD improve access to finance for farmers, who are often the smallest players in the value-added chain of the agribusiness sector.

Asian Development Bank

The Asian Development Bank (ADB) is a regional multilateral financial institution established with the resolution passed at the first Ministerial Conference on Asian Economic Cooperation held by the United Nations Economic Commission for Asia and the Far East in 1963. The ADB is headquartered in Manila (Philippines), and its shareholding structure comprises 49 developing and developed economies in the Asia-Pacific region and 19 countries from outside the regions. As of the end of 2019, the United States (15.6%), Japan (15.6%), China (6.4%), India (6.3%), and Australia (5.8%) were the five largest shareholders of the Bank.

The ADB raises funds by issuing bonds on domestic and international capital markets, and it is rated Aaa/AAA/AAA (Moody's/Standard & Poor's/Fitch, December 2021).

Given the relevance of poverty and climate-change-related risks for the Asia-Pacific region, the ADB has committed to sustainable development through its lending policies. In particular, over 2011–18 it invested US$29 billion in climate-related projects. Over 2019–30, ADB climate finance is planned to reach US$80 billion, focusing on projects related to climate change mitigation and adaptation, including clean energy, sustainable transport, urban development, and managing land use and forests for carbon sequestration.

The ADB launched its green bond program in 2015, and during 2015–18 the Bank raised US$5 billion through green bond issuances. In July 2018, the ABD issued its first green bond denominated in euros, with an issue size of €600 million and maturity in July 2025.

European Bank for Reconstruction and Development

The European Bank for Reconstruction and Development (EBRD) was established in 1991, following the fall of the Berlin Wall. EBRD shareholders include 69 sovereign countries together with the European Union and the European Investment Bank.

As of December 31, 2020, the EBRD's assets were €69.7 billion (€51.9 billion liabilities and €17.8 billion capital). The EBRD raises funds by issuing bonds in the capital markets, and it is rated Aaa/AAA/AAA (Moody's/Standard & Poor's/Fitch, December 2021).

The EBRD offers direct financing to private companies, sovereigns, and sub-sovereigns in the form of loans, guarantees, equity, and quasi-equity investments (including ordinary shares, listed or unlisted, subordinated and convertible loans, income notes, redeemable preference shares, and underwriting of share issues by public or privately owned enterprises). Such instruments are available to a large set of industries and sectors, including infrastructures, manufacturing SMEs, energy, financial intermediation, telecommunications, media & technology, transport, and natural resources.

The amount of EBRD financing in the form of equity and loans generally ranges from €5 million to €250 million, in the form of loans or equity. The EBRD adapts each project to the specific features of the economy, region, or sector. It often complements, rather than displaces, private sources of finance to create synergies with the local and foreign sponsors of the project. The EBRD typically finances up to 35% of the cost of the project in the case of both greenfield investments and long-term capitalization.

The EBRD mainly operates in transition economies, many of which rely heavily on fossil fuels. In July 2020, the EBRD's board of directors approved the Green Economy Transition Plan 2021-2025 to help the countries in which it operates build a green and low-carbon economy. With the implementation of this 5-year plan, the EBRD expects to increase its green financing to more than 50% of its annual business volume to achieve a GHG emissions reduction of at least 25 million metric tons. In July 2021, the EBRD also announced a plan to align all its activities with the goals of the Paris Agreement by 2022.

6.5.3 Summary

Supranationals are large lending institutions, and influence policy in various sectors. They provide lending, but do not have deposits. Therefore, they rely on market funding. Most of their funding is in the form of long-dated bonds, and several have been early adopters of green bond issuance.

These institutions can play an important role in channelizing funding into climate finance. Many supranationals are major players in the global green bond market, and issuance is expected to increase. In their lending role, they also mobilize private sector funds through their credibility, monitoring, risk assessment, and additional guarantees that they sometimes bring to projects.

The biggest multilateral institutions have committed to scale up their efforts to address climate change through their operations, either on adaptation or mitigation. Some supranational institutions are incorporating climate targets into their operations and risk screenings, and promoting the standardization of green finance practices and disclosure standards. The involvement of multilaterals may also help developing countries include climate issues in their development plan.

6.6 THE ROLE OF CENTRAL BANKS

Central banks are key institutions in the international financial system. Their responsibilities include implementing monetary policy and supervising the stability of financial institutions. The climate transition affects the various dimensions of their mandate.

In implementing monetary policy, the central bank sets short-term interest rates to influence bank lending over the business cycle. In most jurisdictions, the central bank also serves as a lender of last resort for the government and banks. Also, around the world central banks have been implementing asset purchase programs, typically referred to as Quantitative Easing (QE). Central bank financing of public debt in the form of QE has become an important part of monetary policy.

In its role of supervising the banking system, the central bank is concerned with financial stability and oversight of banks on parameters such as capital adequacy, liquidity, governance, and risk.

6.6.1 The Central Banks' Mandate and Climate Change

Central banking practices in advanced economies around the world have evolved in the direction of greater independence, autonomy, and transparency. The primary objective of most central banks is to preserve price stability. However, in many jurisdictions, besides inflation control, central banks are also assigned other objectives, such as economic growth, exchange rate stability, and job creation. This can include supporting the economic policies of the government, which may include sustainability.

Examples of Central Banks' Mandates

ECB: "The primary objective of the ECB's monetary policy is to maintain price stability. This means making sure that inflation – the rate at which the prices for goods and services change over time – remains low, stable and predictable. To succeed, we seek to anchor inflation expectations and influence the 'temperature' of the economy, making sure the conditions are just right – not too hot, and not too cold. We do this through our monetary policy."

FED: "The monetary policy goals of the Federal Reserve are to foster economic conditions that achieve both stable prices and maximum sustainable employment."

Bank of England: "We set monetary policy to achieve the Government's target of keeping inflation at 2%. Low and stable inflation is good for the UK's economy and it is our main monetary policy aim. We also support the Government's other economic aims for growth and employment. Sometimes, in the short term, we need to balance our target of low inflation with supporting economic growth and jobs."

People's Bank of China: "As we know, the Law of the People's Bank of China explicitly stipulates that the ultimate goal of China's monetary policy is to maintain currency stability and thereby facilitate economic growth. To maintain currency stability has two tiers of meanings: internally it means to maintain prices stable and externally it means to keep RMB exchange rate basically stable at an adaptive and equilibrium level".

Central Bank of Portugal: "The Bank has two core missions: to maintain price stability and to promote the stability of the financial system."

Central Bank of Brazil: "To ensure the stability of the currency purchasing power, to foster a sound, efficient and competitive financial system, and to promote the economic well-being of society."

In recent years, central banks have been called upon to internalize climate change in their policy frameworks. Climate risk can have significant impacts on the asset side of financial institutions. For example, they could suffer losses from exposure to firms whose assets get stranded because of regulatory changes and technological advancements related to the climate transition. Risks can spill over to the economy at large, especially if the shift to a low-carbon economy is abrupt.

Mark Carney, at the time governor of the Bank of England, delivered a famous speech called "Breaking the Tragedy of the Horizon – Climate Change and Financial Stability"[224] that raised the profile of climate change among central bankers. Carney suggests that "our societies face a series of profound environmental and social challenges. The combination of the weight of scientific evidence and the dynamics of the financial system suggest that, in

---

[224] Carney, M. 2015. "Breaking the Tragedy of the Horizon: Climate Change and Financial Stability." Speech given at Lloyd's of London (29 September).

the fullness of time, climate change will threaten financial resilience and longer-term prosperity. While there is still time to act, the window of opportunity is finite and shrinking." In particular, he argued that financial stability can be affected by the physical risk, the liability risk, and the transition risk.

Financial stability concerns arise whenever asset prices change rapidly, for example, if unexpected transition or physical risks occur. Therefore, central banks and financial regulators are increasingly acknowledging the financial stability implications of climate change. For example, since its inception in 2017, an increasing number of central banks have joined the Network of Central Banks and Supervisors for Greening the Financial System (NGFS) to establish a common benchmark to integrate climate-related risks into supervision and financial stability monitoring.

Following the decision to join the NGFS, Federal Reserve Chair, Jerome Powell, remarked: "We have a supervisory mandate and we have overall responsibility for financial stability with a number of agencies and I think the public expects that we will ensure that the financial system is resilient and robust against the risk of climate change."

In January 2021, the statements of ECB president, Christine Lagarde, echoed those of the FED chair: "Clearly, central banks are not the main actors when it comes to preventing global heating. Central banks are not responsible for climate policy and the most important tools that are needed lie outside of our mandate. But the fact that we are not in the driving seat does not mean that we can simply ignore climate change, or that we do not play a role in combating it".

In addition, François Villeroy de Galhau, president of Banque de France, outlined the financial risks for the central bank arising from climate change: "Let's face it: the ECB's balance sheet is 'exposed' to climate risk through the securities it purchases and the assets pledged as collateral by banks, to an extent that is insufficiently taken into account." He added: "Climate change shocks are potentially difficult for the central bank to manage due to their stagflationary nature, as they can cause both upward pressure on prices and a slowdown in activity." He felt that the ECB should limit its climate risk exposure by buying debt issues from corporates aligned with the Paris Agreement on climate change.

Central banks can set examples and use several tools to influence the climate transition. These tools include implementation of monetary policy and supervision of financial institutions. However, introducing climate issues into their policies also poses trade-offs and choices. Dikau and Volz (2021) analyzed the alignment of the legal mandates of central banks with climate-related policies. Of the 135 central banks in the sample, 12% had explicit sustainability mandates, while another 40% were mandated to support the government's policy priorities, which in most cases include sustainability goals.

KEY LEARNING POINT

Central banks can influence the climate transition through monetary policy and supervision of financial institutions.

6.6.2 Monetary Policy

Monetary policy is the set of actions undertaken by central bank to control money supply and the channels through which new money is supplied. It uses many different tools such as open market operations, conditions for direct lending to banks, bank reserve requirements, unconventional bond purchase programs, emergency lending programs, short-term interest rates, and interventions in the foreign exchange market.

Asset Purchases

Central banks can influence liquidity and interest rates in the government and corporate bond markets. Purchases of government and corporate bonds became more conventional after the Global Financial crisis. To ensure liquidity in the government and corporate bond markets, central banks around the world launched asset purchase programs, conventionally known as Quantitative Easing (QE).

Central banks manage foreign exchange reserves while balancing different objectives: liquidity, safety, and returns. More recently, central banks have started incorporating environmental sustainability objectives into their reserve management, for instance, by allocating part of their foreign exchange reserves to green bonds.

Asset purchases are one way in which central banks can impact the climate transition. A central bank can re-direct purchases to securities selected according to the climate risk embedded in the asset's industry or firm. This can be done through tilting. For instance, through the selection rules for asset purchases, monetary policy can impact the green bond market (as well as other "green" financing instruments). Therefore, the size of asset purchases in industries with high climate risk would be smaller than in industries with low climate risk.

Central banks can also implement negative screening. This means excluding a priori securities from issuers that do not meet certain environmental criteria (such as emissions) from the set of eligible investible securities.

The European Central Bank (ECB) and Bank of England climate change mitigation initiatives

Given the massive purchases of government and corporate bonds already underway, the ECB has recently started investigating options for greening the asset purchases it is making as part of its monetary policy interventions. Despite the absence of an explicit environmental target in the asset purchase programs, the ECB has purchased green bonds under both the Corporate Sector Purchase Programme (CSPP) and the Public Sector Purchase Programme (PSPP). Green bond purchases under CSPP were broadly in line with the growing share of green bonds in the eligible universe.

The Bank of England's involvement in climate change mitigation has gone a step further, compared with most other central banks. The British finance minister, Rishi Sunak, in 2021 asked the Bank of England governor, Andrew Bailey, to give the Bank a new mandate to support the U.K. government's ambition to become a net zero economy by 2050.

The Bank of England was given the mandate to include the purchase of investment-grade green bonds in its QE operations, in compliance with the government's decarbonization strategy. Therefore, both to preserve financial stability and to contribute to CO_2 emissions reduction, the Bank of England will aim to start greening its corporate- bond-buying program and exclude fossil fuel assets.

Refinancing and Collateral

Another tool central banks can use is their lending facilities to banks. In particular, central banks regularly refinance, with repurchase agreements (REPOs), the balance sheet of commercial banks. This in effect is a collateralized loan given by the central bank. To access a REPO operation, a commercial bank has to provide a bond to the central bank as collateral for the loan. These collaterals are typically government bonds, but many central banks also accept high-rated corporate bonds as collateral. The short-term interest rate set by the central bank in REPO operations influences the interbank rate and, finally, the interest rates applied by commercial banks.

Besides the main refinancing operations, central banks also have a set of instruments known as lending facilities, which support banks that need overnight liquidity. The interest rate applied on lending facilities is commonly set at a fixed spread above the rate applied on the main refinancing operations.[225]

Therefore, central banks can stimulate or inhibit bank lending to businesses and households by lowering or raising the short-term interest rate on REPO operations, or by changing the collateral requirements. Sustainability considerations can be implemented through selective interest rate policies:

---

[225] In the case of the ECB, the other two rates are the rate on the marginal lending facility, which is the rate at which banks can borrow from the ECB overnight (this costs them more than if they borrow for one week), and the rate on the deposit facility, which defines the interest banks receive – or have to pay in times of negative interest rates – for depositing money with the ECB overnight.

- o Setting the lending rates for banks conditional on the extent to which a counterparty is contributing to climate mitigation with its lending activity. Thus, banks that are decarbonizing their business model would benefit from better refinancing conditions.
- o Making some lending facilities conditional on a bank counterparty's disclosure of climate-related information
- o Making some lending facilities conditional on a bank counterparty's lending portfolio's carbon profile

The collateral policy of central banks aims to hedge the default risk of the borrower, and it can also influence the behavior of potential counterparties. From the perspective of collateral policy, central banks can do the following:

- o Offer different rates depending on the pledged collateral. Central banks can charge a lower interest rate to banks that provide a higher proportion of low-carbon assets as collateral. Banks pledging more sustainable bonds as collateral will benefit from larger and more favorable funding conditions.
- o Implement negative screening, and exclude from the collateral-acceptable universe assets based on their climate-risk profile.
- o Implement positive screening for some credit lines available only to banks that can pledge some sustainable collateral.

These actions would incentivize banks to lend (directly or through collateral) to borrowers and projects that are environment-friendly.

The Chinese green loan market

The People's Bank of China (PBoC) issued the "Guidelines for Establishing the Green Financial System," which includes several policy and regulatory initiatives to provide the banking system with the incentives to expand their credit portfolio.

To expand the Chinese green loan market, the PBoC has started to accept green loans as collateral for its re-lending facility called the Standing Lending Facility, through which the central bank provides loans with maturity between 1 and 3 months to the banking system. PBoC has also accepts green bonds with rating AA and higher as collateral for its Medium-term Lending Facility, through which the central bank provides loans with maturity between 3 and 12 months. These policy initiatives helped expand the green loan market, whose cumulative amount reached RMB 10.6 trillion (USD 1.5 trillion) in 2019 (Choi et al., 2020).

KEY LEARNING POINT

Central banks can use many tools to influence sustainability considerations, such as the selection rules for asset purchases, refinancing rules, collateral requirements, and selective interest rate policies.

6.6.3 Bank Supervision

In most countries, central banks are usually also designed as the supervisory authority of the banking system. In line with the existing frameworks, supervisory guidance typically covers bank's capital ratios, liquidity requirements, governance, risk management, and disclosure. In some other countries, central banks do not have this supervisory role, and there is a specialized regulator for that purpose.

Banks and regulators are increasingly concerned with the financial risks posed by climate change. Directly, the financial industry is relatively immune to the physical aspects of climate change, and is not a heavy emitter. However, it is strongly affected through the funding it provides to different companies, and thus, the indirect climate risks of its clients. That is, if a bank's borrowers face significant negative financial impacts (due to severe weather events, losses in stranded assets, future cash flows affected by the transition risk, or other factors), that would pose additional risks to the bank.

The rationale for incorporating climate issues into the ambit of a bank's supervisory role is that climate-related risks have financial stability implications. Thus, green prudential policy could play a role in incentivizing a transition to low-carbon assets. Several policy instruments available to central banks could be adjusted to take account of climate risks, including capital instruments and risk weights.

Basel III is an internationally agreed set of measures that aim to strengthen the financial sector. These rules were developed by the Basel Committee on Banking Supervision, and aim to improve the regulation, supervision, and risk management of banks. Basel III is based on three pillars:

- o The first pillar sets the capital adequacy ratio (CAR) for banks, expressed as the ratio of equity to risk-weighted assets. When computing the risk-weighted assets, the riskier the assets, the higher is their weight, and as a consequence, the higher is the equity a bank needs to hold in its balance sheet to comply with the CAR. For example, government bonds are typically assigned a weight of 0. Other assets backed by less strong collaterals, such as mortgages or consumer credit, are assigned a higher risk weighting. Pillar 1 also addresses coverage and liquidity risk (such as securitization, bank exposure to central counterparties, and counterparty credit risk) and balance sheet leverage.
- o The second pillar is intended to ensure that banks develop and use better risk management techniques in monitoring and managing risks.
- o The third pillar focuses on disclosure requirements, beyond those for regulatory capital requirements. For instance, disclosures related to regulatory ratios, or those related to remuneration are now also part of the Pillar 3 framework.

Discussions have emerged concerning how the three pillars of the Basel regulatory framework could integrate climate-related risks. If green assets have lower physical and transition risk, this could imply lower financial risk. In this case, capital ratios could be used proactively by supervisors. In March 2018, the European Commission published its Action Plan on Financing Sustainable Growth, setting an EU strategy on sustainable finance and a roadmap for future work across the financial system. Among the proposals included in the EU Action Plan (Section 6.4.2) is the adoption of a Green Supporting Factor (GSF) in the EU financial regulatory framework (CAR and CRD IV)[226] as a strategy to integrate ESG risk into prudential supervision and expand the size of the green financial market. The GSF entails the reduction of capital requirements for green assets – i.e., loans and bonds – in the balance sheet of credit institutions. This GSF would free up further bank capital to expand green loans and incentivize banks to expand their green loan portfolio.

A further action envisaged by the European Banking Federation to expand the green loan market is the promotion of green loan securitization. The aggregation of small-scale green loans or mortgages into securitized assets could generate an attractive financial product for institutional investors, helping mobilize finance for small-scale businesses and projects.

In Europe, large banks, also called significant institutions, are directly supervised by the ECB within the framework of the Single Supervisory Mechanism (SSM), and other banks are supervised by their national central banks. As of 2021, the ECB directly supervised 115 systemic banks, which accounted for almost 82% of banking assets in the participating countries.

Climate change is seen as a risk that affects different financial institutions' metrics and actions (i.e., underwriting, credit, market, operational, and liquidity risk). In compliance with its supervisory responsibility, the ECB has published the *Guidance on Climate-related and Environmental Risks (2020)*. This guide was developed jointly by the ECB and the national competent authorities, and aims to improve disclosure and management of climate and environmental risks, under the current prudential framework. This includes several building blocks:

o Business model and strategy: When determining and implementing their business strategy, institutions are expected to integrate climate-related and environmental risks that impact their business environment in the short, medium, or long term. This suggests that, in their credit risk management, banks should consider climate-related risks at all stages of the credit-granting process, as well as monitor the risks in their portfolios

---

[226] The Capital Requirements Directive (Directive 2013/36/EU) (OJ L 176/338) (EU CRD IV) and the Capital Requirements Regulation (Regulation (EU) 575/2013) (OJ L 176/1) (EU CRR) (also known collectively as the EU CRD IV package) is the mechanism through which the EU implemented the global capital adequacy framework, Basel III.

- o Risk management: Banks are expected to incorporate climate-related and environmental risks into their existing risk management framework, with a view to managing, monitoring, and mitigating these over a sufficiently long-term horizon. This includes incorporating these risks into their capital planning and liquidity processes, and counterparties' risk ratings, as well as accessing the impact on pricing, collateral valuation, liability, and reputational risk.
- o Governance and risk appetite: Banks are expected to internally report aggregated risk data on their exposures to climate-related risks, so that management bodies can make informed decisions. Climate risk should be incorporated into the risk appetite framework (RAF), and there should be enough senior management knowledge of, and responsibility for, these areas. The board of directors should have significant oversight of the theme.
- o Reporting and regulatory disclosures: Banks will be expected to disclose information and key metrics, often integrated into their non-financial reporting.

KEY LEARNING POINT

Climate risk can have a significant impact on the asset side of financial institutions, and thus have financial stability implications.

6.6.4 Methods, Scenarios, and Sensitivity Analysis

Despite the acknowledgment of the climate-related risk for the banking industry and financial stability, greening the macro- and micro-prudential policy is paved with challenges. There is significant uncertainty around many aspects of climate change. That is why it is well suited for scenario analysis, as many effects are impossible to predict with precision.

Scenario analysis is a method for developing possible future scenarios, and their impact. The goal is not to predict the future accurately, but rather to highlight the fundamental uncertainties (including climate change impacts) and therefore guide key decisions. The TCFD, ECB, and the EBA suggest that scenario analysis is a useful tool for analyzing the implications of climate risk for individual institutions. The main reason to use scenario analysis is to obtain a comprehensive assessment of the risks and opportunities. Using scenario-based analysis to assess climate-change-related risks involves two separate analyses: one on physical risks, another on transition risks. Besides assessing the impact of the shock associated with heat waves, flooding, and other events, scenarios should introduce a GHG emission tax/carbon price on the quality of a portfolio. With proper scenarios, banks can better understand their exposures. This is indeed one of the key values of scenario analysis, to provide visibility on potential outcomes, so that banks can then adapt their strategy, business models, and investments accordingly.

Methodologies to estimate the magnitude of climate-related risks to the financial system are being developed. In 2015, the French Directorate General of the Treasury with support from the Banque de France and the Prudential Supervisory and Resolution published a report on the evaluation methods for climate-related risk in the banking sector. According to the guidelines, scenario-based risk analyses should be based on a certain number of principles that allow for separate assessments of physical risks and transition risks.

More recently, the NGFS has developed scenarios for the possible impacts of climate change. These scenarios differ in how climate policy, emissions, and temperatures will evolve. They aim to provide a common reference point for physical and transition risks, including detailed possible outcomes for different economic and financial variables in each scenario.

Table 6.5 Scenarios by the level of policy ambition, policy timing, coordination, and technology levers

Category	Scenario	Physical risk	Transition risk			
		Policy ambition	Policy reaction	Technology change	Carbon dioxide removal	Regional policy variation
Orderly	Net Zero 2050	1.5 °C	Immediate and smooth	Fast change	Medium use	Medium variation
	Below 2 °C	1.7 °C	Immediate and smooth	Moderate change	Medium use	Low variation
Disorderly	Divergent Net Zero	1.5 °C	Immediate but divergent	Fast change	Low use	Medium variation
	Delayed Transition	1.8 °C	Delayed	Slow/Fast change	Low use	High variation
Hot House World	Nationally Determined Contributions (NDCs)	~2.5 °C	NDCs	Slow change	Low use	Low variation
	Current Policies	3 °C+	None – current policies	Slow change	Low use	Low variation

Higher risk

Moderate risk

Lower risk

Source: 2021 NGFS Climate Scenarios for central banks and supervisors.

In 2021, the NGFS published six different scenarios, which include the effects of the pandemic and shifts in climate policies since 2018. In two scenarios, policies are introduced early and carbon prices are highly affected; two scenarios include policies being delayed or not unified across countries; and two scenarios reflect little change in policies. The NGFS also details the physical and transition risks that can occur in each scenario. Physical risks are higher in scenarios with fewer policies introduced, and the consequent increase in global warming and its effects (see Section 2.3). On the other hand, with stricter policies, transition risks (see Section 2.4) increase. Moreover, they suggest the economic impact that each scenario could have, with some assumptions. Given all the uncertainties around climate change and its many different variables, scenario analysis and stress testing are useful tools. However, several challenges remain. First, there is a need for data. There is not enough reliable data for risk models, nor consistent emissions- or climate-related data across jurisdictions. Also, what are the indicators used to evaluate companies' sustainability levels? One possibility is to analyze the level of emissions per revenue. However, that is a static measure that simply provides a snapshot at a certain moment in time. Alternatively, one could look at the trajectory of emissions over time for a certain company, which would highlight its efforts toward transitioning to a low-carbon economy. The challenge is that, depending on the metric, we may arrive at different conclusions and outcomes. The scale of the company is also important. Often, banks have limited information on their clients. Although reasonable ESG information exists on large publicly listed companies, it is very different for the millions of SMEs that make up most of the world's economy.

The ECB is conducting its first climate stress test in 2022. This will begin with a top-down macroeconomic analysis of the impacts of climate change on companies and banks covering more than 4 million companies and 2,000 banks in Europe. The ECB will use several climate scenarios that look ahead as far as 2100. These scenarios vary in the range of policies to curb emissions, and therefore are based on different climate scenarios. The extreme scenarios are (1) a complete lack of policies to control emissions and (2) strong policy actions in climate-sensitive industries that are introduced very quickly. It will also carry out a bottom-up test on individual banks. This supervisory test will require banks to assess the climate risks they are exposed to, and how they manage them.

6.6.5 Empirical Evidence and Research Findings

Table 6.6 shows the number of central banks that have progressively joined global green banking initiatives, integrated climate risk in their supervisory activities, or implemented green supportive monetary policies during 2010–20.

Table 6.6 Number of central banks that have adopted "green" activities (by type)

	2015	2019
Green/sustainable network membership	10	58
Incorporation of ESG criteria in central bank portfolio management/TCFD supporter	0	7
Integration of climate risk into macroprudential policy (implemented or under development)	1	4
Guidelines on environmental risk management, disclosure requirements, or stress tests for financial institutions	3	18
Green bond support programs	1	14
Green lending guidelines/guidance or "promotional/directed" credit policies for financial institutions	16	23
Total	**31**	**124**

Source: Dikau and Volz (2021).

Further, many central banks are incorporating climate considerations internally. For instance, EU central banks agreed, in February 2021, on a standardized reporting of their own portfolio carbon footprint, along the lines of the TCFD.

However, in many dimensions, there is no strong consensus on the right level of involvement of central banks in climate change topics. On the one hand, it can be argued that their involvement is justified, on risk and financial stability grounds. On the other hand, the involvement of central banks in the low-carbon transition raises some concerns. Some argue that this can blur the separation between the political objectives of elected governments and the central bank as an independent institution. It is true that an independent central bank's mandate typically does not include managing the economic transition and sustainability. Some could argue that using their policy tools to redirect financial flows and resources is beyond their mandate.

The discussion is ongoing. Some want to go faster in terms of changing capital requirements and regulations. Others argue that such changes have to be "data based," and should avoid trapping capital in ways that undermine banks' profitability.

In many instances, policymaking generates significant trade-offs. For instance, introducing a GSF generates incentives to finance "green" companies. This could be seen as a positive move, by providing more favorable financing conditions to these companies. However, it is also possible that these "green" companies are riskier (for instance, due to novel technologies, innovative offerings, etc.), and therefore would require higher capital buffers. For example, a loan for green real estate is not necessarily less risky than a loan for "conventional" real estate. One of the problems is that there is simply not enough data over time. The evidence on the actual risk of green loans is scarce. Also, the definitions of what a green loan is have been evolving over time. For instance, over 2012–18, loans that are considered green according to the Chinese Taxonomy performed better than conventional loans. At the end of 2018, the non-performing loan (NPL) ratio for green loans stood at 0.42%, while the overall credit NPL ratio stood at 1.83%. But "green" is not necessarily a synonym of "less risk." As an example, Dankert et al. (2018) from De Nederlandsche Bank criticized the proposal for a GSF, as green assets (such as green loans or bonds) are not necessarily less risky than their conventional counterparts.

The same argument applies to corporate loans to finance green projects. The green transition can require the financing of new technologies that may not succeed, in which case the creditors would bear the costs of such project defaults. In this scenario, the reduction of capital buffers based on the "greenness" of the assets would lower the aggregate capitalization of the banking system and increase the systemic risk. Consistent with this, De Nederlandsche Bank (2018) argues that lowering capital buffers would be an option only if there is sufficient evidence that green exposures carry lower risk.

Doubts about the effectiveness of the adoption of these measures also concern the criteria using which a green or brown asset would be classified and distinguished by the supervisory authority, before assigning them different risk weights. Although the financial market is "global," the interpretation of what is "green" or "brown" differs across the different jurisdictions (see also the discussion on green bonds in Section 3.1 and on the EU Taxonomy in Section 6.4.2).

Another concern is that the impact of monetary policy decisions is not neutral, and has distributional effects. For example, when the central bank purchases corporate bonds issued from a specific industry, their price tends to rise, ensuring lower borrowing costs for that specific industry or for specific companies within that industry.

On the other hand, the same argument of non-neutrality of monetary policy has been used to advocate for central bank involvement in the low-carbon transition. That is, monetary policy should play an active role in the low-carbon transition because empirical evidence shows that currently, monetary policy is already affecting the financing conditions of companies. The bonds typically purchased through QE policies tend to be from larger firms, including many that do more environmental harm than the average firm in the economy. In this case, QE may be implicitly subsidizing "brown" industries. Piazzesi et al. (2021) showed that the ECB's portfolio is significantly different from the universe of outstanding bonds in the market, and that it overweights heavy-emission industries, which tend to issue more bonds than companies in other sectors. Conversely, sectors that do not issue many bonds (for instance, services and agriculture) but also have lower emissions are underweighted relative to their market weights. Given this portfolio imbalance, the ECB should restore market neutrality by tilting its portfolio toward green industries. However, this is still a contentious topic among central bankers.

> **KEY LEARNING POINT**
>
> *Whether and how central banks should involve themselves in sustainability is under debate, especially given the lack of historical data on the actual risks and consequences of different policies.*

6.6.6 Summary and Challenges

Central banks are important players in financial markets. To begin with, they are responsible for implementing monetary policy, in which role they affect interest rates. Central banks are also large buyers of financial products, namely, bonds for their portfolios. In addition, many of them are responsible for regulating the financial sector and ensuring financial stability. In their different roles, they can use various tools to influence the climate transition.

Many central bankers are talking about climate issues and the need to incorporate them in their policies. For instance, in bond purchase programs, central banks can use portfolio tilts, or exclusion lists, to direct their purchases toward greener assets. That is, while implementing bond purchase programs, central banks can influence the relative size, and rates, of different bond markets. In supervising the financial sector, different operational tools can be used, including reserves requirements, collateral restrictions, and overall prudential regulation tools such as capital ratios and disclosures. As economic advisors to governments, central banks play a key role.

Across all these domains, central banks have tools that can incentivize banks, and the overall economy, to have greener portfolios with less carbon exposure. However, it is important to consider that all these changes have consequences, costs, and distributional effects, and the availability of data that can justify future changes is a significant challenge.

Ultimately, what central banks and financial regulators will do to support a smooth low-carbon transition will depend on what their mandate allows, how this is interpreted, and their willingness to act, and the mandates and policy tools differ significantly across countries.

REFERENCES: CHAPTER 6

Abe, T., J. Bravinder, S. Goodrich, S. Lavos, and A. Leiser. 2015. "Emerging Practices in Internal Carbon Pricing. A Practical Guide." Geneva: World Business Council for Sustainable Development.

Alves Dias, P., K. Kanellopoulos, H. Medarac, Z. Kapetaki, E. Miranda-Barbosa, R. Shortall, V. Czako, et al. 2018. "EU Coal Regions: Opportunities and Challenges Ahead." Petten, The Netherlands: European Commission, Joint Research Centre.

Badia, M., M. Duro, B.N. Jorgensen, and G. Ormazabal. 2021. "Disclosure Regulation and Competitive Interactions: Evidence from the Oil and Gas Industry." *The Accounting Review* 96 (5): 1–29.

Barth, M.E., S.F. Cahan, L. Chen, and E.R. Venter. 2017. "The Economic Consequences Associated with Integrated Report Quality: Capital Market and Real Effects." *Accounting, Organizations and Society* 62: 43–64.

Bartlett, N., T. Coleman, and S. Schmidt. 2021. "Putting a Price on Carbon: The State of Internal Carbon Pricing by Corporates Globally." London: Carbon Disclosure Project (CDP).

Bolton, P., and M. Kacperczyk. 2021. "Do Investors Care about Carbon Risk?" *Journal of Financial Economics* 142 (2): 517–49.

Brandt, U.S., and G.T. Svendsen. 2003. "The Political Economy of Climate Change Policy in the EU: Auction and Grandfathering." IME Working Paper.

Brulle, R.J. 2018. "The Climate Lobby: A Sectoral Analysis of Lobbying Spending on Climate Change in the USA, 2000 to 2016." *Climatic Change* 149 (3): 289–303.

Bucaro, A.C., K.E. Jackson, and J.B. Lill. 2020. "The Influence of Corporate Social Responsibility Measures on Investors' Judgments When Integrated in a Financial Report versus Presented in a Separate Report." *Contemporary Accounting Research* 37 (2): 665–95.

Cameron, A., G. Claeys, C. Midões, and S. Tagliapietra. 2020. "How Good Is the European Commission's Just Transition Fund Proposal?" Bruegel Policy Contribution No. 2020/04.

Christensen, H.B., L. Hail, and C. Leuz. 2019. "Adoption of CSR and Sustainability Reporting Standards: Economic Analysis and Review." Finance Working Paper 623. Brussels: European Corporate Governance Institute (ECGI).

Coase, R.H. 1960. "The Problem of Social Cost." *Journal of Law and Economics* 3 (1): 1–44.

Crêpy, M. 2021. "EU Climate Taxonomy: The Good, the Bad, and the Ugly." Environmental Coalition on Standards (ECOS) (blog). May 5, 2021. https://ecostandard.org/news_events/good-bad-ugly-taxonomy/.

Dankert, J., L. van Doorn, H.J. Reinders, O. Sleijpen, and N. De Nederlandsche Bank. 2018. "A Green Supporting Factor–the Right Policy." SUERF Policy Note 43 (43): 1–8.

De Nederlandsche Bank. 2018. "Lower Capital Buffers for Sustainable Finance Are Only an Option If Sustainable Finance Carries Lower Risk." DNBulletin 2 October 2018.

Del Granado, F.J.A., D. Coady, and R. Gillingham. 2012. "The Unequal Benefits of Fuel Subsidies: A Review of Evidence for Developing Countries." *World Development* 40 (11): 2234–48.

Dikau, S., and U. Volz. 2021. "Central Bank Mandates, Sustainability Objectives and the Promotion of Green Finance." *Ecological Economics* 184: 107022.

Diski, R., A. Chapman, and C. Kumar. 2021. "Powering the Just Transition." London: New Economics Foundation (NEF).

ECB (European Central Bank). 2020. "Guide on Climate-Related and Environmental Risks: Supervisory Expectations Relating to Risk Management and Disclosure." Frankfurt: ECB.

Fan, J., W. Rehm, and G. Siccardo. 2021. "The State of Internal Carbon Pricing." McKinsey & Company | Strategy & Corporate Finance. February 10, 2021. https://www.mckinsey.com/capabilities/strategy-and-corporate-finance/our-insights/the-state-of-internal-carbon-pricing.

Flammer, C., M.W. Toffel, and K. Viswanathan. 2021. "Shareholder Activism and Firms' Voluntary Disclosure of Climate Change Risks." *Strategic Management Journal* 42 (10): 1850–79.

Furceri, D., M. Ganslmeier, and M.J.D. Ostry. 2021. "Are Climate Change Policies Politically Costly?" IMF Working Paper. International Monetary Fund.

Gulbrandsen, L.H., J. Wettestad, D.G. Victor, and A. Underdal. 2019. "The Political Roots of Divergence in Carbon Market Design: Implications for Linking." *Climate Policy* 19 (4): 427–38.

Hahn, R.W., and R.N. Stavins. 2011. "The Effect of Allowance Allocations on Cap-and-Trade System Performance." *The Journal of Law and Economics* 54 (S4): S267–94.

Heflin, F., and D. Wallace. 2017. "The BP Oil Spill: Shareholder Wealth Effects and Environmental Disclosures." *Journal of Business Finance & Accounting* 44 (3–4): 337–74.

Ilhan, E., P. Krueger, Z. Sautner, and L.T. Starks. 2021. "Climate Risk Disclosure and Institutional Investors." *Swiss Finance Institute Research Paper*, no. 19–66.

Khan, M., G. Serafeim, and A. Yoon. 2016. "Corporate Sustainability: First Evidence on Materiality." *The Accounting Review* 91 (6): 1697–1724.

Krueger, P., Z. Sautner, D.Y. Tang, and R. Zhong. 2021. "The Effects of Mandatory ESG Disclosure around the World." European Corporate Governance Institute–Finance Working Paper, no. 754: 21–44.

Kustova, I., C. Egenhofer, J.N. Ferrer, and J. Popov. 2021. "From Coal to Low Carbon: Coal Region Development Opportunities under EU Recovery Programmes." CEPS Policy Insights No PI2021-06/APRIL.

Lyon, T.P., and J.W. Maxwell. 2011. "Greenwash: Corporate Environmental Disclosure under Threat of Audit." *Journal of Economics & Management Strategy* 20 (1): 3–41.

Nordhaus, W.D. 2015. "The Pope & the Market." *The New York Review*, October 8, 2015. https://www.nybooks.com/articles/2015/10/08/pope-and-market/.

Oates, W.E., and P.R. Portney. 2003. "The Political Economy of Environmental Policy." In *Handbook of Environmental Economics: Environmental Degradation and Institutional Responses*, edited by Maler, K.-G. and J.R. Vincent. Elsevier.

OECD and IEA. 2021. "Update on Recent Progress in Reform of Inefficient Fossil-Fuel Subsidies That Encourage Wasteful Consumption." Prepared for Group of Twenty (G20) discussions. Paris: Organisation for Economic Co-operation and Development, International Energy Agency.

Pfaf, N., and O. Altun. 2022. "Ensuring the Usability of the EU Taxonomy." Zurich: International Capital Market Association (ICMA).

Piazzesi, M., M. Papoutsi, and M. Schneider. (2021). "How Unconventional is Green Monetary Policy." Working paper. IMF and AME.

Pigou, A.C. 1932. *The Economics of Welfare*. 4th edition. London: Macmillan and Co.

PRI (Principles for Responsible Investment). 2020. "Testing the Taxonomy: Insights from the PRI Taxonomy Practitioners Group." London: PRI.

Steves, F., and A. Teytelboym. 2013. "Political Economy of Climate Change Policy." Smith School Working Paper Series. Working Paper 13-06.

TFCD (Task Force on Climate-related Financial Disclosures). 2017. "Recommendations of the Task Force on Climate-Related Financial Disclosures." Final Report. New York: TFCD.

TFCD (Task Force on Climate-related Financial Disclosures). 2021. "2021 Status Report." Progress Report. TFCD: New York.

Threlfall, R., A. King, J. Shulman, and W. Bartels. 2020. "The Time Has Come: The KPMG Survey of Sustainability Reporting 2020." Amstelveen, Netherlands: KPMG.

TMX and CPA (Toronto Stock Exchange and Chartered Professional Accountants Canada). 2020. "A Primer for Environmental and Social Disclosure." TMX and CPA: Toronto.

Zhou, P., and M. Wang. 2016. "Carbon Dioxide Emissions Allocation: A Review." *Ecological Economics* 125: 47–59.

Widuto, A. 2019. "EU Support for Coal Regions." European Parliamentary Research Service (EPRS).

INDEX

A

Activism 32, 155, 189, 190, 210, 248, 256, 264, 270, 321, 353
Activist investors 189, 199, 264
Asset purchases 341

B

Basel III 344
Board of directors 169, 176, 181, 190, 196, 205, 258, 264, 337, 346

C

Carbon pricing 202, 237, 296, 303
Carbon tax 66, 84, 93, 296, 304, 310
Central banks 42, 66, 74, 132, 295, 311, 338
Climate Action 100+ 176, 196, 252, 282, 368
Climate risk 52, 58, 76, 80, 85, 127, 144, 154, 160, 164, 178, 180, 195, 200, 206, 213, 222, 237, 240, 246, 264, 275, 287, 292, 295, 311, 317, 331, 340, 344, 353
Climate-related stock indices 233
Coal 20, 25, 46, 66, 69, 122, 130, 230, 255, 272, 280, 305, 352
Collateral requirements 342
Company performance 185, 216, 246
Constituents 217, 226, 230, 241, 271, 311
Corporate bonds 113, 266, 341, 350
Credit rating agencies 41, 101, 105, 113, 133, 188

D

Decarbonization 30, 45, 65, 69, 147, 284, 328
Disclosure 30, 39, 96, 105, 115, 160, 176, 188, 195, 204, 212, 251, 267, 276, 288, 295, 313, 331, 338, 343
Divestment campaigns 263
Due diligence, 156, 161, 202, 287

E

EBRD 99, 332
EIB 63, 98, 111, 332
Emissions per capita 22,
Emissions trading system 296, 303
Employment 6, 14, 34, 56, 124, 206, 305
Engagement 42, 133, 185, 205, 228, 236, 261, 274, 281, 301, 308, 317, 345
Endowments 41, 158, 251, 256, 281, 292
Environmental activism 36, 195
Environmental due diligence 204
ESG criteria 46, 126, 133, 226, 254, 261, 349
ESG funds 46, 246, 267, 271
ESG indices 221, 230, 241, 270
ESG integration 226, 254, 259, 260
ESG investment 48, 196, 215, 240, 246, 268, 280, 323
ESG rating 46, 64, 78, 91, 126, 207, 215, 235, 245, 260, 267, 272, 324
ETF 228, 268
EU Taxonomy 48, 325, 334, 350
European Union Action Plan 325
Exclusion list 230, 255, 263, 351
Executive compensation 39, 169, 176, 182

F

Family firm 155, 206
Family office 78, 110, 155, 282
Financial reporting 140, 147, 221, 311, 320, 346
Forest area 12, 112
Four Twenty Seven 64

G

Global regulations 115, 311
Global warming 1, 20, 26, 56, 196, 348
Globalization 1, 13, 19, 52
Governance 1, 38, 54, 68, 100, 112, 119, 136, 152, 169, 188, 199, 203, 210, 248, 270, 276, 289, 313, 338, 344, 352

LIST OF ACRONYMS

ACA	Absolute Contraction Approach
AGM	Annual General Meeting
BAP	Boardroom Accountability Project
BRIC	Brazil, Russia, India, China
BRICS	Brazil, Russia, India, China and South Africa
CAIT	Climate Analysis Indicators Tool
CAPEX	capital expenditures
CAPM	capital asset pricing model
CAR	cumulative abnormal returns
CCS	carbon capture and storage
CDIAC	Carbon Dioxide Information Analysis Centre
CDP	Carbon Disclosure Project
CDS	credit default swap
CEO	chief executive officer
CFO	chief financial officer
CH4	methane
CNES	Centre National d'Etudes Spatiales
CO2	carbon dioxide
CRA	credit rating agencies
CSR	corporate social responsibility
DCF	discounted cash flows
DJIA	Dow Jones Industrial Average
DNSH	Do No Significant Harm
EBIT	earnings before interest and taxes
EBITDA	earnings before interest, taxes, depreciation, and amortization
EC	European Commission
EGM	extraordinary general meeting
EMEA	Europe, Middle East, Africa
EPA	Environmental Protection Agency
ES or E&S	Environmental & Social
ESG	Environmental, Social and Governance
ESMA	European Securities and Markets Authority
ETF	exchange-traded fund
ETS	emissions trading system
EU	European Union
EU CTB	EU Climate Transition Benchmark

EU PAB	EU Paris-Aligned Benchmark
EV	enterprise value
FAO	Food and Agricultural Organization
FCFF	free cash flow to the firm
FDI	foreign direct investment
G-7	Group of Seven
GATT	General Agreement on Tariffs and Trade
GBP	Green Bond Principles
GCP	Global Carbon Project
GDP	gross domestic product
GHG	greenhouse gas
GP	general partner
GRI	Global Reporting Initiative
GSF	Green Supporting Factor
HNWI	high net worth individuals
IPO	initial public offering
IR	integrated reporting
IRR	internal rate of return
ISS	Institutional Shareholder Services
IT	information technology
KPI	key performance indicator
LBO	leveraged buyout
LGD	loss given default
LP	limited partner
LTIP	long-term incentive plan
M&A	mergers and acquisitions
MDBs	multilateral development banks
MDGs	Millennium Development Goals
MLIs	multilateral lending institutions
MT	metric ton
N2O	nitrous oxide
NDC	Nationally Determined Contributions
NFRD	Non-Financial Reporting Directive
NPL	non-performing loan
P&L	profit-and-loss
PD	probability of default
PE	private equity
PER	price-earnings ratio
PPA	power purchase agreements

PPP	public-private partnerships/purchasing power parity
PRI	Principles for Responsible Investment
QE	quantitative easing
R&D	research and development
RAF	risk appetite framework
REPO	repurchase agreements
ROA	return on assets
ROE	return of equity
SASB	Sustainability Accounting Standards Board
SBTi	Science Based Targets initiative
SCF	supply chain finance
SDG	Sustainable Development Goals
SEO	seasoned equity offering
SFDR	Sustainable Finance Disclosure Regulation
SLB	sustainability-linked bonds
SLL	sustainability-linked loans
SME	small and medium-sized enterprises
SPO	second party opinion
SPT	sustainability performance targets
SPV	special purpose vehicle
SRI	socially responsible investing
SSM	Single Supervisory Mechanism
SWF	sovereign wealth fund
TCFD	Task Force on Climate-Related Financial Disclosures
TSR	total shareholder return
V20	The Vulnerable 20 Group
VC	venture capital
WACC	weighted average cost of capital
WWI	World War I
WWII	World War II
YTM	yield to maturity

LIST OF FIGURES

LIST OF TABLES

LIST OF CASE STUDIES/COMPANIES

Case Box	Section
Wipro and STBi	1.4.3
The importance of clear plans and targets: an example from Carrefour	1.4.3
Greta Thunberg and the Fridays for Future initiative	1.5.1
Chevron's pledge of "ever-cleaner energy"	1.5.3
The Saudi Arabia government's bond and BlackRock ESG index funds	1.5.3
Bank of New York ESG funds	1.5.3
Walmart setting targets	1.5.3
DWS accused of greenwashing	1.5.3
The bankruptcy of PG&E	2.2
Pearl River Delta coastal flooding	2.3
Peabody Energy	2.5.1
The food industry and Nestlé	2.6
The 2007 EIB bond: pioneering the market	3.1.2
Corticeira Amorim – second party opinion (excerpt from Sustainalytics report)	3.1.3
The First Sovereign Green Bond	3.1.5
The Largest Green Sovereign bond issuer	3.1.5
Telefónica S.A	3.1.7
Apple: the first U.S. green bond in the tech industry	3.1.7
Repsol – a problematic green bond	3.1.8
ENEL S.p.A – the world's first SDG-linked bond	3.2.1
Snam S.p.A	3.2.2
Cadent	3.2.2
Marfrig – a controversial transition bond	3.2.2
Porsche: green Schuldscheine	3.3.1
AB InBev ESG-linked loan facility	3.3.2
The European Investment Bank Climate Risk Scores	3.3.3
Walmart's SCF program	3.6.4
Bridgestone-JP Morgan SCF scheme	3.6.4
Lowercarbon Capital	4.1.3
Summa and Sotera Garbage	4.1.3
NextEra Energy	4.2.2
Beyond Meat IPO	4.2.2
Proxy advisors, Dieselgate, and the board of directors	4.3.2
Changing recommendations: Axcelis and ISS	4.3.2
BlackRock's Global Principles	4.3.3

Shell: compensation tied to climate	4.3.4
Rejection of HelloFresh remuneration package	4.3.4
Elliott Management and Evergy	4.4.1
Engine No. 1 victory with Exxon Mobil	4.4.3
The early days: the battle between Shell and Greenpeace for the North Sea	4.4.4
Climate Action 100+	4.4.4
General Battery Corporation and Exide Corporation	4.5.4
Torres winery	4.6.2
Ferrero	4.6.2
Exxon vs. Tesla vs. BMW	5.1.4
Facebook	5.1.4
DJTA: the first stock index	5.2.1
Vanguard: the first index fund	5.2.2
S&P ESG 500 index	5.2.4
Dow Jones Sustainability World Index	5.2.4
MSCI Global Environment Index	5.2.5
The MSCI ACWI Climate Change Index	5.2.5
Norway Pension Fund in 2020	5.4.5
BlackRock and its ESG engagement	5.4.6
The world's largest green bond fund	5.5.1
Vanguard FTSE Social Index Fund	5.5.2
iShares MSCI World Paris-Aligned Climate ETF	5.5.2
Ossiam Food For Biodiversity ETF	5.5.2
The Boardroom Accountability Project (BAP)	5.5.3
The New York State Teachers Retirement System (NYSTRS)	5.5.3
APG (Netherlands)	5.5.3
Canada Pension Plan (CPP)	5.5.3
One Planet: The SWF collaborative initiative	5.5.4
Sweden's Carbon Tax 1991	6.1.2
The EU-ETS	6.1.3
PUMA and International Finance Corporation (IFC)	6.5.2
KCM and the European Investment Bank	6.5.2
IFC green loan to Latin American Agribusiness Development Corporation (LAAD)	6.5.2
Examples of Central Banks' Mandates	6.6.1
European Central Bank (ECB) and Bank of England climate change mitigation initiatives	6.6.2
The Chinese green loan market	6.6.2

Made in the USA
Las Vegas, NV
30 November 2023

81861045R00219